MW01069451

THE PRACTICE OF AMERICAN CONSTITUTIONAL LAW

Americans often think about constitutional law in terms of high-profile decisions by the Supreme Court – decisions that divide the justices by ideology, not law. This focus often leads to the erroneous conclusion that constitutional law arguments are, and can only be, political in substance. In *The Practice of American Constitutional Law*, H. Jefferson Powell demonstrates that there is a longstanding, shared practice of constructing and evaluating constitutional law claims that transcends current political disagreements. Powell describes how lawyers and judges identify constitutional problems by using a specifiable method of inquiry that enables them to agree on what the questions are, and thus what any plausible answer must address, even when disagreement over the most persuasive answers remains. Rather than being simply politics by other means, constitutional law is the successful practice of giving substance to the Constitution as supreme law.

H. Jefferson Powell is a professor of law at Duke University. He is the former principal deputy solicitor general and a former deputy assistant attorney general in the US Department of Justice. His books include *A Community Built on Words: The Constitution in History and Politics* (2003), *Constitutional Conscience: The Moral Dimension of Judicial Decision* (2008), *The President as Commander in Chief: An Essay in Constitutional Vision* (2013), *and Targeting Americans: The Constitutionality of the U.S. Drone War* (2016).

The Practice of American Constitutional Law

H. JEFFERSON POWELL

Duke University, North Carolina

CAMBRIDGE
UNIVERSITY PRESS

University Printing House, Cambridge CB2 8BS, United Kingdom

One Liberty Plaza, 20th Floor, New York, NY 10006, USA

477 Williamstown Road, Port Melbourne, VIC 3207, Australia

314–321, 3rd Floor, Plot 3, Splendor Forum, Jasola District Centre,
New Delhi – 110025, India

103 Penang Road, #05–06/07, Visioncrest Commercial, Singapore 238467

Cambridge University Press is part of the University of Cambridge.

It furthers the University's mission by disseminating knowledge in the pursuit of
education, learning, and research at the highest international levels of excellence.

www.cambridge.org
Information on this title: www.cambridge.org/9781009158848
DOI: 10.1017/9781009158855

© H. Jefferson Powell 2022

This publication is in copyright. Subject to statutory exception
and to the provisions of relevant collective licensing agreements,
no reproduction of any part may take place without the written
permission of Cambridge University Press.

First published 2022

A catalogue record for this publication is available from the British Library.

ISBN 978-1-009-15884-8 Hardback
ISBN 978-1-009-15886-2 Paperback

Cambridge University Press has no responsibility for the persistence or accuracy of
URLs for external or third-party internet websites referred to in this publication
and does not guarantee that any content on such websites is, or will remain,
accurate or appropriate.

To Sarah,
with wonder, laughter, and love

Contents

Preface

The subject of this book is the practice of American constitutional law, the activity of identifying legal problems that arise under the Constitution of the United States and proposing answers to the questions that the problems present. This lawyers' practice should not be of interest to lawyers alone. Constitutional law plays a major role in the life of the American political community, to an extent not wholly paralleled in other countries, and Americans often have strong views about the right answers to high-profile constitutional law questions even if they otherwise have little interest in or knowledge of law. Despite its political and even cultural salience, however, the activity or practice of constitutional law – what it is that lawyers do when they argue over the right answers – has attracted relatively little attention. Most nonlawyers are primarily (and understandably) interested in the answers, not in the means of getting to the answers. Among constitutional lawyers themselves, reflection about the practice tends to focus on theories about how constitutional decision-making *ought* to be done, the assumption being that practitioners and scholars must understand how *in fact* decisions are made. After all, decisions are made!

I do not mean to quarrel with this assumption, but it is incomplete. Mistakes are made too: no constitutional lawyer thinks that even the Supreme Court is infallible, and despite the strong political tenor of much criticism of the high Court's decisions, no serious constitutional lawyer thinks all disagreements over the right answer to a constitutional law question are sheerly political disputes. In practice, if not always in theory, everyone, lawyer or not, thinks that some constitutional law answers are errors of law. (We shall leave for Chapter 6 the question whether the opposite to an error in constitutional law is the *right* answer or the *most persuasive* one. For now, we can treat these adjectives as interchangeable.) Adherents to a normative theory about how constitutional decisions ought to be made measure error by the extent to which a decision deviates from their preferred theory. But most constitutional lawyers are not rigorous adherents to any theory (to the great frustration of the theorists!), and yet they work with the same idea, that there are mistakes, and thus there are right (or better) answers in constitutional law.

This book is an attempt to spell out the implicit standards by which constitutional lawyers, including judges, identify truth and measure error in the practice of constitutional law when the individual lawyer has not subordinated the practice, which is common to all constitutional lawyers, to a theory – and *no* theory is in fact dominant in practice. My objective is to articulate the best (most accurate) description of the accepted practice of American constitutional law from within the practice, speaking as a lawyer who engages in the practice, not as an external observer or critic. The value of such a description for lawyers who accept the legitimacy of the practice is to articulate what they already know but usually leave implicit; for constitutional theorists and external critics, the value is to provide them with a clearer picture of the practice they are seeking to change or to understand.

The activity of judicial review, the exercise by courts of the authority to follow their own views of constitutional requirements and ignore or set aside contrary constitutional understandings, is central to the broader practice of constitutional law. This book, however, is framed in terms of how a conscientious and skillful constitutional lawyer, filling any role in the system, constructs arguments rather than specifically how a judge decides constitutional cases. Discussions of constitutional law reasoning often adopt a court-centric perspective, but I believe it is helpful to take a broader view. What the judge does in coming to a decision in a constitutional case is in fact very similar to what the constitutional advocate does in writing a good brief – the judge is trying to persuade the reader that he or she has given the best answer to the constitutional law question before the court just as the advocate is trying to persuade the judge that his or her arguments are superior to opposing counsel's.

Whatever may be true about other forms of legal advocacy (trying a criminal case to a jury, for example), constitutional law advocacy, whether the lawyer's to the court or the court's to the reader, is a kind of adversarial reasoning that takes into account the arguments for and against a particular answer in advocating a particular conclusion. For this reason, I refer to the forms of constitutional law thought alternatively as "reasoning" or "argument" because the constitutional lawyer (the judge as much as anyone else) is engaged in persuasion, even if the person to be persuaded is the lawyer him- or herself. It is this activity of adversarial, persuasive reasoning or argument that I shall call the practice of constitutional law.

Because my concern is with this intellectual practice in itself and regardless of who is engaging in the practice, I do not discuss the specific professional skills and techniques a litigator must employ in effectively presenting a constitutional argument to a court. Litigators must engage in the practice of constitutional law in my sense – they must persuade themselves which lines of argument are most likely to persuade the court and then attempt actually to persuade the judges – but many constitutional lawyers are not litigators but judges, advisors, or commentators. Each of these roles requires skills peculiar to that role. In Chapter 4, I discuss certain considerations that are specific to the particular perspective that a constitutional lawyer must adopt in carrying out his or her role, but the book as a whole is meant to portray a practice that is broadly the same across all perspectives.

Again, this book is descriptive rather than prescriptive: I explain to the reader what I think the actual practice of constitutional law is rather than what I think it should be. To be sure, the task of description has required me to make many judgments about formulation and emphasis with which other constitutional lawyers might disagree. To give one particularly important example, I think that the actual practice of constitutional law is shaped more by the constitutional text than some may believe. But my objective is to enable the reader to understand a shared public practice of reason and argument that is not determined by my personal opinions, or indeed those of anyone else. Some of the terminology I use is my own, but if I have succeeded in my goal, the content of the book, its description of our practice, is something I share with constitutional lawyers of all shades of opinion on contested questions of substance.

The reader, therefore, should not infer my personal agreement in the abstract with all of the arguments I present to explain specific rules and principles: I am trying to make the most sense out of the practice as I perceive it, and that includes making sense out of aspects of the practice that in my personal opinion represent a wrong turn. I have no doubt failed on occasion completely to exclude personal and contestable judgments, but any such errors are entirely inadvertent and, I hope, limited to minor details. The book also refrains, almost entirely, from discussion of theoretical debates over originalism, "the living Constitution," and so on. As I explain in the excursus at the end of Chapter 1, with specific reference to originalism, those debates are of minimal significance to the project of describing what constitutional lawyers actually do almost all of the time. I am describing the practice we share rather than the contestable and contested theories that divide us.

As my objective is to explain the *practice* of constitutional law, which has remained remarkably consistent since the time of the early Republic, rather than the *substance* of constitutional law, the reader should not expect to find a systematic presentation of current doctrine in any area of constitutional law. At times I have thought it necessary or helpful to summarize briefly some corner of the great, amorphous body of substantive law that American lawyers recognize as the law of the Constitution, but in every instance, my goal is to aid readers' understanding of the practice rather than provide them with a mini-treatise.

This book often explains a point not by citing its most recent articulation by the Supreme Court (as a lawyer writing a brief might do) but by reference to very old discussions: the reader will quickly note that I frequently use expressions such as "long-standing" and "from the beginning," and that the Supreme Court's 1819 decision in *McCulloch* v. *Maryland* repeatedly shows up to ground an assertion. The reason is not mere antiquarian delight in constitutional law's history. Locating a principle or rule in the law's past is meant to provide a basis for the reader (and the author!) to understand the point being made as genuinely part of the shared practice rather than the author's personal choice among claims that are contestable in the present day.

Even more importantly, the invocation of old or deeply rooted authority indicates the historical foundation of the book's basic assumption, which I must now state. The practice of constitutional law is the legitimate, coherent, principled tradition of legal argument over the best answers to questions arising under the United States Constitution, rather than the tool of policy and partisan conflict that on occasion Supreme Court adjudication appears to be. This assumption is, obviously, *not* a mere description. It is instead a normative assertion, a statement of my opinion on how arguments in the practice ought to be evaluated, and not simply my judgment on what the practice actually consists of as a matter of observation. When anyone, including a justice of the high Court, proffers an answer to a constitutional question that fails to meet the demands of the practice, the answer is illegitimate, and in principle, the rest of us should reject it. The only form of advocacy for my opinion that I present in this book – except in this preface and in the Conclusion – lies in the implications of what I believe is a neutral and dispassionate account of the practice that constitutional lawyers actually share and in which they engage.

Adherence to the forms of reasoning that make up the practice of constitutional law does not exclude personal political and moral commitment from playing a role in difficult cases. I think it is undeniable – though there are those who say otherwise – that such commitments influence the judgment of even the most conscientious judge or lawyer on the right answers in highly contestable issues. As a great judge and Supreme Court justice, Benjamin N. Cardozo, once wrote, no matter how objectively we approach legal problems, "we can never see them with any eyes except our own."[1] In a hard case, where there are strong arguments on either side and the disagreement has deep roots in basic constitutional principles, which arguments a lawyer or judge finds persuasive, *as a matter of constitutional law and not simply on political grounds*, can depend on the extra-legal political and moral commitments that shape any person's thinking. This is not a fault in the system or proof that anyone is advancing legal arguments for improperly extra-legal purposes; it is a product of the reality that the practice of constitutional law involves persuasive, adversarial, *legal* reasoning rather than adherence to a species of deductive logic.

The accusation or fear that constitutional law is "simply" politics is, I think, chiefly due to the fact that the most visible constitutional law decision-maker, the Supreme Court, addresses (as it must, given the Court's role) the most contestable constitutional law questions. The result is that the correlation in those cases between the justices' differing legal judgments and their different political and ideological beliefs is unmistakable. That correlation is also unavoidable and in itself no reason to question the justices' good faith adherence to the accepted practice of constitutional

---

[1]   Benjamin N. Cardozo, *The Nature of the Judicial Process* 13 (New Haven: Yale University Press, 1921).

law or to doubt that the practice this book describes is the framework within which the vast majority of constitutional law questions are answered. That there have been individual Supreme Court decisions that were inexcusably political is more than likely, but lapses in fidelity to principle are also a feature of the human condition. The existence and normative force of the practice of constitutional law is the baseline against which such deviations, by the justices or others, can be identified and criticized.

The introduction which follows explains that in practice, what lawyers regularly mean when they refer to "the Constitution" is usually not the document itself but rather what I shall call the Constitution-in-practice, the set of legal rules and principles that lawyers and judges have created in the course of trying to apply the written Constitution to the real world of legal and political conflict. Chapter 1 explains the reason for which the Constitution-in-practice came into existence. The constitutional text and the structures of government it creates or addresses give rise to problems, not only in litigation but also in the activities of legislators and executive officials, for which the text provides no clear solution or, just as vexingly, more than one plausible solution. Because the written Constitution announces itself to be, and is universally understood to be, "the supreme law" of the American political community, the problems demand solutions, and so from the first years of the Republic, lawyers – who are by profession problem solvers – have set out to find the right solutions. In doing so, the lawyers (some of whom, of course, were judges) created the practice of constitutional law.

Chapters 2 through 5 describe the modes of thought and argument that make up this practice. In Chapter 2, I explain that the first step in solving a constitutional problem is to determine exactly what sort of problem it is, and that constitutional lawyers do so by applying what I refer to as a twofold logic of inquiry. All constitutional issues, if one analyzes them carefully, pose one or more questions that fall, invariably, into one of two categories: questions of authorization (does the Constitution-in-practice authorize *this* part of government to take the action at issue?) and questions of prohibition (does the Constitution-in-practice prohibit *this* part of government from doing so?). Questions of authorization apply, almost exclusively, to the federal government, and all federal actions must be constitutionally authorized. In the practice of federal constitutional law, we presuppose that state governments possess a general power of governance that is not derived from the Constitution, the "police power." Constitutional prohibitions, most of which are addressed to both federal and state governments, override constitutional authorizations and the states' police power alike.

In Chapter 3, we turn to the constitutional lawyer's basic toolkit, the forms of argument that the lawyer employs in constructing the answers to the questions that the problem at hand presents. There are two basic forms, arguments directly based on the written Constitution and arguments derived from the precedents that make up the Constitution-in-practice. Reasoning that focuses on the written instrument includes not only straightforward textual claims but also arguments about the text's original meaning and the structures of government it ordains. Despite the logical priority of the written Constitution, however, in most situations, the rules and principles of the Constitution-in-practice are controlling. The Supreme Court's decisions and doctrines are the primary basis of precedential reasoning, but American political practice and legal tradition also play a role. Chapter 4 discusses the varying perspectives that a lawyer may need to adopt in a specific role or in order to answer a specific constitutional question. For example, a lawyer arguing to a court or sitting as a judge must take into account both the limits on the power of courts to interfere with political decisions in the name of the Constitution and the courts' complementary recognition that democratic politics, not judicial decision, is the ordinary mode of governance in the American Republic. Chapter 5 discusses unusual aspects of certain provisions in the written Constitution that the constitutional lawyer may find puzzling.

As I observed previously, the practice of constitutional law is not a form of deductive logic, and intelligent constitutional lawyers thinking in good faith about a difficult problem may not come to the same conclusion about the right solution. Chapter 6 addresses the very difficult question of what makes one constitutional law argument more persuasive than another. A persuasive argument must be well constructed: It must make intellectually honest use of the accepted forms of argument and take into account the perspectives that are relevant to the question and the weight of the reasons for rejecting a proposed answer. When a constitutional law question is relatively straightforward, it may be possible to formulate an argument that most competent lawyers will accept as compelling because no contrary argument seems plausible in comparison. But on a difficult question, professional craftsmanship alone may not determine which answer is most persuasive, and other considerations will play a proportionately larger role.

In the Conclusion, I return to the normative question posed in this preface and restate – in the light of my description of the practice – my belief that the practice of constitutional law merits its role as the established, legitimate, and appropriate means of addressing the problems that invariably arise under the Constitution of the United States.

The Appendix briefly discusses the English common law, which is the intellectual and institutional ancestor of American constitutional law and also addresses the constitutional debate over the existence of a federal common law.

Notes to the Reader

My concern throughout this book is with *federal* constitutional law, the law of the United States Constitution. Much of what I write applies, I think, to the distinct constitutional laws of the states and of the other subnational political communities that make up the United States, but they are not my topic. All references to "the Court" are to the Supreme Court of the United States.

I am deeply indebted in all that follows, not just to those mentioned in the acknowledgments but also to the many writers on constitutional law topics from whose work I have learned over the years. I am grateful to them all, but in a book of this nature, it is not possible to document the sources of my own thinking, even if I could recognize them all. The brief reading list at the end of the book is intended to provide ideas about further reading for those who have found this book helpful.

In quotations, I have adjusted without notice upper case/lower case letters to fit the context except when I am quoting the text of the Constitution. I have removed internal quotation marks and brackets when they seemed unnecessary or distracting, but, of course, the wording is original and unless noted so are any emphases. To reduce the number of footnotes, I have usually provided the citations to all quotations or case references in a paragraph in a single footnote at the paragraph's end.

Acknowledgments

This book reflects from beginning to end what I have learned from my teachers, colleagues in the academy and in government, and my students, and I am grateful to them all.

Two good friends, Henry Paul Monaghan and James Boyd White, read the manuscript with extraordinary care and gave me the great gift of their comments, suggestions, and criticisms. The book is immeasurably better as a result, and I deeply appreciate their time and wisdom. Of course, Henry and Jim are not to be blamed for the faults I failed to correct!

As always, my older daughter Sara was an enthusiastic sounding board as I wrote. I was fortunate indeed to have her advice on questions of structure and approach, advice based in part on her own fascinating work as a scholar of Slavic literatures.

This book would not exist if it were not for my wife Sarah. When I first mentioned the idea, well over a decade ago, her immediate response was that this was a book worth writing. Without her consistent belief in the project and her confidence in my ability to carry it out, I would have abandoned the book on numerous occasions. And as in past work, I have benefitted more than I can say from her lawyerly intellect and insight and her sense of style. Dedicating *The Practice of American Constitutional Law* to her is an inadequate way of expressing my gratitude, but I trust that Sarah will hear what I do not have the words to say.

Introduction

What Is the Constitution?

Americans refer to "the Constitution" easily and often. What exactly they mean is not so clear much of the time.

The term is, of course, short for "The Constitution of the United States of America," which is the title of a document – really, a collection of documents, the original text and the amendments. In some sense, Americans always have the document in the back of their minds when they invoke its title. In ceremonial contexts, and when politicians want to belabor their opponents about the latter's supposed perfidy, "the Constitution" brings up the image of the parchment document housed in the National Archives, with "We the People" in large flowing script at the beginning and George Washington's signature leading the rest at the end; what the document actually *says* between heading and signatures is often immaterial. At the other end of the spectrum, "the Constitution" in a list of university classes might identify a course truly focused on the language drafted in Philadelphia in the summer of 1787, with some attention paid to the text's antecedents and to the intellectual arguments and political struggles over its subsequent ratification by the thirteen original states. Somewhere in between are those many occasions when "the Constitution" stands for the speaker's views on American ideals. Exactly *how* the words of the text express those ideals may be hazy, but *that* the words do so, and in the process safeguard those ideals, is crucially important, indeed, the very point of referring to the Constitution.

When American lawyers say the words "the Constitution," however, if they are speaking as lawyers, what they usually have in mind is not so much the document or its contents or the ideals for which it stands, although the lawyers' "Constitution" is related to those other meanings. A lawyer's statement about "the Constitution" – "the Constitution authorizes Congress to charter a national bank," for example, or "the Constitution prohibits interference with the right to travel interstate" – is the answer (or proposed answer) to a question about how the nation's fundamental law addresses some issue or problem. What lawyers have in mind, when speaking as lawyers, are the precedents, rules, principles, and doctrines that lawyers and judges have developed since 1787, and that in fact generally provide the rules of decision for solving constitutional problems. It is these rules and doctrines, which I shall call the Constitution-in-practice, that function most of the time as the fundamental law of the Republic.

This is no betrayal or repudiation of the document, most of which was written in 1787. The written Constitution refers to itself as "the supreme Law of the Land," and as we shall see, the constitutional text plays a crucial role in the answers lawyers construct in addressing constitutional questions. But it is descriptively inaccurate, or at least misleading, to equate the fundamental law that lawyers argue over with the semantic contents of the 1787 document plus later amendments. Constitutional lawyers, including those who sit on the Supreme Court of the United States, do not answer a constitutional question, in fact they do not even define what counts as a constitutional question, simply by consulting the words of the document, along with (perhaps) Dr. Johnson's great eighteenth-century dictionary. And this is true even of those lawyers and Supreme Court justices who insist most vigorously that constitutional law questions can only be answered properly on the basis of arguments closely related to the text.

All of this is by way of saying that the lawyers' practice of constitutional law – the activity of framing and debating questions that make sense in court and in other settings of legal argument, and whose answers can be stated as what "the Constitution" authorizes/permits/prohibits/limits, and so on – is an activity distinct from the literary examination of the constitutional text, historical investigation into its origins, or the philosophical or political articulation of our society's highest ideals. These other activities overlap with constitutional law, but engaging in them is not engaging in constitutional law. This book is an introduction to the activity of constitutional law that lawyers writing briefs and judges deciding cases actually practice.

The reader may have detected in the previous paragraphs a preference for referring to constitutional law as an action rather than a subject: constitutional lawyers ask (or are asked) questions, they propose answers, they practice or engage in an activity. I have two reasons for doing so. The first is to suggest what the reader should not expect from the book's contents: This is not a summary of the *content* of the Constitution-in-practice, of the set of answers and predicted answers that competent constitutional lawyers believe the Supreme Court would give, or ought to give, to constitutional questions. Along the way we shall encounter many references to constitutional law in this subject matter sense, but supplying answers to such questions is not my goal. There are plenty of introductions to the principles, doctrines, and rules of constitutional law; this book's aim is to explain the intellectual activities by which lawyers and judges identify, analyze, criticize, and construct those principles, doctrines, and rules. I've already rejected the common sense assumption that the words of the written Constitution supply all the content of constitutional law in some straightforward manner; the rest of this book explains the methods by which lawyers and judges determine that content since the text is not, and indeed cannot be, the exclusive basis of constitutional reasoning.

The second and more important reason for describing constitutional law as an activity or process is that thinking of it in those terms rather than as a body of knowledge is a better way to understand what gives constitutional law its coherence and, in principle, intellectual integrity. The methods of constitutional reasoning are also part of the Constitution-in-practice, and indeed the most enduring part. "Ultimately, the law is not something that we know, but something that we do,"[1] and competence in any area of law *always* requires experiential proficiency in how to practice in that area, not simply the possession of information. (To be sure, many areas of law also demand acquaintance with a great deal of technical detail.) This general truth about law is even more salient in constitutional law, which can seem so riven by political and ideological disagreement that one might wonder if it has any coherent or continuing substance. I think the extent of internal disarray and division in constitutional law is often exaggerated, but there is enough, particularly at the Supreme Court level that is all most nonlawyers know about, to raise a genuine concern that "it's all politics." The claim that constitutional law is a genuine form of law and not merely a species of political choice is crucial to the legitimacy of constitutional law in the American governmental system, and the claim, if it is to be vindicated, rests largely on the existence of a coherent, describable set of methods for making and critiquing constitutional arguments. Americans are sharply divided over any number of substantive constitutional issues, a fact that has always been true although the substance of the disagreements changes over time. What transcends these divisions are the tools American lawyers and judges use to raise and answer constitutional law questions. The purpose of this book is to explain those tools.

---

[1] Arthur A. Leff, Law And, 87 *Yale L. J.* 989, 1011 (1978). No, no words are missing from Professor Leff's title.

1

Constitutional Lawyers as Problem Solvers

Lawyers are problem solvers. The problem may already have occurred (the promised delivery of widgets never arrived) or lie in a future that someone wants to address (what shall we do if the widgets get lost in transit?). The goal in mind as the lawyer looks for a solution to the problem varies across areas of law and the differing roles lawyers play. Contract law facilitates social and economic cooperation and addresses breakdowns in agreements (someone is going to be out of pocket if those widgets never show up). In contrast, the systemic purposes of criminal law are punishment and deterrence (it's socially useful to dissuade a would-be thief from stealing the widgets). Within limits the law creates, the criminal defendant's attorney and the prosecutor have diametrically opposed goals, while the judge's purpose is to ensure the lawfulness and, again within limits dictated by the law, the justice of the proceedings.

Constitutional lawyers address problems that arise out of the fundamental governmental structures and political commitments of the United States as a political community. Any human society has a "constitution" in the sense that one can describe its basic organizational arrangements, even if they are nowhere formally defined. Furthermore, all societies tend to adhere to the arrangements that have characterized their activities in the past – a society in which everything is up for grabs is in the process of dissolution. But in any society, disputes arise not only within the accepted modes of conflict resolution but also at times over the fundamental rules themselves. Every society must have some at least tacit means for resolving the problem of disagreement over its basic arrangements or, once again, it is headed for change or collapse.

In the United States, the fundamental arrangements of political society and the mode of resolving conflict about those arrangements are formalized rather than tacit. The written Constitution both symbolizes this fact and provides an incomplete specification of the arrangements that in fact structure and limit American government. By long-standing agreement, those arrangements, whatever their relation to the written text, are generally treated as legal rules and principles that courts can interpret and apply in the course of judicial proceedings that are, speaking broadly, of the same sort as those used to resolve contractual disputes and criminal prosecutions. This practice in turn means that many problems that arise over American governmental structures and activities – problems that in some other society might be thought the province of politicians or philosophers – are treated in this society as legal problems that lawyers must solve using legal tools.

That constitutional disputes are disagreements over law is an almost universal American assumption; it is also a most peculiar one. The "constitution" of a political community is, by definition, political in nature and content. Controversy arising over, or out of, some aspect of the community's basic governmental arrangements will stem from political, moral, economic, religious, and social causes; draw on the passions and ambitions of political persons and groups; and demand a resolution with intensely political consequences. The processes of legal argument and judicial decision are, on the face of it, ill-suited to handle such conflicts: For quite a long time, indeed, English-speaking law's procedures and professional traditions have been shaped with an eye toward *de*-politicizing the judiciary, excluding nonlegal factors from consideration, and eliminating any formal role for passion or ambition in decision. Either the law's limitations will fail to encompass the moral ideals and commitments of the community, it might seem, or the political nature of constitutional disagreements will corrupt the law and the institutions of law.

Despite these potential drawbacks, which did not escape the notice of founding-era Americans, essentially from the beginning, Americans have generally agreed that the written Constitution is law in much the same way that an enactment by the legislature is law, and that "the Constitution" announced by lawyers, the Constitution-in-practice, governs American government. The details of how and why this happened are disputed, but that it did so very quickly is beyond debate, and that fact provides an essential baseline for this book's goal of introducing the reader to the tools twenty-first-century constitutional lawyers and judges employ.

Begin with the concept of law itself. Many of the leading founders had a surprisingly sophisticated understanding of the history of Western political thought, and the Declaration of Independence reflects the widespread acceptance, for some purposes, of certain very general ideas about law. American political freedom, the second Continental Congress informed the world, is an entitlement based on "the Laws of Nature and of Nature's God." The Declaration's famous second paragraph grandly announced the individual's possession of "certain unalienable Rights" as well as the collective "Right of the People to alter or to abolish" government when in the People's judgment the existing government has become destructive of its purpose "to secure these rights" to "Life, Liberty and the pursuit of Happiness." Since the signatories and supporters of those familiar words were at the same time busily committing treason against the sovereign and the governmental system they had acknowledged up until a few months before, clearly they thought it meaningful to use the language of law in ways that do not refer to any mundane and regularly organized legal system. But for other, less revolutionary purposes, when the founders invoked "law," what they often had in mind was the English common law, the very mundane and indeed parochial set of legal institutions, procedures, and ways of thinking the American colonists had imported from Britain.[1]

Once again, there are fascinating historical arguments about hows and whys and wherefores that we cannot discuss here, although it is important to acknowledge that independence brought along with it a deliberate effort on the part of some Americans to escape the gravitational pull of the familiar English legal forms. In the end, the effort was almost wholly unsuccessful, in part because Americans associated the unalienable and natural right of Liberty with such quintessentially English institutions and practices as the jury, the writ of habeas corpus, and the amenability of executive officials to judicial process, and for that reason maintained those institutions and practices. Equally important was the simple fact that few people who played a significant role in founding-era politics knew much detail about any modern legal system other than the common law. They simply assumed that one must think about a legal issue in the ways common lawyers went about answering legal questions. As a result, when Americans assimilated constitutional dispute resolution to legal problem solving in the wake of the adoption of the written Constitution, they immediately and unreflectively adopted the mindset of the common lawyers as the intellectual starting point for reasoning about the constitutional law of the United States. The consequences of that absent-minded nondecision in the Republic's first years continue to shape how contemporary constitutional lawyers solve twenty-first-century problems.

Consider the written Constitution. The text itself creates questions that cannot plausibly be answered by the text alone, and yet if the text is to function as law, it must be possible to find legal answers to those questions. An example will illustrate the point. Article II section 4 expressly makes the vice president subject to removal from office upon impeachment and conviction for "high Crimes and Misdemeanors." From other provisions, we know that the House of Representatives has the power of impeachment and that the Senate tries any impeachment case that the House presents. In addition, Article I section 3 mandates that "when the President of the United States is tried, the Chief Justice shall preside" over the Senate. Who presides when the vice president is on trial? Section 3 also makes the vice president "President of the Senate" and empowers the senator who is president pro tem to take the vice

---

[1] For additional discussion of the common law, see the Appendix.

president's place only "in the Absence of the Vice President," or when latter is serving as president. Does that mean the vice president presides at his own trial? There must be an answer, and it must be an answer of constitutional law since the Constitution, which is law, gives rise to the question. But the text, by itself, provides no clear answer.[2]

---

[2]   There is in fact a straightforward textual answer to the question of who presides over the Senate if one treats the written Constitution as a hermetically sealed collection of answers to be derived by semantics and abstract logic: when the vice president is tried, the vice president presides. The vice president is subject to trial on being impeached (Article II section 4), the Senate has "the sole Power to try all Impeachments" (Article I section 3), and the vice president is the president of the Senate (Article I section 3). This answer is patently absurd. (Lawyers who accept the answer as correct in some linguistic sense generally treat it as proof that the text contains "a few glaring errors." *See, e.g.*, Stephen L. Carter, The Political Aspects of Judicial Power: Some Notes on the Presidential Immunity Decision, 131 *U. Pa. L. Rev.* 1341, 1357 & n. 72 (1983).)

The lawyerly way to make fun of this answer is to point to the background principle of Anglo-American law that no one should be a judge in his own case and to the incontrovertible historical fact that the framers and ratifiers of the written Constitution meant to create a government that made sense, and made sense in part because it respected universally accepted background principles of law. The fact that no adult, lawyer or not, would think that the vice president presides ought to be the right answer is itself a powerful illustration of the fact that the constitutional text does not, on its own, address all constitutional questions, or at least not satisfactorily.

Article I section 3's designation of the chief justice as the presiding officer when the Senate tries the president is obviously intended to avoid the potential conflict of interest a vice president would face in presiding over a trial that might make him president. Since the conflict of interest would be even more severe if the defendant on trial were the vice president himself, the chief justice seems an excellent choice for vice presidential trials as well. But there are serious textual difficulties with that answer. First, on its face, section 3 authorizes the chief justice to preside over a Senate trial in only one circumstance, and a common law canon of construction respected by founding-era American lawyers counsels against expanding the authorization. (*Expressio unius est exclusio alterius*: the statement of one thing forbids the inclusion of others. *See, e.g., In re Bliss*, 9 Johns. 347, 348–49 (N.Y. Sup. Ct. 1812). *Bliss* quoted the *expressio* canon and held that the mention of specific officers of the court in a statute creating exemptions from militia duty implied, "by irresistible inference," that other officers were not exempt.) Second, section 3's involvement of an officer of the Article III branch of the federal government in the work of a part of the Article I branch creates an exception to the general principle of separation of powers established by Articles I, II, and III. Since the text expressly creates the exception for presidential trials, the chief justice's intrusion raises no constitutional problems, but extending the exception to trials of the vice president has no such textual justification for impinging on one of the most important structural features of the constitutional system.

Since the office of president pro tem exists by constitutional authorization, and allowing that senator to preside does not raise "separation of powers" concerns, perhaps that is the best answer. But this answer has textual difficulties as well. It requires us to ignore the fact that Article I section 3 expressly states when the president pro tem can preside – "in the Absence of the Vice President or when he shall exercise the Office of President" – and thus, by the same canon of construction just mentioned, section 3 implicitly prohibits the president pro tem from presiding if the vice president insists on being present. (The legal fiction that the vice president should be deemed absent when on trial is a confession that section 3 has led us into a dead end.) Furthermore, allowing the president pro tem to preside over a trial that might make her president of the Senate all the time, until the vice presidential office can be filled, poses at least to some degree the conflict of interest concern that we confidently infer lies behind the chief justice's role in presidential trials. And finally, if the president pro tem presides, does she lose her vote for or against convicting the vice president, and does she count as a "Member present" for the purposes of determining if the vice president has been convicted by "the Concurrence of two thirds of the Members present" as Article I section 3 also requires?

Founding-era Americans did not have to decide who should preside at a vice president's trial, but they encountered constitutional questions with no clear textual answer from the beginning, and their response was to use the familiar methods of common law argument to construct answers. After the constitutional text went into effect, this turn to common law reasoning to address questions with textually indeterminate answers began no later than 1790, when President George Washington asked Secretary of State Thomas Jefferson, who had been a practicing lawyer before the Revolution, whether the Senate had the power to reject the rank to which Washington proposed to appoint an American diplomat. Article II section 2 of the Constitution vests the president with the power to "nominate, and by and with the Advice and Consent of the Senate, . . . appoint Ambassadors, other public Ministers and Consuls," but it does not explain whether the Senate can properly address any issue beyond the suitability of the president's nominee for the position and rank that the president proposes. Jefferson gave the answer Washington hoped for (the Senate is limited to an up or down vote on the nominee) and justified his answer with a written legal opinion using traditional common law arguments to conclude that the Senate's advice and consent role is a narrow exception to an otherwise exclusive executive power.

Jefferson's turn to common law-like arguments to make workable sense of the written Constitution was not arbitrary. The constitutional text itself clearly invites its readers to assume that English common law provides the legal backdrop for its provisions. Article VI announces that "This Constitution," along with acts of Congress "in Pursuance thereof" and federal treaties, is "the supreme Law of the Land." The immediate point of the provision is to ensure national law's superiority to state law, but its language is a clear invocation of English legal tradition: The most famous clause in Magna Carta was a royal promise to do no harm to any freeman "but by lawful judgment of his peers, or by the law of the land." The text of the original 1787 document and of the Bill of Rights (the first ten amendments, proposed to the states by the First Congress in 1789[3]) repeatedly presupposes that the reader has some knowledge of the common law system simply to understand its terminology; indeed, the seventh amendment directs that no fact "tried by a jury" (an institution defined by the common law!) is to be re-examined in a federal court other "than according to the rules of the common law." And on a different and, for our

---

I think the best answer is that the president pro tem should preside. The perks of being president of the Senate and thus the conflict of interest issue seem fairly minimal, especially since the adoption of the twenty-fifth amendment in 1967, which creates a procedure for replacing the vice president between presidential elections. The constitutional difficulties pointed out at the end of the last paragraph can be addressed by the Senate's adoption of rules addressing them as part of its constitutional duty and power to determine how to conduct impeachment trials. And deciding not to ask the chief justice to preside avoids any separation of powers problems as well as the possibility that the chief justice would refuse on the ground that, whatever the Senate's view, in his opinion he was not authorized to act.

3 In constitutional law as in political history, "the First Congress" refers to the first Congress to convene under the authority of the written Constitution, which sat from 1789 to 1791. For the special significance of the First Congress in constitutional law, see Chapter 3.

purposes, more important level, the assumption that the constitutional text as written and authoritative law is to be read as common lawyers read such texts profoundly shaped the new practice of constitutional law.

In a strict sense, "common law" referred to law announced by the courts rather than ordained by parliamentary enactment. Founding-era Americans sometimes invoked an old notion that the common law's substance ultimately stemmed from popular customs and early "legislative" pronouncements now lost in the mists of time, a fig leaf attractive to those squeamish about the reality that the courts had made and continued to remake the common law, but otherwise of no significance whatever. Early-modern common law judges generally conceded, sometimes with undisguised reluctance, that an act of Parliament could override or supplant a contrary common law rule. That concession, however, did not extend to the modes of argument and decision the courts accepted in applying superior parliamentary law. Instead, the common law courts construed statutory language using (in general) the same techniques of interpretation they applied to other legal instruments (deeds, written contracts, and the like) and recognizing the same forms of argument they considered when applying purely judge-made legal rules. The result was to minimize the intellectual differences between a decision controlled by a statute and one determined by common law per se, and over time to make the statute in practice as much as product of the judicial decisions construing it as of the original statutory text itself.

The same process has occurred in American constitutional law, as already signaled in the distinction I drew in the introduction between the written Constitution and the Constitution-in-practice that lawyers discuss. Where it exists, it is the latter that is the controlling fundamental law of the United States, and on issues that have been much litigated – the scope of Congress's Article I power to regulate interstate commerce or of the first amendment right to freedom of speech, to take two clear examples – it is to the Supreme Court's decisions, not textual exegesis, that one must chiefly look to in order to answer any difficult question. To the great surprise of some first-year law students, therefore, most of the time debate over what "the Constitution" commands is a discussion of judicial precedents and judicially formulated principles and doctrines far more than an investigation into the semantics and history of the document. To be sure, the precedents and principles and doctrines refer, sometimes rather remotely or indirectly, to the written Constitution, but the courts derive them by methods of legal reasoning parallel to those at work in areas of law traditionally governed by the common law proper such as contracts and torts.[4]

---

[4] The same phenomenon occurs in American statutory law as well: Over time the practical meaning of a legislative provision that is frequently litigated increasingly depends on what the courts have made of it, although of course their decisions stem from the original legislative language. Building additional detail into that language limits but cannot eliminate the gradual incrustation of the legislature's handiwork by judicial glosses; indeed, one effect of statutory detail is to invite the courts to determine

None of this is to say that the written Constitution is inconsequential, or that power-mad judges have usurped the authority that properly belongs to the charter adopted by the sovereign People. The observation that in practice constitutional law is the product of common law-like legal reasoning describes *how* the written Constitution serves as law in reality, not a denial that the text is the supreme law. The constitutional text's authority is axiomatic in constitutional law: Questions about the source and propriety of its authority – for example, whether it makes sense in the twenty-first century to treat as authoritative a collection of documents the oldest and longest of which was drafted and approved by groups of eighteenth-century white men – are not questions within constitutional law.[5]

The constitutional text, in addition, limits the scope of the Constitution-in-practice in two important ways. First, the text addresses some basic aspects of American governmental structure so clearly, whether expressly or by obvious implication, that they seldom or never give rise to legal problems: Congress has two chambers, both of which must act in order for a bill to become law, every state regardless of population has two senators, Congress cannot convict someone of violating federal law by enacting a law stating that he or she is guilty of doing so, the president may not appoint members of Congress or a state legislature or fire a federal judge, no state may limit the right to vote to men (or women). Such unproblematic aspects of the written Constitution are extremely important, but they do not play an important role in constitutional law precisely because their clarity heads off the kind of problems constitutional lawyers solve.

Second, the constitutional text plays a vital, although not exclusive, role in identifying just what political and social questions are matters for constitutional lawyers and judges to debate. Taken on its own, the abstract concept of a constitution suggests that a problem or controversy rises to a "constitutional" level insofar as it involves the broadest or most fundamental political issues and societal commitments of the community. As a rough generality, that can be said of American constitutional law, but the existence of the written Constitution creates many exceptions. On the one hand, very important concerns can be outside the realm of constitutional debate because they have no foothold in the constitutional text. The wisdom and political morality of large-scale federal deficit spending is a legitimate and important question, and some deficit hawks argue that it violates fundamental norms of good government, but in the absence of a balanced-budget amendment, the question lies beyond the purview of constitutional law. And on the other hand, if

---

the statute's effect by resort to canons of statutory construction that are themselves the product of judicial decision and applied by judicial reasoning.

5   "The authoritative status of the written constitution is a legitimate matter of debate for political theorists interested in the nature of political obligation. That status is, however, an incontestable first principle [in] American constitutional law. ... For the purposes of legal reasoning, the binding quality of the constitutional text is itself incapable of and not in need of further demonstration." Henry Paul Monaghan, Our Perfect Constitution (1981), in *American Constitutional Law: Selected Essays* 411–12 (Durham, NC: Carolina Academic Press, 2018).

the written Constitution does address an issue, a problem involving it is constitutional ipso facto even if, on balance, one is inclined to think the matter of limited importance. The Justice Department has determined that it was unconstitutional, for example, for an historian employed by the National Archives to serve on a commission of historians funded by a foreign government even though the historian was willing to forego compensation by that government.[6]

The written Constitution, furthermore, has played a significant role in the rise of "judicial review" (court decisions on constitutional issues) as the central institutional mechanism for debating and resolving constitutional law questions. There is no intrinsic reason that such questions cannot be addressed by legislators or executive officials – early Congresses frequently debated constitutional issues with a high level of legal sophistication – and the executive branch has an unbroken tradition of written legal opinions on constitutional matters that began with Secretary Jefferson's opinion for President Washington. But at a very early point, state and federal judges came to the conclusion that they had the obligation not only to entertain claims that an executive officer had violated the law (a duty that colonial and contemporaneous English judges accepted) but also to consider arguments that an act of Congress or a state legislature had violated the supreme law of the Constitution. The existence of written state and federal constitutions that (axiomatically) are the direct voice of the sovereign people was one of the arguments that persuaded judges and others that this expansion of the judicial role was legitimate.

Once judicial review (a modern term) in this broadened form encompassing legislation was generally accepted, it was easy and perhaps inevitable that Americans would come to think of constitutional law questions as not only susceptible to judicial resolution but most properly dealt with by the courts in general. "It is emphatically the province and duty of the Judicial Department to say what the law is," the Supreme Court announced in 1803 in *Marbury* v. *Madison*, the decision now associated in most lawyers' minds (inaccurately as an historical matter) with the "establishment" of judicial review.[7] If the Constitution is law, then the solution to problems arising under it can seem to belong most naturally to the "Department" charged with determining what the law is and how it is to be applied. Over the long haul, this assumption has gelled into a settled political practice. American executive officers enforce the constitutional decisions of the courts, and American legislators usually accept the finality of the Supreme Court's constitutional views, even when these other government officials believe the decisions wrong. The rare exceptions (President Lincoln's refusal to obey an order releasing a suspected secessionist, the

---

[6] See *Applicability of Emoluments Clause to Proposed Service of Gov't Emp. on Comm'n of Int'l Historians*, 11 Op. O.L.C. 89 (1987). The relevant constitutional prohibition is in Article I section 9: "no Person holding any Office of Profit or Trust under [the United States], shall, without the Consent of the Congress, accept of any present, Emolument, Office, or Title, of any kind whatever, from any King, Prince, or foreign State."

[7] 5 U.S. (1 Cranch) 137, 177 (1803).

initial segregationist response to the Supreme Court's desegregation decisions, the ongoing legislative resistance to the Court's abortion cases) prove only that generalizations, in law as elsewhere in human affairs, seldom are universally valid.

While *Marbury* v. *Madison* does not deserve credit (or blame) for inventing judicial review, Chief Justice John Marshall's opinion for the Court in that case did announce the now-canonical rationale for judges following their own views on constitutional questions. Judicial review, as Marshall described it, rests not on the superiority of the courts over the political branches of government but on the superiority of the written Constitution over decisions by any branch of government, including the judiciary. In executing whatever position they hold, all American governmental officials have a duty to respect the binding legal force of the written Constitution, or as Marshall put it, "the principle, supposed to be essential to all written constitutions, that a law repugnant to the constitution is void; and that courts, as well as other departments, are bound by that instrument." A court's duty is to decide the cases that come before it in accordance with law. When a statute (or any other governmental action) is challenged as unconstitutional, if the court agrees that the statute conflicts with a constitutional rule, to follow the statute would be to decide the case not according to law (the superior law of the Constitution) but in obedience to a rule that the judges think legally "void." The "framers of the constitution contemplated that instrument, as a rule for the government of *courts*, as well as of the legislature. Why otherwise does it direct the judges to take an oath to support it?"[8]

Modern lawyers sometimes argue that Marshall's justification for judicial review as an application of the everyday duty of a court to decide cases lawfully does not depend as a matter of logic on the written nature of "the Constitution." Marshall evidently thought otherwise; more importantly, as his invocation of the judicial oath suggests, the idea that the exercise of judicial review is ultimately based on the judge's duty to a written Constitution that is not the creation of the courts subtly changes the moral context in which lawyers and judges use common law-like reasoning and judicial precedent to answer constitutional questions. The constitutional law that courts make must be understood as the means by which courts serve the fundamental commitments of a political community made up overwhelmingly of nonlawyers and governed for most purposes by political rather than legal decision-making. And constitutional doctrines and decisions may be modified, limited, or even repudiated, even though they make up the Constitution-in-practice that actually governs constitutional disputes, because they are *not* the written Constitution.

* * *

Chief Justice Marshall's reference to the moral dimension he perceived in judicial review returns us to where this chapter began, with the problem solving role of constitutional lawyers (including judges deciding constitutional cases) in the

---

[8] *Id.* at 179–80.

American governmental system. Since the Constitution, both the text itself and the Constitution-in-practice, addresses American political structures and normative political commitments, there is a perfectly straightforward sense in which constitutional problems are political. In a different governmental system, such problems might be addressed using the tools of open political debate, encompassing any and all kinds of argument that a participant thought relevant to the issue at hand. The ultimate solution, whatever the mechanism used for determining what it should be, would be what the decision-makers thought best, all things considered.

The American decision to treat the written Constitution as a legal instrument, and constitutional issues as legal questions demanding legal answers, changes all that. Common lawyers, in both England and the United States, have long entertained arguments of varying kinds, and constitutional lawyers have followed suit, but the list is not unlimited. Many factors and modes of argument that are proper in English-speaking political debate can find no place in a constitutional law brief, and courts have a duty to decide cases, including constitutional ones, by resort to properly legal considerations and only through applying those considerations. This is not to deny what is obvious, that lawyers, including judges, sometimes fall short in carrying out their duties, but the obligation to resolve a *constitutional* law problem by constitutional *law* means remains even though we sometimes catch lawyers (including, on occasion, lawyers on the Supreme Court) guilty of dereliction of duty. The problems constitutional lawyers address are inherently political, but their duty is to formulate the solutions out of the more limited and often apolitical sources of legal argument. Of course, different lawyers play different roles, and the duty of the judge in deciding a case differs from that of the litigator trying to craft the most persuasive argument for a client, but all share a common responsibility to employ the tools of constitutional law reasoning. The next four chapters explain what those tools are.

1.1 EXCURSUS: ORIGINALISM

Most of the time constitutional lawyers, including Supreme Court justices, engage in the practice of constitutional law that this book describes without debating the legitimacy of doing so. In recent decades, however, some scholars, lawyers, and judges have argued that the traditional practice is defective or even fundamentally erroneous, and have proposed radical reforms to our accepted forms of reasoning and argument.

The most important group of reformers subscribe to what is usually known as "originalism," an umbrella term referring to variously articulated arguments made since the 1970s that the practice of constitutional law should be changed to give arguments from original meaning greater or even invariably decisive weight in answering constitutional law questions. Originalists often argue or assert that their approach is in fact the real tradition of American constitutional law reasoning, the true path from which Supreme Court decisions deviated at some point in the past.

I think that historical assertion stands on shaky legs at best.[9] A more plausible foundation for originalist reform rests on the accusation that constitutional law as it is usually practiced and described in this book is too unconstraining, too open to manipulation by clever advocates and unscrupulous judges. The originalist proposal is to bind down constitutional law by a method of argument that supposedly will allow no room for manipulation and minimize the need for the constitutional lawyer or judge to exercise personal judgment.[10]

There are several aspects of originalism that make the theory of little importance in a description of the practice of constitutional law. Originalists regularly assume that the pared-down version of constitutional law reasoning they commend would permit lawyers to carry out their role of solving the problems to which the written Constitution gives rise, but that assumption is often incorrect. As we saw in this chapter, the constitutional text generates questions that the text alone cannot answer, even if we ask not only what its words mean to us, at first glance, but also what they meant to those who first read them. There is no original meaning answer to the question of who presides over the trial of the vice president, at least in the sense that historical investigation can determine what founding-era lawyers thought was the answer. I would not argue with someone who pointed out that the background principle about no person being judge in his own case was well-known to the founders and concluded that reasoning on its basis is consonant with founding-era legal thought. Such a line of argument is, however, quite inconsistent with any claim to limit constitutional law reasoning to the historically determined original meanings of the constitutional text.

The second defect in most versions of originalism is that in practice they seem to be more a matter of packaging than substance. Stricter originalists, to be sure, sometimes insist that only text and original meaning arguments based on the written Constitution are truly legitimate, but even they usually make a grudging concession that for practical reasons judicial precedent must play a role. Most originalists, furthermore, accept arguments based on governmental structure as well, which as we shall see in Chapter 3 are arguments focused on the written Constitution but going well beyond a simple application of its language or historically demonstrable original meaning. And when one recalls that Justice Antonin Scalia, for many years

[9]   For my views on this historical issue, see H. Jefferson Powell, On Not Being Not an Originalist, 7 *U. St. Thomas L. J.* 259, 263–66 (2010).

[10] Originalists, and their anti-originalist foes, often overstate the extent to which the traditional practice of constitutional law is subject to manipulation by judicial ideologues. At any given point in time, there is an endless list of constitutional law questions which, if factual disputes are put to one side, have clear answers in the practical sense that a competent constitutional lawyer can predict with almost complete certainty what answer the Supreme Court or another responsible decision-maker would give. The understandable focus on the part of many people on the decisions the high Court reaches in the small number of hotly contested cases it addresses tends to obscure the fact that "in the vast majority of cases judges of different political stripes, genders, religions, races, ages, and experience all reach the same conclusion." David F. Levi, Autocrat of the Armchair, 58 *Duke L. J.* 1791, 1801 (2009).

the leading originalist, also accepted arguments based on American governmental practice and American legal tradition (if narrowly defined), and was himself a skilled and often enthusiastic practitioner of precedent-based reasoning, one could be excused for wondering just how radical originalism really is.[11]

Most importantly, originalism is a theory of minimal relevance in the 99+ percent of constitutional questions that are answered by lawyers or governmental officials not on the US Supreme Court. Few originalists suggest that lower court judges should be able to disregard Supreme Court precedent whenever those judges think that the Court was wrong on originalist grounds. If we are to have a workable government at all, in the judicial system, the Court must be able to explicate rules of law that it can then expect other courts to follow and enforce. Furthermore, the other courts must be able to apply the law the Supreme Court articulates to an endless series of new fact patterns, many of which will require adapting the Court's rulings in ways the justices did not and could not anticipate. Therefore, since an operational system of "vertical" precedent would require something like our form of argument from precedent, as a practical matter originalism is almost entirely a theory about how the Court itself should deal with its own precedents: precedent that is inconsistent with a persuasive original meaning argument ought to be overruled or (more modestly) may be accorded less *stare decisis* scope or weight. And even there, many originalists concede that there are reliance interests that place some precedents beyond rejection no matter how wrong on originalist grounds. To be fair, originalists also think the Court should reject new arguments that conflict with the individual originalist's views on the text's original meaning, but with over two centuries of decisions, the number of truly novel constitutional law issues is limited.[12]

The great debate over originalism is, then, of little importance for the *practice* of constitutional law. This is not to say that weakening the force of the Supreme Court's respect for its own precedents would be unimportant. But originalism would be unlikely to change much beyond its impact on precedent-based arguments in the Court, however significant the specific precedents that might become vulnerable. Whatever the outcome of the originalism debate, therefore, it is likely to leave most constitutional lawyers still engaged in the traditional tasks of identifying

---

[11] On Justice Scalia's acceptance of argument from tradition, see, e.g., *Kerry* v. *Din*, 576 U.S. 86, 93 (2015) (plurality opinion of Scalia, J.). For examples of Scalia as a practitioner of arguments based on precedent and doctrine, *see Maryland* v. *Shatzer*, 559 U.S. 98, 104–12 (2010) (Scalia, J.) (announcing, after considering costs and benefits of various possibilities, a rule that a fourteen day break in custody terminates the *Edwards* v. *Arizona* prohibition on further interrogation of a suspect who has invoked his right to counsel); *Printz* v. *United States*, 521 U.S. 898, 925 (1997) (Scalia, J.) (after discussing original meaning, political practice and structural arguments, "Finally, and most conclusively in the present litigation, we turn to the prior jurisprudence of this Court.").

[12] I discuss the problems with a more radical originalism in H. Jefferson Powell, *Targeting Americans: The Constitutionality of the U.S. Drone War* 193–99 (New York: Oxford University Press, 2016).

constitutional problems and answering questions of authorization and prohibition (see Chapter 2) through the accepted forms of argument (see Chapter 3).

As I indicated in the introduction, the aim of this book is to describe what it is that competent constitutional lawyers actually do (ordinarily) rather than to discuss or adjudicate between the conflicting theories about constitutional law that some of those lawyers believe. The account of constitutional law this book presents is entirely consistent with originalism, and with most of the anti-originalist theories its critics offer, except of course that originalists and their opponents will not agree with my argument in this excursus that the originalism debate is relatively unimportant as a practical matter. Their theoretical disputes are beside the point for my purposes: that constitutional lawyers share the traditional practice I describe is all that is necessary.

The great constitutional lawyer Walter Dellinger has said that all responsible constitutional lawyers are "moderate originalists" in that they (we) recognize the importance of the constitutional text's historical nature and the force that must be given to arguments focused on the written Constitution. Originalism in practice is best understood not as a revolutionary attack on traditional constitutional law reasoning but as a call to exercise intellectual discipline in making arguments and in particular to take seriously the claims of the text's original meaning. No traditional constitutional lawyer would disagree.

2

Identifying the Problem

The Twofold Logic of Constitutional Law

Constitutional law is a problem-solving activity. All problems in constitutional law, without exception, can be analyzed in terms of one or more questions, and all constitutional law questions, without exception, fall into one of two distinct categories: Does the Constitution authorize this governmental action? and does the Constitution prohibit this governmental action? This twofold logic of inquiry into authorization and prohibition guides the constitutional lawyer's analysis of the problem in a constitutional controversy and provides the intellectual skeleton for constitutional law argument and decision. This chapter will first discuss how the logic of inquiry is used, and then will explain how the two questions are the product of the way the written Constitution is worded and of certain background presuppositions about its purposes.

2.1 QUESTIONS OF AUTHORIZATION AND QUESTIONS OF PROHIBITION

The terminology introduced in this chapter is in part my own, but the substance is orthodox and uncontroversial constitutional law thought. Chief Justice John Roberts explained the twofold logic of inquiry very clearly in 2012.[1]

> The Federal Government "is acknowledged by all to be one of enumerated powers." That is, rather than granting general authority to perform all the conceivable functions of government, the Constitution lists, or enumerates, the Federal Government's powers. ... And the Federal Government "can exercise only the powers granted to it."
>
> Today, the restrictions on government power foremost in many Americans' minds are likely to be affirmative prohibitions, such as contained in the Bill of Rights. These affirmative prohibitions come into play, however, only where the Government possesses authority to act in the first place. If no enumerated power authorizes Congress to pass a certain law, that law may not be enacted, even if it would not violate any of the express prohibitions in the Bill of Rights or elsewhere in

[1] *Nat'l Fed'n of Indep. Bus. v. Sebelius,* 567 U.S. 519, 534–36 (2012) (opinion announcing the judgment of the Court), quoting *McCulloch v. Maryland,* 17 U.S. (4 Wheat.) 316, 405 (1819).

the Constitution. . . . The Federal Government has expanded dramatically over the past two centuries, but it still must show that a constitutional grant of power authorizes each of its actions.

The same does not apply to the States, because the Constitution is not the source of their power. The Constitution may restrict state governments – as it does, for example, by forbidding them to deny any person the equal protection of the laws. But where such prohibitions do not apply, state governments do not need constitutional authorization to act. The States thus can and do perform many of the vital functions of modern government – punishing street crime, running public schools, and zoning property for development, to name but a few – even though the Constitution's text does not authorize any government to do so. Our cases refer to this general power of governing, possessed by the States but not by the Federal Government, as the "police power."

The crucial point in this passage is the distinction Chief Justice Roberts drew between *constitutional authorization*, which is a requirement that generally rests only on the federal government ("The Federal Government must show that a constitutional grant of power authorizes each of its actions"), and *constitutional prohibitions*, which generally apply to both the federal and state governments ("affirmative prohibitions, such as contained in the Bill of Rights . . . may restrict state governments" as well as the federal government).

In employing this distinction to analyze the nature of the constitutional problem he or she is addressing, the constitutional lawyer must remember that the relationship between authorization and prohibition is not commutative. As Chief Justice Roberts explained, when the problem at hand concerns the actions of the federal government, "affirmative prohibitions come into play . . . only where the Government possesses authority to act in the first place. If no enumerated power authorizes Congress to pass a certain law, that law may not be enacted, even if it would not violate any of the express prohibitions in the Bill of Rights or elsewhere in the Constitution." An unauthorized action by *any* federal governmental entity or official is a legal nullity.

So, with respect to federal government actions, one must first ask about authorization, and only if there is authorization does one need to ask whether there is a relevant prohibition. And, as the order in which one asks the two questions implies, a constitutional prohibition overrides a constitutional authorization.

Understanding this twofold logic of inquiry is the key to analyzing constitutional problems and determining their most persuasive solutions. What follows is a schematic restatement.

(1) Is the (federal) governmental action authorized under the Constitution?

If the answer to this question is that the action is not authorized by the Constitution, the inquiry is at an end: the federal action is unconstitutional.

As to any federal action, it is always a question whether the action is affirmatively authorized by the Constitution. As Chief Justice Roberts explained, the federal government may exercise only those powers delegated to it by the Constitution, either directly or because the Constitution has authorized one of the government's branches to create rules that the other two branches must follow. (For example, the executive branch must carry out – execute – a constitutionally authorized act of Congress, while a court, federal or state, must enforce it as law.)

With a few exceptions having to do with the states' role in federal elections and the constitutional amendment process, the question of authorization is not one that needs to be asked of state governmental actions in federal constitutional law. As Chief Justice Roberts explained, this is because the state governments do not derive their general powers of governance from the US Constitution, and for the purposes of federal constitutional law we ordinarily assume that state governmental action is affirmatively authorized by the state's constitution. To be sure, the federal government's powers over foreign affairs and national defense are almost all exclusive, and sometimes lawyers refer to this exclusivity in terms of the state governments lacking authority over these subjects. This is, I think, an inaccurate way to characterize our constitutional arrangements for several reasons: perhaps most importantly, Article I section 10 imposes a variety of limitations on the state governments in these areas, an unnecessary precaution if the states lacked authority altogether.

(2) Is the governmental action prohibited by the Constitution?

If the answer is that the governmental action violates such a prohibition, it is unconstitutional. If you have asked the two questions in the right order, the conclusion that the action does not violate a constitutional prohibition means that the action is constitutional.

As to any federal action that is within the scope of a power delegated to the federal government and thus passes question (1), or as to any state governmental action, it is always a question whether that action violates a prohibition mandated by the Constitution.

An important category of prohibited governmental actions that merits separate mention involves state statutes (and other state rules of law or governmental actions) that are inconsistent with valid acts of Congress and US treaties. The supremacy clause of Article VI confers the same supremacy on federal laws, treaties, regulations, and presidential actions that is enjoyed by the Constitution itself, provided of course that the federal measure is itself authorized and not prohibited. The Constitution therefore does not permit the enforcement of inconsistent state measures even if they would otherwise be constitutional. The usual terminology is that the state measure is "preempted" rather than "unconstitutional" because a change in the act of Congress, treaty, or executive action that removed the inconsistency would render the state measure enforceable. But this terminological point should not obscure the fact that preempted state measures are unenforceable because they have run afoul of the constitutional prohibition announced in the supremacy clause.[2]

A simple example may be helpful in understanding constitutional law's twofold logic. Imagine an act of Congress prohibiting the shipment in interstate commerce of Bibles ("the Bible Act"). Since it is a federal governmental measure, we must first ask the question of authorization. It has been settled for over a century that the provision in Article I section 8 that delegates to Congress the power "To regulate Commerce . . . among the several States" authorizes Congress to prohibit altogether the interstate shipment of objects that Congress does not want traveling across state boundaries. So we can conclude that Congress has constitutional authorization to pass the Bible Act.

We turn now to the question of prohibition and immediately run into at least two clauses of the first amendment that are relevant: "Congress shall make no law . . . prohibiting the free exercise [of religion]; or abridging the freedom of speech." Because modern first amendment doctrine is complicated and makes various allowances for governmental regulations that affect religion and speech, the actual analysis necessary to answer the question professionally would take a little time, but the conclusion is not in doubt: The Bible Act is unconstitutional because it violates the prohibitions imposed by the free exercise and free speech clauses.

The constitutional issues raised by the Bible Act are, on the face of it, simple to identify as well as address. But constitutional problems often come wrapped up in complicated facts and cross-cutting claims that can make it difficult to determine just what the constitutional issue or issues are. The twofold logic of authorization and prohibition is a tool not only for determining how to address whatever issues lurk

---

[2]   Article VI states that "this Constitution, and the Laws of the United States which shall be made in Pursuance thereof; and all Treaties made, or which shall be made, under the Authority of the United States, shall be the supreme Law of the Land; and the Judges in every State shall be bound thereby, any Thing in the Constitution or Laws of any State to the Contrary notwithstanding." When we say that a state law is preempted, we mean that the law "is invalid under the Supremacy Clause of the National Constitution owing to its threat of frustrating federal . . . objectives" or policies. *Crosby v. National Foreign Trade Council*, 530 U.S. 363, 366 (2000).

The text of the supremacy clause does not fully express the scope of federal supremacy in the Constitution-in-practice, which encompasses secondary forms of federal law such as agency regulations, as well as executive actions and federal court orders. Furthermore, notwithstanding the clause's specific reference to "the Judges in every State," all state officials and governmental bodies are "bound" by supreme federal law, although the exact obligations this imposes varies somewhat among the branches of the state governments.

The constitutional law of preemption turns on Congress's intentions when the question is whether a federal statute preempts state law. Congress sometimes includes an express preemption provision, which settles the matter within the scope of the provision. Similarly, an act of Congress may also include a "savings clause" providing that the statute does not preempt state legislation within its scope. In the absence of such direct evidence of Congress's intentions, a court will hold the state measure preempted if it is impossible for someone subject to the specific federal and state laws to comply with both ("conflict preemption") or if the relevant congressional legislation appears to show that Congress does not intend for states to legislate on the subject matter at hand ("field preemption"). The Supreme Court has often said that there is a presumption against preemption of state law, although it is fair to say that the presumption does not always seem very strong in what is a complicated body of case law.

in the problem, but also for undertaking the crucial preliminary work of disentangling different constitutional issues so that the constitutional lawyer can address them properly. Let us look at how that works in practice.

In 1819, the Supreme Court decided *McCulloch* v. *Maryland*, one of the most famous cases in American constitutional history, in a decision written by Chief Justice John Marshall. (We shall return to *McCulloch* at many points in this book.) The case began in the county court in Baltimore, Maryland, when a state treasury officer named John James sued James McCulloch, the cashier (branch manager) of the Bank of the United States, the second national bank, which Congress had chartered in 1816. McCulloch was a complete scoundrel, who was simultaneously trying to evade supervision and control by the bank's national officers while manipulating the Baltimore credit market and engaging in outright fraud. A few months after the Supreme Court decided *McCulloch*, the bank's directors fired him, and he was subsequently prosecuted, unsuccessfully despite his guilt.[3]

James's action did not rest on McCulloch's financial misdeeds, however, but on his refusal, on behalf of the bank, to pay a tax enacted by the Maryland legislature in 1817. The tax required any bank not chartered by the state to issue bank notes on paper issued by the state on which a stamp tax had been paid. The national bank could have avoided liability by paying a $15,000 annual fee, but McCulloch issued notes on unstamped paper without paying the fee. The statute imposed a penalty of $500 per note on the bank that was enforceable by an action brought by any plaintiff, who would for his efforts receive half the judgment. James sued for $2500, and the facts being undisputed, the bank's defense was that the state law was unconstitutional. Jones won a judgment in the county court that Maryland's highest court then affirmed, and the bank asked the Supreme Court to vindicate its constitutional claim.[4]

The bank's argument was that the 1817 state tax was invalid under the US Constitution, but the absence from the constitutional text of any provision about state taxes was only part of the puzzle, not an answer. Chief Justice Marshall therefore applied the twofold logic of authorization and prohibition to identify with greater precision what issues lurked in the constitutional problem *McCulloch* had presented the Court. As we have seen, in federal constitutional

---

[3] Chief Justice Marshall's opinion for the Court in *McCulloch* discusses none of the complicated tale of the cashier's shenanigans because those facts were irrelevant to the issues before the Court in 1819. Seven years later, the Court decided *Etting* v. *Bank of the United States*, 24 U.S. (11 Wheat.) 59 (1826), a case that arose directly out of McCulloch's fraudulent behavior. The Court was evenly divided on the issues before it, but in announcing that equivocal result Marshall discussed at length "McCullough's" scheme. On the facts, including the surprisingly difficult issue of how to spell the man's name, see Mark R. Killenbeck, *M'Culloch* v. *Maryland: Securing a Nation* (Lawrence, Kansas: University Press of Kansas, 2006).

[4] See *McCulloch* v. *Maryland*, 17 U.S. (4 Wheat.) 316 (1819). The discussion of *McCulloch* in the text reflects our contemporary understanding of constitutional decision making, which is not precisely that of Chief Justice Marshall and his contemporaries. (See the next footnote for an example.) Marshall and *McCulloch* played a key role in the emergence of what is now our long-standing practice, but for that very reason we should not expect perfect correspondence in details.

law there is ordinarily no question of authorization to be asked about a state statute (so Marshall could assume that the state constitution authorized the tax law), but *McCulloch* necessarily involved another statute as well, the 1816 act of Congress chartering the bank and thereby indirectly authorizing McCulloch's decisions as an officer of the bank about the state tax. (Jones did not claim that McCulloch's refusal was itself a violation of his duties to the bank.) If Congress was not authorized to charter the bank, the 1816 act was a legal nullity, and McCulloch and the bank had no legal defense against a state tax imposed on private banking activity within the state's jurisdiction. No one claimed that the tax was a violation of some other, express constitutional prohibition on state legislation, so any federal constitutional objection to the tax would have to derive from the 1816 federal statute.[5]

By the logic of constitutional inquiry, therefore, the first issue in *McCulloch* did not concern the state tax at all, but instead whether the act of Congress creating the bank was authorized. There is no express grant of power to Congress to charter corporations or create a national bank, and counsel for Maryland argued that the Bank Act was therefore unauthorized, but Marshall concluded that Article I section 8 authorized the act as a "necessary and proper" means "for carrying into Execution" the fiscal powers expressly delegated to Congress by the initial words of section 8. Of course, the Bank Act would still be a nullity if it violated a constitutional prohibition, but Marshall concluded, for reasons we shall discuss later in this chapter, that the only prohibition Maryland invoked, the tenth amendment, did not limit the scope of Congress's authority to enact the 1816 act.

Having concluded that the act of Congress was authorized and not prohibited, Marshall then turned to the only constitutional question that could be asked about the state tax law, whether it was prohibited. The Bank Act itself did not preempt the state law under the Article VI supremacy clause: It included no provision to that effect and the state tax did not prevent the bank from operating in Maryland but only made its operations less profitable. Marshall nonetheless concluded that the tax was prohibited on the basis of a principle related to but broader than Article VI – that states may not impede the achievement of valid federal governmental objectives. Twentieth-century decisions adjusted in various ways Marshall's no-state-interference principle, but *McCulloch* remains the classic demonstration of the way in which the logic of constitutional inquiry breaks down a controversy into specific constitutional questions of authorization and prohibition.

[5] Marshall did in fact consider what he called the "just theory" that the state's taxing power simply did not "extend to those means which are employed by congress to carry into execution powers conferred on that body by the people of the United States." See *id.* at 428–30 (1819). Marshall carefully distinguished that discussion from his analysis of the constitutional issue of the tax's validity that the Court actually had jurisdiction to decide. See *id.* at 428 ("Before we proceed to examine this argument, and to subject it to the test of the constitution, we must be permitted to bestow a few considerations" on the theory) & 430–31 ("waiving this theory for the present, let us resume the inquiry, whether this power can be exercised by the respective states, consistently with a fair construction of the constitution"). To the extent that Marshall's "theory" is relevant to contemporary constitutional law, it is part of the argument that Maryland's tax was inconsistent with federal supremacy.

We turn now to the foundations of the twofold logic of inquiry, which lie in the constitutional text and in some of constitutional law's major presuppositions. An attentive reader of the written Constitution will quickly notice that it includes several broad types of provisions. Some establish the basic structures of the federal government or identify how its officeholders are to be selected:

> All legislative Powers herein granted shall be vested in a Congress of the United States, which shall consist of a Senate and House of Representatives. . . . The executive Power shall be vested in a President of the United States of America. . . . The judicial Power of the United States, shall be vested in one supreme Court, and in such inferior Courts as the Congress may from time to time ordain and establish. . . . The Electors shall meet in their respective states and vote by ballot for President and Vice-President. . . . The Senate of the United States shall be composed of two Senators from each State, elected by the people thereof.

Other provisions complete the structure of the federal government by designating the powers that the various federal entities and officeholders may exercise:

> The House of Representatives . . . shall have the sole Power of Impeachment. . . . The Vice President of the United States shall be President of the Senate, but shall have no Vote, unless they be equally divided. . . . In all Cases affecting Ambassadors, other public Ministers and Consuls, and those in which a State shall be Party, the supreme Court shall have original Jurisdiction.

A very small number of provisions authorize state governmental actions related to the federal government. "Each State shall appoint, in such Manner as the Legislature thereof may direct, . . . Electors" to choose the president and vice president.

Alongside its provisions establishing the federal government, the written Constitution includes provisions that impose limitations on federal and state officers and institutions, or place conditions on their exercise of power:

> No State shall . . . grant any Title of Nobility. . . . The Senators and Representatives before mentioned, and the Members of the several State Legislatures, and all executive and judicial Officers, both of the United States and of the several States, shall be bound by Oath or Affirmation, to support this Constitution. . . . The right of citizens of the United States to vote shall not be denied or abridged by the United States or by any State on account of sex.

Many provisions in the written Constitution fall under more than one of these categories. One of the clauses of Article II section 2, for example, states that the president "shall have Power, by and with the Advice and Consent of the Senate, to make Treaties, provided two thirds of the Senators present concur."[6] At one and the

---

[6] The word "clause" has two technical meanings in constitutional law. It is conventional to cite provisions of the Constitution by article or amendment, section (where there is one) and clause (ditto, with respect to the 1787 document). In citations, the term "clause" refers to one of the sections of

same time, those words authorize the president to enter into treaties on behalf of the United States, and the Senate to give or withhold its approval, while prohibiting the president from making a treaty without obtaining that approval and the Senate from giving its consent in the absence of a supermajority. As this example indicates, constitutional problems involving the constitutional distribution of power among the three branches of the federal government invariably require consideration of both authorization and prohibition issues.

A few parts of the written Constitution do not fit, or fit entirely, into any of these categories. The preamble to the Constitution announces the document's purposes; common lawyers traditionally treated preambular matter in a written instrument as having no legal force and constitutional law has followed suit, although (again following common law tradition) the preamble can be relevant to understanding a legally operative authorization or prohibition. In a somewhat similar way, which we shall discuss shortly, the ninth and tenth amendments do not, on their face, authorize or prohibit anything but are instead textual reminders of important overall features of the constitutional system. Article VII ("The Ratification of the Conventions of nine States shall be sufficient for the Establishment of this Constitution between the States so ratifying the Same.") identifies the condition that the written Constitution set for its own legal inception and has no further significance. Finally, section 1 of the thirteenth amendment reads: "Neither slavery nor involuntary servitude ... shall exist within the United States, or any place subject to their jurisdiction." Based on this language, the Supreme Court concluded long ago that "the amendment is not a mere prohibition of State laws establishing or upholding slavery, but an absolute declaration that slavery or involuntary servitude shall not exist in any part of the United States." The amendment's guarantee of freedom therefore has force against private parties as well as governmental actions.[7]

2.2 THE BACKGROUND PRESUPPOSITIONS OF CONSTITUTIONAL LAW

Constitutional law's twofold logic of authorization and prohibition reflects not only linguistic features of the text but also certain critical presuppositions about the Constitution's purposes and the overall governmental structure of the American Republic. Perhaps the most important is that *the federal government is in all respects the creation of the written Constitution and enjoys only those powers that the text*

---

text that the 1787 transcription sets apart without regard to whether it is grammatically a single clause, several clauses, or not a complete clause at all.

   In discussion, a "clause" refers to a set of words that make up a discrete provision for the purposes of analysis. Thus, a citation to Const. Art. I, § 8, cl. 3 ("[The Congress shall have power] ... To regulate Commerce with foreign Nations, and among the several States, and with the Indian Tribes") includes three distinct "clauses" in analytical terms, often referred to as the Foreign Commerce, Interstate Commerce, and Indian Commerce Clauses.

7   *Civil Rights Cases*, 109 U.S. 3, 20 (1883).

authorizes some part of the government to exercise. "The United States is entirely a creature of the Constitution. Its power and authority have no other source." A lone, mischievous Supreme Court opinion, *United States v. Curtiss-Wright Export Corp.* (1936), long ago endorsed its author's idiosyncratic theory that the federal government's powers over foreign affairs came to it not through the Constitution but directly from the King, but within a few years the Court quietly interred that notion. The powers that the modern federal government exercises are extremely broad, but constitutional law requires that "it still must show that a constitutional grant of power authorizes each of its actions."[8]

The principle that the Constitution is the exclusive source of federal power has no exceptions. At times nonlawyers (or lawyers being inexact) assert that international law authorizes the United States to take a certain action. Such a statement may indeed be accurate as a matter of international law, but as a matter of American constitutional law the federal government would act unlawfully if it took that action without authorization ultimately derived from the written Constitution. International law, for example, permits any nation to exercise jurisdiction over pirates operating outside any state's territorial waters, but the lawfulness of federal prosecutions of "pirates" as defined by international law depends on the existence of federal statutes making piracy a crime pursuant to Article I section 8's grant to Congress of the power "To define and punish Piracies and Felonies committed on the high Seas."

Conversely, a second presupposition that informs the logic of authorization and prohibition is that the Constitution of the United States neither creates the states' governmental structures nor as a general matter provides state governments with authority. Instead, the people of each individual state create and empower that state's government through the state's own constitution. The written Constitution of the United States expressly forbids states from exercising certain powers and the Constitution-in-practice sweeps even more broadly, particularly in the areas of foreign affairs and national security. But on issues of domestic governance, as Chief Justice Roberts wrote in *Sebelius*, federal constitutional law assumes that state governments possess a general or indefinite authority to enact laws. This general power to govern, usually referred to as the police power, sharply distinguishes state legislatures from Congress, which can only act pursuant to a grant of authority by the written Constitution. (The word "police" in "police power" does not refer to law enforcement officers but is an older use of the word to mean the administration of public order.)

---

[8] *Reid v. Covert*, 354 U.S. 1, 5–6 (1957) (plurality opinion); *United States v. Curtiss-Wright Export Corp.*, 299 U.S. 304 (1936); *National Federation of Independent Business v. Sebelius*, 567 U.S. 519, 535 (2012) (opinion of Roberts, C.J.). For the Court's rejection of *Curtiss-Wright*, see *Youngstown Sheet & Tube Co. v. Sawyer*, 343 U.S. 579, 585 (1952) (the president's authority to take actions he thought necessary to protect national security in wartime had to come from the Constitution or from a statute Congress was authorized to enact).

The tenth amendment places in the written Constitution a clear reminder of both principles – that federal powers must derive from or, as it is often put, must be *enumerated* in the written Constitution, and that state governments are assumed to possess a general power of governance that they may exercise without constitutional authorization in the absence of a federal constitutional prohibition. "The powers not delegated to the United States by the Constitution, nor prohibited by it to the States, are reserved to the States respectively, or to the people." I shall refer to these as, respectively, the enumeration and police power principles.

The tenth amendment has a long if intermittent history of being read (or misread) as a limitation on the scope of the powers actually delegated to the federal government – as if it provided that any powers not *expressly* delegated to the United States are reserved to the states, which the parallel provision in the Articles of Confederation did provide. A provision employing that adverb would be fairly read to forbid the federal exercise of any power not unmistakably included within the language of some constitutional text, and in *McCulloch* v. *Maryland*, Chief Justice Marshall argued that the tenth amendment's omission of "expressly" appears worded to avoid just such an effect. Since *McCulloch*, the Supreme Court has generally been skeptical of treating the tenth amendment as limiting what Congress would be authorized to enact if the amendment did not exist. Careful constitutional lawyers therefore avoid invoking the amendment as a prohibition rather than as an express and concise restatement of the enumeration and police power principles, central features of American federalism that are of great importance in constitutional law analysis.[9]

The principles encapsulated in the tenth amendment have three important corollaries. First, the Constitution does not vest Congress with a general power of governance, despite the text's references, in the preamble and in Article I section 8, to "the general Welfare." As we have seen, the preamble does not itself authorize (or prohibit) anything, but section 8 is the written Constitution's primary list of congressional powers, and opens with the assertion that "[t]he Congress shall have Power To lay and collect Taxes, Duties, Imposts and Excises, to pay the Debts *and provide for the common Defence and general Welfare of the United States.*" On a semantic level, the words I italicized could be read to vest Congress with the police power or something very close to it, perhaps excluding extremely local or parochial matters. In the early Republic, it was sometimes argued that federal legislation that did not appear to fit within any other clause in section 8 could be justified by construing the reference to "the general Welfare" as an independent grant of power. The consistent response, as James Madison put it in an 1817 veto message, was that "such a view of the Constitution would have the effect of giving to Congress a general power of legislation" and make "the special and careful enumeration of powers which follow the clause nugatory," an unacceptable conclusion both as a matter of the text and in

---

[9]   For more on the origin of the tenth amendment, see Chapter 5.

light of the general understanding that Congress's legislative powers are constitutionally defined.[10]

Madison's argument rested in part on the sensible rule of common law documentary construction that no part of a legal instrument should be rendered meaningless by construction if there is any way to avoid doing so. What is the function, then, of section 8's statement that Congress may "provide for the common Defence and general Welfare"? From the beginning, Congress repeatedly acted on the assumption that it could lay taxes and spend money to accomplish goals that did not appear to be within any of its powers to enact substantive regulations. Some important constitutionalists, including Madison and Jefferson, objected that doing so was to make an end run around the enumeration principle, and that federal taxing and spending legislation should be limited to purposes within the scope of Congress's express regulatory powers. Others such as Chief Justice Marshall's learned colleague Joseph Story answered that the text of section 8 should be read to authorize any tax or spending law that provides "for the common Defence and general Welfare," even if Congress could not pursue the objective in view by direct regulation. The Supreme Court eventually endorsed Justice Story's view, and thus the enumeration principle does not significantly limit the purposes for which Congress may impose taxes or enact spending programs.[11]

A second corollary to the principles reflected in the tenth amendment is that there is, in general, no federal common law in the sense of substantive legal rules devised by the federal courts. English common law extended to any matter over which the royal courts could take jurisdiction, and thus from a modern perspective amounted to a general power of (judicial) governance – a police power exercised by the courts. The oddity of understanding the Constitution to deny Congress the police power while essentially granting it to the federal courts was obvious early on, and the difficulty was compounded by the assumption that Congress can dictate the substantive law that the federal courts will apply: If the courts can deal with any subject addressed by the common law, then Congress should be able to do so as well, and the enumeration principle disappears. After some initial debate, the Supreme Court held early in the nineteenth century that there is no federal common law of crimes, and thus the federal government may only prosecute anti-social behavior on the basis of an act of Congress that itself must be authorized by the written Constitution. In 1938, the Court held that there is generally no federal common law as to civil matters, although it subsequently recognized that federal courts are authorized, where no act of Congress governs, to create common law rules to address peculiarly federal issues (e.g., the rules governing federal government contracts).[12]

---

[10] Madison, Veto Message (March 3, 1817), in 11 *Papers of James Madison (Presidential Series)* 701, 702 (J. C.A. Stagg ed., Charlottesville, VA: University Press of Virginia, 2020).

[11] See 2 Joseph Story, *Commentaries on the Constitution* § 908 (Boston: Hilliard, Gray, and Company, 1833); *United States* v. *Butler*, 297 U.S. 1, 65–66 (1936) (expressly endorsing Story's view).

[12] For more on the controversy over federal common law, see the appendix.

The third corollary to the tenth amendment's principles is that one cannot infer that the federal government is unauthorized to address a matter from the fact that the state governments can, and vice versa. The police power is a general power of governance and a state may exercise it to address any issue that the Constitution does not make exclusively federal. If the police power were exclusive, therefore, Congress's domestic regulatory powers would be very narrow indeed, and that conclusion is patently incorrect. It has long been settled, therefore, that Congress may address a matter in exercising one of its enumerated powers, most often the power to regulate interstate commerce, despite the fact that the states may also do so under the police power. It is equally long-settled that Congress may adopt the same tools of regulation in carrying out, say, the commerce power that states use in exercising the police power. Conversely, except on topics that are exclusively federal, the fact that one of Congress's enumerated powers authorizes it to legislate on a matter does not imply that the matter is beyond the states' legislative competence. For example, Article I section 8 delegates to Congress the power "To establish ... uniform Laws on the subject of Bankruptcies throughout the United States." For the first century of government under the Constitution, however, a federal bankruptcy law existed only intermittently and for a few years on each occasion, and the Supreme Court held early on that the mere existence of the congressional power did not preclude the states from enacting insolvency laws that dealt with the same social problem.[13]

The constitutional possibility of overlapping legislation creates the practical inevitability of conflicting legislation. As discussed previously, the text of Article VI's supremacy clause addresses this problem by providing that acts of Congress "made in pursuance" of the Constitution are, like the Constitution, "the supreme Law of the Land ... any Thing in the Constitution or Laws of any State to the Contrary notwithstanding." As we saw previously, a state statute or other state rule of law or action is preempted if it conflicts with a valid federal statute.

The third presupposition that informs constitutional law's logic of authorization and prohibition is that the Constitution does not limit or affect a state's decisions about how to structure its government, about the fundamental political commitments it makes through its constitution, or about what laws to enact, except to the extent required by the federal constitutional text or as necessary to carry out federal constitutional commands. Unlike the federal government, American federalism is not a creature of the Constitution, and with certain limitations the people of a state are free to create whatever institutions of government they prefer. Article IV affirms that "[t]he United States shall guarantee to every State in this Union a Republican Form of Government," which clearly puts some governmental choices off limits, but what counts as a republican form of government is just as clearly a broad category. In

---

[13]   As a general matter, this paragraph's observations also apply to the subjects that the federal government may address through the Article II treaty power and that do not lie within the areas of exclusive federal control over foreign affairs. Some peculiarities of the treaty power are discussed in Chapter 5.

addition, the Supreme Court has repeatedly held that the federal courts cannot adjudicate constitutional challenges based on this clause, but as we shall see when we discuss "political questions," this does not mean that such challenges do not present problems of constitutional law.

A state legislature may have one house (Nebraska) or two (all the rest). The state's governor may have the power to veto legislation, but need not (North Carolina's governor did not prior to 1996), and the details of a governor's veto power need not follow the federal model. A state may permit its courts to engage in what amounts to lawmaking by common law decision, or it may adopt a European-style civil code (Louisiana). States may adopt direct democracy mechanisms such as legislation by referendum, and employ popular election for purposes handled differently by the Constitution (e.g., by providing for the election of judges or creating a recall process for judges or governors). The state constitution may create local governments with considerable "home rule" autonomy or leave them dependent on state legislation for their authority. And on and on, indefinitely.[14] Even with respect to the rare instances in which the federal Constitution is the source of the state's authority to act, the Supreme Court has indicated that a state should enjoy broad discretion in structuring how it will exercise its federally based power.[15]

Because of the supremacy clause, a state may not take actions that contravene a political commitment embodied in a prohibition in the written Constitution or the Constitution-in-practice. For example, a state law or constitutional provision that purported to deny the right to vote to eighteen-year olds because of their age would be a dead letter because it contradicts the twenty-sixth amendment. But a state may adopt for itself commitments that go beyond those mandated by the Constitution. For example, the Supreme Court concluded decades ago that the Constitution-in-practice does not guarantee any right to public education, but many states' constitutional arrangements include a judicially enforceable right to education. As a matter of history, recognizing the validity of state constitutional rights that go beyond those protected by the federal Constitution may well be the original point of the somewhat mysterious ninth amendment. If so, the ninth and tenth amendments were meant to have parallel functions, to prevent the written Constitution's announcement of, respectively, federal constitutional rights and powers from suggesting that state law

---

[14] Most states follow some version of the arrangement by which local governments are the creatures of the state legislature, and are thus said to follow "Dillon's Rule." For federal constitutional law purposes, regardless of the state's choice, the actions of local government and local officials are generally treated as those of the state, and subject to the same constitutional prohibitions that apply to the state's central government.

[15] See e.g., *Arizona State Legislature* v. *Arizona Indep. Redistricting Comm'n*, 576 U.S. 787 (2015) (holding that a state constitutional amendment adopted by referendum that placed the power to draw congressional districts in an independent commission was consistent with the clause in Article I section 4 providing that "The Times, Places and Manner of holding Elections for Senators and Representatives, shall be prescribed in each State by the Legislature thereof.").

rights and powers are necessarily abridged. In any event, the ninth amendment has played an insignificant role to date in the practice of constitutional law.[16]

In addition to minimizing the extent of interference through judicial review with a state's choices about its own fundamental structures, the Constitution-in-practice prohibits the political branches of the federal government from treating state governments and state officials as federal agents. The Constitution authorizes Congress to regulate private conduct directly, and to require federal executive officers and agencies to execute its regulations. The Supreme Court has therefore concluded that Congress cannot require state legislatures to enact legislation to carry out congressional goals even if it has the authority to regulate the matter in view directly. This "anti-commandeering principle" equally prohibits Congress from imposing duties on state and local executive officials to execute federal laws even if the laws are themselves authorized by a constitutional grant of power to Congress. The principle does not preclude Congress from regulating states pursuant to an enumerated power, and when Congress does so, it may impose administrative duties on state officials parallel to those such regulation would require private parties to carry out.[17]

Furthermore, states enjoy "sovereign immunity" against lawsuits brought by private parties even when the private plaintiff has a valid federal law claim unless the state legislature chooses to waive that immunity. Congress may not interfere with the state's decision to retain its immunity, even if the decision obstructs the operation of a valid federal statute or the vindication of a federal constitutional right, except in the context of bankruptcy or eminent domain legislation, or congressional abrogation under section 5 of the fourteenth amendment. Because Congress does have the authority to subject state and local officials to lawsuits for prospective relief (chiefly, to compel the officials to obey the federal rule at issue in the future), the main practical significance of the state sovereign immunity principle is to prevent courts from ordering the payment of state funds to plaintiffs with federal claims unless the state legislature has chosen to permit such payments.[18]

The constitutional presupposition of state autonomy operates somewhat differently when Congress attempts to influence state decisions by conditioning the availability or amount of federal funding available to the state on the state's compliance with congressional directives. This use of the spending power (sometimes called, a bit misleadingly, a form of "cooperative federalism") is generally constitutional as long as Congress makes its conditions explicit and relevant in some way to the purposes of the federal spending. For example, the Supreme Court upheld Congress's imposition of a modest reduction in federal funding for state highways if the state legislature failed to set the age for alcohol purchases at twenty-one because the Court thought the age requirement reasonably related to highway safety, but

---

[16] For more on the ninth amendment, see Chapter 5.
[17] See *Reno v. Condon*, 528 U.S. 141, 149–51 (2000).
[18] For more on Congress and state sovereign immunity, see Chapter 5.

a similar reduction in highway funds for failure to mandate physical education in public elementary schools presumably would be invalid.[19]

The practical effect of conditional spending legislation is to induce the state to carry out Congress's program; what makes it consistent with the presupposition of state autonomy is that the state legislature is free to decline the federal funds (or accept the reduction in funding it will receive) and thus in principle remains autonomous. The logical corollary to this reasoning is that the financial inducement must not be so large that the legislature cannot reasonably be thought to have a choice. If Congress's financial carrot or stick leaves the legislature with no practical option other than to comply with Congress's demands, the spending condition is unconstitutional. The same reasoning applies when Congress or a state legislature conditions the receipt of public funds or the exercise of some other privilege on the surrender of an individual constitutional right: The individual's choice to forego the government's largess must be a decision that is possible as a practical and not just a theoretical matter.

The fourth presupposition important to understanding the logic of constitutional inquiry is that the written Constitution, and the constitutional law derived from it that makes up the Constitution-in-practice, are the law that governs the institutions and actions of the United States as a political community, rather than the law governing the people of the United States in their individual and private capacities. The Constitution dictates the basic framework of the federal government and places limits on the lawful actions of all American public institutions and officers. (In addition, as we have already discussed, the Constitution-in-practice presupposes the autonomous role of state constitutions in structuring state governments, authorizing the exercise of the police power, and imposing additional limitations and obligations on state governmental actors.) In turn, federal and state governments create the complex web of public regulation, rights, and duties that make up almost all the law structuring Americans' private lives, centrally though not exclusively through the enactment of federal and state legislation.

The distinction between the law governing government that is the Constitution-in-practice, and the law governing private conduct that is created by government, has two consequences. The first is that constitutional law is not itself directly the product of democratic politics. To be sure, the subject matter of constitutional law is political through and through – it is, after all, the law governing the political authority of the various instrumentalities of government, and constitutional problems often arise out of issues that are political in an ordinary or even partisan sense. But in the United States the basic rules of democratic governance are not laid down by the ordinary democratic processes. This is abundantly clear with respect to the written Constitution. The means by which the original constitutional text was adopted flouted the existing

---

[19]   *South Dakota v. Dole*, 483 U.S. 203 (1987).

procedures for constitutional change at every step. Since then, while Article V authorizes various means by which the People can adopt formal amendments to the Constitution, and all of them involve Congress at least minimally, none of them actually track the usual methods of federal or state lawmaking.[20]

The broader set of rules and principles that make up the Constitution-in-practice are even more clearly distant from what we ordinarily think of as democratic decision making. Their articulation takes place chiefly through constitutional adjudication in the federal courts, a process that is administered by officials who enjoy life tenure and are neither elected nor subject to removal by popular vote. The resulting decisions claim, on their face, to ignore ordinary political considerations entirely and to rest on nonpartisan, apolitical legal reasoning. The recurrent worry that the courts, and above all the Supreme Court, reach conclusions that are in fact political, and that all the lawyer-talk is window dressing, only makes things worse. A nondemocratic institution does not become less inconsistent with democratic governance because those administering it are covertly importing into their supposedly apolitical decisions preferences that we would instantly label political if they were avowed in public.

These are substantive concerns, and in Chapter 6 we shall return to the question whether the possibility of chicanery and bad faith in decision making undermines the claim of the traditional practice of constitutional law to authority. (The answer is no.) But the "counter-majoritarian difficulty," as some constitutional lawyers have labeled the apparently undemocratic and allegedly problematic nature of constitutional law, is not in fact a defect in the American constitutional system, even if it would be unacceptable in a democratic political community with other arrangements. The reason is not (as is sometimes asserted, cleverly but misleadingly) that the founders intended the United States to be a "republic" rather than a "democracy." Some founding-era Americans did use the latter term as a political disparagement, but their point was to reject mob rule or the ancient Athenian system of immediate direct democracy, not the sort of government through elected officials that most twenty-first century Americans assume is part of the actual definition of "democracy."

The democratic legitimacy of constitutional law rests instead on the role it plays in making democracy of the American kind a political reality. The law that governs the ordinary concerns of human life and the personal, economic, and social relationships among individuals is fully democratic in principle, created by or answerable to majoritarian politics on the federal or state level. The constitutional law that governs government is not itself the product of such politics but it makes democratic politics in the United States possible, by creating a stable framework within which those who hold political authority are accountable to voters, and political authority is meaningful because political decisions are carried out.[21]

---

[20] On Article V and amending the Constitution, see Chapter 5.

[21] The extraordinary level of gerrymandering in many states is in my judgment contrary to settled constitutional principles under the first amendment and the equal protection clause, and impairs American government's democratic legitimacy. The Supreme Court concluded in *Rucho* v. *Common*

The Constitution creates the processes of national democratic decision making through the political branches of the federal government and limits the danger that majoritarian politics at the national or state level will impair or limit democracy by empowering courts to protect political and minority rights, and the institutions of constitutional governance themselves. "The irreplaceable value of the power [of judicial review] articulated by Mr. Chief Justice Marshall in *Marbury v. Madison* (1803) lies in the protection it has afforded the constitutional rights and liberties of individual citizens and minority groups against oppressive or discriminatory government action." When controversy arises out of the Constitution's distribution of political power among the structures of federal and state government, constitutional law does indeed prevent the exercise of democratic political power by the losing governmental entity, but that is the unavoidable consequence of having rules of the road in a political community with complex governing arrangements. If Congress votes to require all widgets to be painted blue, and the North Carolina legislature mandates green, both democratic choices cannot prevail.[22]

Finally, the Constitution's protection of individual liberties, including some with no obvious or direct connection to the individual's ability to participate in democratic politics, reflects *this particular* political community's commitment "to withdraw certain subjects from the vicissitudes of political controversy, to place them beyond the reach of majorities and officials." While that is a limitation on a certain purely procedural view of democracy, it is an intrinsic part of democracy as understood in the *American* democratic tradition, and judicial decisions upholding such liberties against political interference are undemocratic in no sense relevant to the American constitutional system. Like the authority of the written Constitution itself, the democratic legitimacy of protection for individual rights is axiomatic.[23]

The presupposition that constitutional law governs American government rather than American individuals has a second consequence, one that constitutional lawyers usually refer to as the state action requirement. ("State action" in this context refers to any governmental action, not to the acts of a state as opposed to the federal government.) Put simply, and with a very few exceptions, the Constitution does not directly address private individuals or nongovernmental entities. The principle is fairly intuitive with respect to the constitutional authorizations that create the branches of the federal government and enumerate their powers, but it may be less so with respect to constitutional prohibitions, and particularly those that protect individual rights. A sentence such as "the first amendment protects my right to freedom of speech" is a natural and for many purposes an accurate enough statement. But if, for example, I work for a private business with a policy against discussing politics at work, the first amendment places no obstacle in the way of

---

Cause, 139 S.Ct. 2484 (2019), that this constitutional problem cannot be addressed by the federal courts because it involves a nonjusticiable political question. On political questions, see Chapter 4.

[22] *Raines v. Byrd*, 521 U.S. 811, 829 (1997).
[23] *West Virginia State Bd. of Educ. v. Barnette*, 319 U.S. 624, 638 (1943).

my employer docking my pay if I violate the policy, although in theory my employment contract might. My employer's enforcement of its policy does not involve state action, and so the first amendment does not address the matter.

Determining whether a particular decision or event involves state action, and thus may be governed by a constitutional prohibition, can itself be a tricky problem in constitutional law. Private persons and entities interact with government in many different ways, and the Supreme Court has long recognized that in some situations, public officials or institutions are so intertwined with nongovernmental actors that what the latter do is "fairly attributable" to the government. If so, the state action requirement is satisfied and a relevant constitutional prohibition such as the first amendment free speech clause applies to the ostensibly nongovernmental party. The case law on state action is unusually complex, in part because of the difficulty of distinguishing the area of private life that is governed only by ordinary law from circumstances in which government really is responsible for certain actions, regardless of the identity of the specific actor, and thus constitutional norms should apply.[24]

There are two important exceptions to the state action limitation on constitutional prohibitions. The wording of the thirteenth amendment that abolished slavery does not address a specific governmental addressee. "Neither slavery nor involuntary servitude ... shall exist within the United States, or any place subject to their jurisdiction." (Contrast the beginning of the first amendment, "Congress shall make no law.") In itself, that should not be dispositive: The appropriations clause of Article I section 9 is phrased in the passive voice ("No Money shall be drawn from the Treasury, but in Consequence of Appropriations made by Law") but no one thinks it applies to freelance thieves of federal funds – the ordinary criminal law addresses them. As noted previously, however, at an early point the Supreme Court read the thirteenth amendment differently, not simply as a prohibition on laws that create or protect slavery but as an affirmative rule "establishing and decreeing universal civil and political freedom throughout the United States." As such, the thirteenth amendment also prohibits purely private behavior that reduces someone to the status of a slave.[25]

Since the mid-nineteenth century, the Supreme Court has recognized that the Constitution prohibits some state interferences with interstate travel. While some justices have rooted the prohibition in a specific provision of the written

---

[24] See *Brentwood Acad. v. Tennessee Secondary Sch. Athletic Assoc.*, 531 U.S. 288, 295 (2001). Courts are obviously state actors, but as a general rule constitutional prohibitions do not constrain the ordinary law claims a private party may raise. The most important exception is that the first amendment free speech clause limits, in some circumstances quite sharply, the ability of a plaintiff to obtain a remedy in an action for defamation and some closely related torts.

[25] *Civil Rights Cases*, 109 U.S. 3, 20 (1883). The eighteenth amendment's prohibition on the sale of alcoholic beverages applied to private conduct, as does the twenty-first amendment's ban on transporting such beverages into a state or territory in violation of its laws. Neither amendment provided any sanction for its violation, and ordinary law legislation was and is necessary to enforce the constitutional rule despite the theoretical absence of a state action limitation.

Constitution, more often the Court itself has treated the prohibition as an inference from the structure of the American political community, which despite its federalism arrangements also creates a direct relationship between the individual citizen and the national government. To make that relationship a reality, the Court has reasoned, Americans must be able to travel to the national capital, as well as throughout the states in order to participate in the duties and privileges of national citizenship. In the late twentieth century, the Court concluded that this same structural reasoning supports application of the prohibition, at least in some circumstances, to private interference with travel across state boundaries.[26]

As we have seen, the Constitution authorizes, and through the anti-commandeering principle requires, Congress to regulate private individuals directly, through federal laws and federal officials, rather than through using state government as a tool. But this general rule applies to the exercise of Congress's enumerated powers in the original constitutional text. Beginning with the thirteenth amendment, amendments imposing new prohibitions (and one structural amendment, the twenty-third granting presidential electors to the District of Columbia) have included a provision delegating to Congress "power to enforce this article by appropriate legislation." (The wording of the enforcement clause of the fourteenth amendment is slightly and immaterially different.)

The enforcement powers are authorizations for Congress to act just as much as are the provisions of Article I section 8. But the enforcement powers, except for the thirteenth amendment (which as we saw applies to private conduct), are limited to congressional regulation of governmental actions. In other words, like the prohibitions they enforce, these powers only address actions by or attributable to governments. The fundamental rationale for this limitation is simple; we can use the newest enforcement power, that of the twenty-sixth amendment, to illustrate it.

(1) Section 1 of the amendment provides that the right to vote (of citizens eighteen and older) "shall not be denied or abridged by the United States or by any state on account of age."

(2) Section 2 provides Congress the power to make sure that section 1 is not disobeyed.

(3) But only the United States or a state can disobey section 1. Therefore, the only federal law that enforces section 1 is a law that prevents the federal or state government from denying or abridging the right to vote for age reasons if the citizen is eighteen or older.

Since private persons cannot, by legal definition, violate section 1 (they aren't "the United States" or "any state"), Congress cannot use its section 2 power to regulate private behavior even if that behavior is directed toward preventing eighteen-year-old citizens from voting because of their age. Under this reasoning, the state action

---

[26] See *Bray v. Alexandria Women's Health Clinic*, 506 U.S. 263, 274 (1993).

limitation on the scope of the relevant prohibitions becomes a limitation as well on the authorized scope of Congress's relevant enforcement powers. As with the state action limitation on judicial enforcement of constitutional prohibitions, the case law discussing the state action limitation on Congress's enforcement powers is complicated, and in some circumstances Congress may in fact address private conduct.[27]

The fifth presupposition that informs constitutional law's logic of inquiry mirrors the first – that the federal government has no extra-constitutional powers. There are no extra-constitutional prohibitions on the federal government in American domestic law. As we have seen, if the federal government is authorized to take an action, and the Constitution-in-practice imposes no relevant prohibition, the constitutional law analysis of the action's validity is at end. The action is constitutionally valid, and its legal force is undeniable as a matter of American domestic law. The domestic law qualification is necessary because international law recognizes a category of "peremptory norms" or *jus cogens* that as a matter of international law cannot be disavowed by a nation-state. Since the early Republic, American courts have recognized international law as in some sense a part of our law, and some international lawyers believe that an American court should have the power to enforce a peremptory norm against authorized governmental action even if its substance is not embodied in a constitutional prohibition or a limitation based on a valid federal statute or self-executing treaty. But this is not the American constitutional rule, and American constitutional law recognizes no source of legal rules superior to those created by the constitutional text and the Constitution-in-practice.

Supreme Court opinions occasionally observe that a particular individual right preexisted the prohibition in the written Constitution that protects it, and that the constitutional text therefore merely "codified" the pre-constitutional right. For example, in *District of Columbia* v. *Heller* (2008), the Court asserted that "it has always been widely understood that the Second Amendment, like the First and Fourth Amendments, codified a *pre-existing* right." Such comments stem from the wording of the provision in question, and to the extent that they have operational meaning, they indicate the importance of the provision's historical background to its legal meaning. They do not imply that a court could enforce the pre-constitutional right against constitutionally authorized governmental action if the right were not "codified" in the text.[28]

A similar conclusion seems to apply to the question whether there are constraints on the scope of the amendment process established by Article V. The text of the article expressly excludes amendments to two sections of Article I section 9 before 1808, as well as any amendment that would deprive a nonconsenting state "of its equal Suffrage in the Senate," but does not otherwise directly identify any

---

[27]   On the fourteenth amendment's section 5 enforcement power, see Chapter 5.
[28]   *District of Columbia* v. *Heller*, 554 U.S. 570, 592 (2008).

limitations.[29] With their own dubiously lawful example in mind, the Philadelphia framers also carefully limited Congress's power to convene a constitutional convention, either at its own behest or that of the state legislatures, to the authority to "call a Convention for proposing Amendments" in contrast to, presumably, proposing an entirely new charter of government. So perhaps Article V does not authorize a repetition of the framers' own maneuver, although it is obviously unclear how effective such a restriction actually can be, between the precedent the framers and ratifiers set and the ability of a convention to propose an "amendment" striking out everything after the Constitution's preamble.

Some constitutional scholars have nonetheless argued that there are nontextual limitations on the amending processes that Article V authorizes. The specifics vary, but the basic argument is that the US Constitution rests on certain basic principles or assumptions that no amendment could disturb or repudiate without delegitimizing the entire constitutional enterprise. Examples suggested include popular election of legislators on the federal and state levels, Article IV's requirement that states maintain a "Republican Form of Government," and the first amendment's prohibition on governmental imposition of an orthodoxy about "politics, nationalism, religion, or other matters of opinion." The argument is probably precluded by precedent; more importantly, if the processes of Article V were to generate any of the plausible candidates for the status of "unconstitutional amendment," it is almost a certainty that this would reflect a constitutional crisis well beyond the ability of constitutional lawyers to solve.[30]

A final note on constitutional prohibitions. There is nothing graven in stone about the distinction between authorizations and prohibitions. As a matter of the constitutional text, one could treat the prohibitions on federal action as, collectively, an incomplete specification of matters over which the federal government is not authorized to act. Some of the Constitution's most important advocates, including Madison, expressed this view during the ratification campaign and in the first years of government under the Constitution. However, from the beginning that understanding had problems. It cannot explain, for example, the existence of textual prohibitions applicable to action by the states with their general power of governance, and it proved an awkward way of describing provisions of the Bill of Rights that

[29] The time-limited exclusions both addressed provisions protecting slavery. The first clause of Article I section 9 prohibited an outright congressional ban on the slave trade prior to 1808, while the fourth clause ensured favorable treatment for property in slaves under any federal "direct" tax. Article V thus prohibited any amendment that would authorize Congress to ban the slave trade or change the required taxation arrangement at an earlier date.

[30] *West Virginia State Bd. of Educ. v. Barnette*, 319 U.S. 624, 642 (1943). The precedent is *Leser v. Garnett*, 258 U.S. 130, 136 (1922) (Brandeis, J.), which rejected an argument that the nineteenth amendment granting women the right to vote was so radical a transformation of a state as "a political body" that it could not properly be imposed on a state without its consent. For that reason, the argument went, the amendment was outside "the power of amendment conferred by the federal Constitution . . . because of its character." The Supreme Court summarily dismissed the idea without significant elaboration.

seem to address matters squarely within the Constitution's affirmative grants of power to the federal government. Over the course of the first few decades, constitutional lawyers and judges gradually abandoned this way of characterizing the relationship between constitutional authorizations and constitutional prohibitions almost entirely. On this matter, as on some others, this book describes the practice of constitutional law as it exists in the early twenty-first century, and does not discuss the sometimes complex history of how the traditional practice came to have its accepted shape.

The sixth and final presupposition informs not only the twofold logic of inquiry but also the entire practice of constitutional law. All constitutional law problems can be resolved by constitutional law means. The axiomatic authority of the written Constitution is matched by the axiomatic completeness of the Constitution-in-practice. That some questions in constitutional law may be very difficult to answer does not mean that they cannot be answered from within constitutional law. There is *never* no law to apply in American constitutional law.

3

Solving Constitutional Problems

The Basic Toolkit

Constitutional law's twofold logic of inquiry into authorization and prohibition provides the basic structure for constitutional law reasoning. It also supplies the method by which constitutional lawyers break down into discrete, manageable questions the complex set of facts and legal claims that a difficult constitutional problem presents. Finally, as Chapter 2 discussed, this logic rests on several presuppositions that further shape the analysis of any constitutional problem. We can now begin to consider how to solve a problem once we have identified the questions of constitutional law it raises. The answer to a constitutional question that is at all perplexing, or controversial among competent lawyers, can seldom if ever be identified by simply pointing to the constitutional text. Questions that can be answered in that fashion (do Wyoming and California really elect the same number of senators?) do not give rise to serious constitutional law debate, however puzzling they may be from other perspectives. If a constitutional question is debatable, a persuasive answer to it must be constructed, assembled through the use of the tools that are traditionally recognized as appropriate in constitutional law discussion. This chapter will discuss the constitutional lawyer's basic toolkit, the forms of thought and argument that he or she must use in answering the questions that make up the constitutional problem at hand.

As we saw in Chapter 1, founding-era constitutionalists immediately turned to the familiar methods of the common law when they began encountering hard-to-answer questions about the distribution and limits of power under the new Constitution. In doing so, they implicitly rejected the idea that the only legitimate constitutional law arguments are those that take a narrowly defined form. At the end of the eighteenth century, common lawyers employed an amorphous variety of argumentative strategies, without any strictly defined orthodoxy about what counted as a valid or persuasive argument, or how different arguments were to be weighed against one another if they appeared to be incommensurable. American constitutional law followed the common law's lead without missing a beat.

The result as an historical matter is that constitutional law has proven intractably resistant to attempts to impose methodological discipline on its debates. This intellectual unruliness was obvious from the very beginning. In 1791, during the debate in the House of Representatives over what became the first National Bank Act, James Madison began a major speech attacking the proposed act as constitutionally unauthorized with an elaborate presentation of the modes of interpretation that he claimed ought to be employed in constitutional argument. Fisher Ames, Madison's most trenchant opponent in the debate, mocked Madison's list of approved forms of argument "as discoveries [that] the acute penetration of that gentleman [has] brought … to light," and dismissed the idea that there could be a single method of answering constitutional questions that leads to incontrovertible answers. Arguments based on Madison's "rules," Ames predicted, "will be found as obscure" as the arguments Madison "condemns[s]; they only set up one construction against another."[1]

Ames's objection was not that constitutional law debate should be unreasoned or without method – in his reply to Madison, Ames offered his own candidate for the right kind of argument to entertain in considering the bank bill – but that it was a mistake to attempt to canonize a single method or orthodoxy. At the time, Ames won both the political debate (Congress enacted the bank act) and the methodological one: Madison's emphasis on considerations of documentary construction and Ames's on constitutional purposes, both of them familiar common law dialectical tools, became regular features of founding-era constitutional debate used indifferently by the same debater depending on which argument seemed most persuasive in a given controversy. This methodological eclecticism has remained characteristic of constitutional law to the present, and is one of the respects in which constitutional law continues to resemble the common law itself.

The constitutional lawyer's toolkit, therefore, contains the forms of argument of the Revolutionary and founding-era common law as those forms, taken up into constitutional law, have evolved or have been elaborated over time. It will be helpful to separate out the various methods that (as a matter of observation) constitutional lawyers employ, and to do so in schematic terms. But it is important for the reader to keep in mind that in actual constitutional debates and opinions, the different methods we discuss will usually be found to be overlapping, intertwined, and often unidentified. The purpose of distinguishing different kinds of argument is not to create a rhetorical taxonomy for its own sake, but to grasp the different ways in which persuasive constitutional arguments can be constructed and rebutted. There is, furthermore, no "official" taxonomy of arguments, and different scholars have suggested somewhat different lists. My presentation differs in various details from others, and is intended to help the reader understand the overall range of

[1] 2 Annals of Congress 1945–46 (Madison), 1954–55 (Ames). Madison was not himself a member of the bar but he appreciated common law methods of reasoning and assumed that they should be employed in constitutional debate.

constitutional modes of argument that one can observe in judicial opinions and other sources rather than to propose a definitive category scheme.[2]

It is also vitally important to realize that the various forms of constitutional argument do not occupy fixed places in an agreed-upon hierarchy of methods. References in debate to the kind of arguments being made often have a polemical rather than a genuinely explanatory point, and despite the written Constitution's axiomatic authority, not even cogent arguments from constitutional text necessarily prevail. These features of the practice of constitutional law are well illustrated in a 1996 decision, *Seminole Tribe* v. *Florida*. In that case, a divided Supreme Court held that Congress is prohibited by state sovereign immunity from using its power over commerce "with the Indian Tribes" to require states to submit to lawsuit by Native American nations. Chief Justice William H. Rehnquist, writing for a majority of the justices, conceded that this holding could not be derived from the texts of Article III or the eleventh amendment. Instead, he argued, constitutional structure and over a century of judicial precedent led to the Court's conclusion. As for the textual argument to the contrary,

> "[m]anifestly, we cannot rest with a *mere literal* application of the words of § 2 of Article III, or assume *that the letter of the Eleventh Amendment* exhausts the restrictions upon suits against non-consenting States. Behind the words of the constitutional provisions are postulates which limit and control."

In dissent, Justice David H. Souter vigorously asserted the superior force of his argument based on the eleventh amendment's text, and responded to Rehnquist's elevation of unwritten principle over "mere literal" contentions in a puckish footnote. "The majority chides me that the 'lengthy analysis of the text of the Eleventh Amendment is directed at a straw man.' But *plain text is the Man of Steel* in a confrontation with 'background principle[s]' and 'postulates which limit and control.'"[3]

Neither Chief Justice Rehnquist nor Justice Souter was stating a universal principle of constitutional reasoning. Souter offered an accurate half-concession: "An argument rooted in the text of a constitutional provision may not be guaranteed of carrying the day, but insubstantiality is not its failing." Rehnquist's reasoning, in turn, is not inconsistent with the assumption that a clear-enough textual argument will usually carry great weight in answering a constitutional question. But *Seminole Tribe* demonstrates that the Constitution-in-practice does not create an ironclad hierarchy of forms of argument.[4]

---

[2] The seminal modern discussion of the forms of constitutional law argument is that originally presented by Philip Bobbitt in his brilliant 1982 book *Constitutional Fate: Theory of the Constitution*. Subsequent attempts to describe the accepted methods of constitutional reasoning, including this book, are all indebted to his work.

[3] *Seminole Tribe* v. *Florida*, 517 U.S. 44, 68 (1996) (quoting *Principality of Monaco* v. *Mississippi*, 292 U.S. 313, 322 (1934)); *id.* at 116 n. 13 (Souter, J., dissenting). All emphases added.

[4] *Seminole Tribe*, 517 U.S. at 116 n. 13 (Souter, J., dissenting).

Seminole Tribe illustrates a final preliminary observation about any categorization of the various modes of argument that American constitutional lawyers employ. Once an argument in any mode has achieved judicial recognition, it has a hybrid quality since it carries with it both its own substantive force and its claim to authority from the principle of stare decisis, adherence to precedent. Put another way, a decision resting on some basis other than argument from precedent itself becomes precedent and thus can be invoked on that basis as well as for the force of its original reasoning. Furthermore, since constitutional law stems not from a line of judicial decisions stretching back into the misty past but begins formally with the adoption of the written Constitution, reliance on any judicial precedent must involve at least one other form of argument. (There are no judicial precedents of any significance in current constitutional law that consist solely of facts and outcome.) The words in the previous block quotation were first used in the opinion of the Court in a 1934 decision, and in their original setting were part of a line of reasoning that invoked the constitutional autonomy of the states and also quoted ratification-era materials on sovereign immunity. Chief Justice Rehnquist's use of the passage in *Seminole Tribe* not only adopted for his reasoning those structural and original meaning arguments but also, and expressly, summoned the force of precedent in support of his conclusion.

At a fundamental level, the accepted forms of constitutional argument fall into two categories: arguments that focus on the written Constitution and arguments that rest primarily on the Constitution-in-practice. Because the contents of the latter are all found in various types of judicial and political decisions, the category could also be called argument from precedent, but I will usually reserve that term for the most important variety of Constitution-in-practice arguments, reasoning that stems from decisions by the Supreme Court. As we have seen, the authority of the written Constitution is axiomatic, and the scope of the Constitution-in-practice is limited (sometimes in complex ways) by the contents of the constitutional text. As a formal matter, provisions of the written Constitution cannot be abrogated except through the amendment process, while in principle judicial and political precedents are subject to rejection by the same processes that created them. It is quite impossible to imagine the Supreme Court overruling *McCulloch* v. *Maryland*, the basic themes of which run throughout American constitutional law, but the precedential force of even *McCulloch* has been somewhat modified as to the scope of its prohibition on state interference with federal programs. It would be easy, therefore, to assume that arguments focused on the constitutional instrument outweigh reasoning based on the Constitution-in-practice when the two conflict.

The assumption is erroneous. As *Seminole Tribe* illustrates, depending on the particular problem under consideration, the Supreme Court sometimes rejects a text-based argument that is cogent in its own terms because the justices (or a majority of them) conclude that precedent-based reasoning provides a more persuasive answer. As a general matter, the existence of over two centuries of judicial and political precedent means that the Constitution-in-practice is the ordinary source of constitutional law reasoning. Arguments that attempt to circumvent the existence of rules, principles, and long-accepted Supreme Court decisions on the basis of novel claims about the meaning, original or otherwise, of a provision in the constitutional text face an uphill battle in persuading constitutional lawyers. Thus, constitutional argument based on precedent enjoys a certain primacy in practice. In what follows, however, I discuss arguments focused on the written Constitution first. Within the category of reasoning derived from the Constitution-in-practice, arguments based on judicial precedent will be discussed last in recognition of the reality that such arguments always involve (at least indirectly) other modes of reasoning because a Supreme Court precedent absorbs into its own authority the nonprecedent-based arguments on which it relied.

3.1 ARGUMENTS FOCUSED ON THE WRITTEN CONSTITUTION

The United States has a written Constitution, and it would be extremely odd if American constitutional law paid no attention to that document's actual language. Because the authority of the constitutional text is axiomatic, as Justice Souter noted in *Seminole Tribe*, in principle arguments focused on the written Constitution are (almost) always substantial. In thinking about how to construct and evaluate such arguments, it can be valuable to distinguish three ways in which a line of reasoning can draw on the authority of the written Constitution. Some arguments are primarily exegetical or expository and involve the use of common law and common sense methods of interpreting a document with legal force. Others derive their force from historical inquiry into the meaning the text's language would have conveyed to informed readers at the time it was adopted. Still other arguments rest on observations about the ways in which the written Constitution outlines the structures of American government. The ways in which these differing versions of written-Constitution reasoning can be given legal weight vary, but each shares the general characteristic of depending directly on the authority of the written Constitution rather than on the rules and principles of the Constitution-in-practice. (The reader should always keep in mind the crucially important point made above, that once accepted by a constitutional decision maker, a written-Constitution argument acquires the force of precedent as well.)[5]

Textual Arguments. I shall use this term to refer to reasoning that is primarily exegetical or expository. "Textual" is not an altogether satisfactory label since all constitutional arguments focused on the written Constitution depend for their force on claims about the meaning of the text, and indeed all arguments derived primarily from the Constitution-in-practice ultimately involve some reference to the text. Furthermore, expository reasoning is not a simple matter of reading the words of

---

[5] *Seminole Tribe*, 517 U.S. at 116 n. 13 (Souter, J., dissenting).

the written Constitution with a dictionary in hand. In the lawyers' "Constitution," the Constitution-in-practice that actually determines the solutions to constitutional problems, the textual arguments that matter, are *legal* arguments, not simply claims about the semantics of a constitutional provision, and thus they are shaped by legal as well as literary considerations. By the end of the eighteenth century, common law courts had developed an extensive body of interpretive principles and canons of construction for dealing with legal instruments of various kinds. The reader has already encountered early constitutional lawyers borrowing common law techniques for interpreting documents, and in particular acts of Parliament, in addressing issues arising under the written Constitution.

Although critics then and now have sometimes suggested that applying common law exegetical tools is a means of making the People's Constitution the preserve of a professional elite, the lawyers' purpose in doing so was rooted in a realistic understanding of the nature of the constitutional text. It was an almost universal founding-era assumption that the written Constitution speaks as clearly as possible since it is act of the People who must be reasonably thought to be able to understand it. But, as the Article VI supremacy clause demonstrates, the written Constitution was drafted so that if adopted it would be "supreme *law* of the land" applied by "the Judges in every state" alongside statutes and treaties. And it was another universal (and realistic) assumption that "from the imperfection of human language" and the impossibility of foreseeing all future questions, it was impossible for even the most careful drafting to eliminate serious legal questions about constitutional meaning.[6]

Early constitutional lawyers thought it a fair conclusion, therefore, that constitutional phrases with settled legal meanings ought to be given that meaning, and that ambiguities and apparent gaps in the text should be resolved using the same means that courts would apply to parallel textual problems in other authoritative legal instruments. After two centuries of constitutional law development, even a well-constructed argument based on the textual interpretation of a provision is likely to give way to arguments based on other forms of argument (*Seminole Tribe*!), but the tools of documentary construction the early lawyers adopted remain part of twenty-first century constitutional law.[7]

To carry weight, a textual argument in the expository sense must take into proper account the nature or aspect of the specific constitutional text on which it relies. The written Constitution, viewed as a whole, is the American political community's basic charter of government, and must play that role – and provide a basis for delineating

---

[6] *Gibbons* v. *Ogden*, 22 U.S. (9 Wheat.) 1, 188–89 (1824) (Marshall, C.J.) (recognizing that "from the imperfection of human language" there can be "serious doubts" about the meaning and scope of constitutional language).

[7] Some modern constitutional scholars distinguish "constitutional interpretation" from "constitutional construction," with the latter term generally paralleling the activities that lead to what this book terms the Constitution-in-practice. However, as a terminological matter, early constitutional lawyers treated interpretation and construction as synonyms, and this modern interpretation/construction distinction is anachronistic when read back into founding-era debates. This book does not make use of it.

the responsibilities of the national and state governments – despite its brevity, and the often laconic wording of key provisions. *McCulloch* v. *Maryland* is the classic statement of both the rationale for employing so spare a document as the nation's written fundamental law, and of the consequences of doing so. As for rationale, Chief Justice Marshall reasoned that a national "constitution, to contain an accurate detail of all" the matters it must address, "would partake of the prolixity of a legal code.... It would, probably, never be understood by the public. Its nature, therefore, requires, that only its great outlines should be marked, its important objects desig-nated, and the minor ingredients which compose those objects, be deduced" by legal reasoning. The fact that *this* particular document is the Republic's basic charter necessarily implies that its provisions will often speak in very broad terms and it should be read accordingly.[8]

Several implications follow. Most fundamentally, the constitutional text is *mis-read* if it is treated as a collection of discrete commands that can be taken apart analytically and read independently of one another and of the text's overall purposes. The written Constitution does indeed address many different issues and distinguish the powers and roles of the different parts of American government. But the text "contemplates that practice will integrate" the entirety "into a workable govern-ment." This fundamental constitutional purpose must guide argument from the text, and such argument, to be persuasive, must keep in view the principle that in the American political community, "a workable government," entails not only govern-mental efficacy but equally government's obedience to constitutional limitations on its powers.[9]

Another important aspect of the written Constitution's nature as *McCulloch* described it concerns the relationship between the document and the rules and principles of constitutional law. If the constitutional text is pitched, much of the time, at the level of broad principle ("great outlines" and "important objects"), then the Constitution-in-practice that brings the text to bear on an ever-increasing number of specific questions will unavoidably include many rules and propositions that go beyond the bare words of the text. Dissenting opinions occasionally complain that the dissenter cannot find the Supreme Court's holding "in" his copy of "the Constitution," but that complaint on its own is empty rhetoric, not a plausible textual argument or even a meaningful objection. Constitutional law must very often go beyond the semantic meaning of the text precisely in order to give the text its proper legal force as the American political community's *constitutional* charter.

An example may be useful. Article I sections 9 and 10 prohibit Congress and the states, respectively, from passing any "Bill of Attainder," a term with a technical

---

[8] *McCulloch* v. *Maryland*, 17 U.S. (4 Wheat.) 316, 407 (1819). The original constitutional document has approximately 4,543 words, including 39 signatures, and the amendments increase the word count to about 7,591. State constitutions vary wildly in length, although all are longer than the US Constitution; their average word count is around 39,000.

[9] *Youngstown Sheet & Tube Co.* v. *Sawyer*, 343 U.S. 579, 635 (1952) (Jackson, J., concurring).

common law definition in the late eighteenth century – a legislative act condemning someone to death without criminal trial. An act imposing a lesser criminal penalty carried a different label (a bill of pains and penalties), and following the traditional common law assumption that language with a settled legal meaning should be read that way would lead to the conclusion that the prohibition of the bill of attainder clauses is limited to that specific parliamentary practice. But already in 1810, the Supreme Court assumed that the bill of attainder clauses were "not to be given a narrow historical reading (which would exclude bills of pains and penalties), but ... instead to be read in light of the evil the Framers had sought to bar," which the Court understood broadly as the retributive imposition by legislation of any harm on specific individuals or groups. Subsequent decisions have applied the clauses to statutes excluding supporters of the Confederacy from law practice, specifically named "subversives" from governmental employment, and members of the Communist Party from holding office in labor unions. Despite their wording, the clauses have been treated as stating broad principles protecting the separation of governmental powers as well as individual liberty rather than a narrow rule barring a specific historical injustice.[10]

The constitutional text's nature as the American political community's basic charter gives force to the argument that a particular answer to a constitutional question is persuasive in part because it is consistent with the Constitution-in-practice as a whole. Thus, even expository arguments from text are usually persuasive only to the extent that they take account of precedent-based reasoning. Without a strong reason to reject the argument, constitutional lawyers should assume that the best solution to today's constitutional problem will be the answer that is reasonable in the light of the solutions accepted in past controversies, and of the overarching themes of the Constitution-in-practice. Again, an example will be useful. Section 2 of the twenty-first amendment prohibits the "transportation or importation into any State ... of intoxicating liquors, in violation of the laws thereof." A few early cases appeared to read that language literally, but on sober second thought, the Supreme Court recognized the consequences of treating that wording as permitting a state to ban the importation of alcoholic beverages on any ground whatever. State legislation intended to protect the state's domestic wine industry from interstate competition would be valid, notwithstanding the very long series of decisions holding that such economic protectionist measures are unconstitutional. Equally and even more importantly, a state law restricting the privilege of importation to a particular racial group, for example, would be shielded against challenge in the teeth of the textual Constitution's fundamental rejection of racial discrimination. The Court's more recent decisions therefore "have held that § 2 must be viewed as one part of a unified constitutional scheme" in which "§ 2 and other constitutional provisions work together," and the

---

[10]   See *United States* v. *Brown*, 381 U.S. 437, 446–49 (1965), discussing Chief Justice Marshall's opinion in *Fletcher* v. *Peck*, 10 U.S. (6 Cranch) 87 (1810).

Court now reads the provision to permit state legislation that serves "the protection of public health and safety" but not laws that protect local industry or violate other constitutional principles.[11]

Constitutional law ought to make sense if it is to be faithful to a text that has the overarching constitutional purpose of creating a workable government. "Constitutions are not themes proposed for ingenious speculation; but fundamental laws ordained for practical purposes." But this type of argument based on the-text-as-a-whole has limits. The original handiwork of the Philadelphia convention reflected compromises among the framers, and subsequent amendments and constitutional precedents have in some ways increased the extent to which the Constitution-in-practice contains principles and purposes that are in tension with one another. For example, the Constitution authorizes the federal government to safeguard the safety of the nation, a task that its prohibitions on governmental interference with personal freedom, privacy, and free speech can make much more difficult. The answer is not, however, to subordinate one principle to the other across the board. "The defining character of American constitutional government is its constant tension between security and liberty, serving both by partial helpings of each." The first amendment almost always prohibits the imposition of prior censorship on speech about public affairs, for example, but its prohibition would give way if the speaker intended to publish "the sailing dates of transports or the number and location of troops" in war time. Overall coherence is not the only goal in constitutional reasoning, or better, the coherence of the US Constitution lies in its ongoing preservation of each of the basic commitments of the American political community, even when they are in tension.[12]

Textual argument based on a specific provision of the written Constitution is dependent for its force on the nature of that provision. *McCulloch*'s description of the instrument as a charter of "great outlines" is itself a broad generalization, and many provisions in fact address specific details. Constitutional reasoning must take note of the difference between, say, the first clause of the fourth amendment, which protects the people's right "to be secure in their persons, houses, papers, and effects, against unreasonable searches and seizures," and its second clause, which provides that "no Warrants shall issue, but upon probable cause, supported by Oath or affirmation, and particularly describing the place to be searched, and the persons or things to be seized." The first clause clearly announces a general principle, and the Supreme Court accordingly has concluded that it addresses an indefinitely broad range of circumstances, the government's use of a cell phone company's records to track a phone user's movements, for example, and equally the employment by police of a drug-sniffing dog standing on someone's front porch. In contrast, the warrant clause's details identify it as a provision laying down specific rules, and the Court has, for example, held invalid a warrant that did

---

[11] *Tennessee Wine & Spirits Retailers Assoc. v. Thomas*, 139 S. Ct. 2449, 2462–63, 2474 (2019).
[12] *State* v. *Manuel*, 4 Dev. & Bat. 20, 29 (N.C. 1838) (Gaston, J.); *Hamdi* v. *Rumsfeld*, 542 U.S. 507, 545 (2004) (Souter, J., concurring in the judgment); *Haig* v. *Agee*, 453 U.S. 280, 308 (1981).

not specify the "things to be seized" even though the magistrate who issued the warrant knew the object of the search and could have issued a valid warrant. And the long-standing rule that a warrantless search generally is presumptively unreasonable gives the amendment as a whole a coherent reading, although one not compelled by its wording.[13]

The distinction between provisions that state general principles and those that ordain specific rules is clear in principle but not always easy to apply, although for most legal purposes the nature of many provisions is long settled by precedent or political practice. The first section of the fourteenth amendment, for example, includes a command prohibiting states from making or enforcing "any law which shall abridge the privileges or immunities of citizens of the United States." That language seems very broad, but early precedent treating the provision as a specific, very narrow prohibition is long-standing and apparently beyond successful challenge. In contrast, as we have seen, the bill of attainder clauses, which on their face seem specific and narrow, have been given an expansive reading.[14]

In some instances, whether a provision is broad or narrow does not matter in practice. Article I section 8 authorizes Congress to "raise and support Armies" and "provide and maintain a Navy." The fact that the text separately mentions each suggests that neither clause should be read as a general grant of power to establish a national military establishment. But section 8 makes no mention of the Marine Corps or, for obvious reasons, of an Air Force (much less a Space Force!), and yet no one seriously doubts the constitutionality of these other military services. But our sense that the answer to a question of authorization is obvious does not make the question pointless. The enumeration principle, a fundamental presupposition of constitutional law, requires that any federal government action be authorized by the Constitution, and so there *must* be an answer to *this* question of authorization: Is Congress empowered to create a separate Marine Corps? How then can we go about answering it?

One very reasonable approach would be to look beyond textual argument to a form of argument derived from the Constitution-in-practice, in this instance an argument from political practice. (See the discussion of such arguments later in the chapter) The Marine Corps has existed for a very long time, first by resolution of the Second Continental Congress in 1775 and then, under the Constitution, by a 1798

---

[13]   See *Carpenter* v. *United States*, 138 S.Ct. 2206 (2018) (cell phone records); *Florida* v. *Jardines*, 569 U.S. 1 (2013) (police dog); *Groh* v. *Ramirez*, 540 U.S. 551 (2004) (defective warrant). Both *Carpenter* and *Ramirez* produced strong dissents, but the general point made in the text would not change if they were overruled.

[14]   The *Slaughter-House Cases*, 83 U.S. (16 Wall.) 36 (1873), construed the privileges or immunities clause to protect only rights stemming from the relationship between the individual citizen and the federal government. Subsequent decisions confirmed that the Supreme Court understood this to be an exceedingly narrow category with little practical significance, but the Court has declined to revisit the issue despite the extreme oddity of treating a broadly phrased constitutional provision as almost meaningless.

act of Congress. The relationship of the Marines to the other services was ambiguous at first, and the Marine Corps continues to be located (in terms of the executive branch's structure) in the Department of the Navy, but from the beginning congressional legislation has assumed the Marines' distinct identity and it is now clearly a fully independent service. Political practice, we may argue, has answered the question.

When the Fifth Congress created the Marine Corps, however, the argument from political practice that it was constitutionally authorized to do so was negligible, and the question of authorization nonetheless demanded an answer, even if no one actually discussed the issue. Let's look again at the army and navy clauses. To read either as a "broad outline" provision is to put in question the need for the other, which appears to contradict the old canon of construction against reducing part of a text to "mere surplusage." But accepting the provisions as relatively specific clauses does not require the further conclusion that they should be given so narrow a construction that we impair the obvious and broad constitutional purpose they clearly serve – the empowerment of Congress to protect the Republic against military threat. "The words expressing the various grants [of power] in the Constitution are words of general import, and they are to be construed as such" and receive "no narrow and technical limitation or construction." That one of the written Constitution's central purposes is to enable Congress to defend the nation is beyond doubt. The text itself clearly indicates this by its references to "the common Defence" in the preamble and the first clause of Article I section 8, and by the various subsequent parts of section 8, including the army and navy clauses, that delegate military powers to Congress. Analogical reasoning is a central mode of traditional common law thinking, and so the common law-like character of constitutional law indicates that even a narrow constitutional provision may address a subject that is analogous to the provision's literal subject.[15]

The Marine Corps, and the Air and Space Forces as well in their turn, are analogous to the Army and Navy: military services that enable the federal government to address potential military threat. Since there is no constitutional meta-rule against an act of Congress being authorized by more than one grant of power, reasoning by analogy suggests that *both* the army and the navy clauses empowered the Fifth Congress to create the Marine Corps. After *McCulloch* v. *Maryland*, furthermore, the Constitution-in-practice clearly authorizes Congress to adopt whatever means it thinks best to achieve a constitutional end as long as its choice is "appropriate [and] plainly adapted to that end." The details of our current military arrangements, such as the existence of three separate military departments (rather than five or six, including the Coast Guard) all within a single Department of Defense (except the Coast Guard, ordinarily), are thus matters of legislative

---

[15] *Fairbank* v. *United States*, 181 U.S. 283, 287 (1901). *Cf. Cohens* v. *Virginia*, 19 U.S. (6 Wheat.) 264, 391 (1821) (Marshall, C.J.) (rejecting an interpretation of Article III because it would reduce part of the Article to "mere surplusage").

discretion rather than constitutional law. In the twenty-first century, finally, over two centuries of political practice make the validity of creating a separate Marine Corps, and indeed whatever separate military services Congress thinks valuable is beyond dispute.[16]

One additional observation: The reader should note that in solving our constitutional problem and coming to the happy conclusion that the Marine Corps is not unconstitutional, we found several different forms of argument relevant – the written Constitution by reasoning from the text and analogy to the text, the Constitution-in-practice in our consideration of political practice and judicial precedent. In this instance, the relevant forms of argument worked together to provide mutual support for the answer to the question of authorization we were considering. But this is not always true by any means. Recall the question in *Seminole Tribe* that we discussed previously: Does the Constitution-in-practice prohibit Congress from abrogating state sovereign immunity pursuant to its plenary power to legislate with respect to Native American nations? Chief Justice Rehnquist argued yes, largely on the basis of judicial precedent and governmental structure; Justice Souter argued no, relying in large part on an expository argument about the text's meaning. In that case, the forms of argument produced conflicting answers. In Chapter 6, we shall return to the difficult question of what makes one of two defensible answers to a constitutional question more persuasive.

The *McCulloch* principle that because the written Constitution is a charter setting out basic outlines of government its language should ordinarily be read broadly underpins a great deal of the Constitution-in-practice. Nevertheless, the reader may well feel that expository argument plays a more modest role than expected. This impression is not altogether unjustified, and if American constitutional law had not been decisively shaped by common law thought, expository and other arguments focused on the written Constitution might play a larger role. But given the common law-like qualities of constitutional law, after more than two centuries of debate, judicial precedent, and political practice, most provisions of the written Constitution that are at all likely to provoke controversy have done so, and plausible arguments based primarily on their wording have been absorbed into the precedents. At the same time, the occasional scholar who suggests that the written Constitution is of only minor significance is, I think, demonstrably wrong. Textual argument is pervasive, but the text is discussed most of the time through the case law.

---

[16] *McCulloch* v. *Maryland*, 17 U.S. (4 Wheat.) 316, 421 (1819). The original constitutional authorization for the Coast Guard was quite different. The Revenue-Marine, as the initial system of revenue cutters was generally known, came into existence through a 1790 statute enacted at the urging of Treasury Secretary Alexander Hamilton, and the cutters' central purpose was to enforce congressional tariffs. Thus the 1790 act was unproblematically authorized by two provisions of Article I section 8 read together: the grants of power "[t]o ... collect Taxes, Duties, Imposts and Excises" and "[t]o make all Laws which shall be necessary and proper for carrying into Execution the foregoing Powers."

But not always. There are, for example, parts of the constitutional text of great significance with respect to which the question whether to read the provision as one of *McCulloch*'s broad outlines remains unsettled. The clause in Article I section 8 preceding the army and navy clauses delegates the power to "declare War." Do those words grant Congress general authority over decisions to use military force, or the formal and narrowly legal power to enter the United States into a state of "war" as defined by the law of nations, or something in between? The constitutional problem posed by uncertainty over the extent to which the president can employ force unilaterally is of tremendous importance, but there is no consensus on how to read the declaration of war clause – or the commander in chief clause in Article II – and the only directly relevant Supreme Court precedents are over two centuries old.[17] Either clause could be read (and is read by some) to state as a general principle that the branch it concerns has final authority over the use of military force; obviously both cannot. Another example: Section 4 of the twenty-fifth amendment provides that the vice president becomes acting president upon submitting to congressional officers a written declaration, joined by the cabinet secretaries or some other statutorily designated body, that "the President is unable to discharge the powers and duties of his office." Is the "inability" to which the amendment refers in the following sentence limited to actual physical or mental incapacity in a medical sense, or is it a concept encompassing other circumstances that might in reality significantly impair the president's functioning? The answer is debatable.

The exegetical or expository forms of constitutional law reasoning that I am labeling textual argument are relevant to solving a constitutional law problem because they bring the (axiomatically authoritative) words of the written Constitution to bear on the problem. But such reasoning is persuasive only if it fits into the overall pattern of constitutional law thought, and some textual arguments that might appear plausible, if considered in isolation from the text as a whole and from tradition and precedent, carry no weight in the practice of constitutional law. We have already encountered a classic example. Even if the better grammatical construction of Article I section 8's words about Congress having "Power To . . . pay the Debts and provide for the common Defence and general Welfare" would be to treat the "provide for" clause as an independent grant of power, the argument to that effect is ludicrous because it would eviscerate the enumeration principle, one of the central presuppositions of constitutional law.

As *McCulloch*'s teaching on the nature of the Constitution implies, textual arguments that rely on an overly literal reading of constitutional language undercut by their literalism whatever persuasive power they might otherwise have. Article III section 2 qualifies the Supreme Court's appellate jurisdiction as subject to "such Exceptions, and under such Regulations as the Congress shall make." As a semantic

---

[17] See, e.g., *Talbot v. Seeman*, 5 U.S. (1 Cranch) 1, 28 (1801) (Marshall, C.J.) ("The whole powers of war [are] by the constitution of the United States, vested in congress").

matter, it could be argued that Congress can exercise its exceptions and regulations power to limit the Court's entire appellate role to the review of, say, federal contracts disputes involving claims of less than a thousand dollars, everything else being excluded as an "Exception." But other arguments based on the written Constitution as well as political and judicial precedent point to the conclusion that "Congress can limit the Supreme Court's appellate jurisdiction only up to the point where it impairs the Court's core functions in the constitutional scheme." Exactly where that line should be drawn is debatable, but the argument that "Exceptions" should be "read so broadly as to swallow the general rule [of appellate jurisdiction] in terms of which it is defined" is implausible.[18]

The substantive prohibitions in the Bill of Rights (the first eight amendments) present two unique issues in textual argument. At an early point, the Supreme Court concluded that the first eight amendments do not limit state governmental actions, even though some of them are written in language that could apply to the states. Its reasoning rested on an argument from original meaning: the First Congress proposed the adoption of the Bill of Rights to allay specific concerns that the *federal* government was not subject to a declaration of rights. However, through a long series of decisions that began at the end of the nineteenth century and has extended up to the very recent past, the Supreme Court has concluded that the due process clause of section 1 of the fourteenth amendment "incorporates" almost all of the Bill of Rights provisions and thereby makes them applicable to state government.

The incorporation doctrine's consistency with the text of the due process clause, and with the original meaning of section 1, remains controversial, but the doctrine seems established beyond practical question. As a result, virtually all of the prohibitions that the first eight amendments impose on the federal government apply equally, and in exactly the same manner, to the states. As a theoretical matter, a Bill of Rights case involving state or local government is decided under the fourteenth amendment due process clause, but this is a technicality that even judges with a particular interest in textual argument generally ignore. At the time I am writing, there are only three Bill of Rights provisions that the Supreme Court has not held to be incorporated: the third amendment ban on quartering soldiers in private homes, the fifth amendment grand jury clause, and the seventh amendment, which addresses the right to a civil jury in federal court. There is no serious contemporary interest in incorporating the grand jury and civil jury provisions, and the Court held them inapplicable to the states long ago. The Court has never considered a third amendment case nor has it been asked to decide if that provision is incorporated, although the one federal appellate court to address the question decided, no doubt correctly, that the amendment is.[19]

[18]   *Constitutionality of Legislation Withdrawing Supreme Court Jurisdiction to Consider Cases Relating to Voluntary Prayer*, 6 Op. O.L.C. 13, 17, 16 (1982) (William French Smith, Att'y Gen.).

[19]   See *McDonald v. City of Chicago, Ill.*, 561 U.S. 742, 765 n. 13 (2010) (plurality opinion of Alito, J.) (indicating that the grand jury and civil jury provisions will remain unincorporated); *Engblom v. Carey*, 677 F.2d 957 (2d Cir. 1982) (third amendment is incorporated).

Second, the fifth and fourteenth amendments both include a due process clause, but the fourteenth amendment also provides that "[n]o state shall ... deny to any person within its jurisdiction the equal protection of the laws." The text and context of the equal protection clause preclude its application to the federal government. But from the 1940s onward the Supreme Court began applying the equality doctrines it was developing under the fourteenth amendment clause to federal actions as well, and identified the fifth amendment due process clause as the textual basis for doing so. By the end of the century the Court had eliminated all but minor differences between the equal protection principle as applied to the federal and state governments. The inclusion of *equal protection* as an aspect of fifth amendment *due process* exemplifies the limited weight that can be given to argument from the semantic features of broadly worded constitutional provisions, even as it demonstrates once more the importance of the *McCulloch* presumption that the constitutional text is to be read when possible to state broad principles rather than narrow rules.

Finally, the purpose of formalizing political arrangements through a written constitutional text is to stabilize and secure those arrangements. As Chief Justice Marshall put it in *Marbury* v. *Madison*, "the constitution is written" so that the definitions and limits of government power "may not be mistaken, or forgotten." Many provisions of the written Constitution do exactly that, and do it with such success that they play little or no role in the lawyers' Constitution-in-practice that is forged through controversy and litigation. But the structure of American government is not the only subject addressed in the written Constitution. By ensuring that the political community's commitments to such ideas as "freedom of speech" and "the equal protection of the laws" cannot easily or permanently be forgotten, the constitutional text, and arguments based on it, are a tool of change as well as stability. Fidelity to the past sometimes involves change, in constitutional law as in other human affairs.[20]

Original Meaning Arguments. The written Constitution did not appear out of the sky, devoid of historical antecedents, context, or purposes. It is instead a collection of historical documents, drafted and adopted at specific times by known groups of people and for purposes that we can state at least in general terms, although as with all political decisions by multiple actors, there are ambiguities and internal tensions in the historical record. The axiomatic authority of the constitutional text is an attribute of *historical* documents and the starting point for constitutional arguments that depend on the text is the meaning the specific part of the text had when it was drafted and adopted. The role of history is clear on the semantic level – Article I section 8's reference to "the Indian Tribes" will continue to refer to the Native American nations even if the adjective is no longer used with that meaning – but it extends beyond that level to broader questions of meaning,

---

[20] *Marbury* v. *Madison*, 5 U.S. (1 Cranch) 137, 176 (1803).

substance, and purpose. As the reader is aware, this book often discusses founding-era thought even though our subject is twenty-first-century constitutional law. Precisely because the American political community governs itself through a set of texts with specific histories, the Constitution-in-practice is shaped by those histories and, in part, constructed out of arguments about the history as well as the wording of the written Constitution.

Arguments based on the original meaning of the written Constitution are therefore as fully arguments from the text as reasoning grounded in semantics or syntax, and constitutional lawyers who put great weight on "textual argument" in the sense of expository or exegetical reasoning often emphasize original meaning claims as well. However, it is useful as well as conventional to distinguish *textual* arguments that focus on the semantic and literary features of the text, including the definitions of its terms and the level of generality of its phrasing, from *original meaning* arguments that rely on historical assertions about the text's antecedents, its drafters' and ratifiers' concerns, purposes and intentions, debates at the time of drafting or adoption over its meaning, and the assumptions that an informed contemporaneous reader would have made in construing the text or thinking about its application to constitutional problems. *Original meaning* as a form of argument focused on the written Constitution should not be confused with *originalist* claims about the correct theory of constitutional decision making. (See the excursus to Chapter 1.) The assertion that original meaning arguments are relevant to constitutional law debate describes a fact: original meaning arguments *in fact* play a role in argument and decision by serious constitutional lawyers.[21] The salience of original meaning arguments stems from the undisputed and axiomatic authority of the constitutional text, not from a disputed theory.

It is also important not to confuse original meaning arguments that draw on historical sources other than the constitutional text itself from what we might call "ceremonial" references to the founders, the framers, original understanding, and the like. The former depend for their cogency on their relationship to actual historical information, but ceremonial references are little more than synonyms for "the Constitution." It has been common practice since the early Republic for constitutional lawyers and judges to present assertions about constitutional law in language that to an unwary reader might sound like an original meaning argument

---

21   The qualifier "serious" is intended only to recognize the fact with which the Introduction begins: Americans talk about "the Constitution" in many ways and some of what is said has little or nothing to do with the constitutional law arguments that one finds in, for example, Supreme Court opinions. There are Americans who believe that the progressive federal income tax is invalid or that "constitutional sheriffs" have the lawful authority to disregard laws they think unconstitutional. Neither claim would find any purchase in Supreme Court arguments or opinions. The range of assertions that serious constitutional lawyers accept as plausible does not remain static. The existence of a constitutional right of state secession was within that range in the early Republic but no longer is. Contemporary talk about secession, whatever its political salience, is beyond the outer bounds of serious constitutional law argument in the twenty-first-century United States.

that the writer then fails to substantiate by offering any historical evidence beyond his or her personal opinion. In these ceremonial invocations of the founding-era, however, no real claim about the past is being made: the apparent historical reference is simply a somewhat grandiloquent way of asserting that the writer is making a correct constitutional law argument.

Chief Justice Marshall, for example, liked to attribute textual and structural arguments he found persuasive to the Philadelphia framers. In *McCulloch* v. *Maryland*, for example, he carefully explained that the framers "reported" to Congress "a mere proposal" with no legal force; the Constitution "derives its whole authority" from the state ratifying conventions. Having reduced the Philadelphia convention (correctly as a formal matter) to the status of a drafting committee, Marshall then proceeded to invoke repeatedly as authority, with slight variations in wording, "the framers of the American constitution," "the convention," and "the intention of the convention." Other Marshall opinions employ similar formulas. In no case does Marshall so much as hint that he is relying on historical knowledge of what went on in Philadelphia. Marshall's reference in *Barron* v. *Baltimore* (1833) to what "the framers of [the Bill of Rights] intended" is probably an exception to this practice, and meant seriously as an appeal to common knowledge about the First Congress's purpose in proposing those amendments.[22]

Marshall, of course, was a founding-era lawyer and a delegate to the Virginia state ratifying convention: he could rightly claim that his personal views on the interpretation of constitutional language and the reasons for adopting the instrument were in themselves evidence of its original meaning. But the practice of expressing arguments based on other reasoning in the language of original meaning did not cease with Marshall's departure. For example, in a 2020 separation of powers case, *Seila Law* v. *CFPB*, the opinion of the Court stated that "the Framers recognized that, in the long term, structural protections against abuse of power were critical to preserving liberty." The sentence, which is "substantiated" by a reference to a famous passage in *The Federalist*, is in fact a quotation from an earlier Supreme Court opinion where it is a mere assertion unsupported by reference to any historical source. The dissent in *Seila Law* also referred to "the Framers' choice to give the political branches wide discretion over administrative offices" without giving any supporting authority at all.[23] Both statements are in fact parts of perfectly sensible, if

---

[22]   *McCulloch* v. *Maryland*, 17 U.S. (4 Wheat.) 316, 403, 407, 408, 420 ("framers"), 413, 414, 416, 419 ("the convention") (1819); *Barron* v. *Baltimore*, 32 U.S. (7 Pet.) 243, 250 (1833). For other examples in Marshall opinions, see *Sturges* v. *Crowninshield*, 17 U.S. (4 Wheat.) 122, 193 (1819) ("the sense of the convention"); *Gibbons* v. *Ogden*, 22 U.S. (9 Wheat.) 1, 200 (1824) ("the opinion of the Convention"); *Brown* v. *Maryland*, 25 U.S. (12 Wheat.) 419, 438, 440 (1827) ("the framers of the [or "our"] constitution").

[23]   *Seila Law LLC* v. *Consumer Fin. Prot. Bureau*, 140 S. Ct. 2183, 2202 (2020) (quoting *Bowsher* v. *Synar*, 478 U.S. 714, 730 (1986)); *id.* at 2225 (Kagan, J., concurring in part and dissenting in part). The Court's quotation from *The Federalist* is apposite but hardly *proof* of anything that the founders as a group recognized.

conflicting, structural arguments (and the quotation invokes precedent as well). But if either were assessed as the framers' intent arguments they both claim to be verbally, it would have to receive a failing grade. This is not a criticism of either the majority opinion or the dissent in *Seila Law*, but an illustration of the fact that references to original meaning, like statements about what "the Constitution" commands, have to be evaluated for their substance, not for their rhetorical clothing.

Let us turn to genuine or substantive original meaning arguments. Such arguments are rooted in history, directly based on the fact that the authoritative written Constitution is a collection of historical documents. Real original meaning arguments are not, however, historical arguments per se; they are legal arguments that bear their ultimate allegiance, as it were, to the law. Let us begin with the role of history. The weight an original meaning argument carries in constitutional law depends on its intelligent and intellectually honest engagement with whatever historical sources are relevant. In principle, and taken as a whole, there is a great abundance of historical source material. Every part of the written Constitution was the product of a deliberative body that drafted it (the Philadelphia framing convention and, for the amendments, Congress), and was in turn given legal force by other deliberative bodies in the states (the state conventions that ratified the original text and the twenty-first amendment, and for the rest of the amendments, the state legislatures). In every instance there were debates. Because the processes of adopting each part of the Constitution were public, there are records of contemporaneous debate in the press and, particularly with respect to the ratification of the original instrument, of private correspondence about the proposed text. Early post-adoption discussion of a constitutional provision is evidence of contemporaneous understandings as well and is available, for some provisions in profusion.

Casting one's net more broadly, the intellectual background to the 1787 text and the Bill of Rights was strongly shaped by pre-Revolutionary English political history and the history of the common law, both somewhat mythologized by Americans so that what matters for constitutional law is the mythology, not a modern reconstruction of the English past. American political and legal history is important to arguments about the original meaning of other parts of the text, especially the three Civil War (or Reconstruction) amendments and the two prohibition amendments. Judicial decisions and political practice under a constitutional provision in the period immediately following its adoption are also relevant.

The wealth of potential source material should not obscure the fact that the evidentiary record is uneven. We have the official journal of the federal convention, and Madison's fairly extensive notes on the debates at the Philadelphia convention have traditionally been seen as reliable of information about "the intentions of the framers," although Madison has been criticized for bias and incompleteness. But while there are extensive records of the 1787–1788 debates in some state conventions, from others we have very little. The discussion of the proposed Bill of Rights in the House of Representatives in 1789 is partially recorded, but the Senate's deliberations were secret. With respect to many of the later amendments, detailed information about the state legislative proceedings is minimal or unattainable from a practicing lawyer's or judge's perspective.

As with all forms of constitutional law argument, whether focused on the written Constitution or derived from the Constitution-in-practice, original meaning reasoning has limitations: none of the accepted modes of argument is the skeleton key that unlocks the answer to every question. The unique characteristic of original meaning thinking is, of course, its foundation in history, and a properly constructed original meaning argument will relate history to law in a way that respects the integrity of both types of thought. The constitutional lawyer therefore must avoid the temptation of trying to force history to be useful when the historical sources are recalcitrant. A court does not refuse to decide a case over which it has jurisdiction because it cannot determine which is the right answer to the dispositive legal question: The court must come to an answer, no matter how finely balanced it thinks the arguments. In contrast, in an historical inquiry, the only intellectually honest conclusion may very well be that we cannot determine the answer to a question about, for example, which of two semantically permissible meanings was *the* historical meaning of a public document. There may have been no consensus on its meaning, and we may be unable to determine which of the competing meanings was more widely shared. Without that essential historical foundation, there is no credible original meaning argument that one of the meanings was the generally accepted public meaning, and if we are to adopt one of the *possible* original meanings, the reasons for doing so must be shown through some other form of constitutional argument.

The Supreme Court's seminal second amendment decision, *District of Columbia v. Heller*, is an example of good constitutional lawyers presenting bad original meaning arguments because they failed to remember that original meaning reasoning is limited by what history can show. Justices Antonin Scalia and John Paul Stevens each presented an elaborate argument that *the* original meaning (singular) of the second amendment supported his conclusion, the problem being that they came to opposite conclusions. I think there is very little doubt that taken together what the evidence Scalia and Stevens amassed actually shows is that there was no founding-era consensus, or even an ascertainable majority view, over how to understand the amendment. Each justice was therefore entitled to argue that history did not exclude his reading of the amendment; unfortunately, each chose to make the stronger but indefensible claim that his view was *the* original meaning.[24]

What the original history sources reveal, most of the time, will not be a direct solution to the problem the constitutional lawyer is addressing. But this does not make the inquiry into the historical sources pointless. The sources may show that a particular provision was included in the constitutional text in response to a specific

---

[24] See *District of Columbia v. Heller*, 554 U.S. 570, 581–610 (2008) (Scalia, J., for the Court); *id.* at 640–70 (Stevens, J., dissenting).

problem or controversy of concern to the provision's drafters. That historical concern, in turn, may be analogous to the issue posed by the modern problem the lawyer
is attempting to solve, or may suggest a principle broad enough to encompass the
modern controversy as well as the problem originally in view. In order to be
persuasive in that situation, of course, the original meaning argument must draw
the analogy convincingly, or explain why the underlying principle should be given
a scope that includes both the historical and the contemporary concerns. In doing
so, however, the argument need not show that the provision's makers or original
readers themselves had already drawn the analogy or worked out the scope of the
principle. The answer to *that* question will usually be unknowable or even meaningless. (No one in the founding era thought that the Constitution authorizes the
creation of a Space Force, but that "fact" is irrelevant.) *McCulloch*'s teaching that
the written Constitution is a broad outline rather than (primarily) a collection of
specific rules applies to original meaning arguments just as fully as it does to textual
arguments in the narrow, expository sense. An example will illustrate these points.

In the same 1819 term in which *McCulloch v. Maryland* came before it, the
Supreme Court decided *Dartmouth College v. Woodward*. The case involved the
validity of an 1816 New Hampshire law that radically reorganized the governance
structure of Dartmouth, converting it from a private college into a state-controlled
university. The old trustees objected, arguing that the statute violated Article
I section 10's prohibition on the state enacting any "Law impairing the Obligation
of Contracts" because it altered the terms of the 1769 royal charter that had created
the college as a corporate body. The new university responded that the original
purpose of that clause was limited to protecting contractual rights between two
private parties from state interference, that a corporation created to serve a public
purpose such as education does not enjoy private rights against the state, and that the
royal charter was not a contract within the meaning of section 10. The Court rejected
those arguments and invalidated the 1816 law.[25]

Writing for the Court, Chief Justice Marshall conceded that the university's
lawyers were probably right that "the great motive for imposing this restriction on
the state legislatures" was to prevent legislative meddling with private parties' ordinary contracts, and that it was therefore unlikely that charters such as the college's
were "particularly in the view of the framers of the constitution." But that argument,
he reasoned, took too narrow a view of the significance of the contract clause's
original meaning. "It is not enough to say, that this particular case was not in the
mind of the convention, when the article was framed, nor of the American people,

---

[25]   The old trustees' lead lawyer was Daniel Webster, a Dartmouth alumnus, and already a famous
political and courtroom orator. At one point in his argument, Webster told the Court, "It is, Sir, as
I have said, a small college. And yet there are those who love it!" and dramatically burst into tears. It
was said afterward, improbably, that Webster's emotional appeal actually swayed Chief Justice
Marshall, which if true nicely illustrates the important truth that constitutional law decisions are
made by human beings whose judgments are not driven solely by logic. I nonetheless would counsel
the reader not to start crying when arguing a point of constitutional law in court.

when it was adopted." The years immediately prior to the Constitution's adoption had seen state legislatures frequently enact debtor relief laws that prevented creditors from enforcing preexisting legal rights, which no one denied was the precipitating cause for the clause's inclusion in Article I section 10. But the clause's wording is not limited to the particular issue of debtor relief legislation, and therefore, Marshall reasoned, its original purpose, understood with the breadth appropriate to a constitutional provision, was to prohibit any legislative interference with preexisting rights originally created by agreement. The college's legal rights as a corporation, and its legal right to property given to it by private donors, were created by agreements with the crown and with the donors, and the 1816 state law impaired those rights and thus violated the contracts clause.[26]

The *Dartmouth College* opinion skillfully interwove historical facts, the debtor relief controversy of the 1780s, and the causative relationship between that controversy and the framers' inclusion of the contracts clause, with the legal principle (articulated in the Court's almost simultaneous decision in *McCulloch*) that the written Constitution is the basic charter of American government and to be read as such. The original meaning argument that Marshall constructed was not itself an historical assertion – whether most readers in 1787–1788 would have thought Dartmouth's charter within the protection of the contracts clause is in reality unknowable – but it persuasively linked the historical facts to the question before the Court by common law-like analogical reasoning. Like the debtor relief legislation of the 1780s, the 1816 law interfered with someone's ability to enforce the legal rights created by private parties entering into agreements. This combination of factual claims based on history, which a modern lawyer must prove from written sources, with legal reasoning that brings the historical facts to bear on the constitutional issue, is characteristic of constitutional arguments based on original meaning.

Dartmouth College exemplifies a second attribute of original meaning argument that is also a corollary of the *McCulloch* presumption that the Constitution articulates principles rather than rules. It was the old trustees' contention that history supported application of the contracts clause to their case, not the university's claim that history showed the clause inapplicable, that persuaded the Court. This illustrates a general feature of original meaning arguments. Most of the time, original meaning reasoning is more persuasive as part of an affirmative argument that the Constitution *does* address a subject on which its text seems to be silent because the subject is within the principle stated by the text than in support of a negative argument that the Constitution *does not* address a matter that otherwise appears to be within the words of the text.

The case law applying the equal protection clause of the fourteenth amendment provides many examples of this common (although not universal) feature of original meaning argument. The historical reason for including the clause in the proposed

---

[26] See *Dartmouth College* v. *Woodward*, 17 U.S. (4 Wheat.) 518, 644 (1819).

amendment was, without any doubt, specifically to protect African Americans against discrimination on the basis of race, but the Supreme Court has always admitted that the clause, and the Civil War amendments generally, go beyond that specific, original purpose. In 1873, the Court stated that "both the language and spirit of these articles are to have their fair and just weight in any question of construction," and immediately added that the thirteenth amendment is not limited to prohibiting the antebellum enslavement of African Americans but "forbids any other kind of slavery, now or hereafter." If "other rights are assailed by the States which properly and necessarily fall within the protection" of the Civil War amendments, the Court added, their "protection will apply, though the party interested may not be of African descent." The twenty-first-century Constitution-in-practice prohibits discrimination based on many criteria other than race as a violation of equal protection because the Court has repeatedly discerned an analogy between such criteria and the racial injustices that were the fourteenth amendment's original focus, and repeatedly rejected arguments that the clause's general wording should be limited by that specific purpose.[27]

The ultimate limitation to argument from original meaning appears when there is no historical source material relevant to the constitutional problem at hand, or what exists is patently inadequate to support any plausible argument. Under those circumstances, like those where the historical sources show the existence of conflicting understandings (as in *District of Columbia* v. *Heller*, discussed previously), history does not allow the construction of an affirmative original meaning argument as to the constitutional answer. A good example is the important question whether, and to what extent, the president is authorized to order combat operations in the absence of congressional authorization or an actual attack on the United States or its armed forces. What evidence from Philadelphia and the ratification debates exists indicates a widespread understanding that the Constitution denies to the president the lawful authority to launch a war of aggression, but neither that history nor early practice and judicial precedent provide a basis for giving an answer either way to the question whether the president may undertake lesser military actions in the absence of congressional authorization or an attack. When the relevant historical information is so scanty or inconclusive, the most that the practice of constitutional law permits a lawyer to conclude is that history does not weigh against an answer that is supported by other kinds of constitutional law arguments.

We turn now to the ways in which original meaning argument goes beyond history because it is, in the end, a form of legal rather than historical reasoning. The most fundamental difference is that original meaning argument, like all forms of constitutional law reasoning, starts from the axiomatic legal premise that the written Constitution, both the original document and the amendments, is the act of the People, the American political community. That is, in no sense, a statement of

---

[27] *Slaughter-House Cases*, 83 U.S. (16 Wall.) 36, 72 (1873).

historical fact, and from an historian's perspective, it is difficult to view it as anything other than a legal fiction, but a constitutional lawyer cannot question the premise while working within the practice. While factual assertions that are defensible on strictly historical grounds are an essential part of any claim about original meaning, the claim itself is ultimately a proposal about the correct answer to a legal question: What does the Constitution, the act of the People, say with regard to the problem the lawyer is trying to solve? Historical reasoning, by itself, *cannot* answer that question because the problem it concerns is not an historical problem. There is nothing mysterious about this point. Consider a close parallel.

Were the American Revolutionaries of 1776 traitors at war with their sovereign, or patriots seeking to secure for the American colonies, as the Declaration of Independence put it, "the separate and equal station to which the Laws of Nature and of Nature's God entitle them?" History can address any number of matters that might be thought relevant to the answer: whether their actions were treason as defined by the common law, what arguments were made for and against declaring independence in the Second Continental Congress, how similar were the colonists' complaints to those which led to the Glorious Revolution of 1688 that many English speakers on both sides of the Atlantic thought a legitimate popular act, and the like. But to answer the question itself requires the exercise of legal or political or moral judgment, and the premises by which anyone makes such a judgment must come from law, political thought, or morality. The question is not an historical one.

Original meaning arguments, then, are shaped by the constitutional lawyer's objective of determining what, as a matter of law, the People should be deemed to have meant by adopting the constitutional text. The relevance of historical facts to that determination is ultimately a legal judgment. (As we have seen, the sources may not permit any judgment on original meaning, in which case the constitutional problem at hand must be solved using other forms of argument.) The ultimate criterion for making that judgment is closely related to the concept of the "reasonable person" familiar to lawyers from its use in other areas of law. The original meaning of a constitutional provision is that understanding of it which, in light of the historically ascertainable facts, it appears a well-informed and reasonable reader would have thought was the provision's meaning at the time it became part of the Constitution. Original meaning argument, properly understood, is not the impossible and incoherent attempt to retrospectively survey public opinion about the Constitution that critics sometimes charge it with being, but the application of a legal concept to facts about the extra-legal world, something that the American legal system does constantly.

The weight of the various historical sources that are available with respect to a question of original meaning depends on how plausible it is to treat a given source as indicative of the views of the reasonable reader. Very often a statement about original meaning is so uncontroversial that it can be adequately supported by reference to any source, or indeed to our general understanding of American constitutional history. The relationship between the inability of the 1780s Confederation Congress to address interstate economic conflict and the delegation to Congress of power to regulate commerce "among the several States," and the common purpose of the Civil War amendments to abolish slavery and protect the former slaves against oppression, are obvious examples. Furthermore, most of the time, any contemporaneous source about the import or purpose of a proposed or newly adopted constitutional provision is relevant as long as it does not appear to be expressing an entirely idiosyncratic viewpoint. Nevertheless, twenty-first-century constitutional lawyers tend to accept, in principle, the proposition that the object of original meaning argument is the "original public meaning" of the reasonable reader, not (say) the intentions of the Philadelphia framers or of the congressional majority that crafted and proposed the fourteenth amendment. Although original meaning reasoning in earlier periods was usually cast in different terms, the rhetorical change does not seem to reflect a substantive change in original meaning as a mode of argument.[28]

Two historical sources for original meaning arguments about the original document and the Bill of Rights deserve special mention. *The Federalist* (or *Federalist Papers*) is the collection of eighty-five newspaper essays published by James Madison, Alexander Hamilton, and John Jay between late 1787 and the middle of

---

[28] For most of American constitutional history, constitutional lawyers paid little or no attention to the language used to describe what in this book, and in contemporary constitutional law, are referred to as "original meaning" arguments. As discussed earlier, many apparent references to the historical meaning of the constitutional text were (and are) ceremonial, and interchangeable with statements about "the Constitution" itself. Everyone understood that it was the state ratifying conventions, not the Philadelphia framers, that gave the original text its authority, and that the meanings that matter in constitutional law are those that can be attributed to the People, but even when a lawyer was making a genuine original meaning argument rather than a ceremonial gesture, the labels were used almost randomly. There was almost never any suggestion that terms such as "the intent of the framers," "the original understanding," what "the convention" intended or understood, and so on referred to distinct concepts of differing constitutional importance. This casual approach to the labels was consistent with the usual character of original meaning arguments before the 1970s: with rare exceptions, most such arguments were based on uncontested historical assertions or on quotations from a small number of familiar sources that were generally assumed to be acceptable. Chief among these were the collections of material on the framing and ratification of the Constitution published by Jonathan Elliot in 1827–1830 and by Max Farrand in 1911, Madison's notes of the framers' debates (first published in 1840 and included in Farrand), and *The Federalist*.

The widespread availability of a broad range of historical sources, and the advent of modern originalism as a normative theory of constitutional decision making, have significantly changed these traditional, rather easy-going practices. The ceremonial invocation of original meaning has not disappeared, but in recent decades, briefs and judicial opinions have become much more likely to include original meaning arguments that go into extensive, heavily footnoted detail, advance highly controversial claims, and (sometimes) display a sophisticated grasp of the relationship between historical sources and constitutional law argument. The advent of greater rigor in dealing with the historical sources is an admirable development, and the practice of making original meaning argument does not seem to be significantly influenced by disagreements over just what aspects of history are authoritative or over the right terminology.

1788 to advocate the ratification of the Constitution. Even before the series was complete, partial editions were published in book form, and it is fair to assume that the essays were widely read, although the extent to which they in fact influenced the ratification struggle is unclear. However, already in the First Congress *The Federalist* was quoted for the light it might shed on a constitutional issue, and the first reference to the essays in a Supreme Court opinion was in 1798. *The Federalist's* status as a highly important historical source for original meaning arguments is thus as old as constitutional law itself. Having been written as political propaganda, the essays are hardly a neutral analysis of the constitutional text's public meaning, but their comprehensiveness, the sophistication of some of their analyses, and the simple fact that they have been treated as an authority since the beginning give *The Federalist* considerable weight in original meaning argument.[29]

The First Congress to convene under the Constitution (1789–1791) played a momentous roll in the translating the constitutional text into a functioning charter of government: It created the executive branch and the lower federal courts, made critical decisions on constitutional issues such as the president's power to remove executive officers and its own authority to charter a national bank, and proposed the adoption of the Bill of Rights. Many of its decisions established political practices that have continued to the present. The House of Representatives publicly debated constitutional issues with a seriousness and sophistication that remains impressive over two centuries later. (The Senate's debates were secret.) For these reasons alone, it is unsurprising that constitutional lawyers, and since at least 1804 the Supreme Court, have treated the First Congress's actions as a "contemporary . . . practical exposition" of the constitutional text that is "strong evidence of the original meaning of the Constitution."[30]

Structural Arguments. The great constitutional lawyer Henry Paul Monaghan once wrote that the US Constitution was "a watershed in the evolution of thinking about the meaning of a constitution" because "it culminated a shift from viewing a constitution as simply a description of the fundamental political arrangements of the society to a conception that the constitution stood behind, or grounded and legitimated, those arrangements – and of course constrained them."[31] The political arrangements of the American political community are not legitimate simply because they exist: they must stand in a legally cognizable relationship to the written Constitution or they lose legitimacy and become unlawful. But it would be an over-simplification of the American conception to think of the constitutional text as a sort of blueprint providing a complete set of directions to which American political

---

[29]   See *Calder v. Bull*, 3 U.S. 386, 391 (1798) (seriatim opinion of Chase, J.).

[30]   *Stuart v. Laird*, 5 U.S. 299, 309 (1803); *Fin. Oversight & Mgmt. Bd. for Puerto Rico v. Aurelius Investment*, 140 S. Ct. 1649, 1659 (2020). The Court has sometimes put weight on the fact that the First Congress included Philadelphia framers and others involved in the adoption of the Constitution.

[31]   Henry Paul Monaghan, Stare Decisis and Constitutional Adjudication, (1988), in Monaghan, *American Constitutional Law: Selected Essays* 539 (Durham, NC: Carolina Academic Press, 2018).

arrangements must conform. The interaction between the written Constitution and the actual structures of American government is correlative rather than simply the one-way application of written instructions to sometimes recalcitrant moving parts.

The written Constitution, as a legal matter, creates and thus legitimates the three branches of the federal government, in broad outline, and orders their relationships with one another and with the states, again in broad outline. But the text did not create the states or the American Union, and it is silent on many practical issues that can arise out of the interactions among the various parts of the system, including those parts it did create. Structural reasoning is the form of argument focused on the written Constitution that starts from the basic assumption that the fundamental political arrangements recognized by the document can and should make sense. Any solution offered to a constitutional problem involving those arrangements must serve the goal of ensuring that that the system is in practice a workable government.

As mentioned previously, this does not mean that the answer to a constitutional question is always whatever would enhance governmental efficiency. Some of the most important constitutional commitments of the American political community are to values such as personal freedom that cut across and sometimes reduce the efficiency of government. A "workable government" in the constitutional sense is a government that respects and safeguards those commitments as well as possessing the power and flexibility to exercise political authority effectively. But the Constitution-in-practice should not be characterized by outright self-contradictions or rules that do not serve any of the authorizations or prohibitions that make up constitutional law. Where a question about the relationship among the structures of American government has no clear answer in the words of the text, the practice of constitutional law sometimes permits constitutional lawyers to infer what the text *must* mean, if the constitutional arrangements are to be workable, from the written Constitution as a whole or from the logical implications of the scheme of government it outlines.

The opinion of the Court in *McCulloch* v. *Maryland* provides the classic example of structural argument. The reader will recall that the constitutional problem the Supreme Court needed to solve in *McCulloch* – was the state tax on the national bank constitutional? – presented both the question of Congress's authorization to create the bank and the question whether, if the bank was authorized, the Constitution prohibited the state from taxing it. The Court's conclusion that the Bank Act was valid did not in itself generate an answer to this second question. Because the Act was authorized, the supremacy clause of Article VI ensured that the Act would override state laws that conflicted with its provisions, but nothing in the Act conferred immunity from taxation on the bank, and the state law did not prohibit the bank's operation – in modern terms, the state tax was not invalid on either express or conflict preemption grounds.

Chief Justice Marshall nonetheless concluded that the Constitution prohibited the Maryland tax, not on the basis of any "express provision" in the text, but as an inference from the principle of national supremacy that the text as a whole (including Article VI) implies, "a principle which so entirely pervades the constitution, is so intermixed with the materials which compose it, so interwoven with its web, so blended with its texture, as to be incapable of being separated from it, without rending it into shreds." The Constitution creates a government chosen by the people of the entire Union and delegated the authority to legislate for the entire Union; it would make no sense of those political arrangements to allow an individual state "to retard, impede, burden, or in any manner control, the operations of the constitutional laws enacted by congress to carry into execution the powers vested in the general government." In later cases, the Court has applied the same principle of national supremacy that *McCulloch* inferred from the structure of American federalism to prohibit interference by state executive officials with federal court orders and to invalidate a state statute that impeded the president's conduct of foreign affairs.[32]

Structural arguments are related to the written Constitution in differing ways. An inference from the structures of government may itself be drawn in part out of some feature or provision of the text, which we might call a text to structure argument. The prohibition on state action that *McCulloch* inferred from national supremacy within the federal system is obviously closely connected to the supremacy clause of Article VI, and indeed it would be perfectly sensible to describe Marshall's reasoning as an example of an argument based on the text of the clause as construed broadly in light of the written Constitution's nature as the basic charter of government, a version of textual argument that *McCulloch* also pioneered. (Once again, recall that the forms of constitutional argument overlap, and that the point of a taxonomy of forms is to understand their logic, not to assign labels.)

A much more recent example of text to structure argument can be found in the Supreme Court's decision in *Zivotofsky* v. *Kerry* (2015) that the president's authority to extend US diplomatic recognition is exclusive and thus beyond congressional infringement. The Court reasoned that as a functional matter, in order for the United States to effectively employ diplomatic recognition to serve American national interests, the recognition power must be located in a single branch and needs to be exclusive. But the Court did not rest its structural reasoning solely on this practical assertion about what a workable government requires on the matter. In addition, it reviewed the relevant constitutional provisions and concluded that the "inference that the President exercises the recognition power is ... supported by" Article II's express conferral on the president of the duty to receive foreign ambassadors, as well as the powers to make treaties and appoint American diplomatic officers with the Senate's advice and consent.[33]

Structural argument, conversely, can make use of an inference from the basic principles of American governmental arrangements to address the meaning of

---

[32] *McCulloch* v. *Maryland*, 17 U.S. (4 Wheat.) 316, 426, 436 (1819). See *Cooper* v. *Aaron*, 358 U.S. 1, 18–19 (1958) (federal court order); *Am. Ins. Assoc.* v. *Garamendi*, 539 U.S. 396, 421, 427 (2003) (presidential foreign policy).

[33] *Zivotofsky* v. *Kerry*, 576 U.S. 1, 13 (2015).

a provision in the written Constitution, which we might call a structure to text argument. One issue before the Court in *United States* v. *Morrison* (2000) was whether the Constitution authorized Congress to allow a victim of gender-motivated violence to sue his or her assailant in federal court on the basis of legislative findings that gender-motivated violence in the aggregate has a substantial negative effect on interstate commerce and the national economy. Several decades earlier the Court upheld Congress's ban on racial discrimination by motels and restaurants on a similar factual record, but the Court reasoned that the earlier decisions were distinguishable because motels and restaurants are themselves engaged in economic activity. Gender-motivated violence, like any other noneconomic criminal behavior, affects the national economy in the aggregate, but the Court thought that inferring constitutional authorization for congressional regulation of such behavior on that basis is "unworkable if we are to maintain the Constitution's enumeration of powers." Doing so would effectively recognize the existence of a federal police power, a conclusion contrary to "the entire structure of the Constitution." Structural reasoning thus provided a convincing reason to limit what precedent indicated might be the scope of the interstate commerce clause.[34]

Morrison employed structural argument based on the enumeration and police power presuppositions that underlie constitutional law's twofold logic in the process of addressing a question of authorization related to a specific clause in Article I section 8. Structural reasoning is not limited, however, to arguments closely linked to specific provisions of the text, whether structure to text as in *Morrison*, or text to structure as in *Zivotofsky*. Structural argument may also establish rules or principles in the Constitution-in-practice that are not dependent on specific provisions in any sense, but are inferred directly from the written Constitution as a whole or from the basic postulates and presuppositions of constitutional law. In *New York* v. *United States* (1992), the Court held that Congress cannot "commandeer" state legislatures by requiring them to enact laws essentially dictated by Congress. The Court relied on a basic structural feature of the written Constitution as a whole, its rejection of the mode of federal legislation ordained by the Articles of Confederation which had required Congress to act through the states rather than regulating or taxing individuals itself. By authorizing Congress to regulate and tax individuals directly, the Constitution eliminated what had proven an unworkable system of congressional government and ensured that Congress's responsibility for policies it ordains is clear to the public. The Court reasoned that the Constitution therefore prohibits Congress from using the Articles model of legislation by proxy, in part because doing so obscures which legislature is politically responsible for Congress's policy.[35]

Printz v. *United States* (1997) addressed the validity of a congressional requirement that local law enforcement officials conduct background checks on would-be

---

[34]   *United States* v. *Morrison*, 529 U.S. 598, 615, 618 n. 8 (2000).
[35]   *New York* v. *United States*, 505 U.S. 144, 165–66, 168–69 (1992).

firearms purchasers until a federal system for carrying out the checks could be set up. The Court did not question Congress's authority to require *someone* to perform the background checks as part of its regulation of the interstate market in firearms, but it held, on the basis of structural argument as well as other considerations, that the Constitution prohibits the imposition of a duty to enforce federal law on state officials. *Printz* relied in part on the argument that the structural reasoning adopted in *New York* was equally applicable to congressional commandeering of state executive officers. But the Court also perceived the relevance of other structural observations. First, federalism's role in reducing the risk of governmental oppression would be weakened substantially if Congress could "impress into its service – and at no cost to itself – the police officers of the 50 States." Second, Congress could circumvent the constitutional assignment to the president of responsibility for (and thus authority over) the execution of federal law if it were free to transfer the duty of execution to officials beyond presidential control. The anti-commandeering principle, which has no specific locus in the written Constitution, is thus a feature of the Constitution-in-practice because it serves multiple constitutional principles, none of which are expressly located in the text.[36]

Although the anti-commandeering decisions demonstrate that structural reasoning need not depend on a tight connection between the proposition argued for and a specific provision in the text, structural arguments are at their most persuasive when the relationship between the argument and the written Constitution is clear. The temptation constitutional lawyers face in structural reasoning is that of invoking a vague or abstract term as if it were an argument rather than a conclusion. The classic examples are "separation of powers" and "federalism." Structural argument, by definition, rests on reasoning about the relationships among the parts of American government in light of the written Constitution, and those relationships are centrally characterized by the existence of both state and federal governments and, within the federal government, of distinct legislative, executive, and judicial branches. There can be no objection, therefore, to a line of argument that presents considerations based on the implications of the written Constitution and the practical demands of maintaining a workable government with these characteristics, *and then* concludes that for those reasons the proposed answer satisfies the Constitution's separation of powers or "our federalism." *New York* and *Printz* do so.

Where structural argument can go wrong is in the use of those conclusions as if they were arguments, which neither by itself is. The language of *separation* is inexact because problems about the constitutional arrangement of powers among Congress, the president, and the federal judiciary more often arise out of the necessity,

---

[36] *Printz v. United States,* 521 U.S. 898, 921–223 (1997). In both *New York* and *Printz,* the Court also referred to "state sovereignty" in explaining its reasoning. The term has no fixed meaning in constitutional law although in these cases it clearly invoked the presupposition that the federal Constitution generally leaves the structuring of state government to the discretion of each state. See Chapter 2.

stemming either from provisions of the written Constitution or from the practical operations of government, of figuring out how two branches' *overlapping* powers are to be coordinated or reconciled, not kept apart. In *Bank Markazi v. Peterson* (2016), for example, the petitioner argued that as a matter of definition the constitutional separation of powers prohibits Congress from enacting a statute that addresses an issue in specific pending cases. The Court responded that precedent and political practice have recognized as "a valid exercise of Congress' legislative power diverse laws that governed one or a very small number of specific subjects." When Congress enacts "a new legal standard" and directs the courts to apply it to pending cases, it does not "impinge on judicial power" to determine what the law is in deciding cases but simply exercises the legislative power to determine what the law shall be.[37]

Similarly, the invocation of *federalism* generally carries with it a strong suggestion that the limitation of national power is the sole point of the Constitution's federalism arrangements. But the maintenance of national unity and of the national government's legitimate authority is at least as much a concern of the written Constitution and the federal system as is the protection of state autonomy. In *Reno v. Condon* (2000), a state vigorously argued that "principles of federalism" exempted it from congressional regulation requiring "time and effort on the part of state employees" in order to comply. The Court's answer was that the federalism principle underlying its anti-commandeering decisions in *New York* and *Printz* was that Congress may "not require the States in their sovereign capacity to regulate their own citizens"; the federal structure of the American political community does not entail that Congress is prohibited from regulating state government activities that fall within the scope of one of Congress's powers.[38]

Structural reasoning can also play a role in problems involving individual rights. As we saw in Chapter 2, the Supreme Court has long recognized the existence of a constitutional prohibition on interference with the right of a citizen to travel interstate, a prohibition so sweeping that it even extends to some private interferences. With respect to the core right simply to cross state borders, none of the efforts to ground the prohibition on state interference with the right in a particular textual provision have proven persuasive: Its real basis, as the first Supreme Court decision upholding the right recognized, is the inference that the structure of the American Union must guarantee the ability of the individual citizen and the federal government to interact in person without state interference. The governmental arrangements created by the written Constitution would not produce a workable government if, for example, a state could burden a citizen crossing state borders in order to carry out federal duties or exercise federal law privileges.[39]

---

[37]   *Bank Markazi v. Peterson*, 578 U.S. 212, 233-34, 230–31 (2016).
[38]   *Reno v. Condon*, 528 U.S. 141, 147, 150–51 (2006).
[39]   See *Crandall v. Nevada*, 73 U.S. (6 Wall.) 35 (1867).

3.2 ARGUMENTS DERIVED FROM THE CONSTITUTION-IN-PRACTICE

The relationship between the written Constitution and the specific forms of argument that focus on the constitutional instrument – argument from text, from the text's original meaning, and from the governmental structures the text creates and orders – is obvious. Their place in the traditional practice of constitutional law is secured by the fact that their force ultimately rests on the formal, axiomatic authority of the written Constitution. We turn now to constitutional law reasoning that is primarily derived from the ideas, rules, and principles that have been articulated by lawyers and judges engaged in solving constitutional problems, what this book refers to as the Constitution-in-practice. Arguments derived from the Constitution-in-practice are weightier, in the end and for many purposes, than written-Constitution reasoning, because as a practical matter they are the main tools by which constitutional lawyers actually solve constitutional problems by answering constitutional questions. The central and most authoritative form of reasoning stemming from the Constitution-in-practice is argument from Supreme Court precedent. I shall deal with it last in this chapter in recognition of the fact that other modes of argument ordinarily become authoritative in practice through their adoption in high Court opinions, but first we must consider two subordinate forms of practice-based reasoning, arguments from tradition and from political practice.

Arguments from Tradition. Constitutional reasoning that centers on the written Constitution often involves reference to legal and political traditions. Many of the words and phrases used in the text of the 1787 document and the Bill of Rights can only be understood properly by looking to English common law tradition: to choose a list almost at random, "Writs of Election, Impeachment, Emoluments, good Behaviour, Cases in Law and Equity, Jury, jeopardy of life or limb, Suits at common law." English and American historical traditions are primary sources for original meaning arguments about many constitutional provisions. And the basic presuppositions of American governmental structures – majoritarian decision making, popular elections, the roles of the judge and jury at trial – are the products of long-standing English-speaking political traditions about free and limited government.[40]

The form of practice-based argument to which we now turn also invokes tradition, but it does so in a different manner. What I shall call argument from tradition proposes answers to constitutional questions on the basis of legal and moral commitments of the American political community that are neither expressly announced by the constitutional text nor directly derived from its implications or original meaning, or from the governmental structures the text creates. Judicial enforcement of such a commitment, its inclusion in the Constitution-in-practice, is

---

[40] For a clear (and succinct) example of the interplay between tradition and textual, original meaning *and* structural arguments, see *Summers v. Earth Island Inst.*, 555 U.S. 488, 492 (2009) ("In limiting the judicial power to 'Cases' and 'Controversies,' Article III of the Constitution restricts it to the traditional role of Anglo–American courts, which is to redress or prevent actual or imminently threatened injury to persons caused by private or official violation of law.").

usually justified in the name of a constitutional provision, most often the due process clause of the fifth or fourteenth amendment, but the substance of the commitment is identified by considering arguments about American traditions that may not have a strong connection to the textual provision that formally legitimates the arguments as within the scope of the practice of constitutional law. As the prominence of the due process clauses suggests, arguments from tradition are usually employed in discussing questions of prohibition.

The role and even the legitimacy of argument from tradition has been the subject of considerable debate at various periods in American constitutional history. Since the authority of the written Constitution is axiomatic, and there can be no extra-constitutional limitations on government authority within the constitutional system, a recurrent temptation has been to assume that constitutional prohibitions can only be identified through textual argument, in the broader sense that includes original meaning and structure. More importantly, the critics of argument from tradition have argued that reasoning based on tradition that is not clearly rooted in the text is inherently and objectionably subjective. Such arguments lack the disciplining force the text exerts in other forms of argument, and its alleged source is too amorphous and contestable to do more than supply its advocate with confirmation of, or camouflage for, personal preferences and commitments. A judicial decision accepting an argument from tradition, the criticism goes, does not enforce the will of the People but the will of the judges. The emptiness of tradition-based reasoning's claim to be "constitutional," some critics have added, is evident from its proponents' resort to the due process clauses as a textual hook on which to hang their claims. The wording of the clauses limits their scope to governmental procedures and cannot serve as an entry point for extra-textual prohibitions on the substance of what American government may do.

These are not insubstantial objections, but the criticisms of argument from tradition have failed to exclude such arguments from constitutional debate. From Chief Justice Marshall's era on there have been Supreme Court decisions that turn on arguments from tradition, and even during the middle of the twentieth century, when the Court seemed least receptive, it did not avoid them altogether. In the twenty-first century, the legitimacy of tradition-based argument, and the identification of the due process clauses as its textual vehicle, appears to be settled. Argument from tradition, or "substantive due process" as the Court usually labels it when those clauses are invoked, clearly has a place in the constitutional lawyer's toolbox as a matter of observation, whatever reservations one may have about it in principle. Present-day controversies concern specific decisions as well as details of the method to be followed in constructing a persuasive argument from tradition.[41]

---

[41] See, e.g., *Washington v. Glucksberg*, 521 U.S. 702, 720–21 (1997) (discussing the Court's "established method of substantive-due-process analysis" and identifying "our Nation's history, legal traditions, and practices" as "crucial guideposts").

Argument from tradition thus brings into constitutional law debate political and legal norms that cannot be directly attributed to the written Constitution. However, the norms are "not simply deduced from abstract concepts of personal autonomy" but depend for their plausibility as arguments *of constitutional law* on their connection to "this Nation's history and constitutional traditions" and "the history of our values as a people." What legitimates the imposition of a tradition-based prohibition on governmental action is not its authority as a principle of moral or political philosophy but its status as a fundamental – and thus constitutional – commitment of the American political community. The logical structure of argument from tradition is therefore parallel to that of original meaning argument. Like the latter, constitutional reasoning from tradition is based on history, and a properly constructed argument from tradition must look outside law to find an adequate basis in the historical sources for the factual claim that the supposed tradition actually exists. And (again like original meaning arguments) an argument from tradition must include a plausible legal claim that a reasonable person would think that the tradition can be attributed to the American political community. Put in the words of a famous opinion often invoked as an objection to tradition-based reasoning, a successful argument from tradition must persuade the reader that "a rational and fair man necessarily would admit that the statute [or other governmental action] would infringe fundamental principles as they have been understood by the traditions of our people and our law."[42]

A good set of examples lies in the areas of marriage and family life. The written Constitution makes no mention of these topics at all, and as a general matter the states' police powers give them plenary authority over matters such as who may marry, how disputes over custody arrangements are to be resolved, and what obligations parents must fulfill in providing for their children's welfare and education. For almost a century, however, the Constitution-in-practice has prohibited state interference with various personal decisions related to marriage and family relationships. From the earliest decisions, the Court has rested these prohibitions on the central importance of marriage and the family to American society, an importance reflected not just in social relationships but in many aspects of American law as well. The historical "traditions of our people and our law" clearly presuppose that government will respect a significant degree of autonomy in private choices about marriage and family matters, and the Court has concluded across a wide range of specific issues that respect for this fundamental American tradition required invalidation of otherwise permissible regulations.

At the same time, the tradition-based decisions on marriage, family, and reproductive choice have generally avoided sweeping pronouncements about the line to be drawn between private choice and public regulation. Although the cases are often

---

[42] The quotations are from, respectively, *Glucksberg*, 521 U.S. at 725; *id.* at 764 (Souter, J., concurring in the judgment); and *Lochner v. New York*, 198 U.S. 45, 76 (1905) (Holmes, J., dissenting).

referred to as privacy decisions, they are best understood not to depend on an abstract or subjective concept of "privacy" but to adhere to a practice of addressing the specific question before the Court by careful attention to the particular intrusion into personal or family autonomy at issue and to the public justifications for the government's action. For example, in *Troxel* v. *Granville* (2000), Justice Sandra Day O'Connor's plurality opinion concluded that it was unconstitutional for a state court to award visitation rights to a child's grandparents over the objections of the custodial parent. O'Connor did not rest this decision on the basis of a general rule that the parent should always prevail. Instead, her opinion's examination of the case's specific facts revealed that the judge had given no weight at all to the parent's judgment, and thus ignored entirely "the traditional presumption that a fit parent will act in the best interest of his or her child." A concurring justice would have gone further and invalidated on its face the law under which the trial judge had acted "because the state statute authorizes *any* person at *any* time to request (and a judge to award) visitation rights," thus undermining the traditional presumption in favor of parental decisions wholesale rather than retail.[43]

In recent decades, the Court has declined to impose hard-edged methodological constraints on arguments from tradition although several have been proposed, such as requiring the analysis to proceed at "the most specific level at which a relevant tradition protecting, or denying protection to, the asserted right can be identified."[44] Instead, the Constitution-in-practice disciplines the potentially open-ended invocation of a fundamental but nontextual principle as the Court did in *Troxel* by focusing on the concrete intrusion on the traditional interest and on the weight of the government's countervailing interest.[45] As the marriage and family decisions

---

[43]   *Troxel* v. *Granville*, 530 U.S. 57, 69 (2000) (plurality opinion of O'Connor, J.); *id.* at 76–77 (Souter, J., concurring in the judgment).

[44]   *Michael H.* v. *Gerald D.*, 491 U.S. 110, 127 n. 6 (1989) (opinion of Scalia, J.).

[45]   The best known example of a decision that failed to observe these disciplining conventions, *Roe* v. *Wade*, is also the most heavily criticized substantive due process case, partly for that reason. It is highly likely that no Supreme Court decision on the constitutionality of legislative restrictions on abortion, regardless of its conclusion or the care with which its reasoning was constructed, could have avoided intense controversy. Be that as it may, the opinion of the Court in *Roe* could hardly have been better designed to invite such controversy. The opinion identified the issue before the Court, and linked the holding to the precedents, in an abrupt and oddly casual fashion. See *Roe* v. *Wade*, 410 U.S. 113, 153 (1973) ("This right of privacy, whether it be founded in the Fourteenth Amendment's concept of personal liberty and restrictions upon state action, as we feel it is, or, as the District Court determined, in the Ninth Amendment's reservation of rights to the people, is broad enough to encompass a woman's decision whether or not to terminate her pregnancy."). The opinion went on to announce a pattern of analysis that had little connection to the specific abortion regulations before the Court, and indeed seemed formulated to address in principle and in advance all conceivable future controversies through a set of rules that gave the appearance of a regulatory code. One of the earliest commentaries on the decision, written by a supporter of a broad legal right to choose an abortion, famously asserted that the opinion in *Roe* was "bad because it is bad constitutional law, or rather because it is *not* constitutional law and gives almost no sense of an obligation to try to be." John Hart Ely, The Wages of Crying Wolf: A Comment on *Roe* v. *Wade*, 82 *Yale L. J.* 920, 926, 947 (1973). From the perspective on the practice of constitutional law presented in this book, Ely's judgment is

demonstrate, once the Court has accepted an argument from tradition, future cases in the same area depend not only on further explication of the tradition that has been identified but also on the scope of the Court's precedent. To be sure, even the most meticulously constructed argument from tradition may fail to persuade constitutional lawyers evaluating it because it does not seem to them to fit the overall shape of the Constitution-in-practice. The same is true of constitutional reasoning that takes other forms, but it is fair to note that tradition-based arguments are especially vulnerable to criticism even when they have the support of stare decisis.

Continuing uneasiness over the allowable scope of arguments from tradition explains what is sometimes known as "the rule in *Graham*," which forbids reasoning from tradition when the constitutional problem at hand is addressed by an express prohibition in the Bill of Rights or presumably any other textual prohibition. "Where a particular Amendment 'provides an explicit textual source of constitutional protection' against a particular sort of government behavior, 'that Amendment, not the more generalized notion of substantive due process, must be the guide for analyzing these claims.'" The Court's explanation for the rule is that where specific provisions of the Bill of Rights apply "in particular situations," it was "through those provisions" rather than through general constitutional reasoning that "their Framers sought to restrict the exercise of arbitrary authority by the Government." The reference to the framers of the Bill of Rights is purely ceremonial, however, and the real source of the rule in *Graham* appears to be the Court's preference to avoid the use of even well-constructed arguments from tradition whenever possible.[46]

The precedent governing a substantive due process challenge to actions by executive officials that is not barred by the rule in *Graham* defines the constitutionally "cognizable level of executive abuse of power as that which shocks the conscience." As a means of applying the due process clauses to executive action, the "shocks the conscience" standard is rooted in the original meaning of "due process," a concept that goes back to Magna Carta and as such is centrally concerned with prohibiting arbitrary or oppressive government actions. But the inquiry whether the challenged action was sufficiently egregious to satisfy the conscience-shocking standard is not based on history: "the threshold question is whether the behavior of the governmental officer is so egregious, so outrageous, that it may fairly be said to shock the *contemporary* conscience." The purpose of the "shocks the conscience" inquiry is to avoid converting the constitutional prohibition into "a font of tort law" by making every mistake by an executive officer a violation of the Constitution.[47]

indisputable. Two decades later, the controlling opinion in *Planned Parenthood* v. *Casey* presented a professionally defensible argument for recognizing the constitutional status of a right to choose an abortion, but debate over the issue continues to be shaped by the accusation that *Roe* v. *Wade* originally created the right by an act of judicial willfulness rather than the exercise of defensible, if also contestable, constitutional judgment. See *Planned Parenthood* v. *Casey*, 505 U.S. 833 (1992) (joint opinion of O'Connor, Kennedy, & Souter, J.).

[46] *Albright* v. *Oliver*, 510 U.S. 266, 273 (1994) (quoting *Graham* v. *Connor*, 490 U.S. 286, 295 (1989)).

[47] *Sacramento* v. *Lewis*, 523 U.S. 833, 846, 847 n. 8 (1998) (emphasis added).

The introduction of an element of contemporary moral judgment by courts also raises the question whether substantive due process as tool for formulating and answering questions of constitutional prohibition can reach beyond argument from tradition to include, under some circumstances, the direct application of moral norms that have no basis in either text or tradition. The traditional answer, I think, is clearly no. Moral convictions are not, in themselves, propositions of constitutional law. In a case involving what would generally be thought of as extreme injustice, the *McCulloch* principle that the Constitution states broad principles might make it appropriate to stretch the nearest relevant provision or precedent as far as reasonably possible, but the link to the text or earlier decision would be essential.[48] The "shocks the conscience" decisions are not themselves an example of a direct application of moral norms both because they have a clear basis in the original meaning of due process and also because historical tradition is relevant to the ultimate decision whether the executive official violated the Constitution: the contemporary time frame of the "shocks the conscience" requirement is a threshold consideration only.

That the practice of constitutional law does not allow the direct importation of moral reasoning into constitutional argument follows from one of the basic presuppositions of the twofold logic of constitutional inquiry discussed in Chapter 2 – that there are no extra-constitutional prohibitions on authorized exercises of federal power or on the states' exercise of their undefined powers of governance. The impulse to say that a repugnant or inhumane governmental action *must* be unconstitutional arguably stems from a quintessentially American confusion (perhaps a morally attractive confusion) between constitutional law and political morality, which are distinct normative realms. The Constitution permits American

---

[48]   Professor (and former solicitor general and Massachusetts high court justice) Charles Fried once wrote that the main reason the Supreme Court did not in the end reject most of the controversial, rights-protecting decisions of the Warren Court despite the inadequacy of many of the Warren era opinions was that the cases had "a core coherence that few on the Court, in the bar, or in the country wanted to do without. It was not a theory, but it was a promise: that the Constitution of the United States somewhere, somehow, provided a basis for holding back the most palpable abuses and indecencies of organized government." Charles Fried, Foreword: Revolutions? 109 *Harv. L. Rev.* 13, 74 (1995). Fried was not criticizing the Warren Court "promise." An express judicial example of this line of thought – in a dissent, to be sure – can be found in a 1987 case, *United States v. Stanley*. In *Stanley*, the Supreme Court held that a former soldier had no constitutional cause of action to seek damages for the serious psychological injuries he allegedly suffered as a result of the Army's administration of LSD without his consent as part of a secret study of the drug's effects. The majority reasoned that the fact that the plaintiff incurred the injuries incident to his military service precluded the courts from inferring a constitutional remedy and that Congress had not authorized such legal actions. In dissent, Justice O'Connor conceded that ordinarily the military context would bar such a judicially created cause of action, but she went on to argue that in her view "conduct of the type alleged in this case is so far beyond the bounds of human decency that as a matter of law it simply cannot be considered a part of the military mission." Human decency, in other words, set a limit to what the army clause of Article I can properly be read to authorize. See *United States v. Stanley*, 483 U.S. 669, 709 (1987) (O'Connor, J., concurring in part and dissenting in part). (I have ignored details not germane to this discussion.)

government to violate moral principles just as it authorizes American government to violate international law, unless in doing so government also violates a norm ordained by the Constitution-in-practice. It would be an error, however, to understand this to mean that the practice of constitutional law demands of those involved a commitment to moral relativism. American constitutionalism rests on political commitments that are themselves infused with moral substance. That the American political community can and should "establish Justice," in the words of the Preamble, and that it ordinarily does so through the processes of democratic politics, are two such commitments. That Supreme Court justices and other judges can interfere with democratic governance in the name of the Constitution only when they can do so conscientiously and in good faith reliance on legal argument is another.

Arguments from Political Practice. In *McCulloch* v. *Maryland*, Chief Justice Marshall introduced his discussion of whether Congress was authorized to create the Bank of the United States with the observation that "this can scarcely be considered as an open question, entirely unprejudiced by the former proceedings of the nation respecting it." Marshall then provided the reader with an outline history of national bank legislation in the early Republic. He put particular weight on the fact that the first bank act was the work of the First Congress, that the issues about its constitutionality had been aired "in the fair and open field of debate, and afterwards, in the executive cabinet," and finally, that the arguments in its favor "convinced minds as pure and as intelligent as this country can boast [so that] it became a law." (The plural "minds" was stylistic: as Marshall expected his readers to know, the one mind that mattered in the end was George Washington's.) The opinion went on to point out that the inconveniences experienced after the first bank's charter expired had "convinced those who were most prejudiced against the measure of its necessity" and led to the enactment of the second Bank Act. Again, Marshall assumed it was common knowledge that James Madison opposed the first bank bill in Congress as unconstitutional, but, as president, argued that the validity of a national bank was settled by history, and signed the second bank bill into law in 1816. Marshall concluded his historical discussion with the droll comment that it "would require no ordinary share of intrepidity, to assert that a measure adopted under these circumstances, was a bold and plain usurpation" of authority, although he also assured his readers that he was not saying the bank would be invalid if the question were "entirely new."[49]

McCulloch was the clearest early judicial discussion of constitutional law argument based on political practice by Congress and the executive, and Marshall's reasoning anticipated major themes in later explanations of the role of political practice in constitutional thought. Such arguments are, as Marshall wrote, of the

---

[49] *McCulloch* v. *Maryland*, 17 U.S. (4 Wheat.) 316, 401–02 (1819). The quotations in the following paragraph in the text are from the same pages.

greatest importance on "a doubtful question" about which other lines of constitutional reasoning give inconclusive answers, and where the constitutional problem at hand involves the scope or interaction of governmental powers rather than "the great principles of liberty." The weight to be given to a political practice depends on how old the practice is, how long it has endured, and the extent to which both political branches have accepted or acted on it. A history of political action carries more force as an argument in support of the action's constitutionality if the political actors recognized the constitutional issues involved and therefore can be said to have acted on a deliberate constitutional decision. A practical "exposition of the constitution, deliberately established by" the First Congress (which "fully understood" the constitutional issues), and "recognised by many successive legislatures" is, for Marshall and still today, the paradigm of a convincing political practice argument. Because the constitutional understandings on which a political decision rests are often opaque, and different political actors may have agreed on an outcome without agreeing on the reasoning, the fact that Washington and Madison signed the bank bills into law on the clear understanding that the bills were constitutionally authorized further underscored the weight of the political practice argument as to Congress's powers. *McCulloch* did not involve any issue about the distribution of power among the branches of the federal government, but Marshall's allusion to Madison's change of view anticipates the point often made in later separation of powers discussions that a political decision should only be viewed as a constitutional one when those with reason to oppose it had the opportunity to do so.[50]

The Supreme Court's 2014 decision in *NLRB* v. *Noel Canning* provides good examples of argument from political practice. The issues in *Noel Canning* involved the scope of the president's Article II section 2 authority to appoint officers, without obtaining the Senate's advice and consent, to fill "all Vacancies that may happen during the Recess of the Senate." The Court thought that "the constitutional text is … ambiguous." Which breaks in the Senate's activities count as a "Recess," and does the president's power extend only to vacancies that first occur during a "Recess" or include those which were ongoing when the "Recess" began? As the Court noted, while it had never construed the clause, there was "a great deal of history to consider" because "Presidents have made recess appointments since the beginning of the Republic." The opinion of the Court therefore inquired at length into political practice with respect to both constitutional questions, examining the history of Senate recesses and of presidential appointments under the clause, executive branch

---

[50] See, e.g., *Youngstown Sheet & Tube Co.* v. *Sawyer*, 343 U.S. 579, 610–11 (1952) (Frankfurter, J., concurring) ("a systematic, unbroken, executive practice, long pursued to the knowledge of the Congress and never before questioned, engaged in by Presidents who have also sworn to uphold the Constitution, mak[es] as it were such exercise of power part of the structure of our government"); *The President and the War Power: South Vietnam and the Cambodian Sanctuaries*, 1 Op. O.L.C. Supp. 321, 326 (1970) (Rehnquist, Ass't Att'y Gen.) (presidential action "to which there was no opportunity for the Legislative Branch to effectively object cannot establish a constitutional precedent").

legal opinions on the president's power and Senate objections to its exercise, and the fact that the Senate had passed over many opportunities to resist a broad reading of the power. With so long a history, political practice under the clause was not entirely uniform, but the Court concluded that the weight of the historical evidence about political practice pointed to the conclusion that the president may make recess appointments during any recess of more than *de minimis* length to any vacant office regardless of when the vacancy occurred. Thus, "the actual practice of Government," along with the Court's view of the clause's text and purposes, resolved the constitutional problem.[51]

In constructing a persuasive argument from political practice, the constitutional lawyer must take into account the reasons that such arguments are part of constitutional law. The written Constitution, as we have seen, is to be understood as a practical instrument of governance, and a solution to a constitutional problem that renders the system more effective is, by that very fact, stronger than a solution that does not. The constitutional text "contemplates that practice will integrate the dispersed powers into a workable government." A history of political practice may be convincing evidence that the arrangements the political branches have settled on accomplish this central constitutional purpose. (As I have noted previously, the American constitutional system's effectiveness is measured not solely by governmental efficiency but also by government's compliance with constitutional limitations on its powers.) "The Constitution is a framework for government. Therefore the way the framework has consistently operated fairly establishes that it has operated according to its true nature. ... It is an inadmissibly narrow conception of American constitutional law to confine it to the words of the Constitution and to disregard the gloss which life has written upon them."[52]

The same constitutional objective of practical or workable government provides a second, converse reason to give weight to political practice arguments: to reject settled political practice is to retrospectively invalidate what was done under it and to replace an arrangement that has been working with one that is untried. *Noel Canning* stated that the Court would "hesitate to upset the compromises and working arrangements that the elected branches of Government themselves have reached," and pointed out that rejecting the history of political practice "would render illegitimate thousands of recess appointments reaching all the way back to the founding era." For the same reason, on issues where the Court has spoken,

---

[51] N.L.R.B. v. *Noel Canning*, 573 U.S. 513, 526, 557 (2014). The Court ruled *against* the president, nonetheless, because he made the recess appointments at issue in a recess of less than three days between two pro forma sessions of the Senate. The executive argued that as a practical matter a pro forma session attended by almost no senators should not count as a break in what amounts to a longer recess, but the Court disagreed, relying on the principle that courts "generally take at face value the Senate's own report of its actions" and on the fact that under its rules the Senate can act during a pro forma session and occasionally does. *Id.* at 551–53.

[52] *Youngstown Sheet & Tube Co.* v. *Sawyer*, 343 U.S. 579, 635 (1952) (Jackson, J., concurring); *id.* at 610 (Frankfurter, J., concurring).

political practice pursuant to the Court's decisions may powerfully support stare decisis in "counseling" the Court "not to call in question the essential principles now in place" on which Congress and the president have relied.[53]

The traditional practice of constitutional law sets limits on the scope of argument from political practice. As Chief Justice Marshall noted in *McCulloch*, such arguments are not ordinarily persuasive when addressed to questions involving "the great principles of liberty." Constitutional prohibitions that have as their core purpose the protection of individual rights set an outer limit on the exercise of political power, and constitutional reasoning should not accept the erosion of that limit through the repeated use of the very power meant to be limited. Even when addressed to issues of constitutional authorization or the demarcation between the powers possessed by different parts of American government, argument from political practice cannot properly be used to justify practice that is questionable on other grounds and that cannot fairly be treated as involving a deliberate decision that the practice is legitimate. If an arguable constitutional error passed unnoticed, or there was no effective means by which critics could contest a practice's constitutionality, the bare fact of successful repetition is not a constitutional argument entitled to any weight: reasoning based on political practice is not a form of constitutional adverse possession but a recognition that political actors can and should make constitutional decisions and that such decisions are relevant in future constitutional debate under appropriate circumstances.

Arguments from Precedent. We turn finally to the subset of arguments derived from the Constitution-in-practice that is central to the traditional practice of constitutional law. In solving the great majority of problems in constitutional law cases, the proper resolution of the problem must be based on arguments from judicial precedent, and ultimately the decisions of the Supreme Court. This is utterly unsurprising. As we saw in Chapter 1, from the beginning American constitutional law took on the forms and methods of reasoning of the common law. In the twenty-first century, most of the Constitution-in-practice is made up of rules, principles, and doctrines found in, argued over, constructed by, and reconstructed out of judicial decisions that constitutional lawyers treat very much as their colleagues treat precedents in contract or tort law. A nonlawyer idly examining the table of contents in most casebooks could be forgiven for assuming that constitutional law is a prime example of judge-made law rather than the law of a written and authoritative text. And therein lies the reason for the otherwise odd tendency of constitutional lawyers, on and off the bench, to express uneasiness on occasion about the commanding role in practice of argument from precedent: It might seem to dethrone the written Constitution and to substitute the judiciary – and ultimately nine specific judges – for the People as the ultimate decision maker. To understand constitutional law as it is traditionally

---

[53] *Noel Canning*, 573 U.S. at 526; *id.* at 556; *United States* v. *Lopez*, 514 U.S. 549, 574 (1995) (Kennedy, J., concurring).

practiced, however, one must put aside such worries. In the conclusion, we shall return to the issue of the practice's legitimacy; our present concern is with how to construct the precedent-based arguments that are at the heart of the practice.

Horizontal and Vertical Precedent. A preliminary point of importance is that not all precedents are created equal. Stare decisis, the principle of adherence to precedent, "imparts authority to a decision ... merely *by virtue of the authority of the rendering court* and independently of the quality of its reasoning. The essence of stare decisis is that the mere existence of certain decisions becomes a reason for adhering to their holdings in subsequent cases." Following common law tradition, the Supreme Court treats its own decisions as "horizontal" precedent that binds the Court itself unless the Court finds there are pressing reasons to overrule a particular precedent – and mere disagreement with the earlier decision is not enough in itself.[54]

Supreme Court precedent enjoys unique authority in all federal law, including constitutional law, and is constitutionally binding on all other American courts, state as well as federal, as to federal law. This is often called "vertical" precedent. Any high Court decision on the merits is precedent for lower courts. Even if the Court appears to have undermined its own precedent in later cases, lower courts are still bound by the decision if it "directly controls an issue before them, leaving to [the Supreme] Court the prerogative of overruling its own decisions." Since executive branch legal opinions also accept the authority of Supreme Court precedent, it is fair to say that the Court's decisions are at the heart of arguments from precedent, which (again) make up the majority of constitutional law arguments in practice.[55]

Not everything the Supreme Court does has the same effect for stare decisis purposes. For a century the Supreme Court's docket has been mostly and is now almost entirely discretionary. The Court often treats the few remaining areas in which its appellate jurisdiction is mandatory as if it had discretion not to decide by summarily affirming or (rarely) reversing the lower court's decision without oral argument or opinion. Despite this absence of reasoned elaboration, however,

---

[54] *Midlock v. Apple Vacations W., Inc.*, 406 F.3d 453, 457 (7th Cir. 2005) (Posner, Cir. J.) (emphasis added).

The Supreme Court purports to adhere to stare decisis more strictly when its precedent concerns the construction of an act of Congress, and less rigorously when the decision is a constitutional ruling, its explanation being that Congress can simply amend a statute it thinks the Court has mangled, while the abrogation of an erroneous constitutional decision requires the difficult Article V amendment process or a change of mind on the Court. Neither of these justifications is entirely convincing. On the one hand, the political process necessary to amend an existing statute in order to eliminate the effect of a judicial decision that members of Congress think misconstrued the law may be very difficult, and (assuming that the decision was a genuine error) puts the burden on proponents of the law's correct interpretation once again to run the gantlet of bicameral passage and presentment. On the other hand, reducing the force of stare decisis for constitutional precedents may well reduce the need for resorting to Article V at the risk of making constitutional law *too* responsive to intellectual fashion or changing membership on the Court. The fact that five justices this year firmly believe that last year's decision got the constitutional answer wrong does not, of itself, prove them right.

[55] *Rodriguez de Quijas v. Shearson/American Express*, 490 U.S. 477, 484 (1989).

summary decisions *are* precedents on "the precise issues presented and necessarily decided" by the judgments below that the Court affirms or reverses. In contrast, in cases within the Court's (genuinely) discretionary jurisdiction by writ of certiorari, a decision by the Court to deny review produces *no* high Court precedent: It is not a decision on the merits. If the sitting justices in a case divide equally, the decision below is affirmed but the Supreme Court's action sets no precedent.[56]

In the federal system, the principle of vertical precedent applies to the decisions of a court of appeals as well, which are therefore binding on district courts and other federal adjudicatory bodies acting within the jurisdiction of that court of appeals. Because the courts of appeals ordinarily decide cases in panels of three judges rather than in a plenary session (en banc), a later panel has no authority to overrule precedent set by an earlier panel or by the appeals court sitting en banc. Only the en banc court can do so. Finally, "a district court decision does not have stare decisis effect; it is not a precedent. It may be a wise, well-reasoned decision that persuades by the quality of its reasoning, but in that respect it is no different from a persuasive article or treatise. The fact of such a decision is not a reason for following it." The federal courts of appeals do not stand in a vertical relationship with state courts, and therefore the ultimate authority on a question of federal constitutional law that arises in a state's legal system is the state's highest court, subject of course to the US Supreme Court.[57]

In this chapter, almost all references to argument from precedent have primarily in view argument from US Supreme Court precedents because the rule of vertical precedent gives that Court's articulation of the Constitution-in-practice unique authority. But the reader should not lose sight of the facts that the vast majority of federal appellate decisions on constitutional issues come from the courts of appeals, and that as a result the individual federal circuits necessarily develop their own body of constitutional law that is supposed to be consistent with the high Court's precedents but in numerous ways supplements those precedents by addressing questions that the Court has not yet addressed or providing additional guidance for the application of the Court's answers.

The Supreme Court itself is not a vertical "superior" to the political branches of the federal government: The Constitution allocates the federal government's "power among three coequal branches." Furthermore, "each branch of the Government has the duty initially to interpret the Constitution for itself, and . . . its interpretation of its powers is due great respect from the other branches." Presidents therefore have

---

[56] *Metromedia, Inc.* v. *San Diego*, 453 U.S. 490, 499 (1981). See *Ramos* v. *Louisiana*, 140 S. Ct. 1390, 1404 n. 56 (2020) ("The significance of a denial of a petition for certiorari ought no longer . . . require discussion. This Court has said again and again and again that such a denial has no legal significance whatever bearing on the merits of the claim."); *Exxon Shipping Co.* v. *Baker*, 554 U.S. 471, 484 (2008) (if the Court divides equally on a case or issue, "the disposition here is not precedential").

[57] *Midlock* v. *Apple Vacations W., Inc.*, 406 F.3d 453, 457–58 (7th Cir. 2005) (Posner, Cir. J.). See *Johnson* v. *Williams*, 568 U.S. 289, 305 (2013) ("the views of the federal courts of appeals do not bind [a state] Supreme Court when it decides a federal constitutional question").

occasionally argued that the Court's constitutional decisions do not bind Congress or the executive within the political branches' respective spheres. The premise that both Congress and the president have a duty to make their own conscientious judgments about constitutional issues that arise in the course of discharging their duties is sound, but it does not follow that Congress or the president may simply disregard Supreme Court precedent regardless of circumstances. The guiding principle is that a political branch may act on a view of constitutional law that differs from the Court's if doing so does not lead to a result that is unconstitutional under the Court's precedents. Let us see how that works out in practice.[58]

On the one hand, neither Congress nor the president can lawfully interfere with the judiciary's enforcement of its view of the law. As we shall see later in the chapter, the courts will ignore an act of Congress that attempts to require the judiciary to act on a constitutional rule contrary to the Court's constitutional precedent. Since 1809, furthermore, the executive has acknowledged its duty to enforce the Supreme Court's *orders* even if the president genuinely thinks the Court's decision was wrong or even unconstitutional. Speaking broadly, the same duty exists with regard to the orders of the lower federal courts; the rule could not be otherwise if the system is to be workable. Modern executive branch legal opinions, furthermore, accept that "the constitutional structure obligates the executive branch to adhere to settled judicial doctrine that limits executive and legislative power" and that the executive's solutions to constitutional problems are "guided and, where there is a decision of the Court on point, governed by the Supreme Court's decisions" even when the executive's actions are not subject to judicial review.[59]

Conversely, either political branch may act on a narrower view of its constitutional authority than the Supreme Court holds or interpret a constitutional prohibition as more constraining than the Court's precedents require, because in those situations the outcome of the political branch's act is not unconstitutional on anyone's view. *McCulloch v. Maryland* settled the question of the national bank's

---

[58] *Nixon v. Adm'r of Gen. Servs.*, 433 U.S. 425, 442–43 (1977).

[59] *The Constitutional Separation of Powers Between the President and Congress*, 20 Op. O.L.C. 124, 127–28 (1996). On the invalidity of acts of Congress that attempt to "overrule" Supreme Court decisions, see later in the chapter. Executive practice as to the enforcement of federal court orders was set when a state governor asked President Madison to prevent the execution of the Supreme Court's order in *United States v. Peters*, 9 U.S. (5 Cranch) 115 (1809), because in the governor's view the Court was acting unconstitutionally. Madison refused even to consider the governor's constitutional arguments, explaining that it was his duty to "carry into effect any such decree." Very early in the Civil War, President Lincoln, it is true, defied an order of Chief Justice Taney, exercising the habeas corpus jurisdiction of the federal circuit court, that the executive release a suspected secessionist. Lincoln's action was almost certainly erroneous under the Supreme Court's decision in *Hamdi v. Rumsfeld*, 542 U.S. 507, 525, 537 (2004) (plurality opinion) (habeas corpus available "absent suspension of the writ by Congress").

The modern executive does not defy lower court orders as Lincoln did, although federal regulatory agencies do not always acquiesce in the legal reasoning of a court of appeals decision beyond the immediate case. See, e.g., *Heartland Plymouth Ct. MI v. NLRB*, 838 F.3d 16, 21–25 (D.C. Cir. 2016) (discussing the propriety of agency nonacquiescence in various circumstances).

constitutionality from the Court's perspective, but when President Andrew Jackson subsequently vetoed a bill rechartering the bank partly on constitutional grounds, he did not violate the Constitution-in-practice. The existence of a national bank is not a constitutional necessity, and *McCulloch's* holding as to the scope of Congress's powers set no limits to the grounds on which a president may veto a bill. Similarly, Congress's enactment of the Religious Freedom Restoration Act, which imposes on the federal government limitations on interference with religious freedom more protective than the Court's interpretation of the first amendment required, was constitutional even though Congress's original reason for doing so was direct disagreement with the Court's interpretation. In requiring special respect for religious free exercise, Congress exercised the same powers that enabled it to authorize the government to act in the first place, and it does not violate the Court's understanding of the first amendment for the government to give broader scope to its liberties than the amendment as interpreted by the Court requires.[60]

The Scope of Constitutional Precedents. Precedent-based reasoning obviously presupposes a perspective on how judicial precedents function in constitutional law, which is similar but not identical to precedent's role in other areas of American law. Every Supreme Court case is in form a legal action involving opposing parties who claim to have conflicting, legally cognizable interests that the Court must resolve by applying the controlling legal rule – the Court has always understood the Article III authorization of federal court adjudication to be limited to cases in this sense and as we saw in Chapter 1, the now-settled justification for judicial review is an American court's duty to resolve controversies before it by following the Constitution's supreme rule of law when applicable. For many purposes, therefore, it may seem adequate to think of constitutional precedents as parallel to precedents in an area of the common law, and therefore to be analyzed in terms of the Court determining the specific controlling rule of law and relating it to the particular facts presented by the parties. From this common law perspective, the holding of the Court that is precedent for lower courts and its own future decisions consists of the rule and its application, and other things the Court may say along the way to reaching the holding would "just" be dicta (*obiter dicta*, things "said in passing"). "It is a judicial decision's reasoning – its *ratio decidendi* – that allows it to have life and effect in the disposition of future cases." The scope of a decision as precedent, on this view, is bounded by the holding/dictum distinction and by the necessary relationship of the case's reasoning to its facts.[61]

This description of precedent is not exactly wrong, but at least in constitutional law and as applied to Supreme Court decisions it is oversimplified. The Court's

---

[60]   Jackson's veto sparked a constitutional controversy for reasons not germane to this discussion. On the validity of the religious freedom law, see *Burwell* v. *Hobby Lobby Stores, Inc.*, 573 U.S. 682, 695 (2014). ("As applied to a federal agency, RFRA is based on the enumerated power that supports the particular agency's work.") As enacted, RFRA applied to the states as well, but *City of Boerne* v. *Flores*, 521 U.S. 507 (1997), held that Congress lacked the authority to extend its rules to state and local government.

[61]   *Ramos* v. *Louisiana*, 140 S. Ct. 1390, 1404 (2020) (opinion of Gorsuch, J.).

opinions in constitutional cases are neither written nor read, most of the time, as if the justices were merely resolving the particular dispute before them. This is not a recent development: Chief Justice Marshall's opinion in *McCulloch v. Maryland* painted with a broad brush, and subsequent constitutional decisions have followed suit. While it might be desirable for the Court to make more of an effort to avoid *unnecessary* disquisitions on constitutional topics, in a constitutional case the Court is articulating what the Constitution-in-practice will be for the entire Republic and it would fail to do so effectively if it wrote, or the rest of us read, its opinions as narrow resolutions of specific cases. What the justices write is going to be read by other judges, constitutional lawyers, government officials, and private citizens who want or need to know how the Court's decision today will affect other cases and constitutional controversies tomorrow. An important corollary of the bedrock constitutional goal of creating a workable government is that the Republic's system of constitutional law must be coherent and administrable, and one of the Court's most important tasks is to make that possible. It does so, in part, by explaining its decisions in the broad terms suitable to thinking about the fundamental commitments of the American political community.

For these reasons, the holding/dictum distinction and the assumption that the facts of the case substantially limit its scope as precedent are imprecise ways of thinking about constitutional precedents. (A Supreme Court justice who invokes the holding/dictum distinction is often making a polemical point against a colleague: "I'm relying on the holding, you're just quoting dicta.") Decisions often rest on the complex interweaving of different forms of constitutional argument or on the judgment that a particular outcome is persuasive because it makes sense in light of the Constitution-in-practice as a whole. Opinions often create or modify doctrines, patterns of analysis that govern an entire topic, or attempt to bring order to an entire area of constitutional law. (On doctrine, see later in the chapter.) In constitutional law, therefore, a Supreme Court precedent's scope extends beyond its specific holding to include the entire constitutional discussion that led to that holding. "When an opinion issues for the Court, it is not only the result but also those portions of the opinion necessary to that result by which we are bound. ... As a general rule, the principle of *stare decisis* directs us to adhere not only to the holdings of our prior cases, *but also to their explications of the governing rules of law.*" A discussion that is "technically dicta" but is "an important part of the Court's rationale for the result it reached" is part of the precedent the result establishes.[62]

An example may be helpful. In *United States v. Lopez* (1995), the Supreme Court invalidated an act of Congress making it a federal crime to carry a firearm into a school zone. The government's argument from precedent in defense of the Gun-Free School Zones Act was that the prohibited behavior, if all potential instances were aggregated, would have the substantial effect on interstate commerce that

---

[62] *Seminole Tribe v. Florida*, 517 U.S. 44, 67 (1996) (emphasis added).

earlier cases held will support commerce clause legislation. The Court's "holding," stated narrowly, was that the government had failed to show the required effect, and specifically that the possible impact of guns in schools on the quality of education, and thus on the future productivity of school children, did not do so. At first glance, this conclusion appeared in considerable tension with precedent. The Court's extensive commerce clause case law included opinions describing the commerce power in very broad terms, and the decision in *Lopez* was the first in almost sixty years to hold that the commerce clause did not authorize a statute predicated on it.

Chief Justice William H. Rehnquist, writing for the Court, clearly thought it important to explain how such an outcome fit into the Constitution-in-practice as a whole. In order to do so, Rehnquist reviewed the history of commerce clause thinking, systematized the entire body of post-1937 commerce clause decisions into three analytically useful categories originally outlined in an earlier case, showed that none of the prior decisions provided direct authority for finding a substantial effect on commerce by aggregating instances of a noneconomic activity, and pointed out that the government had offered no limiting principle to its argument that such aggregation is permissible in commerce clause analysis.

> To uphold the Government's contentions here, we would have to pile inference upon inference in a manner that would bid fair to convert congressional authority under the Commerce Clause to a general police power of the sort retained by the States. Admittedly, some of our prior cases have taken long steps down that road, giving great deference to congressional action. The broad language in these opinions has suggested the possibility of additional expansion, but we decline here to proceed any further. To do so would require us to conclude that the Constitution's enumeration of powers does not presuppose something not enumerated.

Rehnquist's objective clearly was to persuade the reader that the Court's narrow (and to some surprising) ruling that the Constitution did not authorize the Gun-Free School Zones Act was the proper conclusion to reach in light of the precedents and of the enumeration principle, a basic presupposition of constitutional law.[63]

It would be wrong to suggest that *Lopez*'s significance as precedent is limited to future controversies involving the use of the concepts of aggregation and substantial effect in commerce clause analysis, important as that is in itself. If *Lopez* were a common law decision meant only to resolve the case before (albeit consistently with other cases), the Court's extensive review of the commerce clause case law, its discussion of the reasons that the Court had modified earlier approaches after 1937, and its discussion of the two categories it found irrelevant to the case before it could be dismissed in whole or part as dicta unnecessary to the specific decision. To do so, however, would be to misunderstand the role of Supreme Court precedent in the Constitution-in-practice. The *Lopez* opinion's sweeping "explication of the governing rules of law" (the three categories of decisions), its justifications for the existing

[63]   *United States v. Lopez*, 514 U.S. 549, 567 (1995).

precedents (they make sense out of text and history), and its explanation for the Court's refusal to extend those precedents to the school zones law (the enumeration principle is fundamental) were all "part of the Court's rationale" and "necessary to the result" if the result was to be the logical constitutional law conclusion rather than a fluke. Accordingly, a future controversy that involves any of these aspects of Chief Justice Rehnquist's opinion falls "within the *ratio decidendi* – or *rationale*" of *Lopez*, and an argument based on *Lopez* as precedent is relevant and perhaps decisive.[64]

And what about the facts in *Lopez*? The scope and application of a precedent in American law often depend on the specific facts that the court was addressing. The court's identification of which legal rules or principles governed the dispute will have been guided by the factual controversy that gave rise to the case, and argument based on the decision as precedent may rely on the degree to which the precedent's facts are analogous to those in the later controversy. These common features of legal reasoning in other areas, however, do not always apply in constitutional law, and in particular to Supreme Court constitutional precedents, because constitutional law involves fundamental principles of American government, and as we have seen, the Court has a particular role and responsibility in the governmental system. "The Supreme Court is not, and never has been, primarily concerned with the correction of errors in lower court decisions. ... The function of the Supreme Court is ... to resolve conflicts of opinion on federal questions that have arisen among lower courts [and] to pass upon questions of wide import under the Constitution, laws, and treaties of the United States," and by doing so to maintain the coherence and integrity of federal law. The modern Supreme Court's almost entirely discretionary appellate jurisdiction reflects and carries out its unique mission of resolving problems in the law itself rather than being focused, as are other courts, on resolving disputes between particular litigants. Since a Supreme Court constitutional decision addresses issues of broad legal significance almost by definition, it is unsurprising that the specific facts are frequently of little importance (except, of course, to the actual parties to the case!) and do not materially affect the case's meaning as a precedent.[65]

This generalization about the lessened importance of a Supreme Court precedent's specific facts has three important limitations. First, the actual substance of some provisions in the constitutional text and some principles of the Constitution-in-practice can only be applied by close attention to the specific facts in the constitutional problem that the lawyer is attempting to solve. The fourth amendment's prohibition on "unreasonable searches and seizures" is a clear example: The scope as precedent of a decision that a governmental action did or did not violate the prohibition necessarily depends on the facts of the decision as well as on

---

[64] *Ramos*, 140 S. Ct. at 1404 n. 54 (opinion of Gorsuch, J.).

[65] *Boag v. MacDougall*, 454 U.S. 364, 368 (1982) (Rehnquist, J., dissenting). Then-Associate Justice Rehnquist was quoting a 1949 speech by Chief Justice Fred Vinson. See also *San Francisco v. Sheehan*, 575 U.S. 600, 610 (2015) (the Court's discretionary "certiorari jurisdiction exists to clarify the law").

the legal reasoning the Court used in relating those facts to earlier decisions and to the constitutional text. *Carpenter v. United States*, the decision holding that government acquisition of cell phone records from the service provider violated the fourth amendment, reached its conclusion by examining the factual parallels between the government's investigatory actions in the case before it and the fact patterns in earlier Supreme Court precedents. In turn, lower courts must determine the scope of *Carpenter* itself as precedent in part by comparing its facts to those in the cases they must decide.[66]

Second, Congress sometimes enacts legislation that expressly limits its enforcement to situations in which the executive can demonstrate that the particular incident in question is within the scope of Congress's authorizations of power, most often by requiring proof of a connection to interstate commerce. Under *United States v. Lopez*, inclusion of such a "jurisdictional element" in the statute ensures the constitutionality of enforcement on a case by case basis. *Lopez* itself occasioned an example. In the wake of the Court's decision striking down the statutory ban on guns in schools, Congress amended the statute to include a requirement that the prosecution prove that the gun in question "has moved in or ... otherwise affects interstate or foreign commerce." The federal courts of appeals uniformly upheld the amended law against constitutional challenge because part of every successful prosecution under it is proof that the specific action was related to interstate commerce.[67]

Of necessity, the precedential scope of a decision applying a statutory jurisdictional element, including a decision by the Supreme Court, is tied to the particular facts which the decision held did or did not meet the statutorily required demonstration that the particular enforcement action has adequate connection to a constitutional authorization. In *Taylor v. United States* (2016), for example, the Court affirmed a conviction under the Hobbs Act, which makes robbery a federal crime when it affects interstate or foreign commerce or any "other commerce over which the United States has jurisdiction." The attempted robbery in question was an attempt to rob drug dealers of marijuana and proceeds from its sale, but the defendant argued that there was no proof that either he or his would-be victims had any connection to interstate commerce. However, the Court reasoned that precedent had established Congress's plenary legislative jurisdiction over intra- as well as interstate commerce in marijuana because of the existence of an interstate market for the drug and thus the jurisdictional element was satisfied. *Taylor* stated its "holding" as "limited to cases in which the defendant targets drug dealers for the purpose of stealing drugs or drug proceeds," and lower courts have generally treated it as precedent for analogous cases only, although they have properly extended the analogies beyond the robbery of drug dealers.[68]

---

[66] See *Carpenter v. United States*, 138 S. Ct. 2206, 2214–19 (2018); *United States v. Moalin*, 973 F.3d 977, 989–92 (9th Cir. 2020) (discussing the scope of *Carpenter* and other fourth amendment precedents with reference to their facts).

[67] See, e.g., *United States v. Dorsey*, 418 F.3d 1038 (9th Cir. 2005); *United States v. Danks*, 221 F.3d 1037 (8th Cir. 1999).

[68] *Taylor v. United States*, 136 S. Ct. 2074, 2082 (2016). The Court's apparent effort in *Taylor* to set a formal limit to the arguments that can be made based on the decision (to cases involving robbery

Third, the extent to which a Supreme Court constitutional precedent is tied to its particular facts can vary depending on whether the party arguing for the invalidity of a law or other governmental action made a facial or an as-applied challenge. Determining which category a given challenge falls in is not always easy, and a challenger can make both claims at once, but the general idea is clear: A facial challenge is a claim that there is no set of circumstances in which the statute or other action would be constitutional, while an as-applied challenge is limited to the claim that, under the particular factual circumstances the challenger alleges, the application of the law or policy is unconstitutional. *United States* v. *Lopez* was a facial challenge: The claim was that the commerce clause simply did not authorize Congress to enact the Gun-Free School Zones Act, and since the Court agreed, it held that the statute was flatly invalid. As we have already seen, the specific facts of *Lopez* are immaterial to its scope as a precedent.[69]

and drug dealers) was doomed to failure. Supreme Court decisions are read by many lawyers with advice to give and briefs to write, and by lower court judges anxious to reach correct decisions, all interested in any argument from precedent that seems valuable or relevant. At the time I am writing, at least one court of appeals has made extensive use of *Taylor* (as well as other precedents) in concluding that the federal Hate Crimes Prevention Act "may be constitutionally applied to an unarmed assault of a victim engaged in commercial activity at his place of work." In doing so, the court took account of the built-in role of facts in *Taylor*'s scope as a precedent, noting for example that *Taylor* upheld the Hobbs Act conviction even though there was no proof that either the robber or his victims had any interstate connections. But the court simply ignored *Taylor*'s attempted self-limitation to cases involving "drugs or drug proceeds." See *United States* v. *Hill*, 927 F.3d 188, 198–202 (4th Cir. 2019). Another good example of a lower court giving a sensible interpretation to *Taylor*'s scope as precedent is *United States* v. *Woodberry*, 987 F.3d 1231, 1235 (9th Cir. 2021), which rejected the argument that robbery of a state-licensed marijuana dispensary was not within the Hobbs Act because *Taylor* specifically referred to the robbery of "drug dealers."

The best-known example of the Court trying without success to control the use of a case as precedent is *Bush* v. *Gore*, the decision that resolved the controversy over the outcome of the 2000 presidential election. Several aspects of the opinion of the Court betray the justices' understandable worry that the Court's entry into such a politically charged controversy would damage its reputation and encourage the participants in future political struggles to bring similarly unwelcome cases to the Court: the opinion was unsigned, said as little as possible about its reasoning, ended with an apologia for the Court's involvement ("None are more conscious of the vital limits on judicial authority than are the Members of this Court . . . When contending parties invoke the process of the courts, however, it becomes our unsought responsibility to resolve the federal and constitutional issues"), and dropped a strong hint that the decision was a ticket good for one ride only: "Our consideration is limited to the present circumstances." The Court's efforts to render the decision invisible, however, have failed: While as yet no opinion of the Court and only two separate opinions have cited *Bush* v. *Gore*, by the end of 2020 more than 500 lower court decisions had. The bottom line is that the Court cannot prevent determined constitutional lawyers from finding grist for their mills in the Court's decisions. See *Bush* v. *Gore*, 531 U.S. 98, 111, 109 (2000).

[69] The facial/as-applied distinction plays a significant role in constitutional law, and has its clearest application when someone claims that a law clearly authorized by the constitutional text or within the scope of a state's police power clashes with a constitutional prohibition. If the only choices were to strike the law down entirely or flatly reject the right protected by the prohibition, constitutional decisions would swing between undue judicial interference with the democratic process of legislation and undue judicial timidity in the vindication of individual rights. The facial/as-applied distinction allows litigants and judges to make finer-tuned arguments in identifying the specific constitutional problem by the two-fold logic of inquiry into authorization and prohibition. But the distinction is not

In contrast, in *United States* v. *U.S. Shoe Corp.* (1998), the constitutional claim involved a federal Harbor Maintenance Tax that is levied on commercial cargo moving through American ports. The challenger did not argue that the statute imposing the Tax is unauthorized or that any constitutional prohibition renders it generally invalid, but only that as applied to cargo for international export the Tax violates the export clause of Article I section 9 ("No Tax or Duty shall be laid on Articles exported from any State."). The government argued that the so-called Tax was actually a valid user fee "designed to defray the cost of harbor development and maintenance," but after reviewing the Tax's specific characteristics, the Court concluded it fell within the export clause prohibition because it did not "fairly match the exporters' use of port services and facilities." The Court therefore held the Tax unconstitutional as to exporters, leaving it in force as to importers and domestic shippers. *U.S. Shoe* as a precedent is thus shaped not only by its holding's limitation to exporters in accordance with the text of the export clause, but also by the specific facts that persuaded the Court that the Tax is not a user fee as applied to exporters.[70]

Whether a Supreme Court precedent is on its face broad or narrow, its application as precedent in subsequent cases can itself raise a difficult question of constitutional law. When a precedent's scope is not obvious, the constitutional lawyer has several means for determining the best answer. The first and in some ways the primary method is that workhorse of common law thought, reasoning by analogy: How closely does the constitutional resolution in the precedent resemble the constitutional problem in the matter at hand? When the precedent is shaped by its facts, the process of deciding if it is closely analogous to the new situation will closely resemble an argument over a precedent in contract or tort law. But analogical reasoning is also useful in determining the scope of the many constitutional precedents that do not turn on the original case's specific facts.

One of the issues in *United States* v. *Morrison*, which we discussed earlier, was whether *United States* v. *Lopez* as precedent supported the conclusion that the commerce clause did not authorize Congress to create a federal civil remedy for victims of gender-motivated violence. The argument that *Lopez* did not dictate that answer was, in part, that *Morrison* was not closely analogous to *Lopez*: The statutory provision under review was not (as in *Lopez*) a federal criminal law; there were express congressional findings detailing the effect of gender-motivated violence on

confined to such constitutional problems, and the Court's cases administering it are not entirely consistent. The Supreme Court frequently asserts that facial challenges are disfavored, but in fact often decides them, and there is in addition a special and generous rule permitting facial challenges based on the free speech clause of the first amendment. Furthermore, the Court usually states that a party bringing a facial challenge must show that there are "no circumstances . . . under which the Act [or other action] would be valid," but asserts at times that the challenger need only establish that the statute lacks a "plainly legitimate sweep." See, e.g., *Washington State Grange* v. *Washington State Republican Party*, 552 U.S. 442, 449–50 (2008).

70   *United States* v. *U.S. Shoe Corp.*, 523 U.S. 360, 370 (1998). See also *Trafigura Trading LLC* v. *United States*, 485 F. Supp. 3d 822, 825–26 (S.D. Tex. 2020), *appeal pending* (applying *U.S. Shoe Corp* in light of the Court's discussion of the specific characteristics of the Harbor Maintenance Tax).

interstate commerce (there were no such findings in *Lopez*), and earlier precedent that *Lopez* expressly reaffirmed had upheld commerce clause legislation addressing other kinds of discriminatory behavior. The Court was persuaded nonetheless that the issue in *Morrison* fell within the scope of *Lopez*. In both cases the argument that the commerce clause authorized the federal law depended on the permissibility of aggregating individual instances of noncommercial criminal behavior in order to show a substantial effect on interstate commerce. Neither *Lopez* nor earlier precedent had approved such reasoning, and allowing it in *Morrison* would pose the same threat to the enumeration principle that was of central concern in *Lopez*. Since the features of *Lopez* parallel to *Morrison* were more crucial than the dissimilarities, the Court found the two cases analogous and thus *Lopez* was controlling precedent in *Morrison*.

The reasoning in *Morrison* just summarized is obviously not an exercise in deductive logic. The arguments that *Lopez* was distinguishable – the technical term for the conclusion that a precedent is not sufficiently analogous to be controlling – were strong, and indeed persuaded the four justices who dissented. Analogical reasoning in constitutional law arguments from precedent requires the lawyer to make judgments about the fundamental point of the precedent *and* the precedent's fit with the Constitution-in-practice as a whole that are not susceptible to logical demonstration but depend on the lawyer's own judgment that the proposed analogy (or disanalogy) between precedent and present problem is more persuasive than the opposite argument. Competent constitutional lawyers trying in good faith to find the best solution to a constitutional problem will sometimes come to different judgments about the scope of precedent without either being guilty of inept reasoning. An example will illustrate the point.

One of the issues in *Manning v. Caldwell*, a 2019 decision by a federal court of appeals, was whether a 1962 Supreme Court decision, *Robinson v. California*, was controlling precedent. *Robinson*'s holding was that the cruel and unusual punishment clause of the eighth amendment prohibited a state law criminalizing the status of being addicted to narcotics without any proof of possession, use, or antisocial behavior related to narcotics. *Robinson* has long since been understood to state a more general principle – that mere status unrelated to any specific action cannot be the basis for criminal punishment. In *Manning*, the challengers, who were homeless alcoholics, claimed that under *Robinson* and as applied to them, a state alcohol regulatory scheme violated the eighth amendment. One statute provided for a civil adjudication that an individual was an "habitual drunkard"; other provisions made it a crime for an individual subject to such a judgment to obtain, possess, or consume alcoholic beverages, along with other negative consequences.

The challengers argued that the habitual-drunkard scheme effectively criminalized their status because they were addicted and unable to obey the prohibitions on possession and consumption, and being homeless, as a practical matter they could not conceal their actions. Thus their status as habitual drunkards after the civil adjudication inevitably led to their liability for criminal punishment, and *Robinson* was precedent for the conclusion that as applied to them the state regime was unconstitutional. A majority of the judges on the appeals court agreed that *Manning* was within the scope of *Robinson's* holding. "Virginia's two-pronged statutory scheme may be less direct than the statute at issue in *Robinson*, but it yields the same result: it effectively criminalizes an illness." In the judgment of the majority, the analogy between *Robinson* and *Manning* was sound because *Robinson* stated a *constitutional* principle, and it makes sense to accord such a principle a generous rather than parsimonious interpretation. A dissenter came to the opposite judgment. "The core dispute in this case is whether *Robinson* prohibits only the criminalization of status, or also of conduct compelled by status. I am satisfied that *Robinson* is better understood as distinguishing status from conduct," a conclusion he thought consistent with most other cases applying *Robinson*, and with a lower court's obligation to respect the limits inherent in the Supreme Court precedent. Either judgment – in *my* judgment (!) – is defensible.[71]

Doctrine. Important as analogical reasoning is in argument from precedent, what we shall call doctrinal reasoning is perhaps even more central to this form of argument derived from the Constitution-in-practice. The Supreme Court often employs the word "doctrine" in discussing constitutional law, but it has never offered a definition of the term. The word is sometimes used very broadly and quite sensibly to refer to all the "rules and principles of constitutional law . . . that are capable of statement and that generally guide the decisions of courts, the conduct of government officials, and the arguments and counsel of lawyers," the idea that in this book is referred to as the Constitution-in-practice. However, I am going to reserve "doctrine" to refer to the particular subset of precedent-based argument that is characterized by adherence to *formal* rules and principles that the precedent *expressly* announces. Doing so will enable us to identify important, shared features of all such arguments.[72]

As discussed earlier, because of the Supreme Court's unique, structurally essential role in ensuring that constitutional law is principled, coherent and reasonably uniform across the Republic, stare decisis requires the Court and other constitutional decision makers "to adhere not only to the holdings of [the Court's] prior

---

[71] *Manning v. Caldwell*, 930 F.3d 264, 283 (4th Cir. 2019) (en banc); *id.* at 307 (Diaz, Cir. J., dissenting). It is unnecessary for the purposes of this discussion to decide which judgment is correct, but in case the reader is curious, I believe the majority had the better of the argument. The dissent expressed the concern that the majority's decision was an extension of the holding in *Robinson* and that whether to do so was a decision for the Supreme Court. This seems to me to misunderstand the duty owed to vertical precedent. Except in a case factually indistinguishable from a Supreme Court precedent, any lower court that applies the precedent as the controlling rule of law could be described as "extending" the high Court's decision, but that is not ordinarily viewed as illegitimate. The majority's conclusion that *Manning* was analogous to *Robinson* seems to me to take better account of the concerns animating *Robinson* and of its fit within the overall shape of the Constitution-in-practice. But again, I think either conclusion is a plausible interpretation of *Robinson*.

[72] Charles Fried, Constitutional Doctrine, 107 *Harv. L. Rev.* 1140 (1994).

cases, *but also to their explications of the governing rules of law.*"[73] Many governing rules of law are themselves straightforward statements of the substantive law. *Robinson v. California* announced a rule of constitutional law that criminal punishment may not be imposed on someone because of status rather than actions. The question in *Manning v. Caldwell* was whether that rule applied to the punishment of someone for actions he could not avoid doing on the basis of a status imposed on him by government. But the Supreme Court often formulates rules that do not dictate specific answers to constitutional questions but instead govern the line of reasoning to be used in addressing a question. It is these formally structured patterns of analysis that the Court most often means when it refers to constitutional law doctrines, and it is in this sense that I am going to use the term.

From the beginning, the justices have recognized the value of providing substantive criteria that not only explain today's result but also provide guidance for resolving tomorrow's problem. In *Calder v. Bull*, decided in 1798, Justice Samuel Chase outlined the four categories of criminal law that he thought were included in the common law definition of "ex post facto law" and thus within the clauses forbidding such laws in Article I sections 9 and 10. Chase's reasoning on the matter was an original meaning argument and unnecessary to the resolution of *Calder* itself, which did not involve a criminal law at all and thus could be decided (as Chase himself recognized) on the ground that the prohibition is limited to criminal laws. Chase was speaking to the future, to later questions about just what criminal laws are within the scope of the ex post facto clauses. Later decisions adopted his "explication of the governing rules of law" under the clauses, which thus acquired the authority of argument from precedent. His four categories remain the framework that the Supreme Court and other courts follow in analyzing claims under the ex post facto clauses: The categories are doctrine and as such, with the various adjustments later precedents have made (a process we shall discuss below), are an authoritative part of the Constitution-in-practice.[74]

Doctrine can take several different forms and can be built out of varying materials. Some doctrines affirmatively indicate the various situations to which a provision of the constitutional text applies: Justice Chase's four ex post facto categories, derived from the common law, are one example, as are the three categories of legislation into which Chief Justice Rehnquist systematized the Supreme Court's commerce clause

---

[73] *Seminole Tribe v. Florida*, 517 U.S. at 66–67 (emphasis added).

[74] See *Peugh v. United States*, 569 U.S. 530, 538–39 (2013) (the Supreme Court's later ex post facto precedents "build on Justice Chase's formulation of what constitutes an '*ex post facto* Law,'" and have given the term additional "substance by an accretion of case law"); *Calder v. Bull*, 3 U.S. (3 Dall.) 386, 390–91 (1798) (seriatim opinion of Chase, J.). There was no opinion of the Court in *Calder*, and Justice William Johnson later objected, vehemently but unsuccessfully, to treating the decision or any of the opinions as precedent on the meaning of the ex post facto clauses. See *Satterlee v. Matthewson*, 27 U.S. 380, 416 & n. a (1829) (Johnson, J., concurring in the judgment). Johnson's arguments were not trivial, but the precedential status of *Calder* and the authority of Chase's four categories as doctrine have long been settled ... by precedent.

precedent. Conversely, other doctrines define the scope of constitutional language by identifying boundaries to its application. Article III grants the federal courts "judicial Power" to decide "Cases" and "Controversies," language that the Supreme Court has "always taken ... to mean cases and controversies of the sort traditionally amenable to, and resolved by, the judicial process." The Court has given that concept operative meaning through a set of complex "justiciability" doctrines that function to limit the federal courts to such matters.[75]

Most provisions of the constitutional text, read in isolation, appear to authorize or prohibit a set of governmental actions without apparent regard to the fact that the American political community is committed to a variety of distinct, often overlapping, and sometimes conflicting, constitutional commitments. The first clauses of Article I section 8 authorize Congress to lay taxes and spend money for the general welfare, but make no mention of the obvious fact that a truly unlimited spending power could be used to undermine state autonomy or induce the surrender of individual liberties by creating effectively irresistible financial incentives. The free speech clause of the first amendment seems on its face to prohibit interference with freedom of speech no matter how pressing the justification and limited the intrusion.

Another kind of doctrine responds to the written Constitution's often absolute language by building into constitutional reasoning a recognition of the overall commitments the Constitution-in-practice incorporates. Such doctrines instruct constitutional lawyers as to the factors that must be taken into account in answering questions that arise out of specific constitutional provisions or principles. In Chapter 2, we encountered the coercion limitation on the spending power. The law of the free speech clause presents a remarkable profusion of different though sometimes overlapping doctrines that Supreme Court precedents ordain for use in different sets of circumstances. Most of them require that the analysis give some consideration to other constitutional commitments besides that of free expression because the Court has concluded that the other commitment should not simply be dismissed as irrelevant when the free speech clause is at issue.

When a court is reviewing a governmental regulation of the "time, place or manner" in which people may engage in speech, for example, the relevant doctrine is that "the government may impose reasonable restrictions on the time, place, or manner of protected speech, provided the restrictions are justified without reference to the content of the regulated speech, that they are narrowly tailored to serve a significant governmental interest, and that they leave open ample alternative channels for communication of the information." Thus, even though the written Constitution speaks in absolute terms ("Congress shall make no law ... "), the doctrine allows for "reasonable" governmental measures that in fact forbid protected

---

[75]   *Steel Co. v. Citizens for a Better Env't*, 523 U.S. 83, 102 (1998). On the justiciability doctrines, see Chapter 4.

speech at certain times (2 A.M., say) or certain places (residential streets) or in certain manners (cranking up a loudspeaker above 140 decibels). A ban on driving vehicles playing very loud sound systems in a sleeping neighborhood in the wee hours of the morning, the case law has concluded, serves the government's significant interest in protecting people from annoyance in their homes without unduly diminishing freedom of expression. On the other hand, in order to take into account the weight of the constitutional prohibition on abridging free speech, the doctrine limits how far even apparently reasonable regulations may go. A municipal ordinance banning only political messages from the neighborhood is not a valid time, place, or manner regulation because it is in effect (and no doubt in intent) an attempt to censor a certain kind of speech rather protect people's rest, and an ordinance banning all audible message from all vehicles on all city streets at any time probably constrains the channels of protected communication more broadly than can be justified by even legitimate concerns about noise.[76]

Yet another category of doctrine builds into the analysis of constitutional problems considerations derived from the basic constitutional arrangements of the American political community. Supreme Court precedent, for example, often requires that a court examining the constitutionality of legislative or executive actions approach the analysis by applying a "standard of review" that guides and constrains the court's decision. The equal protection principle, for example, addresses governmental discriminations between individuals but it cannot rationally be thought to forbid all discrimination since most laws, even the most benign, draw distinctions (= discriminate). A rule that only people who pass a driving test can lawfully drive discriminates against those who fail or decline to take the test. At an early stage, equal protection precedent often went no further than to say that equal protection prohibits only "invidious" discriminations, but that formulation provides next to no guidance, and the Supreme Court eventually developed different standards of review to govern analysis in different kinds of controversies. Because the American political norm is that the community is governed by rules created by democratic politics, the default equal protection standard sharply restricts judicial interference with those rules: The court must presume their constitutionality, and a challenger can only prevail by proving that there is no "rational basis" for the discrimination in question. But it is also an American political norm that government must not harm an individual based on his or her race and that the judiciary must intervene if government does so and its actions are challenged in court: In a case about racial discrimination, the court must apply "strict scrutiny," and government can prevail only if it can overcome a presumption of *un*constitutionality and demonstrate that its action meets specified, and demanding, requirements. (We shall discuss standards of review again in Chapter 4.)

---

[76] *McCullen v. Coakley*, 573 U.S. 464, 477 (2014).

Not all doctrines derived from structure are the product of reflection on the relationship between the federal courts and the political branches of the federal and state governments. The Supreme Court has also created doctrines that address complex questions about the interaction between Congress's powers and those of the president, and between the federal government's sphere of action and that of the states. An important example is the pattern of analysis that governs questions about the lawfulness of presidential action. The underlying constitutional principle is that the Constitution embodies a fundamental asymmetry between Congress's powers and those of the president. The texts of Articles I and II express this asymmetry. On the one hand, Article I section 8 expressly authorizes Congress to enact "*all* Laws which shall be necessary and proper for carrying into Execution the foregoing Powers, and all other Powers vested by this Constitution in the Government of the United States, or in any Department or Officer thereof." *McCulloch v. Maryland* was only the first of many decisions holding that this language gives Congress very broad leeway in deciding what measures it thinks necessary: I added the italics but Chief Justice Marshall long ago endorsed the idea. The reader will also note that the necessary and proper clause extends Congress's legislative authority to the execution of any power that the Constitution vests in the president, again with the same breadth of discretion recognized in *McCulloch*.

On the other hand, Article II section 3 expressly imposes on the president the duty to carry out Congress's laws: "[H]e shall take Care that the Laws be faithfully executed." Neither text nor precedent permits us to read the take care clause as an exceptionless command that the president carry out any law that Congress happens to enact. For example, it would render pointless Article II's express delegation to the president of the power to appoint principal officers (with the Senate's advice and consent), to conclude that the president must execute an act of Congress, naming whom the president should appoint or requiring the president to obtain the agreement of the House as well as the Senate. But the take care clause does ordain what must be the ordinary rule if the overall system is to work in accordance with the text of the written Constitution and the institutional relationship it creates: It is Congress's prerogative to make the laws, and the president's obligation to obey and execute them.

The pattern of analysis that precedent recognizes for carrying into effect this asymmetry between legislative and executive authority was first articulated in *Youngstown Sheet &Tube Co. v. Sawyer*, the famous 1952 Steel Seizure Case that held invalid President Truman's seizure of American steel mills during the Korean War. The executive justified Truman's order as the only effective means of averting a nation-wide strike that would shut the mills down and immediately put the nation's war measures in peril: Existing legislation authorizing the president to intervene in a labor dispute, the Justice Department argued, was too slow and cumbersome to meet the crisis. Justice Hugo Black's official opinion of the Court rested the decision to invalidate the order entirely on the enumeration principle: The president simply could not point to any source of authority, constitutional or statutory, for his action. But every other member of the six-justice majority also filed a separate opinion, and it is clear that most of them did so because they thought Black's reasoning incomplete. By the 1980s the Court as a body had come to the same conclusion, and adopted the analysis proposed by Justice Robert H. Jackson in his *Youngstown* concurrence as the controlling doctrine.

Justice Jackson built his analytical framework on the basis of two structural principles, the asymmetry between the powers of the two branches and the constitutional objective of creating and maintaining a workable government. "While the Constitution diffuses power the better to secure liberty, it also contemplates that practice will integrate the dispersed powers into a workable government. Presidential powers are not fixed but fluctuate, depending upon their disjunction or conjunction with those of Congress." The constitutional lawyer with a constitutional problem involving the president's power must therefore ask what Congress has done *and* what it is authorized to do, as well as source of the president's power to act.

> Justice Jackson's familiar tripartite framework ... divides exercises of Presidential power into three categories: First, when "the President acts pursuant to an express or implied authorization of Congress, his authority is at its maximum, for it includes all that he possesses in his own right plus all that Congress can delegate." Second, "in absence of either a congressional grant or denial of authority" there is a "zone of twilight in which he and Congress may have concurrent authority." Finally, when "the President takes measures incompatible with the expressed or implied will of Congress ... he can rely only upon his own constitutional powers minus any constitutional powers of Congress over the matter." To succeed in this third category, the President's asserted power must be both "exclusive" and "conclusive" on the issue.

Put another way, Congress's will prevails *if* Congress is authorized to act (the asymmetry principle), *but* the president can act if authorized to do so and Congress approves or is silent or the Constitution gives the president exclusive power over the matter (the workable government principle). The doctrine thus ensures that the analysis of a specific problem does not overlook either of the underlying constitutional principles that is relevant, and provides a solution if the principles point in different directions: If Congress exercises any constitutional power it possesses, the Constitution prohibits the president from acting contrary to the statute, while the president may only act against a statute when Congress is not authorized to address the matter at issue.[77]

Finding and reading the controlling opinion. Although his role is often ignored, Oliver Ellsworth, chief justice from 1796 to 1800, was largely responsible for the

---

[77] *Zivotofsky v. Kerry*, 576 U.S. 1, 10 (2015) (quoting *Youngstown Sheet & Tube Co. v. Sawyer*, 343 U.S. 579, 635 (1952) (Jackson, J., concurring)).

Supreme Court abandoning an original practice of sitting justices explaining their reasoning in seriatim opinions in most cases. Ellsworth and then John Marshall successfully persuaded or pushed their colleagues into acquiescing in the announcement of the Court's judgment and reasoning through a single opinion of the Court. The custom continues to this day, and when it works as Ellsworth and Marshall intended, it simplifies the work of determining the decision's meaning as precedent – a logical, internally consistent rationale for the Court's judgment can (or at least should) be found in a single opinion.[78]

In reality, however, things are often not that simple. There may be no opinion of the Court because a majority of the justices agree on the judgment, but not on the reasons for the judgment, or the lead opinion may command a majority on some issues but not on others, so that one must keep careful score to be sure which parts of the opinion are "of the Court."[79] Or on closer examination of one or more concurring opinions written by justices in the majority, it may turn out that the arguments presented in the supposed opinion of the Court did not in fact command a majority, or by some were thought insufficient on their own. As noted previously, all six justices who agreed with the judgment in the Steel Seizure Case – that President Truman's order was unlawful – filed separate opinions. One of them expressly noted that he did not join Justice Black's official opinion of the Court, but three of the other concurrences (including Justice Jackson's) gave reasons for the judgment that indicate less than complete agreement with Black even though they purportedly joined Black's opinion.

Even more complicated patterns occur. In *Goldwater* v. *Carter* (1979), a court of appeals upheld President Carter's decision to terminate a mutual defense treaty with Taiwan without obtaining the advice and consent of the Senate. The Supreme Court was unanimous in granting Senator Goldwater's petition for review, but that was the only matter on which there was unanimity. A five-justice majority agreed that the Court should not allow briefing or argument on the merits: In their view, the appeals court's decision should be vacated immediately (eliminating it both as a judgment and as a lower court precedent) and the case should return to the district court with directions to dismiss Goldwater's complaint. But these justices did not agree on the reason that Goldwater had failed to present a viable lawsuit. Then-Associate Justice

[78]   On Chief Justice Ellsworth's role in establishing the custom, see William R. Casto, *The Supreme Court in the Early Republic: The Chief Justiceships of John Jay and Oliver Ellsworth* 110–11 (Columbia, SC: University of South Carolina Press, 1995).

[79]   In modern practice, the tendency toward this sort of fragmentation has accelerated. See, e.g., *Ramos* v. *Louisiana*, 140 S. Ct. 1390, 1391 (2020): "Justice GORSUCH announced the judgment of the Court and delivered the opinion of the Court with respect to Parts I, II–A, III, and IV–B–1, an opinion with respect to Parts II–B, IV–B–2, and V, in which Justice GINSBURG, Justice BREYER, and Justice SOTOMAYOR join, and an opinion with respect to Part IV–A, in which Justice GINSBURG and Justice BREYER join." The unwary reader can easily miss the fact that in *Ramos*, subsections IV-A and IV-B-2 speak only for (respectively) three and four justices, while section IV-B-1 is part of the reasoning of "the Court." This is rather clearly not what Chief Justices Ellsworth and Marshall had in mind, and few constitutional lawyers not actually on the high Court find it a happy development.

Rehnquist, writing for four justices, thought the constitutional issue in the case was a "political question" inherently beyond the power of the federal courts to decide. (The political question doctrine is discussed in Chapter 4.) The fifth, Justice Lewis Powell, thought that Goldwater's suit was not yet "ripe" because the Senate as an institution had not yet taken action to object to Carter's action; if it did, the courts presumably could hear the case. Two justices thought the Court should allow the parties to brief the case and refrain from taking further action until after it was argued. The eighth justice filed a Delphic notice that he concurred "in the result" without further explanation – for some undisclosed reason the right outcome was for Goldwater to be out of court, period. And the ninth justice thought the Court did not need briefing or argument because the appeals court judgment was patently correct and should be summarily affirmed.[80]

As a matter of preserving clarity and consistency in the Constitution-in-practice, *Goldwater v. Carter* was clearly a disaster. But the Supreme Court exercised jurisdiction over the case and issued an order with a substantive result – Senator Goldwater lost and President Carter won – so the decision sets a precedent and cannot simply be ignored. Given the range of conflicting viewpoints among the justices, one possibility would be to treat *Goldwater* as precedent only as to its outcome (future plaintiffs in Goldwater's shoes will lost). But that approach won't work if the future Goldwater has the formal support of the Senate or of both houses, since on Rehnquist's political question reasoning he still has no case, while on Powell's ripeness theory the federal courts should now proceed to decide the constitutional issue. Keep in mind as well that constitutional law questions are not just issues for courts but are the concern of nonjudicial actors as well: What should lawyers for a future Carter or Goldwater advise their client, given that *Goldwater v. Carter* is a Supreme Court constitutional decision? Unless we have stumbled on a glitch in the constitutional law system, *Goldwater* must be precedent not just as to result but as to (some) reasoning.

Happily, there is a solution. Several decades ago, in a case called *Marks v. United States*, the Supreme Court settled on a method of determining the holding in a case such as *Goldwater*. "When a fragmented Court decides a case and no single rationale explaining the result enjoys the assent of five Justices, the holding of the Court may be viewed as that position taken by those Members who concurred in the judgments on the narrowest grounds." Applying the rule in *Marks* to *Goldwater*, we can immediately eliminate the views of four justices from consideration, the three who actually disagreed with the judgment ordering the suit dismissed immediately and the one who agreed "with the result" but gave no reason why. As between Justice Rehnquist's political question and Justice Powell's ripeness rationales, Rehnquist clearly applied a broader constitutional rule, that the constitutionality of the president's unilateral abrogation of a treaty can *never* be addressed by a federal court, than

---

[80]   *Goldwater v. Carter*, 444 U.S. 996, 996–97 (1979).

did Powell, who joined the judgment on the ground that *given the particular facts* in *Goldwater*, the legal action could *not yet* be decided. *Goldwater* v. *Carter* is therefore constitutional precedent that Article III authorizes the federal courts to entertain a challenge to the president's power to terminate a treaty unilaterally if the legislative branch has formally challenged a treaty termination ... and *Goldwater* is irrelevant to resolving the constitutional issue whether the Constitution-in-practice actually authorizes the president to do so since the Court's judgment did not address that issue. That question, the reader knows, must be answered in a future controversy by employing the doctrine Justice Jackson created in the Steel Seizure Case.[81]

When constitutional lawyers address the meaning and application of a constitutional precedent, they not only take into account the broad themes in an opinion but also its specific details as a document. This is obviously necessary when the opinion presents a doctrine in the sense discussed previously, since the very purpose of doctrine is to define with some precision the analysis to be applied in addressing a particular constitutional issue. But the practice of parsing the language of a Supreme Court opinion is not limited to precedents that announce doctrines: As a general matter, the Court's opinions play "a canonical role not unlike that played by the words in a statute" or in the written Constitution, and "in the lower courts, application of a pithy statement, a summary of a holding, or a three-part test [in a Supreme Court opinion] is likely to look very much like application of a statute. The language will be carefully analyzed, and discussions of why one word rather than another was used will be common," as if the opinion were part of the constitutional text.[82] Cases applying *United States* v. *Lopez* illustrate such discussion at a fine-grained level. Chief Justice Rehnquist's opinion grouped the Court's commerce clause decisions into three categories and provided citations to cases falling into each category. In applying *Lopez*, lower court judges have carefully scrutinized the language Rehnquist used in defining the categories, and also weighed the significance of which cases he cited under each.[83]

---

[81] *Marks* v. *United States*, 430 U.S. 188, 193 (1977). Applying the rule in *Marks* can be difficult, and on rare occasions may not appear to generate a rationale at all. See *Ramos* v. *Louisiana*, 140 S. Ct. 1390, 1403 (2020) (opinion of Gorsuch, J.) (concluding that an earlier decision "yielded no controlling opinion at all" and so was not amenable to analysis under *Marks*).

[82] Frederick Schauer, Opinions as Rules, 53 *U. Chi. L. Rev.* 682, 683 (1986).

[83] See, e.g., *United States* v. *MacEwan*, 445 F.3d 237, 246 & n. 8 (3d Cir. 2006) (concluding that the internet is both a channel and an instrumentality of interstate commerce while observing that "because the Internet is a worldwide communications system composed of an interconnected network of computers, data lines, routers, servers, and electronic signals, it is difficult to discern when the instrumentality component of *Lopez*'s Category Two ends and the channel component of *Lopez*'s Category One begins."); *United States* v. *Shahani-Jahromi*, 286 F. Supp. 2d 723, 735 n. 23 (E. D. Va. 2003) ("*Heart of Atlanta Motel* [a 1964 commerce clause decision] was decided long before the Supreme Court delineated the three permissible categories" of commerce clause legislation, but *Lopez*'s citation of *Heart of Atlanta* under the first category "implicitly sanction[s]" a particular understanding of its precedential force); *United States* v. *Cruz*, 2013 WL 3833033, at *5 (E.D. Cal. 2013) ("Defendant correctly notes that the *Heart of Atlanta* Motel and *Darby* cases, cited by the *Lopez*

On its face, scrutinizing the exact wording and even the placement of citations in Supreme Court opinions seems somewhat odd. After all, such opinions, including unanimous opinions of the Court written by Chief Justice John Marshall, are *not* "the Constitution" in the sense that the words of the 1787 text and its amendments are. Even the justices sometimes remind their readers (and themselves) that "the ultimate touchstone of constitutionality is the Constitution itself and not what we have said about it." As a warning against putting undue weight on the semantic features of a judicial opinion, this is good counsel for all constitutional lawyers, including the Court's members. The warning is especially valuable since the Court sometimes uses even what seem to be technical terms in casual or ambiguous ways. But given the role Supreme Court precedent plays in constitutional law, it is unavoidable and indeed necessary that constitutional lawyers parse the justices' language with special care. The Court's explications of constitutional law *are* the Constitution-in-practice, and the ultimate touchstone of constitutionality as long as they remain unchanged.[84]

Change and the authority of precedent. The reality that the Supreme Court's precedents *are* central to the Constitution-in-practice imbues constitutional law to some degree with a characteristic of the common law as modern lawyers understand the common law: Since the precedents are judge-made law, what the judges made they can unmake, or remake. It would be a gross exaggeration to push that expression too far. The weight of reasoning focused on the written Constitution, in addition to the principle of stare decisis, sharply limits the extent to which even the Court can break new ground, and the constraints on other constitutional law decision makers are still greater. The perception that the Court is unharnessed from authority that it must respect as a general matter stems from the public's (and many lawyers') understandable but misleading focus on the relatively small set of hot-button constitutional issues that are unsettled. But it nonetheless is true that the judicial power to say what the law of the Constitution is amounts in a real sense to the power to make constitutional law interstitially. As a result, the law of the Constitution-in-practice changes over time, as the justices confront new questions and revisit old answers.

The creation of precedent involves new and creative thought as does its modification, and both creation and modification are a reality in constitutional law even though we do not usually speak of the fact in terms of the Court changing the law. Recognition of this truth is not limited to those constitutional lawyers who, like Justice Oliver Holmes, are willing to say bluntly that "judges do and must legislate." Justice Antonin Scalia, a champion of close adherence to the written Constitution, authored one of the Court's clearest statements about the creative aspect of constitutional law reasoning:

'The judicial Power of the United States' conferred upon this Court and such inferior courts as Congress may establish, must be deemed to be the judicial

court as representative of category one, both upheld statutes that targeted economic conduct found to be injurious to interstate commerce").

[84] *Graves v. New York ex rel. O'Keefe*, 306 U.S. 466, 491–92 (1939) (Frankfurter, J., concurring).

power as understood by our common-law tradition. That is the power 'to say what the law is,' *Marbury* v. *Madison*, not the power to change it. I am not so naive (nor do I think our forebears were) as to be unaware that judges in a real sense 'make' law. But they make it *as judges make it*, which is to say *as though* they were 'finding' it – discerning what the law *is*, rather than decreeing what it is today *changed to*, or what it will *tomorrow* be.[85]

The realities that (a) constitutional rules and doctrines created by precedent are not simply restatements of the semantic contents of the written Constitution, and (b) over time the Supreme Court almost invariably finds it appropriate to change the original scope of a rule or doctrine in order to take into account considerations it did not at first recognize, do not change the character of the rule or doctrine as authoritative parts of the Constitution-in-practice. Lower courts must therefore follow these rules and doctrines, and the political branches cannot change or "overrule" them. The Court's already classic discussion is in *Dickerson* v. *United States* (2000), which addressed the status of the famous rule of *Miranda* v. *Arizona*, decided in 1966, that a confession cannot ordinarily be used in a criminal prosecution if the defendant did not receive the warnings about the right to remain silent and be given a lawyer familiar to anyone who has watched a police procedural on television or in the theater. In 1968, Congress enacted a statutory provision that purported to require federal courts to admit many confessions that violated *Miranda*, but the provision was often ignored, and of course had no application in that vast majority of the cases involving *Miranda* that arose in state courts. In *Dickerson*, a federal court of appeals, acting *sua sponte*, relied on the statute to admit a confession in violation of *Miranda*.[86]

---

[85] *James B. Beam Distilling Co.* v. *Georgia*, 501 U.S. 529, 549 (1991) (Scalia, J., concurring in the judgment) (*quoting Marbury* v. *Madison*, 5 U.S. (Cranch) 137, 177 (1803)) (emphases in original). Justice Holmes's words are quoted from a dissent in which, like Justice Scalia in *Beam Distilling*, Holmes carefully qualified the "legislative" aspect of judicial decision making: "I recognize without hesitation that judges do and must legislate, but they can do so only interstitially; they are confined from molar to molecular motions." *Southern Pacific Co.* v. *Jensen*, 244 U.S. 205, 221 (1917) (Holmes, J., dissenting).

[86] See *Dickerson* v. *United States*, 530 U.S. 428 (2000). Did the court of appeals violate the rule of vertical precedent in applying the statute rather than *Miranda*? Since the Supreme Court had never addressed the validity of the 1968 provision, one could argue that as a technical matter that issue was not foreclosed by high Court precedent. Not all technical arguments in law are *good* technical arguments, however, and I think this one is entirely unpersuasive. When the appeals court decided to consider the question whether the statute had abrogated *Miranda*, for thirty years the Supreme Court had consistently applied *Miranda* in reviewing state court decisions, an action beyond the Court's lawful authority unless *Miranda* was a constitutional decision. And no one would have argued that Congress had the power to overrule a Supreme Court decision enforcing the fifth amendment. *Cf. City of Boerne* v. *Flores*, 521 U.S. 507, 536 (1997) ("When the political branches of the Government act against the background of a judicial interpretation of the Constitution already issued, it must be understood that in later cases and controversies the Court will treat its precedents with the respect due them under settled principles, including *stare decisis*, and contrary expectations must be disappointed.").

Although the Justice Department declined to defend the 1968 statute in *Dickerson*, the Court entertained the question of its validity and held that it was an unconstitutional congressional attempt to overrule a Supreme Court precedent. *Miranda*, Chief Justice Rehnquist explained for the Court, was a constitutional decision: the opinion of the Court in *Miranda* was explicit on the matter, the reasons *Miranda* gave for the rule about the warnings were constitutional, and the Court would not have had the power to impose the rule on state courts if the rule had been not constitutional in status. In concluding that *Miranda* was *not* a constitutional rule, the appeals court had thought significant the existence of post-*Miranda* decisions cutting back on its scope; the Court responded that other decisions had expanded the situations to which *Miranda* applies, and that in any event constitutional precedent is subject to change.

> These decisions illustrate the principle – not that *Miranda* is not a constitutional rule – but that no constitutional rule is immutable. No court laying down a general rule can possibly foresee the various circumstances in which counsel will seek to apply it, and the sort of modifications represented by these cases are as much a normal part of constitutional law as the original decision.

It is inherent and in fact desirable, in a body of law that is continually built and adjusted over time by judicial decisions, that change in the operative rules will be "a normal part" of the law.[87]

As to the dissent's claim that the 1968 statute was binding unless "the *Miranda* warnings are required by the Constitution, in the sense that nothing else will suffice to satisfy constitutional requirements," Rehnquist answered that this argument misconceived the nature of constitutional rules or doctrines created by precedent. Such rules are not justified by their repetition of words from the written Constitution (which is never all they do) or because they are inexorable deductions from the text, but because they serve as a means of enforcing the requirements of the text. Of course, the words of the fifth amendment do not somehow contain the *Miranda* warnings if only you stare at them long enough, but the *Miranda* justices correctly held that the amendment requires "a procedure that is effective in securing" the privilege against self-incrimination, and concluded that the rule followed before *Miranda* was not fulfilling that genuinely constitutional demand. The rule requiring the warnings if a self-incriminatory statement is to be admissible in court was the means *Miranda* adopted for ensuring that the self-incrimination clause is law in practical reality. Creating such rules is one of the Supreme Court's chief

---

[87] *Dickerson*, 530 U.S. at 438–41. As Rehnquist explained, *Miranda* itself stated that the rationale for its warnings requirement was the need to ensure that courts can adequately enforce the self-incrimination clause, and acknowledged that the underlying constitutional requirement was "a procedure that is effective in securing Fifth Amendment rights" rather than that "the police administer the particular *Miranda* warnings." *Id.* at 440 n. 6. See *Miranda v. Arizona*, 384 U.S. 436, 467 (1966).

responsibilities, and a rule such as *Miranda* that proves workable is entitled to be given stare decisis effect.[88]

As *Dickerson* explained, *Miranda* as a precedent in 2000 was the basis for a "constitutional rule" that covered a somewhat different range of situations than would have appeared when the decision was first announced, in some ways sweeping more broadly and in others more narrowly than the Court's original discussion implied. But the constitutional concern that *Miranda* addressed, the need for an effective means of enforcing the self-incrimination clause, and the original means *Miranda* adopted, the requirement that the warnings be given if a confession is to be used, remain the same. In applying *Miranda* the precedent to new situations, the rationale – the holding in a basic sense – is unchanged, and the question is whether that rationale should govern the new circumstances. As Chief Justice Rehnquist observed, this is all "a normal part of constitutional law" and entirely consistent with *Miranda*'s ongoing status as a constitutional precedent.

At times however, the change in a precedent goes more deeply and reaches the rationale itself. This is a critical point and merits our consideration of an example at some length. In 1965, the Supreme Court held in *Griswold* v. *Connecticut* that a state law criminalizing the use of contraceptives could not be applied constitutionally to their use by a married couple. There were several separate opinions by justices who joined in the judgment, including notably an opinion by Justice John Marshall Harlan II, who thought that the decision should rest on the substantive due process analysis he had proposed in an earlier case about the same statute, *Poe* v. *Ullman* (1961). (The Court did not reach the merits in *Poe* for justiciability reasons.) The opinion of the Court in *Griswold* expressly rejected a due process rationale, however, and reasoned instead that the law violated a marital couple's "right of privacy," the existence of which the Court inferred from several different provisions in the Bill of Rights. Most 1965 readers would have had little doubt that the right recognized in *Griswold* was specifically linked to marriage, which the Court lauded as "an association for as noble a purpose as any involved in our prior decisions."[89]

From the beginning, however, the Court's opinion was vulnerable to criticism both for its odd rhetoric – the opinion asserted that "specific guarantees in the Bill of Rights have penumbras, formed by emanations from those guarantees" – and for its unconvincing attempt to distinguish its reasoning from substantive due process. As one of the *Griswold* dissenters wrote later, conceding that the decision had become precedent: "[I]t was clear to me then, and it is equally clear to me now, that the *Griswold* decision can be rationally understood only" on substantive due process grounds, not the Bill of Rights rationale the Court ostensibly invoked. In *Eisenstadt*

---

[88] *Dickerson*, 430 U.S. at 442, responding to *id.* at 452–54 (Scalia, J., dissenting). The Court's application of stare decisis to *Miranda* is in *id.* at 443–44.

[89] 381 U.S. 479, 486 (1965). A few years later, a student note correctly observed that "all the opinions [in *Griswold*] carefully limit the scope of the decision to the marital bed." Note, Hallucinogens, 68 *Colum. L. Rev.* 521, 552 (1968). See also *Poe v. Ullman*, 367 U.S. 497 (1961).

v. *Baird* (1972), furthermore, the Court extended the rule in *Griswold* to protect *unmarried* persons' access to contraceptives, asserting that "if the right of privacy means anything, it is the right of the individual, married or single, to be free from unwarranted governmental intrusion into matters." *Eisenstadt's* casual assertion that the right protected in *Griswold* necessarily extended to unmarried persons if it was "to mean anything" was a striking non sequitur in a legal tradition that has always accorded marriage a special legal status. It also effectively eliminated the marriage-centered reasoning in the 1965 *Griswold* opinion of the Court from future consideration as the rationale for *Griswold* as precedent.[90]

After *Eisenstadt*, *Griswold* no longer had any clear rationale despite the fact that it was now clearly more than a narrow rule based on the unique constitutional status of marriage. But constitutional law, like its parent the common law, cannot tolerate for long a precedent that lacks reasoned content and yet does not fade away. The Supreme Court's duty to explicate the principles governing constitutional law rather than simply announce conclusions quickly led individual justices to the conclusion that Justice Harlan's dissent in *Poe* provided the most satisfactory intellectual basis for *Griswold* as a precedent. In 1992, the Court formally recognized *Griswold* as a substantive due process decision and Harlan's reasoning as its rationale. Much more recently, in holding that due process prohibits laws limiting the right to marry to opposite-sex couples, *Obergefell* v. *Hodges* (2015) quoted the description of marriage in the *Griswold* opinion of the Court, but it cited Justice Harlan's dissent in *Poe* as authority for its approach to substantive due process reasoning and for "the basic reasons why the right to marry has been long protected." *Griswold* as precedent now has very little overlap with what the Court in *Griswold* originally said.[91]

The transformation of *Griswold* v. *Connecticut* into a leading substantive due process precedent with a much broader sweep than a right of privacy protecting martial intimacy is somewhat more dramatic than the norm, but it illustrates a crucial point about precedents that a constitutional lawyer must take into account. The meaning and scope of a precedent are always determined by how the Supreme Court *now* understands the case, and subsequent decisions may significantly change the original controlling rationale. The rationale for which the case stands is, after all, what the precedent actually amounts to *as authority* in constitutional argument. The original decision's facts and reasoning do not disappear, of course, and can play a role in debate on the Supreme Court about how to understand and apply the

---

[90] *Griswold*, 381 U.S. at 384; *Roe* v. *Wade*, 410 U.S. 113, 167–68 (1973) (Stewart, J., concurring); *Eisenstadt* v. *Baird*, 405 U.S. 438, 453 (1972).

[91] See *Moore* v. *City of East Cleveland*, 431 U.S. 494, 499, 501–04 (1977) (plurality opinion of Powell, J.); *id.* at 542–45 (White, J., dissenting); *Planned Parenthood* v. *Casey*, 505 U.S. 833, 848–50 (1992); *Obergefell* v. *Hodges*, 576 U.S. 644, 666–67 (2015) (quoting *Griswold*, 381 U.S. at 486), *id.* at 663–65 (citing the *Poe* dissent). See also *id.* at 701–02 (Roberts, C.J., dissenting) (noting that "the majority . . . relies on Justice Harlan's influential dissenting opinion in *Poe* v. *Ullman*" while asserting that Harlan's reasoning did not support the majority's approach).

precedent, but that too is always a debate about present-day constitutional law rather than a discussion of the case's original meaning for its own sake.

In *Washington v. Glucksberg* (1997), for example, Chief Justice Rehnquist described *Griswold* as a case about "marital privacy" and challenged the authority of the *Poe* dissent. In rebuttal, Justice Souter treated *Griswold* as one in a long line of cases on various matters, all of which should be understood to rest on "the modern justification for such judicial review found in Justice Harlan's dissent in *Poe*." But Rehnquist's argument was an interpretation of how *Griswold* as a reconfigured substantive due process precedent should be understood, not a call for a return to the reasoning of the original *Griswold* opinion of the Court, an opinion that abjured substantive due process. And as already noted, the Court's 2015 decision in *Obergefell v. Hodges* adhered to the understanding of *Griswold* as precedent that incorporates Harlan's reasoning in *Poe*.[92]

Constitutional precedent is central to the governing law of the Constitution-in-practice, and neither the fact that it goes beyond the letter of the written instrument nor the fact that it has a history in which change plays a normal part renders precedent-based reasoning illegitimate, or inconsistent with the existence of a written Constitution that does not change except rarely and through a nonjudicial process. The self-incrimination clause's wording has not changed since the fifth amendment was adopted in 1791, but the precedents have which ensure its efficacy as law by defining its operative meaning. That the practice of constitutional law is an historical tradition that involves change in its operative rules of law is no new discovery. In *Davidson v. New Orleans* (1877), for example, the Court defended the propriety of "ascertaining ... the intent and application" of the due process clause of the fourteenth amendment "by the gradual process of judicial inclusion and exclusion, as the cases presented for decision shall require, with the reasoning on which such decisions may be founded." The Court suggested that the process of building constitutional law over time through precedent is an open-ended one. "This court is, after an experience of nearly a century, still engaged in defining the obligation of contracts, the regulation of commerce, and other powers conferred on the Federal government, or limitations imposed upon the States." Argument from precedent reflects the American choice, from the beginning, to give legal efficacy to the written Constitution through the flexible tool of common law-like argument from precedent: "constitutional provisions ... acquire[] substance and meaning when explained, elaborated, and enforced in the context of actual disputes."[93]

Overruling Precedent. Change in the law may occur not only through the application or modification of precedent but also through the repudiation of

---

[92]   *Washington v. Glucksberg*, 521 U.S. 702, 720, 721–22 & n. 17, 727 n. 19 (1997); *id.* at 756 & n.4 (Souter, J., concurring in the judgment).

[93]   *Davidson v. New Orleans*, 96 U.S. 97, 104 (1877); *Arizona Christian Sch. Tuition Org. v. Winn*, 563 U.S. 125, 145 (2011).

precedent. American courts have always claimed the authority to overrule their own precedents, and stare decisis thus is not an inexorable command. The official rule in the federal system, however, is that there is a strong presumption against the Supreme Court overruling a precedent. The Court has asserted, for example, that "precedent is to be respected unless the most convincing of reasons demonstrates that adherence to it puts us on a course that is sure error." A conviction that the precedent was wrongly decided is necessary (obviously) but not sufficient to the conclusion that there is a convincing reason to overrule the decision, since the very point of obeying stare decisis is to preclude, or at least avoid ordinarily, reconsidering precedents on their merits. "Respecting *stare decisis* means sticking to some wrong decisions. ... Indeed, *stare decisis* has consequence only to the extent it sustains incorrect decisions; correct judgments have no need for that principle to prop them up." Different opinions propose slightly varying lists of what reasons support or counsel against adherence to a decision. In general, a decision to overrule erroneous precedent might be appropriate if there is experience showing that the decision is unworkable, in the sense that the lower courts are unable to apply it consistently or its application interferes with other, legitimate interests. Similarly, changes in related areas of law or in the Court's perception of the facts may indicate that the precedent is "no more than a remnant of abandoned doctrine" or no longer has "significant application or justification" in light of the facts as now understood.[94]

We began our examination of argument from precedent with the observation that this mode of reasoning is both the most important in terms of the actual practice of constitutional law, and a form of argument that can seem remote from the written Constitution. As the discussion has shown, however, the fear or accusation that Supreme Court decisions based on precedent-based reasoning are simply "legislating from the bench" is an overblown and imprecise description of this mode of constitutional law argument. The precedents themselves are constructed out of materials from other forms of argument and, taken as a whole and with individual exceptions, the Supreme Court's decisions are the record of a sustained and ongoing effort to be faithful to the written Constitution and to the principles that inform it while enabling constitutional lawyers and judges to address specific constitutional problems that the letter of the written instrument cannot resolve. We shall return to the arguments over the legitimacy of the practice of constitutional law in the conclusion, but when we do the reader should keep in mind the many indications we have seen that the Constitution-in-practice is, the occasional lapse notwithstanding, the product of disciplined legal thought in service of the written Constitution.

---

[94]   *Citizens United v. Fed. Election Comm'n*, 558 U.S. 310, 362 (2010); *Kimble v. Marvel Entertainment*, 576 U.S. 446, 455 (2015); *Planned Parenthood v. Casey*, 505 U.S. 833, 855 (1992).

4

Solving Constitutional Problems

The Importance of Institutional Perspective

Judicial review is central to the Constitution-in-practice, and in the American system of vertical precedent this necessarily gives the Supreme Court, because it is the final voice in the primary American process of articulating constitutional law, the most important role in solving constitutional problems. It does not follow, however, that all constitutional questions are to be answered by the Supreme Court or that all constitutional answers are the ones that a majority of the justices think are correct *in the abstract*. The practice of constitutional law involves a web of principles, doctrines, and practices that make the perspective from which one is addressing a question a significant factor, much of the time, in the reasoning the constitutional lawyer should employ. The "judicial Power" exercised by the federal courts does not extend to all constitutional issues in principle or in practice, and the courts impose rules on their resolution of cases within their reach that limit the extent to which they may set aside political actions or that structure their response to an invalid law. The executive branch, which has a tradition of answering constitutional questions through formal legal opinions that is slightly older than the Supreme Court's, observes its own set of norms. Congress, which has no such tradition, has its own practices of embedding views on constitutional meaning into the process and products of lawmaking. In this chapter, we shall review the ways in which institutional perspective influences the shape of the questions and the answers that make up constitutional law.

4.1 THE CONSTITUTIONAL PERSPECTIVE FROM WITHIN THE FEDERAL COURTS

The perspective on constitutional problems that shapes constitutional reasoning in the federal courts is informed by two principles. First, the Article III judiciary is limited to actions authorized by Article III, and second, the ordinary means by which the American political community governs itself is not by federal court adjudication but through decisions by elected officials and those answerable to them. With minor exceptions, the "judicial Power of the United States" extends only to the resolution of legal disputes between particular parties, and as we saw in Chapter 1, the power of American courts to review the constitutionality of the actions of other parts of American government is a by-product of their duty to decide the cases before them according to law, including the law of the Constitution. None of this takes away from the centrality of judicial review or the finality of Supreme Court decisions in the Constitution-in-practice. But it does mean that the federal court perspective transforms what could be stated as an abstract inquiry about constitutional meaning into a concrete question about how to resolve a legal issue raised by a case within the court's power to decide. Equally, the perspective from within the federal courts demands that constitutional answers take into account the everyday priority of democratic governance by the political branches of the federal government and by the states.

Article III Limitations. Fundamental to the federal courts' perspective is the judiciary's duty to ensure its own compliance with the enumeration principle: Like the rest of the federal government, the federal courts can act lawfully only within the bounds of the authority the Constitution grants them. The rules of justiciability – the doctrines the Supreme Court has developed to enable the federal courts to limit themselves to the written Constitution's grant of power to decide "Cases" and "Controversies" – are gatekeepers that prevent the courts from deciding any aspect of a controversy (including any constitutional dimensions) if the conflict does not take the shape of a case within the scope of the Article III grant of "judicial Power." But in doing so, justiciability rules influence the content of constitutional law from the federal courts' perspective. An example will be helpful.[1]

One of the justiciability requirements is that in order to sue in federal court, a plaintiff must have "standing," that is, allege a particular injury to the plaintiff's individual and legally protected interests. The Court's decisions indicate that with rare exceptions, members of Congress and the president lack standing to sue officials of the other political branch over alleged violations of the Constitution, including violations of the president's constitutional duty to take care that acts of Congress are faithfully executed. Because the Court has also consistently held that private plaintiffs lack standing if the injury they assert is "only a generally available grievance about government – claiming only harm to ... every citizen's interest in proper application of the Constitution and laws," the result is to leave some constitutional principles and provisions beyond federal court enforcement.[2]

In *Schlesinger* v. *Reservists Committee* (1974), the plaintiffs sued the civilian leadership of the Defense Department, claiming that certain members of

---

[1] By the text of Article III and in accordance with the presupposition of constitutional law about the states' autonomy in arranging their governmental structures, "the state courts are not bound by the limitations of a case or controversy or other federal rules of justiciability even when they address issues of federal law." *ASARCO Inc.* v. *Kadish*, 490 U.S. 605, 617 (1989).

[2] *Lujan* v. *Defenders of Wildlife*, 504 U.S. 555, 573 (1992).

Congress were ineligible to serve in the legislature because they continued to hold reserve commissions as US military officers in violation of the Article I section 6 incompatibility clause ("no Person holding any Office under the United States shall be a Member of either House during his Continuance in Office"). They argued that they had standing to sue as citizens because "citizens were meant to be protected by the Incompatibility Clause," and thus they were injured by the defendants' failure to enforce the clause by discharging sitting members of Congress from the reserves. The Court held that the case was nonjusticiable for lack of standing: "every provision of the Constitution was meant to serve the interests of all [but such] a generalized interest . . . is too abstract to constitute a case or controversy." The possibility that in that event no one could sue to enforce the clause did not change the analysis. "The assumption that if [plaintiffs] have no standing to sue, no one would have standing, is not a reason to find standing."[3]

The outcome in *Schlesinger* left the constitutional question in the case – does the presence in Congress of members with reserve commissions violate Article I section 6? – unanswered and indeed unanswerable by the federal courts except perhaps in the unlikely event that the Defense Department discharged a reservist-member over objection. It is difficult, to be sure, to see much danger of executive branch self-aggrandizement in a few military reservists sitting in Congress. But the practical efficacy of the principle of asymmetry between the legislative and executive branches and of other limitations on presidential authority is obviously affected on more important matters by executive freedom from judicial review. In some extremely important areas of presidential responsibility, especially foreign affairs and military matters, it is often the case that no one will have standing to sue even though the executive's actions give rise to serious constitutional questions.

The practical consequences of the standing doctrine's limitation on federal court review are not all one-sided: Self-aggrandizement is not a constitutional vice limited to the executive branch. A subtler but more far-reaching issue, however, stems from standing doctrine's conceptual effect on the Constitution-in-practice. In areas where constitutional problems do not usually produce plaintiffs with standing, arguments from judicial precedent often can play only a small role. The answers to many constitutional questions about the president's authority to initiate military conflict, for example, are less than clear in part because standing has precluded most challenges to unilateral presidential action. From the federal court perspective, the constitutional law of war and peace is largely invisible, and the paucity of Supreme Court precedent makes it more difficult for legislative and executive branch legal advisors to give sound advice. Short-sighted policy makers may welcome their lawyers' inability on occasion to assert limitations rooted in the high Court's decisions but the risk that genuine limitations will therefore be under-enforced is obvious.

---

[3] *Schlesinger v. Reservists Committee to Stop the War*, 418 U.S. 208, 226–27 (1974).

None of this is meant to suggest that the Supreme Court's standing decisions are fundamentally wrong. The Supreme Court has consistently explained that the purpose of each of the justiciability doctrines is to give meaning to Article III's statement that "The judicial Power shall extend to . . . Cases [and] Controversies." From the beginning, the Court has understood this to mean that Article III's grant to the federal courts of "The judicial Power of the United States" is the authority to adjudicate lawsuits "of the sort traditionally amenable to, and resolved by, the judicial process." That definition, in turn, flows directly from the wording of Article III, which the Court has interpreted not simply by relying on the ordinary understanding of "cases" and "controversies" but on the basis of structural considerations ("the Constitution's central mechanism of separation of powers depends largely upon common understanding of what activities are appropriate to legislatures, to executives, and to courts") and an argument from original meaning (Article III's language limits the "judicial Power" to "matters that were the traditional concern of the courts at Westminster and only if they arose in ways that to the expert feel of lawyers constituted 'Cases' or 'Controversies'").[4]

The separation of powers rationale makes the definition a two-way street. Congress cannot confer on other federal entities the Article III power to decide issues involving private rights of property, contract, and the like over which the eighteenth-century royal courts exercised jurisdiction, although federal courts may adjudicate cases involving "public rights" if Congress chooses and the case is justiciable. The justiciability doctrines thus ensure that all federal court litigation resembles in procedural form an action at common law or suit in equity, and exclude from the purview of the Article III courts issues that can only be addressed through forms of reasoning with no analogy in traditional Anglo-American legal thought, and at the same time ensure that controversies over private rights are decided by Article III courts if they come before any federal tribunal.[5]

While the basic concept of justiciability is quite straightforward, the law of justiciability is extremely complex. To put a long and demanding course into a grossly over-simplified outline: Federal courts cannot issue advisory opinions on questions of law at the request of Congress, the president, or anyone else (some state high courts have an advisory opinion power), and so they cannot decide nonadversarial or "friendly" cases in which the parties are not truly opposed but would like the judiciary to settle some question of law. The party that initiates a federal action must have "standing" and plead a judicially cognizable "cause of action," and the action must be "ripe" (not hypothetical or premature, but a legal disagreement on present

---

[4]   The first two quotations in the preceding paragraph are from *Steel Co.* v. *Citizens for a Better Env't*, 523 U.S. 83, 102 (1998), and third is an often-quoted observation of Justice Felix Frankfurter. See *Vermont Agency of Nat. Res.* v. *U.S. ex rel. Stevens*, 529 U.S. 765, 774 (2000) (quoting *Coleman* v. *Miller*, 307 U.S. 433, 460 (1939) (opinion of Frankfurter, J.)).

[5]   See also *Oil States Energy Servs.* v. *Greene's Energy Grp.*, 138 S. Ct. 1365, 1372–73 (2018) (private/public rights distinction).

facts). The action cannot be "moot" (the legal disagreement must be ongoing) and it cannot ask the court to decide a "political question."[6]

Some critics of the justiciability doctrines, at least as they currently are stated and applied, argue that the doctrines are too pliable and in particular that they invite the courts to dismiss as nonjusticiable cases that the judges would rather avoid deciding on the merits. Other critics insist that the doctrines create practical obstacles to the Supreme Court's fulfillment of its vital role in overseeing the coherence and consistency of federal law, including constitutional law. Both lines of criticism probably have some basis in fact, but in the end neither demonstrates that the doctrines are fundamentally flawed. As to the first, any legal rule or principle can be misapplied (inadvertently or otherwise), and as to the second, it will surprise no reader of this book to find, once again, that the Constitution-in-practice contains principles and doctrines that cut against one another and thus interfere with the full accomplishment of either.

In application, the justiciability doctrines (except for the political question doctrine) include what the Supreme Court terms a "prudential" aspect – limitations on the exercise of the judicial power that are not mandated by Article III but that the Court deems appropriate in order to preserve the federal courts' role as dispute-resolution adjudicators rather than forums for political or policy dispute. Prudential limitations, "unlike their constitutional counterparts, . . . can be modified or abrogated by Congress." The Court has also developed a parallel set of "abstention doctrines" that limit federal court intrusion into state court systems: These doctrines "may, in various circumstances, permit or require the federal court to stay or dismiss the federal action in favor of the state-court litigation." Finally, federal courts have also traditionally exercised authority over certain nonadversarial or ex parte matters that cannot easily be explained in terms of the case or controversy requirement. The justification for these otherwise anomalous instances of "non-contentious jurisdiction" lies in their long-standing existence (an argument from political and judicial practice), and in their combination of practical value and limited scope. (The Constitution is an instrument of practical governance!)[7]

Two of the usual justiciability requirements merit additional comment in this context. As discussed previously when we considered the *Schlesinger* case, standing is the requirement that in order for a federal court to exercise jurisdiction over a controversy, the party that files suit must be someone who can properly assert a legal claim that the court has the constitutional authority to decide. The standing

---

[6] It is possible for a plaintiff to have a cause of action (be able to plead a legal harm) and yet not have standing because he or she cannot plead any actual injury. See *Thole* v. *U.S. Bank N.A*, 140 S. Ct. 1615, 1620–21 (2020) (plaintiffs' cause of action was expressly created by statute but they lacked standing because they could not plausibly plead any concrete injury).

[7] For these points, see, respectively, *Bennett* v. *Spear*, 520 U.S. 154, 162 (1997); *Exxon Mobil Corp.* v. *Saudi Basic Indus. Corp.*, 544 U.S. 280, 292 (2005); and James E. Pfander & David D. Birk, Article III Judicial Power, the Adverse-Party Requirement, and Non-Contentious Jurisdiction, 124 *Yale L.J.* 1346 (2015).

requirement must also "be met by persons seeking appellate review, just as it must be met by persons appearing in courts of first instance." At its historical core, standing serves the goal of limiting the federal courts to cases in which the plaintiff has a genuine, personal grievance with the defendant analogous to a claim for damages based on tort or breach of contract. However, standing doctrine now includes broader themes that supplement the requirement of a grievance with additional, overlapping requirements that relate to the substance of the plaintiff's claim: "The standing inquiry ... often turns on the nature and source of the claim asserted. ... We have also stressed that the alleged injury must be legally and judicially cognizable. This requires, among other things, that the plaintiff have suffered an invasion of a legally protected interest ... [that is not] too abstract, or otherwise not appropriate, to be considered judicially cognizable." Standing doctrine thus plays a critical role in limiting judicial review to situations in which the federal courts are asked to resolve practical disagreements rather than exercise an "amorphous general supervision of the operations of government."[8]

Another aspect of justiciability is the political question doctrine. "The doctrine ... is one of 'political questions,' not one of 'political cases,'" and the mere fact that there is a political aspect to a lawsuit does not put it outside the Article III power. A political question, in the constitutional sense, is an issue of constitutional law that the federal courts cannot address because of its substance, even if there is a plaintiff who meets the other justiciability requirements. At first glance, the idea seems odd: How can there be questions of *law* that can't be answered by the branch of government that has as its "province and duty ... to say what the law is"? The explanation, as with the rest of the justiciability doctrines, lies in the enumeration principle. Article III vests the general power in the federal courts to articulate the law (including constitutional law) in the course of deciding cases, and to set aside contrary judgments about the law reached by the legislative and executive branches. But the written Constitution at times vests exclusive power to decide specific questions of constitutional law in the political branches, and when it does, Article III does not authorize the courts to resolve those questions.[9]

Nixon v. United States (1993) is a rare example of such "a textually demonstrable constitutional commitment of the issue to a coordinate political department." The question in *Nixon* was whether the Senate had violated Article I section 3 by appointing a committee of senators to receive evidence in an impeachment trial rather than doing so in plenary meetings of the Senate. A former judge who was convicted through that process argued that the constitutional text specified that the "*Senate* [not

---

[8]   *Seila Law LLC* v. *Consumer Fin. Prot. Bureau*, 140 S. Ct. 2183, 2195 (2020); *Raines* v. *Byrd*, 521 U.S. 811, 818–19, 829 (1997).

[9]   *Baker* v. *Carr*, 369 U.S. 186, 217 (1962); *Marbury* v. *Madison*, 5 U.S. (1 Cranch) 137, 177 (1803). As discussed below, the modern Supreme Court's decisions identify a second category of political questions, legal questions that cannot be answered using "judicially discoverable and manageable standards." *Baker*, 369 U.S. at 217.

a committee] shall have the sole Power to *try* all Impeachments," and that the reception of evidence is a crucial part of any trial. The Supreme Court held that the question of what counts as an impeachment trial under Article I section 3 is textually committed to the Senate, pointing to the wording of the clause (the Senate enjoys "the *sole* Power" over the trial), the vagueness of the word "try," and the structural problem that would be created by federal courts sitting in judgment on the process by which the legislative branch can remove federal judges. The Court concluded, therefore, that the federal courts were not authorized to answer the dispositive constitutional question in the former judge's suit but could only dismiss his complaint.[10]

A critical aspect of the political question doctrine is what it does *not* mean. The doctrine, as is obvious from the *Nixon* case, does not preclude the courts from interpreting the provision of the constitutional text in question and determining "whether and to what extent the issue is textually committed" to another branch: Whether an issue of constitutional law involves a political question "is itself a delicate exercise in constitutional interpretation, and ... a responsibility of [the Supreme] Court as ultimate interpreter of the Constitution." A decision by the Court that a constitutional claim is a political question, furthermore, is not a substantive ruling in favor of the party resisting the claim. *Nixon v. United States* did not uphold the constitutionality of the Senate's evidentiary committee procedure, and the defendant in a future impeachment trial should be able to challenge application of the same procedure, presumably by motion presented to the officer presiding over the Senate, without *Nixon* weighing against his or her challenge at all as a matter of law.[11]

It is important to realize that *Nixon* did not deny that the question it held nonjusticiable was a genuine issue of constitutional law. Indeed, the question "does X senatorial process satisfy the Senate's constitutional duty in trying an impeachment?" is self-evidently a question of constitutional law. Stated precisely, it is the question whether X is within the power that Article I section 3 authorizes the Senate to exercise, and of course it is a bedrock principle that the Senate, like all the rest of the federal government, cannot lawfully take any action that it is not constitutionally authorized to take. To say that the substantive question in *Nixon* is not a constitutional one is to misunderstand the logic of constitutional law. To be sure, the opinion of the Court in *Nixon* also doubted the existence of "judicially discoverable and manageable standards" for deciding the case, but two concurring justices took sharp issue with that argument. In any event, as the reader knows, it is an axiomatic assumption of the Constitution-in-practice that any genuine constitutional law question has a constitutional law answer, even in situations where discerning the right answer is difficult and any proposal is likely to be hotly contested.[12]

---

[10]   *Nixon v. United States*, 506 U.S. 224, 228 (1993).
[11]   *Id.* at 228, 238.
[12]   *Compare id.* at 230 ("the word 'try' in the first sentence of the Impeachment Trial Clause lacks sufficient precision to afford any judicially manageable standard of review of the Senate's actions")

In addition to the rare situations in which the written Constitution gives exclusive authority to answer a question of constitutional law to another branch of government, the Supreme Court's cases state that a federal lawsuit contains a political question in the even rarer circumstance where there are no "judicially discoverable and manageable standards for resolving" a constitutional law issue it presents. The basic idea underlying this second prong of the political question doctrine is clear. A federal court can only resolve a constitutional problem through constitutional law reasoning, employing the twofold logic of authorizations and prohibitions to identify the questions, and the accepted forms of argument derived from the written Constitution and from precedent to identify persuasive answers. If the court would be driven outside the limits of legal reasoning to give an answer, or would be forced to announce its decision in conclusory terms – the law requiring widgets to be green is (or isn't) fair and therefore it isn't (or is) unconstitutional – the court would have left the domain of law for some other realm of discourse. Its answer might well make sense (the idea of fairness is not empty) but it would not be an answer of constitutional law and, if a Supreme Court decision, could not serve as a precedent providing meaningful guidance for later courts and controversies.

It is not clear that the "no-manageable-standards" version of the political question doctrine is much more than a theoretical possibility. The Court invoked the idea in *Nixon v. United States*, but the core holding in that case was that the written Constitution commits the resolution of the constitutional issue in question to the Senate. As the reader has seen, constitutional law reasoning in the American tradition is characterized by its extraordinary capacity to enable constitutional lawyers – on and off a court – to resolve constitutional problems by identifying the issues of authorization and prohibition they present and providing persuasive answers based on legal arguments to the questions raised. On occasion, to be sure, someone files a federal lawsuit that cloaks a sheerly political disagreement in constitutional terminology. The issue before the Supreme Court in *Gilligan v. Morgan* (1973), for example, was whether a state national guard's "pattern of training, weaponry and order" led inevitably to the unnecessary use of lethal force when the guard was engaged "in suppressing civilian disorders." That issue was clearly not justiciable, as the Court held, for the simple reason that it was not a question of constitutional law at all but a political question in the nontechnical sense, a question about the wisdom of political decisions.[13]

The modern Supreme Court, in fact, has relied exclusively on the "no-manageable-standards" idea to dismiss a true constitutional law question in only a single decision, *Rucho v. Common Cause* (2019). In *Rucho*, the Court agreed that the substantive issue

with *id.* at 248 (White, J., concurring in the judgment). ("The majority's conclusion that 'try' is incapable of meaningful judicial construction is not without irony. One might think that if any class of concepts would fall within the definitional abilities of the Judiciary, it would be that class having to do with procedural justice.")

[13] *Nixon v. United States*, 506 U.S. 224, 228–29 (1993) ("the lack of judicially manageable standards may strengthen the conclusion that there is a textually demonstrable commitment to a coordinate branch"); *Gilligan v. Morgan*, 413 U.S. 1, 4 (1973).

before it (whether partisan gerrymandering can violate the first amendment or the equal protection clause) was "an important question of constitutional law," and that severe partisan gerrymandering is "incompatible with democratic principles," but concluded that there are "no legal standards to limit and direct" federal courts in determining an allegedly unconstitutional gerrymander's validity. The dissenters vigorously contested that conclusion, and the underlying explanation of *Rucho* may be that it rested more on concern about involving "the unelected and politically unaccountable branch of the Federal Government" in an especially political and partisan aspect of state legislation. As originally formulated by the modern Court, the political question doctrine included as nonjusticiable "circumstances in which prudence may counsel against a court's resolution of an issue presented" as presenting a political question, but the Supreme Court's current view appears to limit the doctrine's formal reach to "textual-commitment" and "no-manageable-standards" cases, thus precluding *Rucho* from directly relying on prudential considerations.[14]

For the purposes of this book, the no-manageable-standards idea is less a significant part of the Constitution-in-practice – except of course as a rule currently barring federal court challenges to political gerrymanders – than as a reminder that the constitutional perspective from within the federal courts involves a rigorous commitment to legal reasoning as critical to resolving constitutional problems.[15]

The conclusion that a constitutional issue is a political question does not mean that the political branch in a position to act is free to do whatever it chooses without regard to constitutional concerns. "Rather, the issue in the political question doctrine is . . . whether the Constitution has given one of the political branches final responsibility for interpreting the scope and nature of [a specific] power." The "claim of unlawfulness" does not disappear when the federal courts determine that the claim involves a political question; instead, its resolution "is entrusted to one of the political branches." As we shall see later in this chapter, both the executive branch and Congress have a duty to answer constitutional questions – and act on the answers – when constitutional issues arise in the exercise of their functions. By making a political branch's constitutional answer final, the political question doctrine makes that duty, if anything, even more imperative. The absence of "judicial scrutiny or intervention . . . does not mean [political] officials are free to disregard the Constitution and the rights it proclaims and protects. The oath that all officials take to adhere to the Constitution is not confined to those spheres in which the Judiciary can correct or even comment upon what those officials say or do." The

---

[14]   *Rucho v. Common Cause*, 139 S. Ct. 2484, 2494 (2019).

[15]   *Rucho*, 139 S. Ct. at 2494, 2506, 2507. In *Vieth v. Jubelirer*, 541 U.S. 267 (2004), a four-justice plurality dismissed a political gerrymandering lawsuit on political question grounds, but the reasoning of the crucial fifth justice is better read as a conclusion that the particular challengers had failed to make a persuasive argument. See *id.* at 306 (Kennedy, J., concurring in the judgment). See also *Zivotofsky v. Clinton*, 566 U.S. 189, 204–07 (2012) (Sotomayor, J. concurring in the judgment) (arguing that the political question doctrine should include a prudential prong).

Constitution-in-practice, the Constitution as the law governing government, leaves no aspect of government outside its authority, even if it sometimes requires a political branch to serve as the ultimate mechanism for enforcing a constitutional norm.[16]

The Priority of Democratic Governance. The judicially enforceable constitutional commitments of the American political community supersede conflicting everyday decisions of its legislatures and executives, but one of the most basic of those commitments is that American government's ordinary mode of governance is through democratically elected officials, and those responsible to them. The perspective on constitutional law from within the federal courts reflects the norm of democratic governance by modulating the extent to which the courts are obliged to displace democratic choice by judicial enforcement of other constitutional commitments.

At the most basic level of constitutional authorization, democratic politics takes priority over judicial decision through the limitations on federal court jurisdiction. The text of Article III defines the outer range of the federal courts' authority, but except for the Supreme Court's original jurisdiction, Article III does not actually confer the power to decide cases on any federal court. The structure, jurisdiction, and very existence of the lower federal courts rest on a statutory basis. The Supreme Court's appellate jurisdiction, the means by which the Court carries out its unique role in the articulation of constitutional law, is subject to "such Exceptions, and under such Regulations as the Congress shall make." The Constitution "most assuredly envisions a role for all three branches when individual liberties are at stake," but in certain circumstances Congress may suspend the power of the federal courts to issue writs of habeas corpus to inquire into the lawfulness of an individual's detention. The federal courts limit political restrictions on their ability to carry out their function to those restrictions permitted by the Constitution, but the existence of the restrictions is a presupposition of the federal courts' constitutional perspective that situates the courts' exercise of judicial review in a framework largely the product of congressional choice.[17]

---

[16] *Nixon*, 506 U.S. at 240 (White, J., concurring in the judgment); *Vieth*, 541 U.S. at 277 (plurality opinion of Scalia, J.); *Trump v. Hawaii*, 138 S. Ct. 2392, 2424 (2018) (Kennedy, J., concurring). Justice Kennedy had immediately in mind situations where the courts' standard of review is highly deferential, but his comments apply even more fully to issues that fall within the political question doctrine.

[17] *Hamdi v. Rumsfeld*, 542 U.S. 507, 536 (2004) (plurality opinion of O'Connor, J.). See *Boumediene v. Bush*, 553 U.S. 723, 733 (2008) (statute divesting federal courts of jurisdiction over certain claims for habeas corpus relief "operates as an unconstitutional suspension of the writ"). Congress may divest the federal courts of jurisdiction over ongoing litigation and enact new substantive law that the courts must apply instead of the law as it stood at the onset of the litigation, but Article III forbids some forms of legislative interference with the courts' decisional processes: Congress cannot order the courts to reopen final judgments or direct that "in 'Smith v. Jones,' 'Smith wins.' Such a statute would create no new substantive law; it would instead direct the court how pre-existing law applies to particular circumstances." *Bank Markazi v. Peterson*, 578 U.S. 212, 225 n.17 (2016).

From a very early point, the Supreme Court has consistently asserted that the federal courts have a duty to avoid deciding a case on constitutional grounds if another basis for its resolution is fairly available. The Court often discusses this duty in terms of "the constitutional decision-avoidance principles articulated by Mr. Justice Brandeis in *Ashwander v. Tennessee Valley Authority.*" The *Ashwander* principles supposedly require a federal court not only to seek a nonconstitutional basis for decision if possible, but also to give as narrow an answer as possible if a constitutional question is unavoidable: The federal "courts should neither 'anticipate a question of constitutional law in advance of the necessity of deciding it' nor 'formulate a rule of constitutional law broader than is required by the precise facts to which it is to be applied.'" And the duty to avoid unnecessary constitutional law decisions is closely linked to the presumption of constitutionality the Court purports (most of the time) to attach to statutes. The presumption ostensibly tips the judicial balance in favor of upholding the political decision to enact the law.[18]

The reader may sense a certain skepticism in the previous paragraph. There is, in reality, a long list of constitutional decisions in which the Court did not strictly observe a duty to minimize constitutional decision making, and the presumption of constitutionality often seems remarkably weak. But this does not make the presumption or the *Ashwander* principles – or the related preference for as-applied rather than facial challenges to statutes and policies discussed in Chapter 3 – meaningless. Together they reflect the Court's long-standing awareness that the preservation of constitutional principles is not the exclusive responsibility of the judiciary, and that constitutional law should reflect, in its substance and in the courts' decisional processes, the role of political decision making in the constitutional system. "Great constitutional provisions must be administered with caution. Some play must be allowed for the joints of the machine, and it must be remembered that legislatures are ultimate guardians of the liberties and welfare of the people in quite as great a degree as the courts."[19]

"Rational basis" analysis is in practice the most important aspect of the Constitution-in-practice that stems from the federal courts' recognition of the priority of democratic politics in American governance. As we saw in Chapter 3, rational basis names one of the doctrines or standards of review that the Supreme Court has created to govern judicial analysis of claims that a law or other governmental action violates a constitutional prohibition, most commonly the principle of equal protection and the due process clauses in their substantive role. Under both equal protection and substantive due process, rational basis scrutiny is the default mode of

---

[18]   *Mayor of City of Philadelphia v. Educ. Equal. League*, 415 U.S. 605, 629 (1974) (citing *Ashwander v. TVA*, 297 U.S. 288, 345–48 (1936) (Brandeis, J., concurring)); *Washington State Grange v. Washington State Republican Party*, 552 U.S. 442, 450 (2008) (quoting Justice Brandeis in *Ashwander*). See also *Davies Warehouse Co. v. Bowles*, 321 U.S. 144, 153 (1944) ("State statutes, like federal ones, are entitled to the presumption of constitutionality").

[19]   *Missouri, Ky. & Tex. Ry. Co. v. May*, 194 U.S. 267, 270 (1904) (Holmes, J.).

analysis, and is usually articulated formally as a requirement that the government's action (treating similarly situated persons differently in equal protection; infringing someone's liberty in due process) is a rational means of achieving a legitimate governmental interest. The basic idea is that making and enforcing law is not in itself constitutionally problematic, and most laws draw distinctions and limit people's freedom of action. If equal protection and substantive due process principles are not to undercut the ordinary primacy of democratic lawmaking, they must generally be limited to an inquiry into whether the governmental action in question is reasonable in light of the underlying constitutional concerns with unjust discriminations and oppressive interferences with liberty.

Rational basis scrutiny imposes this self-limitation on judicial review by denying courts the power to depreciate the constitutional dignity of political decision making by overturning a political decision simply because the judges have come to a different conclusion than the legislators or executive officials about its reasonability. Rather than asking the same question the political actors originally did (e.g., do I think it is a reasonable highway safety measure to require an applicant for a driver's license to pass a road test if under age 18?), rational basis scrutiny limits the judge to asking whether a rational political actor could have thought the action reasonable (could a not-irrational legislature view the age requirement as a reasonable highway safety measure?). The inquiry into the government's purpose is purely hypothetical: The question is not, for example, whether the actual members of the legislature had highway safety in mind, but rather whether they might have, given the law they enacted.[20]

Rational basis scrutiny is an extraordinarily deferential form of judicial review. The court assumes the existence of facts supporting the legislation and the challenger thus must prove facts that "preclude the assumption" that the law has "some basis within the knowledge and experience of the legislators." "The burden is on the one attacking the legislative arrangement to negative every conceivable basis which might support it." If the court concludes that there are "plausible reasons" for the government's action, judicial "inquiry is at an end." The Supreme Court's usual explanation for enforcing constitutional prohibitions with such an undemanding standard is constitutional respect for democratic politics: Rational basis scrutiny "presumes that, absent some reason to infer antipathy, even improvident decisions will eventually be rectified by the democratic process and that judicial intervention is generally unwarranted."[21]

---

[20] Standards of review are part of the Constitution-in-practice and thus state courts addressing issues of federal constitutional law must apply the same standard, if one exists, that would have governed a case in federal court.

[21] *United States* v. *Carolene Products Co.*, 304 U.S. 144, 152 (1938); *Armour* v. *City of Indianapolis*, 566 U.S. 673, 685 (2012); *FCC* v. *Beach Communications*, 508 U.S. 307, 313–14 (1993). A contrary suggestion has been made that in equal protection and substantive due process cases, "rational basis is not just the standard of scrutiny, but the very substance of the constitutional guarantee" because those "constitutional commands ... are themselves prohibitions on irrational laws." *District of*

Rational basis scrutiny is so deferential that one might wonder if it is even possible for governmental action to flunk the test? There are, in fact, occasional cases in which a court decides that a governmental action is sheerly irrational, in the sense that it makes no sense whatever. In recent decades, the Supreme Court has decided a single case on that ground under equal protection and none analyzed under substantive due process. In a handful of other equal protection cases, for various reasons the Court has held that the actual purpose of the law under review was constitutionally illegitimate and invalidated the law on that ground. In one case, the state courts authoritatively stated the purposes of a state law in the course of the litigation, and the Court invalidated it because those purposes were illegitimate under the federal Constitution. On the other occasions when the Court has struck "down a policy as illegitimate under rational basis scrutiny," the "common thread has been that the laws at issue lack any purpose other than a bare . . . desire to harm a politically unpopular group." The Court has not as yet fully explained when rational basis scrutiny allows a court to look beyond legitimate but entirely hypothetical purposes to act on its perception that government's actual goal was constitutionally illegitimate. Its decisions suggest that a stark disproportion between any legitimate justification that can be imagined and the infliction of "immediate, continuing and real injuries" on those affected negatively is an important clue.[22]

In addition to its role in identifying one of the standards of review the federal courts apply in answering questions of prohibition, the language of "rational basis" plays a role in the judicial review of some issues of authorization. The answer to the question whether Congress is authorized by one of its enumerated powers to address a matter sometimes requires an evaluation of Congress's judgment on the relationship between the power's scope and the facts of the world. Recall the third category of situations over which *United States* v. *Lopez* held Congress can exercise its interstate commerce power: activities which have a substantial effect on interstate commerce. Determining whether a federal statute is valid under this analysis requires a judgment about the match between facts about the world and the commerce clause concept of "*substantial* effect." The Supreme Court decided long before *Lopez* that the federal courts should not disturb Congress's judgment on that issue as long as it has a rational basis. Similarly, the Court has used the term rational basis in describing the connection the necessary and proper clause requires

---

Columbia v. *Heller*, 554 U.S. 570, 628 n. 27 (2008). The great weight of precedent supports the position articulated in *Beach Communications*.

[22] *Trump* v. *Hawaii*, 138 S. Ct. 2392, 2420 (2018); *Romer* v. *Evans*, 517 U.S. 620, 635 (1996). The lone example of a completely irrational law coming before the Court was *Allegheny Pittsburgh Coal Co.* v. *Commission of Webster County*, 488 U.S. 336, 341 (1989) (invalidating a county tax assessor's practice of determining property values based on the property's last sale, which resulted in the petitioner being "taxed at approximately 35 times the rate applied to owners of comparable properties"). The decision based on the state courts' construction of state law was *Metro. Life Ins. Co.* v. *Ward*, 470 U.S. 869, 880, 882 (1985) (holding that the purposes of "promotion of domestic business within a State" and "encouragement of capital investment" by "discriminating against foreign corporations that wish to compete by doing business there" are not legitimate state interests).

between an express enumerated power and the matter over which Congress seeks to exercise an implied power. Finally, when Congress exercises its power to enforce the thirteenth amendment's prohibition on slavery, the Court has held that Congress's decision that a practice (not itself literally involving the enslavement of a person) is one of "the badges and incidents of slavery" is subject to rational basis review.[23]

These uses of the concept of rational basis are not precisely identical to one another. In the commerce clause and necessary and proper clause contexts, rational basis analysis preserves for Congress a broad range of discretion about, respectively, what intrastate economic activities affecting interstate commerce are substantial enough to warrant federal legislation, and what legislation is needed to implement fully an express power, subject only to federal court review to ensure that its decision is defensible. The thirteenth amendment judgment, in contrast, involves deciding if the legal and social customs that undergirded slavery historically (its "badges and incidents") are sufficiently analogous to some contemporary social ill to warrant treating the latter as within the scope of the thirteenth amendment enforcement power. Rational basis analysis in that instance accords judicial respect for a congressional judgment that clearly involving comparing the historical facts about slavery's badges and incidents to present-day facts. But in all three situations, as with rational basis as an equal protection or substantive due process standard of review, precedent has built into the federal courts' constitutional perspective a respect for the role and dignity of democratic decision making in the American constitutional system.[24]

The Supreme Court has often stated a reluctance, as we have seen, to infer the existence of constitutional prohibitions that protect individual rights on the basis of argument from tradition in the absence of a textual basis for doing so other than the due process or equal protection clauses. The Court often explains its caution as rooted in respect for democratic politics as the ordinary mode of American governance. "By extending constitutional protection to an asserted right or liberty interest,

[23] *Katzenbach v. McClung*, 379 U.S. 294, 303–04 (1964) (commerce clause); *United States v. Comstock*, 560 U.S. 126, 134 (2010) (necessary and proper clause); *Jones v. Alfred H. Mayer Co.*, 392 U.S. 409, 440 (1968) (thirteenth amendment). On possible differences between rational basis thought in answering questions of authorization and prohibition, see *Comstock*, 560 U.S. at 152 (Kennedy, J., concurring in the judgment) ("The rational basis referred to in the Commerce Clause context is a demonstrated link in fact, based on empirical demonstration. While undoubtedly deferential, this may well be different from the rational-basis test" used in equal protection and due process cases).

[24] The Supreme Court has not revisited the rational basis component of thirteenth amendment enforcement power analysis in decades, but the thoughtful opinion in *United States v. Hatch*, 722 F.3d 1193 (10th Cir. 2013) is instructive. The court upheld a provision of the Hate Crimes Act criminalizing the infliction of bodily injury on the basis of the "race, color, religion or national origin" of the victim because it concluded that Congress had a rational basis for determining that such crimes fall within the constitutional idea of badges and incidents of slavery. The provision's scope is limited to "aspects of race as understood in the 1860s when the Thirteenth Amendment was adopted" (which could include what we would call religious identity), and reflects the fact that antebellum slave state case law treated "master-on-slave violence as one of slavery's most necessary features." *Id.* at 1205–06.

we, to a great extent, place the matter outside the arena of public debate and legislative action. We must therefore exercise the utmost care whenever we are asked to break new ground." The complementary justification for this caution, that the Court is hesitant extend its precedents "lest the liberty protected by the Due Process Clause be subtly transformed into the policy preferences of the Members of this Court," is put in terms more closely aligned with the theme of adhering to the limitations built into Article III, but those limitations themselves demarcate the judiciary's vital but limited sphere of final decision from the general realm of political choice.[25]

Heightened Scrutiny. The constitutional perspective of the federal courts recognizes the American political community's fundamental commitment to democratic decision making as the ordinary form of decision making in American government. But democratic politics is not the community's only commitment, and the second step in constitutional law's twofold logic of inquiry asks whether an otherwise lawful political decision has transgressed a constitutional prohibition that overrides the decision. In order to give full effect to some of those prohibitions, the Supreme Court has devised doctrines that it refers to as "standards of review," generally when, as a formal matter, the doctrine requires some kind of means/ends analysis. We have already examined one such standard of review, rational basis scrutiny, which is purposefully designed to give wide berth to political decisions. But in some circumstances, the Court has concluded that the presumption should be against political decision making. In those situations, one of a number of different standards of review applies; collectively they are usually referred to as forms of "heightened scrutiny." These heightened standards of review share two characteristics. First, they all turn rational basis scrutiny's deferential stance on its head: The burden of persuasion usually rests on the defender of the governmental action, the purpose that matters is the *actual* goal government was pursuing, and to uphold the challenged action the court must satisfy *itself* that the constitutional requirements are met rather than accept a plausible (and perhaps hypothetical) political judgment. Second, the Supreme Court has ordained the various forms of heightened scrutiny in matters where it is convinced that the relevant constitutional prohibition largely excludes a role for democratic politics. Some prohibitions are deliberately countermajoritarian. "The very purpose of a Bill of Rights was to withdraw certain subjects from the vicissitudes of political controversy, to place them beyond the reach of majorities and officials and to establish them as legal principles to be applied by the courts." Others, in particular the equal protection principle, are a safeguard against the possibility that animus against a disfavored group will "curtail the operation of those political processes ordinarily to be relied upon to protect minorities."[26]

---

[25] *Washington v. Glucksberg*, 521 U.S. 702, 720 (1997).
[26] *West Virginia State Bd. of Educ. v. Barnette*, 319 U.S. 624, 638 (1943) (Jackson, J.); *United States v. Carolene Products Co.*, 304 U.S. 144, 152 n. 4 (1938).

In the context of equal protection, some form of heightened scrutiny applies when the governmental discrimination under review falls into certain categories: classifications by race, national origin or ethnicity, noncitizen status, gender, and nonmarital birth status ("illegitimacy" in the older cases), as well as classifications that affect "fundamental rights."[27] Putting the last category to one side for the moment, the Court views each of these bases for classification as "suspect" (or "quasi-suspect" in the case of the last two) and therefore subject to careful scrutiny. The Court has sometimes explained that classifications employing race, ethnicity, or national origin "are deemed to reflect prejudice and antipathy" and for that reason they are subject to strict scrutiny – the usual formula being that in order to be valid, the classification must be a narrowly tailored means to achieving a compelling governmental interest. Somewhat similarly, laws "distributing benefits and burdens between the sexes in different ways," the Court has said, "very likely reflect outmoded notions of the relative capabilities of men and women," and therefore are subject to intermediate level scrutiny – a test requiring that the classification be substantially related to an important governmental interest. In 1996, the Court decided *United States* v. *Virginia* in an opinion that described the test for gender classifications as demanding "an exceedingly persuasive justification" to sustain the classifications although the older formula continues to be used as well. A version of intermediate level scrutiny applies to nonmarital birth status, and the Supreme Court's decisions since the mid-1990s would support the conclusion that discrimination on the basis of sexual orientation is also subject to heightened scrutiny, although as of the time of writing the Court has not expressly said as much.[28]

There has been recurrent criticism, on and off the Court, of the three-tier (or more) system of equal protection standards of review, and some of its details are difficult to defend: What, for example, is the difference between a "compelling" governmental interest and one that is merely "important?" But taken as a whole, the system makes sense and seems reasonably workable. The core original purpose of the fourteenth amendment equal protection clause was to protect African Americans against hostile discrimination based on race. The Court's gradual expansion of heightened scrutiny beyond this original "suspect" classification rested on its

---

[27]   The reader should avoid confusing classifications based on national origin/ethnicity with those based on "alienage," which is the status of being a noncitizen. (The terms "alien" and "alienage" in this sense are now passing out of use, but are still found in judicial opinions and federal statutes.) The Supreme Court's case law addressing discrimination against noncitizens is complex and does not in fact apply heightened scrutiny to congressional classifications because Congress has plenary authority over which noncitizens may be in the United States and on what conditions, subject to other applicable constitutional prohibitions.

[28]   *City of Cleburne* v. *Cleburne Living Center*, 473 U.S. 432, 440–41 (1985); *United States* v. *Virginia*, 518 U.S. 515, 531 (1996). Cf. *Obergefell* v. *Hodges*, 576 U.S. 644, 675 (2015). ("Especially against a long history of disapproval of their relationships, this denial to same-sex couples of the right to marry works a grave and continuing harm. The imposition of this disability on gays and lesbians serves to disrespect and subordinate them.")

application to the clause of the *McCulloch v. Maryland* principle that the provisions of the written Constitution are ordinarily to be treated as statements of broad principle rather than narrow rules. In time, the Court concluded – very quickly in the case of discrimination against other racial groups or on the basis of national origin or ethnicity, very belatedly with respect to gender – that each of these other forms of discrimination is sufficiently analogous to hostile racial classification to merit similar treatment under the equal protection prohibition treated as a broad principle. The differing terms used in the specific standards of review are not of great practical significance and reflect slightly varying judgments on the extent to which a given, presumptively invalid, classification is permissible in some circumstances.

As mentioned previously, Supreme Court cases sometimes inform the reader that equal protection strict scrutiny also applies to nonsuspect classifications that impinge on "fundamental rights." This poses the obvious problem: What are these fundamental rights? If the right that the governmental classification infringes is, or is closely related to, a liberty expressly protected by a constitutional prohibition such as the free speech and press clauses of the first amendment, an equal protection analysis seems unnecessary: Ordinarily, the constitutional issue can and should be resolved on the basis of the express constitutional prohibition. There are cases that nonetheless use the language of equal protection but even when a court does so, the substance of the analysis comes from the express constitutional liberty. This means that, in effect, the only "fundamental rights" independently addressed by equal protection are "fundamental in the equal protection context only: rights that need be granted to none, but if granted to some must be granted to all." On the face of it, this seems a rather odd notion, and one that might be hard to apply, and in *San Antonio Ind. School District v. Rodriguez* (1973), which rejected the argument that equal protection includes a fundamental right to education, the Court effectively put an end to further expansion of fundamental rights analysis. This branch of equal protection doctrine therefore appears to be a fossil, limited for practical purposes to the two fundamental-if-granted rights identified before *Rodriguez*, the right to vote and the right of access to the courts.[29]

The courts also employ heightened standards of review in many situations involving specific constitutional prohibitions that protect enumerated individual rights. All of the (many) first amendment free speech doctrines, for example, are forms of heightened scrutiny and sometimes (not always) use the same language as equal protection doctrine, although not always with the same meaning. As an historical

---

[29] Charles Fried, *Saying What the Law Is: The Constitution in the Supreme Court* 224 (Cambridge, MA: Harvard University Press, 2004); *San Antonio Ind. School District v. Rodriguez*, 411 U.S. 1 (1973). See also *Minneapolis Star & Tribune Co. v. Minn. Comm'r of Revenue*, 460 U.S. 575, 585 n. 7 (1983) (differential taxation of the press should be decided "directly under the First Amendment" rather than by employing equal protection analysis). On the right of access to the courts, see, e.g., *Tennessee v. Lane*, 541 U.S. 509, 533–34 (2004) (the fourteenth amendment protects "the fundamental right of access to the courts"). The Supreme Court no longer automatically applies strict scrutiny in right to vote cases. For more on the right to vote, see Chapter 5.

matter, the Supreme Court seems initially to have borrowed equal protection concepts without careful reflection, although their use can now be explained as a means of according freedom of speech a very high level of protection, while declining to accept Justice Hugo L. Black's view that the first amendment's prohibitions are absolute.

> The First Amendment embodies an overarching commitment to protect speech from government regulation through close judicial scrutiny, thereby enforcing the Constitution's constraints, but without imposing judicial formulas so rigid that they become a straitjacket that disables government from responding to serious problems. This Court, in different contexts, has consistently held that government may directly regulate speech to address extraordinary problems, where its regulations are appropriately tailored to resolve those problems without imposing an unnecessarily great restriction on speech.

As is true in other contexts, the Court's free speech case law reflects its recognition that the constitutional goal of maintaining a workable government often demands respect both for the community's government-limiting commitments and for the goals of effectiveness and efficiency.[30]

The specific first amendment doctrine that applies in a particular case sometimes depends on the nature of the intrusion on freedom of speech; for example, discrimination against speech based on its content is subject to strict scrutiny. In other circumstances, the Court's rules turn on the content of the speech involved: Advocacy of unlawful action is protected "except where such advocacy is directed to inciting or producing imminent lawless action and is likely to incite or produce such action," whereas defamatory statements about public officials or figures are protected unless published with "actual malice" (a misleading technical term). In still other situations, the standard of review is designed to address a particular kind of government action – regulations of the time, place, and manner of expression do not violate the first amendment if they are "reasonable" and do not refer "to the content of the regulated speech ... are narrowly tailored to serve a significant governmental interest, and ... leave open ample alternative channels for communication of the information." Similar differences attend the doctrines implementing other prohibitions.[31]

---

[30] *Denver Area Educ. Telecommunications Consortium* v. *FCC*, 518 U.S. 727, 741 (1996) (plurality opinion of Breyer, J.). On the equal protection origins of first amendment strict scrutiny, see *Simon & Schuster, Inc.* v. *Members of New York State Crime Victims Bd.*, 502 U.S. 105, 125 (1991) (Kennedy, J., concurring in the judgment) ("the Court appears to have adopted this formulation in First Amendment cases by accident rather than as the result of a considered judgment"). See also *Ginzburg* v. *Goldwater*, 396 U.S. 1049, 1052 (1970) (Black, J., dissenting) ("the First Amendment bars in absolute, unequivocal terms any abridgment by the Government of freedom of speech and press").

[31] *Reed* v. *Town of Gilbert*, 576 U.S. 155, 163 (2015); *Virginia* v. *Black*, 538 U.S. 343, 359 (2003); *New York Times Co.* v. *Sullivan*, 376 U.S. 254, 279–80 (1964) (defining "actual malice" not as ill will but as "knowledge that [the statement] was false or with reckless disregard of whether it was false or not"); *Ward* v. *Rock Against Racism*, 491 U.S. 781, 791 (1989).

In discussing heightened scrutiny, the Supreme Court's use of similar or identical technical terminology such as "strict (or intermediate) scrutiny" across different areas of constitutional law reflects similarities in analysis but that truth should not be pressed too far. Since the rest of us are going to worry over the very words that the justices employ in opinions with authority binding on other courts, it would simplify our work if they would employ apparently precise doctrinal language, technical-sounding terms, and so on, consistently – if, for example, "narrowly tailored" always meant the same thing every time one encountered it in a Supreme Court opinion discussing "strict scrutiny." Alas, the justices have not chosen to be so precise. In *Boos* v. *Barry* (1988), for example, the Supreme Court held that a D.C. ordinance limiting protests near foreign embassies violated the first amendment because the ordinance was "not narrowly tailored; a less restrictive alternative is readily available" to achieve the District's goals. However, when a court of appeals subsequently invalidated a New York City noise regulation because there were less restrictive alternatives available, the Supreme Court reversed. The Court explained in *Ward* v. *Rock Against Racism* (1989) that the lower court's error lay in assuming that "narrowly tailored" in cases like *Boos* has the same meaning in a case like *Ward* involving a "time, place or manner" regulation of speech such as a noise ordinance. "While time, place, or manner regulations must also be 'narrowly tailored' in order to survive First Amendment challenge … the same degree of tailoring is not required of these regulations." The moral of the story? Don't assume automatically that all the meaning the Court gives a term or phrase in one setting travels along with the term or phrase into another setting. Maybe so, maybe not.[32]

Balance and Balancing. Supreme Court opinions often use the metaphor of a "balance" in describing some aspect of the Constitution-in-practice or refer to the judicial task in answering certain constitutional law questions as one of "balancing" different interests or factors. The metaphor is so common that it would be challenging to list all the ways it is used, but three basic categories can be distinguished and the constitutional lawyer may sometimes find it useful to take note of their distinctive characteristics.

As discussed later in the chapter, one of the background principles the federal courts employ in construing acts of Congress is the presumption that Congress does not intend to change the usual balance between federal and state responsibilities in such areas as criminal law without a clear statement. The "balance" meant in such statements reflects one of the fundamental structural features of the constitutional system as a whole, "the constitutionally mandated balance of power between the States and the Federal Government." The Court similarly refers to the Constitution's "balance in political mechanisms through separation of powers."

---

[32]   *Boos* v. *Barry*, 485 U.S. 312, 329 (1988); *Ward* v. *Rock Against Racism*, 491 U.S. 781, 798 n. 6 (1989). I do not intend to suggest that *Ward* was wrong to apply a less demanding standard in its context, but one sympathizes with the court of appeals for assuming that a technical term used in one area of constitutional law had the same meaning when used in another.

When the balance metaphor is used to refer to broad structural principles providing for dispersed governmental powers, it does not dictate specific answers to specific questions. The image instead counsels caution in accepting answers that deviate from long-standing institutional relationships and spheres of responsibility.[33]

The second category of references to constitutional "balance" uses the metaphor to refer to the Supreme Court's creation of legal arrangements or judicial doctrines that attempt to reconcile potentially conflicting constitutional principles or textual provisions by ensuring that neither is simply swallowed up by the other. For example, the Court has explained the distinction drawn in copyright law between ideas (which cannot be copyrighted) from specific forms of expression (which can) as a "dichotomy" that "strikes a definitional balance between the First Amendment and [Congress's power to create a copyright system] by permitting free communication of facts while still protecting an author's expression." Or again, substantive due process doctrine "represents the balance which our Nation, built upon postulates of respect for the liberty of the individual, has struck between that liberty and the demands of organized society." The metaphor of "balance" in statements like these justifies what might otherwise be unconvincing or overnice distinctions by pointing to the Court's need to distinguish constitutional commitments that must both be honored. The underlying thought is that constitutional law sometimes requires the Court to draw "a line where no important distinction can be seen between the nearest points on the two sides, but where the distinction between the extremes is plain."[34]

Finally, the Court sometimes articulates the way in which a court is to answer a specific type of constitutional question by describing the court as "balancing" two or more factors or interests. An illustration is the test the Court has ordained for determining when a governmental employee has a constitutional claim under the first amendment based on an adverse personnel action allegedly taken in response to something the employee said. Government generally may control what an employee says as a public servant without violating the first amendment's prohibition on abridging freedom of speech because in that circumstance, the employee is speaking for the government. But even when the employee is speaking on a matter of public concern and the free speech clause is implicated, the precedents require a court to "balance . . . the interests of the public employee, as a citizen, in commenting upon matters of public concern and the interest of the State, as an employer, in promoting the efficiency of the public services it performs through its employees." This test obviously reflects the Court's refusal to choose a blanket answer to the question

---

[33] *Federal Maritime Comm'n v. S.C. State Ports Authority*, 535 U.S. 743, 769 (2002); *Roper v. Simmons*, 543 U.S. 551, 578 (2005). Supreme Court opinions sometimes link separation of powers with the historically rather different idea of "checks and balances" although in current constitutional law it is difficult to discern any specific additional content in the latter term.

[34] *Harper & Row Publishers v. Nation Enterprises*, 471 U.S. 539, 556 (1985); *Planned Parenthood v. Casey*, 505 U.S. 833, 850 (1992), quoting *Poe v. Ullman*, 367 U.S. 497, 542 (1961) (Harlan, J., dissenting); *Klein v. Bd. of Tax Supervisors*, 282 U.S. 19, 23 (1930) (Holmes, J.).

whether the first amendment or efficiency should prevail in safeguarding the Constitution's objective of maintaining a workable government. The difference between this category and the prior one is that when used in this way, the "balance" is not simply a way of describing the respect-both-commitments basis of the Court's doctrine but is in addition part of the doctrine itself, a direction to the courts to make decisions, on a case by case basis, by evaluating how weighty the court thinks each interest is in light of the specific facts of the case.[35]

The primary criticism of "balancing" in this third sense of a method of judicial analysis is that it requires a court to make "quintessentially legislative judgments."

> The burdens and the benefits are always incommensurate, and cannot be placed on the opposite balances of a scale without assigning a policy-based weight to each of them. It is a matter not of weighing apples against apples, but of deciding whether three apples are better than six tangerines. ... Of course you cannot decide which interest "outweighs" the other without deciding which interest is more important to you.

This is by no means a trivial objection, and a doctrinal test that falls within its terms has little claim to respect beyond the bare (if formidable) authority of precedent.[36] But as a general argument for rejecting what the Supreme Court terms "balancing" as a method of constitutional thought, the objection is not persuasive because it depends on treating the metaphor too literally. Most balancing tests identify a clearly superior constitutional commitment that should prevail unless on the specific facts the lesser commitment seems to the court significantly more *at risk*. An example may be useful.

The quotation in the previous paragraph is from a critique of one of the tests case law ordains under the dormant commerce clause, which is discussed in Chapter 5. If a state law does not discriminate against interstate commerce but nonetheless impedes commerce significantly, a doctrine often called "*Pike* balancing" applies. "Where the statute regulates even-handedly to effectuate a legitimate local public interest, and its effects on interstate commerce are only incidental, it will be upheld unless the burden imposed on such commerce is clearly excessive in relation to the putative local benefits." As the Court's statement of the test shows, the Court has identified the state's police power responsibility for local governance as the superior constitutional commitment in such cases, to be upheld by the courts unless on the facts of a specific case, the constitutional goal of protecting interstate commerce is palpably more at risk.[37]

In *Kassel* v. *Consolidated Freightways Corp.* (1981), the Supreme Court reviewed an Iowa statute limiting truck lengths on state highways. The state's main defense of the limitation was as a highway safety measure, but the factual record developed in the district court seriously undercut the argument that the law actually improved

---

[35] *Lane* v. *Franks*, 573 U.S. 228, 236 (2014).
[36] *Kentucky Dept. of Revenue* v. *Davis*, 553 U.S. 328, 360 (2008) (Scalia, J., concurring in part).
[37] *Pike* v. *Bruce Church, Inc.*, 397 U.S. 137, 142 (1970).

highway safety. The controlling opinion in the Supreme Court also pointed out that the statute included exceptions permitting longer trucks when engaged in services for Iowa residents and that its legislative history indicated that "Iowa's statute may not have been designed to ban dangerous trucks, but rather to discourage interstate truck traffic." The statute's value as a safety measure thus was seriously questionable. On the other hand – the "balancing" factor – Iowa was the only upper Midwest state with such a truck-length limitation, and the practical effect of the law was force interstate shipping that would have gone through Iowa to be rerouted or face delays in conforming to the law, in either case imposing a significant financial burden on interstate commerce. The Court therefore invalidated the law.[38]

Pike balancing *does* require constitutional lawyers, on and off the bench, to advance judgments about the degree to which the state law at issue serves legitimate state goals and to consider that public benefit alongside the degree to which the law burdens interstate commerce. In that sense, the critics maintain that the doctrine requires an apples and tangerines comparison. But constitutional law, like other areas of law, often demands judgments about questions of degree, and *Pike* balancing does not invite individual judges to engage in an ad hoc quasi-legislative debate over the pros and cons of the state statute, but to determine if, giving the facts known about the law's purpose and operation, the statute in operation is analogous to a facially discriminatory law, which would almost certainly be prohibited by the dormant commerce clause. If the analogy is not persuasive, the law is constitutional.

Balancing in this sense is sometimes employed to supplement ostensibly very different forms of analysis. As the Supreme Court has observed, even a bright-line constitutional rule can require difficult judgments about whether cases "at the boundary of the rule" are controlled by it or not. For example, governmental action that involves "a permanent physical occupation" of private property "*is* unquestionably a taking" per se for the purposes of the fifth amendment's requirement of just compensation. In some situations, however, it may not be clear if the government has permanently intruded onto someone's property, or its intrusion (e.g., by causing intermittent flooding) may be temporary. Determining whether the bright-line rule applies in those cases, the Court has concluded, can be aided by "a more complex balancing analysis" that takes into account specific facts in determining if the government action is sufficiently analogous to situations that would unquestionably involve a taking that it should treated as a permanent intrusion. The general point is that constitutional lawyers should understand references to "balance" and "balancing" that fall into this third category not as suggestions that a court step outside the judicial role but as indications that the court should follow a specified line of

---

[38] *Kassel v. Consolidated Freightways Corp.*, 450 U.S. 662, 672–75 (1981) (plurality opinion of Powell, J.) (record evidence); *id.* at 677 (quotation about the state's arguable motivation). The concurrence treated the *Pike* analysis as a tool for determining whether the state law had a protectionist purpose, and thought that the record in *Kassel* proved such a purpose. *Id.* at 680–85 (Brennan, J., concurring in the judgment).

analysis that takes into account both the constitutional commitments that are in tension and the facts of the particular case.[39]

Specific Rules Regarding the Judicial Review of Statutes. The perspective that federal courts bring to constitutional law decisions has generated specific rules governing how the courts should deal with statutes about which a serious constitutional question has been raised. Their general purpose is to limit judicial interference with legislation to that which is necessary to ensure the invalidation of statutory provisions that clearly violate the Constitution-in-practice.

The canon of constitutional avoidance applies to statutory provisions of dubious validity but ambiguous meaning. If the court can give the provision a construction that avoids the constitutional problem, it should do so. The canon does not license judicial rewriting of the legislature's language, however, and it therefore has no application if the statute's meaning is unambiguous and unconstitutional. Some opinions state that the avoidance canon comes into play only when the statutory language is "equally susceptible of two constructions, under one of which it is clearly valid," but that does not seem to be the usual practice, which asks not whether the constitutional reading is "the most natural interpretation" of the provision "but only whether is it a fairly possible one." There is an ongoing debate over the propriety of invoking the canon not only in cases where the statute would otherwise be invalid, but also "to avoid the need even to address serious questions about [its] constitutionality."[40]

The avoidance canon, at least in principle, serves the legislature's objectives by preserving its handiwork. The Supreme Court has evolved a second set of presumptions or principles of construction applicable to federal legislation that, at least in practice, serve a rather different objective, that of resolving ambiguities in statutes to preserve what the Court assumes is the normal operation of the constitutional system.

> Among the background principles of construction that our cases have recognized are those grounded in the relationship between the Federal Government and the States under our Constitution. It has long been settled, for example, that we presume federal statutes do not abrogate state sovereign immunity, impose obligations on the States pursuant to section 5 of the Fourteenth Amendment, or preempt state law. Closely related to these is the well-established principle that it is

---

[39]   *Loretto* v. *Teleprompter Manhattan CATV Corp.*, 458 U.S. 419, 435 n. 12 (1982). As a logical matter, the various forms of heightened scrutiny discussed above are a form of balancing in this third sense. See, e.g., *Heller* v. *District of Columbia*, 670 F.3d 1244, 1281–82 (D.C. Cir. 2011) (Kavanaugh, Cir. J., dissenting) (heightened "scrutiny tests" are "quintessential balancing inquiries" because they "always involve at least some assessment of whether the law in question is sufficiently important to justify infringement on an individual constitutional right").

[40]   *Crowell* v. *Benson*, 285 U.S. 22, 76, 52 S. Ct. 285, 302 (1932) (Brandeis, J., dissenting); *Nat'l Fed'n of Indep. Bus.* v. *Sebelius*, 567 U.S. 519, 563 (2012) (opinion of Roberts, C.J.); *United States* v. *Davis*, 139 S. Ct. 2319, 2332 n. 6 (2019) (referring to the latter idea as a separate, "more modern (and more debated) constitutional doubt canon").

incumbent upon the federal courts to be certain of Congress' intent before finding that federal law overrides the usual constitutional balance of federal and state powers.

A clear statement in the statute that Congress intends the result that is contrary to the background assumption defeats the relevant presumption.[41]

In some situations, these background principles bring constitutional considerations to bear on the construction of an act of Congress even in the absence of a clear constitutional problem. In *Gregory v. Ashcroft* (1991), one of the issues was whether the Age Discrimination in Employment Act applied to state court judges. The Court invoked the requirement that Congress include a "plain statement" of its intention to change the usual federal–state balance as a reason to construe the Act not to cover the judges even though it acknowledged that precedent constrained its "ability to consider" any substantive limits that the federal–state balance places on Congress's commerce power. In other cases, the background principles obviate the need to address a difficult constitutional question, thus serving as particularized avoidance canons. For example, the defendant in *Bond v. United States* (2014) was prosecuted under the act of Congress implementing an international treaty banning chemical weapons after she used small quantities of two toxic substances in a personal vendetta. Bond argued that the act, as applied to her, was beyond Congress's Article I power to implement treaties, a claim that threatened to put in issue as well the scope of the Article II treaty power and the basic police power presupposition that petty crime is a matter for state law. The wording of the statute, read literally, covered Bond's actions, but the Court reasoned that because the literal reading would extend the law to "purely local crimes," it was appropriate to construe the statute not to extend to Bond's petty criminal assault since the statute did not include a clear statement that Congress intended to reach so far.[42]

Statutes, especially modern acts of Congress, can be very complex. Some lengthy statutes are grab bags of titles and individual sections related (perhaps) by general subject matter but otherwise consisting of discrete units of legislation, often with

---

[41] *Bond v. United States*, 572 U.S. 844, 857–58 (2014). The Supreme Court's reports include many other specially crafted rules of statutory construction. Some of the uniquely federal rules have a constitutional dimension, while others reflect assumptions about the overall tendencies of congressional legislation. See, e.g., *Chickasaw Nation v. United States*, 534 U.S. 84, 93–95 (2001) (in interpreting a confusing tax provision, the canon that "statutes are to be construed liberally in favor of the Indians [was] offset by the canon that warns us against interpreting federal statutes as providing tax exemptions").

[42] *Gregory v. Ashcroft*, 501 U.S. 452, 464 (1991); *Bond*, 572 U.S. at 859–60. I have simplified somewhat the statutory construction arguments in both cases. The particular facts of a case can influence a court's willingness to reach a decision based on a background principle of construction. In *Bond*, for example, the petitioner's constitutional arguments raised potentially far-reaching issues about the treaty power of the federal government, while the specific case involved the use of small quantities of two toxic chemicals in repeated attempts to cause a personal enemy to "develop an uncomfortable rash"; on the petitioner's one semi-successful attempt, the victim "suffered a minor chemical burn on her thumb, which she treated by rinsing with water." *Id.* at 852.

their own, title-specific, names: The annual National Defense Authorization Act is an example. Even if advised by executive branch lawyers that one or more specific provisions in a bill are unconstitutional, the president might understandably not want to send an otherwise valid and important bill back to Congress, and established executive branch practice does not regard a veto as a duty in those circumstances. It would be a massive and regrettable judicial interference with Congress's work for the federal courts to hold the entire act invalid because of some perhaps minor or technical flaw buried among many valid provisions. In contrast, other sprawling laws such as the Affordable Care Act of 2012 establish intricate systems in which individual components are part of a carefully interconnected and operational whole. It is arguable with regard to such a law that some of its provisions cannot be excised for constitutional reasons without seriously undermining Congress's overall goals. "Severability" analysis is the means by which the federal courts determine how much of a statute must be invalidated if one or more provisions are unconstitutional.

The key to severability is sometimes said to be Congress's intent. As with congressional preemption of state law, Congress itself may clearly decide the question of severability by including in a statute a provision expressly providing that the invalidity of one section should not affect the rest of the law, or a nonseverability provision which indicates that the unconstitutionality of one provision means that all or part of the statute should be struck down as well. But the Court has recognized the difficulties with judicial speculation about what Congress would have wanted the courts to do in the absence of an express severability or nonseverability clause, and the "normal rule" in current law is to apply "a strong presumption of severability" that embodies the Court's own early practice. "Generally speaking, when confronting a constitutional flaw in a statute, we try to limit the solution to the problem, severing any problematic portions while leaving the remainder intact." To apply the presumption, the federal court must conclude that "the remainder of the statute is capable of functioning" without the invalid provision and thus would be "fully operative as a law," but it is unusual for a statute to fail that test.[43]

In its 2012 *Sebelius* decision, the Court held that one aspect of the Affordable Care Act's extension of the Medicaid program was unconstitutional. The Act authorized the Secretary of Health & Human Services to withdraw part or all of a state's existing Medicaid funds if the state declined to expand its Medicaid program on terms dictated by the Act. The Court concluded that this use of the spending power to induce state legislation was coercive and therefore invalid under the anti-commandeering principle. This raised the question whether the provision giving the Secretary the power to penalize uncooperative states was severable from the rest of the Medicaid expansion and from the Act as a whole. The Court held that a pre-existing severability statement

---

[43]   *Barr v. Am. Assoc. of Political Consultants*, 140 S. Ct. 2335, 2350, 2352 (2020) (plurality opinion of Kavanaugh, J.). As Justice Kavanaugh pointed out, the Court's "preference to partially invalidate a statute" rather than strike it down entirely "has been firmly established since *Marbury v. Madison*." *Id.* at 2350.

in the part of the US Code into which the penalty provision had been inserted indicated that the penalty provision could be severed from the Medicaid expansion, and that even in the absence of power to compel states to expand Medicaid, Congress's "other reforms" in the health care system "will still function in a way consistent with Congress' basic objectives in enacting the statute."[44]

The federal courts' constitutional perspective is reflected, finally, in their treatment of Congress's expression of its opinion on constitutional issues, and in particular on the validity of its own legislative acts. Congress is not ordinarily obligated to indicate which of its enumerated powers it intends to carry into effect in enacting a statute, and as discussed previously the courts ordinarily presume that federal statutes are constitutional. The Supreme Court has explained the presumption of constitutionality as based on Congress's "duty to make its own informed judgment on the meaning and force of the Constitution" when it "acts within its sphere of power and responsibilities." The Court has also noted at times that the presumption is particularly appropriate when Congress in fact expressly considered the constitutional issues, but the presumption applies regardless of the existence of congressional deliberation: The presumption is a rule expressing the federal courts' respect for the role of democratic politics rather than an expression of deference to the quality of constitutional law debate in the legislative branch.[45]

For the same reason, it is immaterial whether Congress has correctly identified, in an express provision or the legislative history, the source of its authorization to enact a law if in fact – and "in fact" here means "in the judgment of the federal courts" – the law is authorized. "The question of the constitutionality of action taken by Congress does not depend on recitals of the power which it undertakes to exercise." Judicial review, to make the point another way, does not involve grading Congress's constitutional homework. Another constitutional issue in the *Sebelius* Affordable Care Act case discussed previously was the constitutionality of the Act's mandate that most individuals have a specified level of health care insurance or pay what the Act consistently termed a "penalty" rather than a "tax." As a "penalty," the individual mandate was more naturally read as a commerce clause regulation, and (viewed as such) a majority of the justices thought it unauthorized. But a different majority reasoned that "Congress's choice of label" did not "control whether [the] exaction is within Congress's constitutional power to tax" and, affording the Act "the full measure of deference owed to federal statutes," the Court concluded that the individual mandate was within the scope of the taxing power.[46]

[44] *Nat'l Fed'n of Indep. Bus.* v. *Sebelius*, 567 U.S. 519, 586, 587–88 (2012) (plurality opinion of Roberts, C.J.).

[45] *City of Boerne* v. *Flores*, 521 U.S. 507, 535 (1997). See *Rostker* v. *Goldberg*, 453 U.S. 57, 64 (1981) (presuming the law under review valid against equal protection challenge because, in part, "Congress specifically considered the question of the Act's constitutionality").

[46] *Woods* v. *Cloyd W. Miller Co.*, 333 U.S. 138, 144 (1948); *Sebelius*, 567 U.S. at 563–64 (opinion of the Court).

Procedural Due Process and the Rule of Law. The perspective on constitutional law particular to the federal courts is shaped by the need to address constitutional questions with an awareness of the relationship of the courts to the realm of democratic politics, an awareness that often dictates deference to political choices. But this relationship does not automatically dictate that the courts defer to elected politicians, or that the substance of constitutional law must always allow the broadest defensible scope for democratic decision making. Many areas of the Constitution-in -practice reflect the American political community's commitment to placing certain constitutional values outside political control. Of central importance in this regard are the due process clauses of the fifth and fourteenth amendments, which prohibit federal and state governments, respectively, from depriving anyone of "life, liberty, or property, without due process of law."[47]

As is true of substantive due process, procedural due process has its roots in the written Constitution's historical antecedents, which date back to Magna Carta, and the doctrines share the basic purpose of prohibiting governmental oppression. Unlike its twin doctrine, however, which addresses alleged arbitrariness and injustice in the substance of legislative and executive action, procedural due process enforces the principle that executive and judicial action must follow known, regular procedures in acting to an individual's detriment. Fussing over procedural details is, of course, a quintessentially lawyerly business and easily disparaged by nonlawyers, but the existence of fair procedures to which courts and executive agencies must adhere is at the core of the rule of law. Congress is not itself ordinarily under procedural due process constraints because, except in the context of impeachment proceedings, Congress as an institution cannot generally cause legally cognizable harm to individuals outside the legislative branch.[48] The bill of attainder clauses of Article I sections 9 and 10 prohibit both the federal and state legislatures from imposing criminal and criminal law-like penalties by legislation. The due process clauses also prohibit statutes that would permit executive officials or courts to act in violation of procedural due process.

In his Steel Seizure Case opinion, Justice Jackson stressed the constitutional importance of due process in rejecting the government's argument that the president's power to seize the steel mills stemmed from the take care clause of Article II section 3.

> That authority must be matched against words of the Fifth Amendment that "No person shall be ... deprived of life, liberty, or property, without due process of law." One gives a governmental authority that reaches so far as there is law, the other gives a private right that authority shall go no farther. These signify about all there is of the

[47]   On the meaning of "life, liberty, and property," see Chapter 5.
[48]   The Senate and House of Representatives can enforce subpoenas and punish contempt by direct action through their respective sergeants at arms, but this legislative power is essentially theoretical under modern practice.

principle that ours is a government of laws, not of men, and that we submit ourselves to rulers only if under rules.

Jackson likely had both the substantive and the procedural aspects of due process in mind, but later in his opinion he emphasized the importance of the procedural due process concept of notice: "Government by law" depends on the ability of the public and of "persons affected" to "know the extent and limitations of the powers that can be asserted" by the executive and to be "informed . . . of their rights and duties." Other Supreme Court opinions have often stressed the "centrality" of procedural due process to the American system of government, even when the constitutional issue at hand involves the gravest of national security concerns.[49]

Hamdi v. Rumsfeld provides a clear example of the Supreme Court's insistence that procedural due process is at the heart of the rule of law maintained by the Constitution-in-practice. The petitioner, a US citizen, challenged his detention as an unlawful enemy combatant captured during the American military operations in Afghanistan in the wake of September 11, 2001, over his protests that he was an innocent bystander. The executive branch declined to provide Hamdi an opportunity to contest his identity as a combatant, and before the Court it argued that the most due process required was that the executive provide the federal courts with an affidavit by an executive official stating that Hamdi was in his opinion an enemy combatant. Justice O'Connor's controlling opinion flatly rejected that argument: "[W]hile we do not question that our due process assessment must pay keen attention to the particular burdens faced by the Executive in the context of military action," Hamdi was "entitled to [a] process" by which he could effectively challenge "the factual basis for his detention by his Government." Unless Congress lawfully suspends the writ of habeas corpus, the Constitution "most assuredly envisions a role for all three branches when individual liberties are at stake," and the federal courts therefore must ensure that a detainee receives procedural due process.[50]

The central importance of procedural due process is reflected in several specific rules the federal courts apply in addressing constitutional problems. The courts and the executive must afford an individual procedural due process even if the outcome of the procedure appears clear before it begins: "[T]he right to procedural due

[49] *Youngstown Sheet & Tube Co. v. Sawyer*, 343 U.S. 579, 646, 662–63 (1952) (Jackson, J., concurring). See *Boddie v. Connecticut*, 401 U.S. 371, 375 (1971) ("the centrality of the concept of due process in the operation of [the judicial] system" entails that observance of procedural due process is necessary to make the system "acceptable under our scheme of things"); *Kennedy v. Mendoza-Martinez*, 372 U.S. 144, 164–65 (1963) (affirming the "fundamental" and "imperative necessity for safeguarding these rights to procedural due process" even when the executive is acting pursuant to "the great powers of Congress to conduct war and to regulate the Nation's foreign relations").

[50] *Hamdi v. Rumsfeld*, 542 U.S. 507, 536–37 (2004) (plurality opinion of O'Connor, J.). Justice O'Connor's opinion acknowledged that the executive branch itself could establish an intra-executive procedure that would satisfy procedural due process subject to review by the federal habeas court for its conformity to the constitutional requirements. She did not discuss the question whether the executive would still be obligated to afford a detainee procedural due process if Congress lawfully suspended the writ of habeas corpus.

process is absolute in the sense that it does not depend upon the merits of a claimant's substantive assertions." Many other provisions of the Bill of Rights also impose requirements and prohibitions on judicial procedures, especially in the enforcement of criminal law, but the rule in *Graham* that limits the application of substantive due process analysis does not apply to procedural due process. A specific Bill of Rights prohibition and an independent procedural due process requirement thus may both apply to a controversy and lead to different outcomes in litigation. And although Congress is authorized to establish rules of procedure for the federal courts and executive branch entities, the procedures that either it or a state legislature ordains must meet the procedural due process standards established by Supreme Court precedent.[51]

The procedures familiar to English-speaking lawyers provide the historical baseline for the Court's procedural due process standards, but the Court has long since rejected the argument that history either limits what process is due in a given situation or insulates a traditional procedure against challenge. The core constitutional requirements are that the individual receive "notice of the factual basis for [the government's action], and a fair opportunity to rebut the Government's factual assertions before a neutral decision maker ... at a meaningful time and in a meaningful manner." The procedures necessary in a given situation are determined by the test articulated in *Mathews* v. *Eldridge* (1976), which requires "a judicious balancing" of the individual and governmental interests at stake, and an analysis of both the risk of error posed by less process and the potential value of additional procedures. In *Hamdi* v. *Rumsfeld*, Justice O'Connor agreed that the executive had a weighty interest "in ensuring that those who have in fact fought with the enemy during a war do not return to battle against the United States," but she pointed out that Hamdi was asserting "the most elemental of liberty interests – the interest in being free from physical detention by one's own government." Furthermore, she and a majority of the justices were not persuaded that according Hamdi a genuine opportunity to contest his detention would significantly impair the executive's conduct of the war. Accordingly, he was entitled to an adversarial hearing and the assistance of counsel.[52]

---

[51] See *Hamdi*, 542 U.S. at 530 (O'Connor, J.); *Dickerson* v. *United States*, 530 U.S. 428, 444 (2000) (due process prohibition on admitting involuntary confessions in court and self-incrimination clause *Miranda* doctrine may both apply to challenged confession); *Cleveland Bd. of Educ.* v. *Loudermill*, 470 U.S. 532, 540–41 (1985) (procedures ordained by statute do not define what process is constitutionally due).

[52] *Hamdi*, 542 U.S. at 533 (O'Connor, J.) ("These essential constitutional promises may not be eroded."); *id.* at 528–29 (discussing *Mathews* v. *Eldridge*, 424 U.S. 319, 335 (1976)); *id.* at 531, 529–30; *id.* at 534 ("We think it unlikely that this basic process will have the dire impact on the central functions of warmaking"). Two justices thought that Hamdi was entitled to immediate release under an act of Congress forbidding the detention of citizens without specific statutory authority but joined in Justice O'Connor's disposition of the case. See *id.* at 553 (Souter, J., concurring in the judgment) (assuming the detainee is not immediately released, "someone in Hamdi's position is entitled at a minimum to

A Charter of Negative Liberties. In *DeShaney* v. *Winnebago County Dept. of Social Services* (1989), the Supreme Court held that substantive due process had not been violated by the failure of a local governmental child welfare agency to intervene effectively to prevent child abuse of which its employees were aware despite the fact that the end result was to leave the child with profoundly disabling brain damage. The Court recognized that the case's facts were "undeniably tragic," but reasoned that the dispositive fact for constitutional purposes was that the harm was not inflicted by the state agency. "The most that can be said of the state functionaries in this case is that they stood by and did nothing when suspicious circumstances dictated a more active role for them." That inaction, the Court concluded, did not violate the fourteenth amendment.

> Nothing in the language of the Due Process Clause itself requires the State to protect the life, liberty, and property of its citizens against invasion by private actors. The Clause is phrased as a limitation on the State's power to act, not as a guarantee of certain minimal levels of safety and security. It forbids the State itself to deprive individuals of life, liberty, or property without "due process of law," but its language cannot fairly be extended to impose an affirmative obligation on the State to ensure that those interests do not come to harm through other means.

While the Court acknowledged the precedents holding that the Constitution requires government affirmatively to provide necessary care and protection for prisoners, individuals in police custody, and involuntarily committed mental patients, it explained that the rationale of those decisions was that when the government has interfered with someone's ability "to act on his own behalf," that restraint on the individual's "personal liberty . . . is the 'deprivation of liberty' triggering the protections of the Due Process Clause."[53]

DeShaney is the leading Supreme Court decision exemplifying the broader proposition that, taken as a whole, "the Constitution is a charter of negative liberties; it tells the state to let people alone; it does not require the federal government or the state to provide services, even so elementary a service as maintaining law and order."[54] *DeShaney* suggested (in the context of the due process clauses) that as a general matter, the courts should not order political actors to assume affirmative responsibilities, and in that respect it is closely related to the idea that federal courts should respect democratic processes by avoiding unnecessary interference. But the negative-liberties idea cannot be taken too literally, for two reasons.

---

notice of the Government's claimed factual basis for holding him, and to a fair chance to rebut it before a neutral decisionmaker").

[53]   *DeShaney* v. *Winnebago County Dept. of Social Services*, 489 U.S. 189, 191, 203, 200 (1989). The Court did not reach the question whether state child welfare legislation had given the child an entitlement to state intervention protected by procedural due process because the claim was not properly presented before the Court. *Id.* at 195 n. 2.

[54]   *Bowers* v. *DeVito*, 686 F.2d 616, 618 (7th Cir.1982) (Posner, Cir. J.).

First, constitutional prohibitions often require affirmative action if government is to avoid violating the prohibition or satisfy remedial court orders when it has done so. The right to counsel, which extends to indigent criminal defendants whose lawyers must be paid for by the government, is an obvious example: The only way Congress or a state legislature could avoid financing a system for indigent representation would be to eliminate criminal law altogether or excuse indigents from prosecution (thus raising an equal protection problem by discriminating against those accused of felonies with the misfortune to be able to hire counsel!). Similarly, if a federal court determines that a government agency has engaged in unconstitutional racial or gender discrimination in hiring employees, the court may order remedial action, including expensive changes in hiring practices, in order to remedy the constitutional violation.

Even more fundamentally, the "charter of negative liberties" characterization of the Constitution is too limited a description of the American political community's basic governmental arrangements. The constitutional objective of creating a workable government presupposes more than a government that *could* work in the abstract. *McCulloch v. Maryland* explained that the Constitution grants Congress broad discretion in choosing how to exercise its powers so that it can fulfill its "high *duties*" to secure "the happiness and prosperity of the nation" through their "due execution," and in the immediate wake of the adoption of the Civil War amendments, some judicial opinions intimated that both the federal and state governments may have an affirmative duty to protect Americans against private as well as governmental harm. This is not to suggest that *DeShaney* was wrong or should be overruled, but to point out that the "charter of negative liberties" idea stems from the constitutional perspective of the federal courts with its respect for the role of democratic governance in American government. It is not the business of the courts, generally, to order democratic decision makers to fulfill affirmative constitutional duties, but that does not mean such duties do not exist. Constitutional argument over those duties is meaningful, regardless of whether it is constitutional *law* argument in a narrow sense, but it is usually argument that belongs in political rather than judicial forums.[55]

4.2 THE CONSTITUTIONAL PERSPECTIVE FROM WITHIN THE EXECUTIVE BRANCH

Hamdi v. Rumsfeld, which held that the executive branch must follow the Court's view on the requirements of procedural due process even in a time of war and in a situation where the executive thought due process should be curtailed, suggests some significant differences between the perspective on constitutional law shaped by the position in the constitutional system of the federal judiciary and the

---

[55]   *McCulloch v. Maryland*, 17 U.S. (4 Wheat.) 316, 421, 408 (1819). See *United States v. Hall*, 26 F. Cas. 79, 81 (C.C.S.D. Ala. 1871) ("Denying includes inaction as well as action, and denying the equal protection of the laws includes the omission to protect, as well as the omission to pass laws for protection.").

constitutional perspective of the president, other executive branch officers, and their legal advisors. The executive branch's tradition of addressing constitutional problems through formal, written legal opinions is slightly older than the Supreme Court's debut with *Chisholm v. Georgia* in 1793, since it began with Secretary of State Thomas Jefferson's 1790 opinion on the Senate's role in diplomatic appointments, and continued with the 1791 opinions Jefferson, Treasury Secretary Alexander Hamilton, and Attorney General Edmund Randolph gave President Washington on the constitutionality of a national bank almost three decades before *McCulloch v. Maryland*.[56]

The constitutional perspective that this section discusses is primarily that of the president and of the executive branch lawyers who give constitutional law advice, prepare the Justice Department's comments on pending legislation, and formulate the executive's legal responses to congressional inquiries. The lawyers who represent the executive branch in court must construct their arguments, for the most part, from within the constitutional perspective of the federal courts that will govern the courts' decisions, although of course the executive branch's constitutional law views should ultimately be consistent across all its functions.

The Sources of Constitutional Reasoning in the Executive Branch. The first president sought constitutional advice from many sources – in fact on the diplomatic appointments question about which Jefferson wrote in 1790, Washington also consulted more informally with Congressman James Madison and Chief Justice John Jay, both of whom gave him the same answer that Jefferson reached. But from an early point, the attorney general, as the official "law officer" of the executive branch, came to have a near-monopoly on providing the president and other executive branch policy makers formal legal advice on constitutional questions. The only significant exception at present is that on occasion the Office of the Legal Adviser in the Department of State ("L") issues formal, public statements about that office's views on legal and constitutional issues involving foreign affairs.[57]

When the First Congress created the office of attorney general, that officer was not head of a department, and indeed for a number of years did not even have a clerk. Although Attorney General Randolph began the practice of writing formal legal opinions, neither he nor his immediate successors made a systematic attempt to preserve and consult earlier opinions, and it was Attorney General William Wirt (1817–1829) who regularized the practice and established the principle that the attorneys general treat their opinions and those of their predecessors as precedent

---

[56] On these early constitutional law opinions, see H. Jefferson Powell, *A Community Built on Words: The Constitution in History and Politics* 12–19, 21–30 (rev. ed. Chicago: University of Chicago Press, 2005).

[57] See *id.* at 14–15. The reader should not overlook the qualification "formal" in the text. The actual processes of legal deliberation and debate within the executive branch are much more complicated than any simple model centered on formal opinions can capture. On the role of the Department of State's legal adviser, see, e.g., Harold Hongju Koh, The State Department Legal Adviser's Office: Eight Decades in Peace and War, 100 *Geo. L. J.* 1747 (2012).

with similar force to that of judicial precedent. With the establishment of the Department of Justice in 1870, a process began by which the actual writing of formal opinions shifted from the attorney general himself to his subordinates. Since the 1950s, the Office of Legal Counsel (OLC) has generally carried out the attorney general's duties as the executive's chief legal advisor. Official Justice Department constitutional law opinions are now written and published by OLC, although occasionally, and for no overarching reason, an opinion will be signed by the attorney general.[58]

The Justice Department treats presidential decisions as important factors in its constitutional thinking, and so presidential statements that include constitutional law reasoning or conclusions are especially significant. Since in the modern era the statements themselves were likely drafted by OLC, there is a certain happy circularity to their authority. OLC also draws on its unpublished written advice in answering constitutional questions, a practice that is often criticized, with considerable justification, as reliance on "secret law" that has not been subjected to the test of criticism and rebuttal by others.[59]

Distinctive Features of Executive Branch Constitutional Law Reasoning. First, formal executive branch legal opinions on constitutional issues are almost always advice rather than quasi-adjudications. (OLC does adjudicate disputes between executive branch agencies on request, but those disputes seldom involve constitutional issues.) OLC's advice does not bind the attorney general, and the attorney general's views do not bind the president, although by long-standing custom the Justice Department's stated legal positions become those of the executive branch as a whole unless repudiated by the president. Executive branch opinions therefore may range more widely than most judicial opinions, since the officer who requested the advice may have been interested in a broader overview of some area of law rather than the answer to a narrow question. On the other hand, an opinion is probably shaped in important ways by the political context in which the lawyer's advice was sought, and thus the reasonable scope to be given its arguments may be limited by that context. To say this is not to criticize the executive branch's lawyers, but to note the importance of recalling that an attorney general or OLC opinion is in important ways more like a brief than it is a judicial opinion: The executive's legal advisors are

---

[58]   See 1 Op. O.L.C. Supp. Foreword vii–viii.

[59]   The reader should not confuse the Office of Legal Counsel, a component of the Department of Justice, with the White House Counsel's office. The "Assistant to the President and Counsel to the President" (the White House Counsel's official title) heads an office that is part of the Executive Office of the President (the president's staff) and provides legal advice to the president. (The Counsel is not the personal and private lawyer of the individual who is president.) The issues that OLC and the White House Counsel address overlap, but the Counsel does not issue formal, written opinions, or as a general rule give official advice to other executive branch officials. Unlike OLC opinions, the legal conclusions of the Counsel have no formal authority (leaving to one side the work the Counsel's office does to ensure that the president and immediate staff comply with various ethics requirements), although obviously there are good reasons why other people might be extremely interested in the views of a lawyer who is part of the president's immediate circle of advisors.

not supposed to be neutral decision makers. But of course in order to provide useful advice, the attorney general and OLC must make responsible constitutional law arguments that, especially when they reach contestable conclusions, are professionally defensible explications of what the Constitution-in-practice commands.

An example may be helpful. For much of the time the United States actively participated in the Vietnam War, the government of Cambodia was officially neutral, and the North Vietnamese government and its Viet Cong allies made extensive use of bases just inside the Cambodian border because American unwillingness to push the Cambodian government into the arms of the North Vietnamese made those bases almost inviolate sanctuaries from American or South Vietnamese attack. However, a coup in March 1970 put in a place a Cambodian military government that was willing to act as a de facto ally of the United States, and so the Nixon administration decided to take military action on the ground against the sanctuaries. On April 30, American and South Vietnamese troops began undertaking large-scale operations on Cambodian soil, provoking massive demonstrations in the United States, and a White House request for his legal views to OLC Assistant Attorney General William H. Rehnquist, later chief justice of the United States.

If Rehnquist had concluded that the Cambodian operation was unlawful, we may assume that he would not have been allowed to publish his opinion. That assumption may be incorrect: President Nixon laid emphatic claim to a broad power to impound congressionally appropriated funds but did not interfere with Assistant Attorney General Rehnquist providing Congress a public opinion disagreeing with Nixon's views. But even on the further assumption that Rehnquist, like the author of a brief, knew the conclusion he needed to reach, his opinion, like a good brief, did so only by presenting a powerful argument that the conclusion was the right answer to the question posed. Rehnquist reviewed the history of presidential uses of military force and concluded that political practice supported the existence of some presidential authority to engage in hostilities without congressional authorization. But he also acknowledged the argument from the written Constitution's original meaning and governmental structure that "if the contours of the divided war power contemplated by the framers of the Constitution are to remain, constitutional practice must include Executive resort to Congress in order to obtain its sanction for the conduct of hostilities which reach a certain scale." Rehnquist further conceded Congress's power to set limits on its authorization for the use of military force that the executive must obey.[60]

On the particular issue before him, Rehnquist defended the legality of the Cambodian operation on the ground that it did not violate any congressional limit and was a tactical decision in the conduct of the congressionally authorized defense

---

[60] *The President and the War Power: South Vietnam and the Cambodian Sanctuaries*, 1 Op. O.L.C. Supp. 321, 331–32 (1970). *See Presidential Authority to Impound Funds Appropriated for Assistance to Federally Impacted Schools*, 1 Op. O.L.C. Supp. 303 (1969) (concluding that the president has no general power to impound appropriated funds).

of South Vietnam rather than an expansion of the war. In its immediate context, this advice provided a legal justification for the president's decision; as an executive branch precedent, the opinion was an emphatic rejection of broad claims of unilateral presidential war-making authority. And most importantly for our purposes, Rehnquist's opinion demonstrates the nature of responsible executive branch constitutional thought: responsible both to the task of serving as legal advisor to politicians and to the constitutional lawyer's obligation to construct legal arguments rather than mere public relations statements.

The proposition that in important respects a formal executive branch legal opinion is more like a brief than a judicial opinion is contested, but I believe that disagreement is rooted in an inadvertent misunderstanding of the role of legal advice, and indeed, of legal argument generally. One of the fundamental practical circumstances that attends all constitutional law is that the federal courts are incapable of addressing all constitutionally questionable federal laws, regulations, and executive actions. As the reader knows, some such issues (particularly in such vital areas as the constitutional law of foreign affairs and national security) can never come before the courts because of standing or other justiciability or jurisdictional limitations. And even if an issue could be raised in theory by a plaintiff with standing and in a form that a federal court could address, there are simply too many such issues. The role of Supreme Court precedent in executive branch legal thought must be, most of the time, to serve as guidance for the executive's own decisions, decisions that will generally not be reviewed by any court. The fundamental twofold logic of constitutional law rests on the bedrock principle that *all* federal governmental actions must be authorized to be lawful, and that *none* can be lawful if they are prohibited. If the Constitution-in-practice and the rule of law are to be an across-the-board reality in the executive branch's operations, the executive itself must act to make them so.

The executive's legal advisors cannot act as neutral and detached constitutional decision makers precisely because the ultimate objective of their legal advice is to aid the president and other policy makers in fulfilling their oaths to uphold the Constitution. The goal of the Constitution is to create and maintain a workable government, and (as this book has observed more than once) part of what it means to be a workable government in the American system is that the government respects the fundamental constitutional commitments of the American political community, some of which deliberately cut against efficiency and similar concerns. But another of those commitments is to create a government that can effectively address the needs of the community as those needs are perceived by policy makers in the political branches.[61] Political decisions do not begin with the question "what is

---

[61] *Cf. McCulloch v. Maryland*, 17 U.S. (4 Wheat.) 316, 407–08 (1819) ("The sword and the purse, all the external relations, and no inconsiderable portion of the industry of the nation, are intrusted to [the federal] government. It . . . may with great reason be contended, that a government, intrusted with such ample powers, on the due execution of which the happiness and prosperity of the nation so vitally

lawful?" and then cast about for action within the limits of the law. Policy and politics are the driving forces – rightly – and it serves the Constitution's purposes to enable policy makers to seek advice from lawyers whose goal is to help them find a constitutional path to their objectives if one exists. An executive branch lawyer who was uninterested in the ability of his or her advisees to advance their policy determinations would make government less workable, and would soon be a lawyer whose advice no one sought.

None of this is to say that responsible executive branch lawyers should give advice or take positions that are unprincipled or designed simply to provide the president or other officers with legal cover. Fortunately, however, we do not face a binary choice between neutral and uninvolved decision maker and unprincipled and partisan hack. Constitutional law reasoning is *always* built on arguments designed to persuade rather than on proofs of the sort available in Euclidean geometry. On a great many issues, there are no plausible arguments on one side, and all competent constitutional lawyers will come to the same conclusion. But on contestable issues, what makes the lawyer's answer a responsible and principled one is its foundation in arguments that other lawyers can take seriously, not the answering lawyer's Olympian indifference as to the answer.

If the lawyer is a judge, the goal is to persuade any reader that the arguments and answer are the most compelling that can be given to the question, period. If the lawyer is a litigator, the goal is to present a court with the arguments and answer that are the most compelling that can be made for the client. And if the lawyer is an executive branch legal advisor, the goal is to persuade any reader (once again) that the arguments and answer presented are the most compelling that can be made in answer to the question asked, which sometimes is simply "what's the right answer?" (in which case the advisor's answer will converge with the judge's) and sometimes "is there a plausible constitutional justification for this decision?" (in which case the advisor's answer will resemble that of a litigator). The advisor's success in providing useful advice depends in part on resisting the temptation to overclaim. Assistant Attorney General Rehnquist's opinion on the Cambodian sanctuaries operation clearly fell into the second category, and Rehnquist's careful combination of defensible arguments on behalf of President Nixon's order with repeated, clear acknowledgments of Congress's power to limit presidential discretion is an excellent example of responsible executive branch constitutional advice.

It is too obvious to require elaboration that some policy makers sometimes ask inappropriate questions ("how can we circumvent this law and avoid sanctions?") and that executive branch lawyers may sometimes feel the temptation to give advice based on arguments that do not rise to the level of responsible, defensible legal

depends, must also be intrusted with ample means for their execution. The power being given, it is the interest of the nation to facilitate its execution. It can never be their interest, and cannot be presumed to have been their intention, to clog and embarrass its execution, by withholding the most appropriate means.").

analysis. We need not be naïve about political decision makers or their lawyers, although it is my sense that critics are often too cynical about the intra-executive process of constitutional law reasoning. But regardless of the risk of lapses in responsibility, legal advice advanced from the perspective just outlined is an indispensable part of the arrangements which provide the only practical means in many circumstances of ensuring that American government acts in conformity with the Constitution-in-practice.

Second, some popular impressions to the contrary, the presidents have almost always accepted the binding force of Supreme Court decisions, and the Justice Department formally recognizes an obligation to accept the authority of the Supreme Court's constitutional decisions. "We believe that the constitutional structure obligates the executive branch to adhere to settled judicial doctrine that limits executive and legislative power. While the Supreme Court's decisions interpreting the Constitution cannot simply be *equated* with the Constitution, we are mindful of the special role of the courts in the interpretation of the law of the Constitution." But the Court's decisions have not addressed all issues, and as we have seen cannot do so. The case law therefore constrains the arguments the executive's lawyers can responsibly advance – they are not free to advise disregard for constitutional limits the Supreme Court has asserted – but they may appropriately construct arguments or base advice on lines of reasoning or conclusions that the Court has neither reached nor rejected.[62]

Third, executive branch constitutional lawyers generally use the same basic toolkit as their colleagues in other settings, but with some additions and slight modifications in emphasis. The most obvious and important addition is the weight the Justice Department puts on attorney general and OLC opinions as executive branch precedents. While the federal courts do not entirely ignore those opinions, when the courts do refer to them, it is usually as part of an argument from political practice. For the executive's lawyers, however, the opinions play a role as precedent similar to the practice in the judiciary, although it must be conceded that the commitment of Justice Department lawyers to executive branch stare decisis varies over time and across administrations. Furthermore, executive branch lawyers accord presidential decisions, and statements on legal issues signed by presidents a role as direct sources of constitutional reasoning and not simply as evidence of political practice. Additionally, executive branch constitutional law argument puts greater weight on actual arguments from political practice and from structure than does the Supreme Court's constitutional case law, taken as a whole. This is in part because a far broader swath of the constitutional problems the executive's legal advisors attempt to solve involves issues of structure than is true of the Court, which addresses a myriad of other issues such as individual rights that formal executive branch

---

[62]   *The Constitutional Separation of Powers Between the President and Congress*, 20 Op. O.L.C. 124, 127 (1996).

opinions do not usually address. (In implementing policy and in litigation, executive branch lawyers deal with individual rights questions frequently.)

Finally, a great deal of executive branch constitutional law thought is specifically directed toward the perceived problem of congressional aggrandizement. A contemporary political scientist is unlikely to view the modern presidency as the weaker of the two political branches. As a matter of constitutional law, however, Congress has the upper hand on most issues, if as a political matter it can muster the will to exercise its power. (The reader should recall the fundamental asymmetry of power between Congress and the president.) And even in conditions of partisan divide and congressional deadlock, legislation sometimes includes provisions that infringe legitimate presidential authority or are inconsistent with the Constitution-in-practice even though they are not part of a deliberate legislative attack on the executive, and that will go unaddressed unless the executive identifies them and responds.

It is in that context that the executive's lawyers understand themselves to be under "a constitutional obligation" not simply to act on behalf of "parochial institutional interests" but "to assert and maintain the legitimate powers and privileges of the President against inadvertent or intentional congressional intrusion."

> Since the organization of the Government, Presidents have felt bound to insist upon the maintenance of the Executive functions unimpaired by legislative encroachment, just as the legislative branch has felt bound to resist interferences with its power by the Executive. To acquiesce in legislation having a tendency to encroach upon the executive authority results in establishing dangerous precedents.

The obligation is thought to be especially weighty with respect to legislation that violates acknowledged separation of powers principles but is "unlikely to reach the courts in a form or context in which the judiciary will be able to identify or remedy the constitutional problem."[63]

The executive branch has a variety of means by which to appropriately carry out this duty to resist congressional intrusions on presidential authority or violations of separation of powers limitations on Congress's powers. The least controversial is the president's power to veto legislation, and from the Washington administration on, presidents have regarded the veto as designed, in part, to enable the executive to protect the constitutional structure against legislative impairment. Because

---

[63] *The Constitutional Separation of Powers Between the President and Congress*, 20 Op. O.L.C. 124, 126, 128 (1996). OLC gave as examples "legislation that attempts to structure the very details of executive decision making, or that imposes onerous and repetitive reporting requirements on executive agencies. . . . The overall effects of such micromanagement for the constitutional separation of powers obviously can be tremendous, and yet it is unlikely that judicial intervention can or would preserve the constitutional balance. The executive branch thus has the primary responsibility for presenting, in as forceful and principled a way as possible, the separation of powers problems." *Id.* at 181. The block quotation in the text is from *Constitutionality of Proposed Legislation Affecting Tax Refunds*, 37 Op. Att'y Gen. 56, 64 (1933).

executive branch legal tradition does not view the president as under an obligation to veto legislation when it includes provisions thought to be unconstitutional, particularly in recent decades, presidents sometimes sign into law such legislation while issuing concurrently a signing statement identifying the constitutional problems. The president may then go on to invoke the avoidance canon and instruct subordinate executive branch officers to give the apparently invalid provision a constitutional interpretation or, if that is impossible, to decline to execute the provision.[64]

Both the practice of issuing signing statements and the asserted power to refuse to execute provisions of acts of Congress are highly controversial. The objection to signing statements per se is ill-founded since it is clearly desirable from constitutional and good-government perspectives for the president to announce publicly a decision not to give an act of Congress the force its text seems to require. In contrast, there are significant objections to the claim that the president can decide not to obey a statutory provision, whether in new legislation or a long-standing law, because the president and the executive branch's lawyers think it unconstitutional. The take care clause of Article II section 3 commands the president to "take Care that the Laws be faithfully executed," which no doubt implies that the president has the constitutional authority to do so. OLC has argued that the Constitution is one of "the Laws" that the president must see executed, but the more natural reading of that plural noun is that it is a reference to *Congress's* "Laws," a reading supported by the historical background of English objections to the Stuart kings' claim that they could suspend acts of Parliament or dispense with an act's application in particular cases. As Justice Oliver Wendell Holmes summed up this objection: "The duty of the President to see that the laws be executed is a duty that does not go beyond the laws or require him to achieve more than Congress sees fit to leave within his power."[65]

Despite the weight of the arguments against it, the existence of a presidential power to decline to execute an unconstitutional statute is settled within the executive branch, and is accepted as a pragmatic matter by Congress and the courts. Presidents have exercised the power and defended its legitimacy since at least 1860. While the Supreme Court has never squarely held that the Constitution gives the president this authority, the Court has also refrained from criticizing the executive for refusing to execute an unconstitutional provision or for failing to defend a statute in litigation. (In the opinion just quoted, Justice Holmes was dissenting from a decision invalidating a statute that the president had disobeyed on constitutional grounds, although the Court did so without expressly approving the president's

---

[64]　See *INS v. Chadha*, 462 U.S. 919, 942 n. 13 (1983) ("it is not uncommon for Presidents to approve legislation containing parts which are objectionable on constitutional grounds"); *Presidential Signing Statements*, 31 Op. O.L.C. 23 (2007) (discussing the roles of signing statements); *The Dep't of Homeland Security's Authority to Prioritize Removal of Certain Aliens Unlawfully Present in the United States & to Defer Removal of Others*, 2014 WL 10788677, at *6 (OLC 2014) ("under the Take Care Clause, the President is required to act in accordance with the laws – including the Constitution, which takes precedence over other forms of law").

[65]　*Myers v. United States*, 272 U.S. 52, 295 (1926) (Holmes, J., dissenting).

action.) And in 2002, Congress responded to the increasing number of presidential decline-to-execute decisions not by attempting to prohibit them but by enacting a requirement that the attorney general submit a report to Congress whenever the Justice Department acts on such a decision or decides not to defend or (more aggressively) actually to challenge an act of Congress in court.[66]

Any Article II presidential authority to decline to execute a provision of law enacted by the Article I legislative branch obviously must have limits if the authority is not to devolve into a lawless power to nullify any statutory provision that interferes with the president's discretion in a sufficiently objectionable fashion. The Justice Department has responded to that imperative by creating what is in effect a standard of review. If the president and his/her legal advisors think that the Supreme Court would uphold the provision, the president cannot refuse to enforce it. But if "the President, exercising his independent judgment, determines both that a provision would violate the Constitution and that it is probable that the Court would agree with him, the President has the authority to decline to execute the statute." The president is not obliged to decline execution, and the decision whether to exercise the authority should take into account which course of action would be most likely to lead to a judicial determination of the issue, since it is preferable for reasons of stability and political acceptance that the ultimate constitutional decision be made by the federal courts.[67]

The fact that the executive branch's own perspective leads it to recognize judicial review as the ordinary and most satisfactory means of answering constitutional questions does not mean that executive branch constitutional law opinions are temporary expedients, valuable only while we await a resolution from the federal courts. In part because of the courts' justiciability limitations, an executive branch opinion sometimes provides the only express, reasoned answer with any institutional authority to an important constitutional question. Consider this example. Congress often prescribes qualifications of various kinds for appointment to offices in the executive branch, which raises the question whether the appointments clause of Article II section 2 permits such a limitation on the appointing authority. The

---

[66] *Memorial of Captain Meigs*, 9 Op. Att'y. Gen. 462, 469–70 (1860) (advising the president that a condition in an appropriations law was unconstitutional and that "you are therefore entirely justified in treating this condition ... as if the paper on which it is written were blank."). President Buchanan accepted the attorney general's advice. Modern Justice Department opinions agree. See, e.g., *The Attorney General's Duty to Defend and Enforce Constitutionally Objectionable Legislation*, 4A Op. O. L.C. 55, 59 (1980). For a clear statement of approval in a Supreme Court opinion joined by four justices, see *Freytag* v. *Commissioner*, 501 U.S. 868, 906 (1991) (Scalia, J., concurring in part and concurring in the judgment) (the Constitution provides the president "the means to resist legislative encroachment upon [executive] power [including] the power to veto encroaching laws, or even to disregard them when they are unconstitutional." The 2002 statute is codified at 28 U.S.C. § 530D.

[67] *Presidential Authority to Decline to Execute Unconstitutional Statutes*, 18 Op. O.L.C. 199, 200–01 (1994). The Justice Department view is that the president's authority is not limited to statutes encroaching on executive powers, although the executive has a special responsibility to defend legitimate presidential prerogatives.

Supreme Court has never squarely addressed the issue, and the leading discussion for a century and a half has been an 1871 opinion by a great attorney general, Amos T. Akerman.

Attorney General Akerman was asked to opine whether Congress could limit appointments to some civil offices to those individuals who scored a prescribed score on a civil service examination. Akerman's answer was yes and no. He agreed that "the unquestioned right of Congress to create offices implies a right to prescribe qualifications for them," but reasoned that this implied congressional power should not be construed to render the Article II appointment power a formality. Statutory qualifications must leave "scope for the judgment and will of the person or body in whom the Constitution vests the power of appointment." Anticipating the objection that the doctrinal rule he was proposing leaves the extent to which Congress can narrow the field of potential nominees uncertain, Akerman agreed that he had no bright-line answer. "But the difficulty of drawing a line between such limitations as are, and such as are not, allowed by the Constitution, is no proof that both classes do not exist. In constitutional and legal inquiries, right or wrong is often a question of degree." A twenty-first-century constitutional lawyer addressing a constitutional problem involving qualifications for office can profitably consult Akerman's opinion.[68]

Who Is the Solicitor General's Client? The solicitor general of the United States is required by act of Congress, uniquely, to be "learned in the law," and his or her most prominent duty (shared with the attorney general by statute) is to "conduct and argue suits and appeals in the Supreme Court" and certain other courts "in which the United States is interested." The solicitor general's briefs ordinarily designate the party represented as "the United States," a practice that has its origins in the Judiciary Act of 1789, which imposed both the requirement of legal learning and the duty of representing "the United States" on the attorney general. (When the Justice Department and the office of solicitor general were created in 1870, Congress mysteriously deleted the learning requirement from the statutory definition of the attorney general's office.)[69]

As William Wirt, the greatest of the early attorneys general, had already realized, designating an executive branch officer's duty as one of representing the interests of "the United States" is ambiguous in a constitutional system that disperses the federal government's powers among three branches and ultimately serves the American political community as a whole. In most circumstances, the difficulty of identifying the client is mostly theoretical: The solicitor general (an executive branch officer) advocates the executive's legal position, defends the validity of acts of Congress, and (out of both prudence and principle) recognizes the authority and prerogatives of the federal courts. But conflict among the branches and indeed within the executive branch occurs, and in those situations Attorney General Wirt's riddle can become a problem.

---

[68]   *Civil-Service Commission*, 13 Op. Att'y Gen. 516, 520, 525 (1871).
[69]   28 U.S.C. §§ 505, 518(a).

In 1988, the Supreme Court provided a general answer in *United States v. Providence Journal Co.*, a case in which a special prosecutor brought a criminal contempt proceeding against a newspaper for disobedience to a federal district court order. When the court of appeals reversed the contempt judgment, the solicitor general refused permission for the prosecutor to petition the Court for a writ of certiorari, but the prosecutor nonetheless petitioned and the Court agreed to review the appeals court's decision. Before the justices, both the prosecutor and the solicitor general argued that the case was not one "in which the United States is interested," because that statutory language "refers solely to those cases where the interests of the Executive Branch of the United States are at issue." The Court sharply disagreed.

> We find such a proposition somewhat startling. . . . It seems to be elementary that even when exercising distinct and jealously separated powers, the three branches are but co-ordinate parts of one government. Congress is familiar enough with the language of separation of powers that we shall not assume it intended, without saying so, to exclude the Judicial Branch when it referred to the "interest of the United States." Moreover, while there may well be matters that are uniquely Executive Branch concerns, we do not think they would be fairly described by the broad statutory language of § 518 (a).

On that reasoning, the Court concluded that "a criminal contempt prosecution brought to vindicate the authority of the Judiciary . . . is a suit 'in which the United States is interested,'" and dismissed the writ of certiorari because the statute gave the solicitor general control of whether a petition should be filed.[70]

At least since *Providence Journal*, it has been clear that in principle the solicitor general should attempt to protect the interests of the federal government as a whole, but in a practical sense (and particularly where there are separation of powers issues) the executive branch's interests will ordinarily predominate. By long tradition, the solicitors general hold themselves to high standards of principled argument, respect for Congress and the Court, and the principle that the executive branch's "chief business" in litigation "is not merely to prevail in the instant case . . . but to establish justice." But the solicitor general is nonetheless "not a neutral, he is an advocate." It is no disparagement of the solicitors general and their assistants to suggest that it is odd, and probably a disservice to constitutional law, that Congress has never established an ongoing institutional means for presenting its views to the Court.[71]

---

[70] *United States v. Providence Journal Co.*, 485 U.S. 693, 701, 707–08 (1988). See also *Duties of the Attorney General*, 5 Op. Att'y Gen. 720 (1820) (Wirt, Att'y Gen.).

[71] Simon E. Sobeloff, Attorney for the Government: The Work of the Solicitor General's Office, 41 A.B. A.J, 41 A.B.A.J. 229 (1955). Sobeloff, solicitor general (1954–56) and then a federal appellate judge, was echoing a famous statement by his predecessor Frederick W. Lehmann (1910–1912). Questioned by a judge why his argument seemed to help the opposing party, Solicitor General Lehmann responded that "The United States wins its point whenever justice is done its citizens in the courts."

4.3 THE CONSTITUTIONAL PERSPECTIVE FROM THE STANDPOINT OF CONGRESS

The enumeration principle and the oaths members of Congress take to support the Constitution place on Congress the obligation to consider and decide responsibly questions about the constitutionality of proposed legislation.

> When Congress acts within its sphere of power and responsibilities, it has not just the right but the duty to make its own informed judgment on the meaning and force of the Constitution. This has been clear from the early days of the Republic. In 1789, when a Member of the House of Representatives objected to a debate on the constitutionality of legislation based on the theory that "it would be officious" to consider the constitutionality of a measure that did not affect the House, James Madison explained that "it is incontrovertibly of as much importance to this branch of the Government as to any other, that the constitution should be preserved entire. It is our duty."

Early Congresses took this duty very seriously and engaged in extensive and impressively sophisticated debates about constitutional problems. The emergence of judicial review as the central mechanism for constitutional law articulation and enforcement was accompanied by a decline in the frequency of such debates, and modern Congresses generally leave constitutional issues to committee consideration or simple neglect.[72]

In itself, congressional debate over constitutional questions partly discharges the members' personal and collective duty to the Constitution but does not state the constitutional views of *Congress*: The members speak for themselves, committee reports (whatever their weight in statutory construction) are not actually statements by Congress itself, and there are likely to be many reasons why a majority in both houses voted to enact legislation despite constitutional issues – at least some will have come to a conscientious conclusion that the concerns are unwarranted but others may have decided to ignore the problem or assume that judicial review will correct any constitutional errors. Unlike the federal courts and the executive branch, Congress has no tradition of issuing or approving written legal opinions discussing constitutional issues, and indeed no institutionalized means of doing so. In contrast to the other two branches, which have been explaining their perspectives on constitutional law for over two centuries, there are scarcely any sources at all that would allow us to give a coherent account of the constitutional perspective of

---

[72]   *City of Boerne* v. *Flores*, 521 U.S. 507, 535 (1997) (quoting 1 Annals of Congress 500 (1789)). The Department of Justice provides Congress with comments on legal issues, including constitutional ones, in proposed legislation, which provides Congress with an opportunity to address constitutional concerns as perceived by the executive branch. The classic study of the early constitutional law debates in Congress is 1 & 2 David P. Currie, *The Constitution in Congress* (Chicago: University of Chicago Press, 1997, 2001).

"Congress," a two-chambered, hydra-headed body with no means of authoritatively declaring what "its" views are.

The fact that there is no congressional perspective in the sense that there are judicial and executive ones does not mean that we cannot speak meaningfully, for some purposes, about how constitutional issues appear if we take Congress's standpoint in thinking about them. Indeed, both the federal courts and the executive branch's lawyers approach constitutional issues on the assumption that they can properly speak of Congress's constitutional views. The Supreme Court has often asserted that "judging the constitutionality of an Act of Congress is 'the gravest and most delicate duty that this Court is called on to perform.'" In explaining why, the Court has made the structural point that "Congress is a co-equal branch," but it also has invoked the fact that Congress's "[m]embers take the same oath we do to uphold the Constitution of the United States," and asserted its assumption that the members of Congress carry out their independent duty to answer constitutional questions that arise in the course of lawmaking. But how can we treat a statute, which most of the time will be barren of any constitutional reasoning, as if it were a constitutional argument on its own behalf?[73]

The answer that constitutional lawyers tacitly assume can be stated in terms parallel to our discussion of the method they use in constructing arguments from original meaning. Those arguments require some means of assembling out of diverse sources a meaning that can be ascribed to a single decision maker, in that case the People. Recall that the constitutional lawyer making such an argument must find a significant basis in the historical sources that supports the argument. But the plausibility of arguing that the historical evidence should be treated as establishing the original meaning of the constitutional provision in question is measured not by history but by law. So here, we attribute a particular constitutional answer to Congress by applying a postulate of constitutional law to whatever relevant facts there are. *Congress's constitutional views are those that can be ascribed to a reasonable Congress, informed about the contents of the Constitution-in-practice and committed to acting only with constitutional authorization and without violating any constitutional prohibition.* This is only a presumption, and it is overcome when an act of Congress cannot be defended by any arguments that a responsible constitutional lawyer would make. But it provides the legal bridge between facts about congressional action (statutory texts, committee reports, even floor debates) and conclusions about the constitutional positions that can be ascribed to Congress.

The primary and for most purposes the only formal means by which Congress speaks is of course the enactment of legislation. Acts of Congress and joint resolutions (there is no constitutional distinction between the two, both of which enact

---

[73] *Northwest Austin Mun. Util. Dist. No. One v. Holder*, 557 U.S. 193, 204 (2009) (quoting *Blodgett v. Holden*, 275 U.S. 142, 148 (1927) (separate opinion of Holmes, J.)); *City of Boerne v. Flores*, 521 U.S. 507, 535 (1997). See also *The Constitutional Separation of Powers Between the President and Congress*, 20 Op. O.L.C. 124, 128 n. 13 (1996) ("From the beginning of the Republic, the executive branch has interpreted the Constitution with a due regard for the constitutional views of Congress.").

law) are presumed to reflect a constitutional decision on its part that the legislation is authorized and not prohibited, but in itself the presumption of constitutionality only generates a bare conclusion. Congress occasionally supplements that conclusion with an express statement about constitutional law. Section 2 of the War Powers Resolution, for example, states that "the framers of the Constitution" intended that the lawful use of military force be the product of "the collective judgment of both the Congress and the President." Applying the postulate italicized in the previous paragraph, we should ascribe to Congress the additional reasoning needed to fill out this skeletal argument from original meaning. More controversially, I think that the same analysis should be used when Congress passes a concurrent resolution expressing its views. Such resolutions, which are not presented to the president and do not have the force of law, are clear expressions of position by a majority in both houses, and deserve to be treated as expressing the views of Congress.

Congress more frequently provides a basis for working out the constitutional reasoning to be ascribed to it by including in the statutory text factual findings that implicitly suggest a constitutional argument. For example, a finding that the manu-facture and distribution of green widgets adds $10 billion annually to the national economy implies the argument that green widgets are within Congress's commerce power because their manufacture and distribution have a substantial effect on interstate commerce. Other features of a statutory text that seem to refer to a rule or principle of constitutional law, such as the inclusion of an obvious jurisdictional element, may also provide a basis for a conclusion about the reasoning that can be said to be Congress's. And other statutes on related subjects may, together with the provision under review, provide a basis for inferring what constitutional arguments a constitutionally well-informed Congress would have made in defense of the provision.

Legislative history is another source. A committee report or floor debate may show that a particular line of constitutional law reasoning was at least considered in the lawmaking process. If a competent constitutional lawyer would find the reasoning plausible on the basis of the postulate discussed previously, then it may rightly be treated as expressing Congress's congressional view in the absence of evidence to the contrary.

Taking Congress's standpoint thus provides us a method of filling out the idea that an act of Congress is also, implicitly, a constitutional *argument* by Congress about why the act is authorized and not prohibited. There is additionally another useful sense in which constitutional law can benefit from looking at a problem from the standpoint of Congress, not to infer the reasoning to be imputed to Congress but to enable the constitutional lawyer to take into account Congress's position in the overall structure of American governmental arrangements.

The Supreme Court has observed that its separation of powers decisions are "animated" by concern over the dangers of "encroachment and aggrandizement [resulting from] the hydraulic pressure inherent within each of the separate

Branches to exceed the outer limits of its power." As we have seen, a major theme in the executive branch's constitutional perspective is fear of congressional interference with the constitutional authority of the president, although as we have also seen, the *Youngstown* doctrine rests on the federal courts' cautious approach to presidential actions that disregard Congress's authority. Parallel concerns emerge when constitutional problems arise out of federalism and the enumeration principle's limitation on federal – and in particular congressional – powers. Decisions such as *United States* v. *Lopez* explicitly invoke the danger of congressional aggrandizement impairing the role of the states, although, as *McCulloch* v. *Maryland* showed long ago, state governments can also impede the federal government's ability to exercise its legitimate authority. The metaphor of hydraulic pressure applies to every part of the American system of government.[74]

Congress is, at one and the same time, extremely powerful and remarkably dependent. It enjoys an asymmetric relationship not only with the executive branch but also with the federal courts. Its powers override those of the other branches where they overlap, and its legislative authority enables it to enact laws on any matter within executive or judicial power: "The Congress shall have Power ... [t]o make all Laws which shall be necessary and proper for carrying into Execution ... all ... Powers vested by this Constitution in the Government of the United States, or in any Department or Officer thereof." Congress's authority when acting within its authorized powers is equally superior to that of the states: "the Laws of the United States which shall be made in Pursuance [of the Constitution] shall be the supreme Law of the Land." At the same time, Congress is hemmed in by its need to achieve agreement among a majority of members in two distinct chambers, by the president's veto power, by the judicially enforced limitations on its powers and prohibitions on their exercise, by its dependence on the executive branch to make virtually anything it does more than a dead letter, and by the states' ability to frustrate the achievement of congressional objectives by their frequent and endlessly creative efforts to minimize federal interference and protect their parochial interests.

A perspective on constitutional problems from Congress's standpoint should reflect this combination of power and dependence, and in so doing encourage the constitutional lawyer to understand the practical limitations on Congress's powers. Congressional legislation regulating domestic matters often appears, and sometimes is, overly aggressive in its assertion of national authority in situations where it might be more sensible, and more consonant with American constitutional arrangements, to leave the concern to the state governments. Congressional legislation providing for the federal government's response to emergencies usually appears, and very often is, too permissive in the power it gives the president to set aside ordinary rules on the basis of loosely defined "emergency" conditions. It is easy to explain the former as the product of political willfulness and the latter in terms of the political instinct to

---

[74] *Mistretta* v. *United States*, 488 U.S. 361, 382 (1989).

shirk responsibility, and both observations may be true, but there is a constitutional dimension as well. Painting with a broad brush is an unavoidable by-product of the difficulties attendant on action when taking action depends on bicameral passage and presentment to a third party, and then must rely for its practical implementation on action or noninterference by others. Put another way, taking into account Congress's standpoint suggests that for American government to be workable, the other actors in the system should allow the national legislature considerable leeway, and flaws in its handiwork should often be viewed as political issues to be addressed politically rather than constitutional infractions to be resisted or nullified. *McCulloch* v. *Maryland* said as much long ago. After a federal court has satisfied itself that Congress's exercise of an implied power is "an appropriate mode of executing" its express powers, Chief Justice Marshall wrote, judicial review under the necessary and proper clause is at an end. More fine-tuned debate whether the statute is truly "necessary" belongs in Congress, or as Marshall put it with elegant indirection, "the degree of its necessity . . . is to be discussed in another place."[75]

---

[75] *McCulloch* v. *Maryland*, 17 U.S. (4 Wheat.) 316, 423 (1819).

5

Solving Constitutional Problems

Specific Clauses in the Written Constitution

In order to solve a constitutional problem, the constitutional lawyer will always use the basic toolkit of arguments discussed in Chapter 3, and as we saw in Chapter 4, the lawyer must also consider the ways in which institutional perspective affects how questions are shaped and answers constructed. There are, furthermore, specific clauses in the written Constitution that merit special attention.

Article I Section 8: The Dormant Commerce Clause. Article IV of the Articles of Confederation purported to guarantee to the citizens of every state free entry to and "all the privileges of trade and commerce" in any other state. But the Confederation Congress had no effective means of protecting these rights.

> Removing state trade barriers was a principal reason for the adoption of the Constitution. Under the Articles of Confederation, States notoriously obstructed the interstate shipment of goods. ... The Annapolis Convention of 1786 was convened to address this critical problem, and it culminated in a call for the Philadelphia Convention that framed the Constitution in the summer of 1787. At that Convention, discussion of the power to regulate interstate commerce was almost uniformly linked to the removal of state trade barriers, and when the Constitution was sent to the state conventions, fostering free trade among the States was prominently cited as a reason for ratification.

Article I section 8's grant of power "To regulate Commerce ... among the several States" was the written Constitution's solution.[1]

If the interstate commerce power were exclusive, the commerce clause would provide a clear basis for invalidating state laws affecting the national common market, but such a reading of the clause is impracticable, given the wide range of benign state legislation that affects interstate commerce. By the 1850s, therefore, the Court settled on an intellectual compromise: The constitutional text's authorization of congressional regulation of the national common market implicitly prohibits some but not all state laws that interfere with interstate commerce. The doctrinal

---

[1] *Tennessee Wine & Spirits Retailers Assoc. v. Thomas*, 139 S. Ct. 2449, 2460 (2019).

framework for enforcing this "dormant commerce clause" (or "negative commerce clause" if you are a critic) has changed over time, and current case law recognizes two categories of legislation affected by the doctrine.[2] State laws that directly discriminate against that commerce and are thus closely parallel to the protectionist state legislation of the 1780s are subject to "a virtually *per se* rule of invalidity": They are constitutionally prohibited unless they are the only effective means of achieving an extremely weighty and nonprotectionist state interest. State legislation that addresses legitimate, nonprotectionist state concerns but incidentally has some constraining effect on interstate commerce is reviewed using "*Pike* balancing" and is invalid only if "the burden imposed on [interstate] commerce is clearly excessive in relation to the putative local benefits."[3]

The dormant commerce clause is obviously a somewhat unusual feature of the Constitution-in-practice. On its face, the text of the clause is an authorization of congressional action rather than a prohibition on state legislation, and critics of the doctrine argue that there simply is no proper textual basis for invalidating state laws under the commerce clause, unless of course Congress has enacted affirmative legislation pursuant to the clause that preempts the state legislation. But as the Court has observed, "the proposition that the Commerce Clause by its own force restricts state protectionism is deeply rooted in our case law." Four arguments converge to provide a strong basis for adherence to that case law. First, a doctrine that the Court has adhered to for over a century and a half has great weight simply on stare decisis grounds. Second, as we saw, the doctrine has a very close connection to one of the major historical reasons for the written Constitution's existence. Third, that the clause is phrased as an authorization is hardly a reason in itself for refusing not to treat it as an implicit prohibition as well: Constitutional lawyers sometimes treat other clauses granting authority to one branch of the federal government as implicitly prohibiting action by the other branches or by the states without any such objection being raised. Finally, inferring the existence of a national common market with constitutional status from the Republic's federal structure is parallel to inferring the existence of the right of interstate travel on the same basis: In both instances, the inference makes better sense of American constitutional arrangements than the counter-argument. The dormant commerce clause is a legitimate aspect of the Constitution-in-practice.[4]

---

[2]   The foreign commerce clause of Article I section 8 also has a "dormant" aspect. The case law articulating that doctrine is broadly similar to the dormant (interstate) commerce clause analysis discussed in this paragraph. See *Barclays Bank PLC* v. *Franchise Tax Bd. of California*, 512 U.S. 298, 310–11 (1994) (explaining dormant foreign commerce clause doctrine).

[3]   *Granholm* v. *Heald*, 544 U.S. 460, 476 (2005); *Pike* v. *Bruce Church, Inc.*, 397 U.S. 137, 142 (1970). *Pike* balancing is discussed in Chapter 4.

[4]   *Tennessee Wine & Spirits Retailers Assoc.* v. *Thomas*, 139 S. Ct. 2449, 2460 (2019). See, e.g., *Hamdan* v. *Rumsfeld*, 548 U.S. 557, 591–92 (2006) (quoting Chief Justice Chase that the Constitution prohibits the exercise by Congress and the president of those war powers exclusively vested in one or the other); *Michigan* v. *Bay Mills Indian Cmty.*, 572 U.S. 782, 788 (2014) ("The Constitution grants Congress powers we have consistently described as 'plenary and exclusive' to legislate in respect to Indian

Dormant commerce clause doctrine is unusual in more respect. The Supreme Court recognizes Congress's power to permit states to enforce legislation that the Court would hold unconstitutional on dormant commerce clause grounds. Since as a practical matter this means that Congress can "overrule" the Court, this feature of the doctrine is sometimes treated as suspect (or further proof the entire doctrine is wrong-headed) but the criticism is unpersuasive. An act of Congress that allows a state to discriminate against interstate commerce (or go beyond what *Pike* balancing would allow) does not reject a judicial decision that such state legislation violates the *dormant* commerce clause. The very purpose of the doctrine is to protect the national common market over which the commerce clause gives Congress plenary power; an act of Congress permitting state regulation of some aspect of the national market is simply an exercise of Congress's power. Congress doing so is no more a case of the legislature overruling the Court than is congressional repeal of federal legislation that the Court has held preempts state laws: In both situations, Congress has validly lifted the constitutional bar on state action that the Court had previously and validly enforced.[5]

Article II Section 2: The Treaty Power and the Enumeration Principle. In *Missouri v. Holland* (1920), the Supreme Court rejected a constitutional challenge to a federal statute enacted to enforce the Migratory Game Birds Treaty. The Court thought it beyond question that Congress was authorized to implement the treaty if the latter was itself within the Article II power of the president and Senate, so the case turned on the scope of the Article II treaty power. The Court rejected arguments that the treaty power cannot address matters that are outside the scope of Congress's Article I powers and that this particular treaty was prohibited by "some invisible radiation from the general terms of the Tenth Amendment." In the process of doing so, the Court observed that under Article VI "acts of Congress are the supreme law of the land only when made in pursuance of the Constitution, while treaties are declared to be so when made under the authority of the United States" and that the phrase "the authority of the United States" might refer to nothing "more than the formal acts prescribed to make" a treaty. The Court's holding and its comment about the language of Article VI provoked a several decades-long debate whether the decision implied that treaties and their implementing legislation are exempt from constitutional prohibitions or left the treaty power without limits, thus undermining the enumeration principle.[6]

---

tribes"); *Hannegan v. Esquire, Inc.*, 327 U.S. 146, 156 n. 18 (1946) (post office power is exclusively congressional). Critics also attack *Pike* balancing as illegitimate judicial legislation.

[5] See, e.g., *Prudential Ins. Co. v. Benjamin*, 328 U.S. 408 (1946).

[6] *Missouri v. Holland*, 433–34 (1920). *Holland*'s assumption that Congress is authorized by the necessary and proper clause to carry treaties into effect has been challenged, but political practice and Supreme Court precedent (including *Holland*) uniformly support the assumption. Compare *Bond v. United States*, 572 U.S. 844, 874–76 (2014) (Scalia, J., dissenting) *with* Jean Galbraith, Congress's Treaty-Implementing Power in Historical Practice, 56 *Wm. & Mary L. Rev.* 59, 108–09 (2014) ("Congress's treaty-implementing power" has "a straightforward textual basis in the Necessary and Proper Clause

The former argument was a bizarre misreading of the opinion in *Holland*, which said nothing implying that either treaties or implementing legislation can override a constitutional prohibition, but caused sufficient alarm in the 1950s to spark calls for a constitutional amendment until the Supreme Court laid the worry clearly to rest. The latter argument about the treaty power as a means of circumventing the enumeration principle is a more serious issue, exacerbated by the understanding from the beginning that if they do so clearly, the president and Senate can create domestic law by treaty without any need for implementing legislation. Once again, however, a careful reading of Justice Holmes's opinion for the Court in *Holland* should have dispelled the concern. After noting the supremacy clause's different language about laws and treaties, Holmes immediately added that the Court did "not mean to imply that there are no qualifications to the treaty-making power; but they must be ascertained in a different way." Later in the opinion, he explained that the natural resource protected by the treaty and statute was "a national interest of very nearly the first magnitude" that could be "protected only by national action in concert with that of another power," and for that reason both treaty and law were authorized.[7]

Justice Holmes was an elegant but often laconic writer, and in this instance his preference for brevity misled years of unwary readers. The limits to Congress's Article I legislative powers are "ascertained" by interpreting Article I section 8's long list of express and specific subjects as to which "[t]he Congress shall have power" to legislate. Since Article II does not include a similar list of subjects that the treaty-making power may address, its limits "must be ascertained in a different way," and Holmes assumed the reader would consult the nineteenth-century Supreme Court opinions about the treaty power, which had uniformly concluded that "the treaty power of the United States extends to all proper subjects of negotiation between our government and the governments of other nations." A natural resource that can be conserved only by joint action with another nation is clearly within this understanding of the treaty power's scope, and the enumeration principle is respected because the treaty power is limited by its own definition, even if the definition is not express in the constitutional text.[8]

Article V: Amending the Constitution. Article V outlines several processes for adopting formal amendments to the Constitution: "The Congress, whenever two thirds of both Houses shall deem it necessary, shall propose Amendments to this Constitution, or, on the Application of the Legislatures of two thirds of the several States, shall call a Convention for proposing Amendments, which, in either Case,

---

combined with the Treaty Clause, as these clauses were read by virtually all who considered the issue").

[7] *Id.* at 433, 435. Treaties that have domestic law effect on their own are usually termed "self-executing." A "non-self-executing" treaty imposes international law obligations on the United States but creates no domestic law enforceable in federal court unless implemented by Congress.

[8] *De Geofroy v. Riggs*, 133 U.S. 258, 266–67 (1890).

shall be valid to all Intents and Purposes, as Part of this Constitution, when ratified by the Legislatures of three fourths of the several States, or by Conventions in three fourths thereof, as the one or the other Mode of Ratification may be proposed by the Congress."

With one exception, every amendment to the Constitution to date has been adopted by congressional proposal followed by ratification by the state legislatures, which we may therefore call the ordinary method. The exception, the twenty-first amendment repealing Prohibition, resulted from Congress's decision to make an end run around potentially recalcitrant pro-prohibition state legislative majorities: Section 3 of the amendment submitted it to "conventions in the several States, as provided in the Constitution," for ratification.

Although the ordinary method of adoption involves the federal and state legislatures, they act in highly unusual ways. Congress can propose an amendment only by a supermajority in both houses, and no state legislature's ratification matters unless it is part of an even larger supermajority of state legislatures. Furthermore, unlike the process for enacting federal legislation, the amending process does not involve the president, and the power of a state's legislative houses (or single house in Nebraska) to ratify a proposed amendment is not subject to variation by the state constitution. The other methods involve popularly elected conventions and thus are even more remote from ordinary lawmaking processes.[9]

Article V is plainly intended, as a matter of argument from the text, to provide an exclusive list of the means by which the Constitution can be amended. Some scholars have nonetheless argued that there are other methods. The Civil War amendments, for example, are sometimes thought to demand the recognition that the written Constitution itself can be amended by means outside Article V, the argument being that the federal government secured their ratification by the required three quarters of the state legislatures by extra-legal means. That the means employed in ensuring ratification were highly irregular is true. On December 18, 1865, when the secretary of state declared that the thirteenth amendment had been ratified by the required supermajority, he could do so only by counting the votes of legislative bodies in several ex-Confederate states that were of debatable legality for various reasons, and most of which were eventually dissolved by Congress as part of Reconstruction, in part because they had refused to ratify the fourteenth amendment. The process by which the fourteenth and fifteenth amendments were ratified in 1868 and 1870, respectively,

---

[9] See *Hollingsworth* v. *Virginia*, 3 U.S. (3 Dall.) 378 (1798) (president has no role in proposal or adoption of amendments); *Hawke* v. *Smith*, 253 U.S. 221 (1920) (state constitution cannot require submission of a proposed amendment to a popular referendum); *Arizona State Legislature* v. *Arizona Indep. Redistricting Comm'n*, 576 U.S. 787, 808 (2015) ("In the context of ratifying constitutional amendments ... 'the Legislature' has a different identity, one that excludes the referendum and the Governor's veto.").

included the enactment of congressional legislation forcing specific Southern state legislatures to vote yes.

It does not follow, however, that somehow Article V is not, or no longer, the exclusive set of lawful means by which the written Constitution can be amended. First, no one in the 1865–1870 period claimed that the three amendments became part of the Constitution by any but the ordinary amendment process. The federal government's arguably high-handed methods were intended to fulfill Article V at least as a formal matter, not to circumvent it. Second, the amendments were the Republic's formal constitutional response to secession, Civil War, and the institution of slavery, and were intended to secure what the first Justice John Marshall Harlan, himself a Union army veteran, later called the "legitimate results of the war," the end of slavery and the protection of African Americans from political and legal oppression. Given their origin in the nation's greatest political and constitutional crisis, the existence of irregularities in the amendments' adoption is hardly surprising, and not a precedent for other situations. Finally, all three branches of the federal government have, from the beginning, treated all three amendments as regularly adopted, and the Supreme Court long ago flatly rejected the idea that the fifteenth amendment "was incorporated in the Constitution, not in accordance with law, but practically as a war measure which has been validated by acquiescence." The same conclusion should apply to other two Civil War amendments as well, and the specific details of their ratification processes have never been of any significance in the practice of constitutional law.[10]

I also think unpersuasive (if more interesting) the rather different argument that the Supreme Court's repudiation of several major lines of reasoning and precedent in the period from 1937 to the mid-1940s can only be defended by treating the Court's actions as part of a broader political movement that amended the Constitution informally. Again, the argument has an historical foundation. The New Deal Court's overthrow of pre-1937 doctrines that put significant judicial limitations on congressional legislation under the interstate commerce clause and on federal and state economic regulation was broad, lasting, and of great practical importance. But the Court did so on the basis of pre-1937 decisions as well as dissenting opinions by extremely distinguished justices sometimes writing in cases decided by 5–4 votes. The doctrinal changes in the period were less a revolutionary break with the past than a decision to adhere to certain pre-existing lines of thought that had a strong presence on the pre-1937 Court. The argument underestimates, to put the point more abstractly, the capacity of the traditional practice of constitutional law to

---

[10] *Plessy* v. *Ferguson*, 163 U.S. 537, 560–61 (1896) (Harlan, J., dissenting); *Leser* v. *Garnett*, 258 U.S. 130, 136 (1922) (Brandeis, J.). *Leser* involved a challenge to the legitimacy of the nineteenth amendment, which the Court met in part by analogizing the nineteenth to the fifteenth; the validity of fifteenth amendment, the Court noted, "has been recognized and acted on for half a century." *Leser* also held that the executive's proclamation that an amendment has been ratified "is conclusive upon the courts." *Id.* at 136, 137.

accommodate change without breaking faith with the past. In any event, as with the argument based on the Civil War amendments, the idea has no practical significance in constitutional law.

Fifth and Fourteenth Amendment Procedural Due Process: "Life, Liberty, or Property". The historical origins of the fifth amendment due process clause's reference to "life, liberty, and property" are surprisingly uncertain. The term "due process" is a somewhat later version of Magna Carta's original "law of the land," and so it is logical enough to assume that the fifth amendment also reflects, perhaps at a considerable remove, the first part of the 1215 document's promise that "[n]o free man is to be arrested, or imprisoned, or disseised, or outlawed, or exiled, or in any other way ruined, nor will we go against him or send against him, except by the lawful judgment of his peers or by the law of the land." Already in 1215, as a textual matter, the principle being announced was ambiguous: Is the series of passive constructions a capacious description of all the ways the king might cause someone to be ruined, or are they discrete references to particular forms of harm, to be interpreted separately?[11]

Common law authorities such as Coke and Blackstone, in addition to quoting Magna Carta, gave similarly ambiguous formulations close but not identical to the fifth amendment's wording, as did John Locke, often thought to be a major philosophical forebear of the Constitution. The Declaration of Independence proclaimed "Life, Liberty and the Pursuit of Happiness" as its list of "unalienable Rights," a phrase that seems very difficult to read as a list of separate, technical legal rights, and the nineteenth-century Supreme Court generally treated the language of the fifth and (after 1868) the fourteenth amendment as a general reference to "public and private rights." At times, indeed, the Court echoed the Declaration by glossing "life, liberty, and property" as "all that [a person] is accustomed to call his own, all in which he has placed his happiness, and the security of which is essential to that happiness."[12]

For most of the twentieth century, the Supreme Court adhered to this nontechnical understanding of "life, liberty, and property," and eventually began defining the interests that procedural due process protects simply in terms of the interest's practical importance to the individual; in 1971, for example, *Bell v. Burson* held that because "continued possession" of a driver's license "may become essential in the pursuit of a livelihood," a state decision to suspend someone's license "adjudicates important interests" of the licensee and is subject to procedural due process. A year after *Bell*, however, the Court held that due process required no procedure

---

[11] Magna Carta chapter 39, using the Magna Carta Project's translation. See https://magnacarta .cmp.uea.ac.uk/read/magna_carta_1215/Clause_39.

[12] *Hurtado v. California*, 110 U.S. 516, 536, 537 (1884) (quoting *Citizens' Savings & Loan Assoc. v. City of Topeka*, 87 U.S. 655, 662 (1874)). This approach to the tripartite formula is very old. See *Ware v. Hylton*, 3 U.S. (3 Dall.) 199, 268 (1796) (seriatim opinion of Iredell, J.) (equating "life, liberty, property" with "every thing dear to man").

whatsoever when a public university decided not to rehire a professor at the end of his one year contract. *Board of Regents* v. *Roth* explained that "the range of interests protected by procedural due process is not infinite," and that "liberty and property" is not a way of referring to everything in addition to life that matters to a person, but instead covers discrete, legally protected interests. Since the former professor "remain[ed] as free as before to seek another job" and neither his employment contract nor any state law or university policy gave him any "possible claim of entitlement to re-employment," the university's decision was not a deprivation of liberty or property regardless of how arbitrary or seriously injurious it was in fact.[13]

Current constitutional law follows the *Board of Regents* understanding of "life, liberty, and property" and thus limits the requirement of procedural due process to governmental injury to specific individual interests that can lay claim to an identifiable legal source other than the due process clauses themselves. The Supreme Court recognizes as exceptions an individual's interest in life, freedom from physical detention, and some aspects of bodily security, which the Court treats as guaranteed by the clauses' text, and liberties that are protected by other constitutional provisions are also not subject to deprivation without due process. But other claims to procedural due process protection depend on nonconstitutional rules. "Property interests, of course, are not created by the Constitution. Rather they are created and their dimensions are defined by existing rules or understandings that stem from an independent source such as state law." Federal and state laws and policies may also create protected liberty interests if they confer a freedom to act on individuals that if removed would alter their "legal status." What procedural due process therefore prohibits, the Court explained in *Paul* v. *Davis* (1976), is the alteration or extinction of "a right or status previously recognized by state law" without adequate procedures, and for that reason the threshold requirement for a valid procedural due process claim is the demonstration that governmental action has "officially remov[ed] the interest from the recognition and protection previously afforded by the State."[14]

The reader should not misread the Court's references to *state* law. Congress is the source of general property rights where it has a general power of governance (the District of Columbia, federal territories), and Congress and federal agencies acting within their lawful authority can create liberty and property interests. The Court's point was to exclude the constitutional law articulated by federal courts as the source of such due process-protected interests. *Paul* v. *Davis* therefore restated the holding in *Bell* v. *Burson* as turning on the state's creation of a property "right" to possession of a nonsuspended driver's license; as originally written, *Bell* rested on the Court's decision, as a matter of federal constitutional law, that the injury caused by license suspension triggered on its own procedural due process protections.[15]

---

[13]   *Bell* v. *Burson*, 402 U.S. 535, 539 (1971); *Board of Regents* v. *Roth*, 408 U.S. 564, 570, 575, 578 (1972).

[14]   *Board of Regents*, 408 U.S. at 577; *Paul* v. *Davis*, 424 U.S. 693, 708, 710–11 (1976).

[15]   *Paul* v. *Davis*, 424 U.S. at 711. There does not seem to be any analytically significant difference between liberty and property interests for procedural due process purposes. The Court tends to use the term "liberty" in situations when "property" would sound odd. See *id.* (in an earlier decision, state law

Board of Regents v. *Roth* marked a significant change in the Supreme Court's understanding of the interests that procedural process protects; even the language of "interests" rather than "rights" would have puzzled a nineteenth-century constitutional lawyer. One interpretation of the Court's shift is that it was a reaction to cases such as *Bell* v. *Burson* that seemed to portend an ever-broadening range of situations in which the federal courts would be obligated to require state and local government to provide at least minimal procedures whenever taking any action detrimental to an individual in ways that a judge thought seriously harmful. This seems unworkable since government is constantly doing things that disadvantage individuals, often quite seriously. *Paul* v. *Davis* suggested as much when the Court commented that the courts should not read due process to make the fourteenth amendment "a font of tort law" by constitutionalizing individual wrongs done by state officials to private persons. The Court pursued that goal in *Paul* by reasoning that our nineteenth-century constitutional lawyer would have thought flatly wrong. (The Court held that the claimant in *Paul*, who alleged that he had been defamed, had suffered no injury to a legally protected interest. At common law, the right to one's reputation was thought a core element of personal liberty.) But the Court's concern rested on a legitimate and arguably compelling basis: The creation of "a body of general federal tort law" by way of "the procedural guarantees of the Due Process Clause" would violate the enumeration principle and the police power principle, two basic presuppositions of constitutional law.[16]

Fifth and Fourteenth Amendment Substantive Due Process. The substantive due process cases in what we now refer to as the *Lochner* era after the Court's 1905 decision striking down a state maximum-hours labor law in *Lochner* v. *New York* generally protected economic rights rooted in contract and property. New Deal-era opponents of the *Lochner* line of decisions treated Justice Holmes's dissent in that case as the iconic response to judicial overreaching. What they sometimes ignored was the fact that Holmes did not actually reject the idea of recognizing a substantive dimension to due process, or the propriety of looking to tradition in deciding substantive due process cases. His point in *Lochner* was that, in his view, the majority's protection of freedom of contract rested not on a widely shared American tradition but "upon an economic theory which a large part of the country does not entertain." As Holmes explained, substantive due process prohibits laws that "infringe fundamental principles as they have been understood by the traditions of our people and our law," and he accordingly was willing to invalidate state laws taking private property and abridging freedom of speech.[17]

had conferred on parolees the interest "to remain at liberty as long as the conditions of their parole were not violated" and therefore parole revocation required due process).

[16] *Paul* v. *Davis*, 424 U.S. at 701.

[17] *Lochner* v. *New York*, 198 U.S. 45, 75–76 (1905) (Holmes, J., dissenting). See also *Pennsylvania Coal Co.* v. *Mahon*, 260 U.S. 293 (1922) (Holmes, J.) (regulatory taking of property); *Gitlow* v. *People of State of New York*, 268 U.S. 652, 672 (1925) (Holmes, J., dissenting) ("the general principle of free speech"). Modern lawyers would conceptualize Holmes's position in these cases as resting on, respectively, the

The most influential rationale for associating argument from tradition with provisions worded in terms of "due process of law" was written by Justice John Marshall Harlan II in *Poe v. Ullman* (1961). Harlan pointed out that the phrase's origins lay in chapter 39 of Magna Carta, where it was in fact what we would call a procedural guarantee against lawless *executive* action, but he further noted that in the English context such a guarantee could not be extended to limit Parliament's substantive *legislative* powers, since Parliament is the sovereign source of law and by definition cannot be a lawless tyrant. But American legislatures are not sovereign and there is no conceptual difficulty with the ideas of unlawful legislation or legislative tyranny: Indeed, binding the legislature by a fundamental law adopted by the sovereign People is a central purpose of the written Constitution. Therefore, Harlan concluded, if the due process clauses are to accomplish their historical purpose of prohibiting tyranny, they must prohibit oppression through legislation as well as unfair or inadequate procedure in executive and judicial action. "Thus the guaranties of due process, though [originally] considered as procedural safeguards against executive usurpation and tyranny, have in this country become bulwarks also against arbitrary legislation." Courts should therefore answer a question of prohibition based on the idea of substantive due process by examining the "balance struck by this country" between individual liberty and governmental authority in light of "what history teaches are the traditions from which it developed as well as the traditions from which it broke." Harlan thus attempted to justify substantive due process and to discipline its application by rooting both justification and application in the historical materials out of which much of the Constitution-in-practice is made.[18]

The Ninth Amendment. Opponents of the Constitution's ratification often attacked the document for lacking a declaration of rights similar to those that prefaced or were included in many early state constitutions. In response, some proponents of ratification defended the proposal by arguing that such a declaration would be unwise because it might imply that the People had surrendered any rights not included in whatever list was devised. When he introduced in the First Congress a draft of a bill of rights to allay worry over the Constitution's lack of one, Madison explained that he thought this objection plausible and had included a provision intended to address that concern. Our ninth amendment is the text that emerged from an extensive revision of Madison's draft. Scholars writing about the amendment's origins disagree sharply about just how Madison or anyone else thought the amendment would do this, and its wording gives no clear answer to

---

takings and free speech clauses incorporated into the fourteenth amendment, but Holmes himself understood them as (correct) applications of due process in its substantive dimension.

[18] *Poe v. Ullman*, 367 U.S. 497, 541–42 (1961) (Harlan, J., dissenting). The reader will note that Justice Harlan's defense of the legitimacy of substantive due process weaves together textual, original meaning, structural, and tradition-based arguments.

their debates: "The enumeration in the Constitution, of certain rights, shall not be construed to deny or disparage others retained by the people."

The amendment has played a significant role in only one Supreme Court decision, *Griswold v. Connecticut*, the 1965 case striking down a state law that criminalized the use of contraceptives by a married couple. The opinion of the Court briefly mentioned the ninth amendment in explaining, most subsequent readers have thought unsuccessfully, that the law's invalidity stemmed from the interplay between several provisions in the Bill of Rights, but three members of the Court joined a concurring opinion, arguing that to reject the claim that the Constitution does not protect a right of marital privacy because the constitutional text mentions no such right "is to ignore the Ninth Amendment and to give it no effect whatsoever."[19]

The *Griswold* concurrence is, to date, the high-water mark of the ninth amendment's judicial career. Its reasoning gives the amendment a meaning consistent with its wording, but no later Supreme Court opinion has built on the concurrence in any significant way. Why? Beyond the historical uncertainties about its meaning, I suggest that the amendment has lain fallow because it doesn't really help a constitutional lawyer solve any practical problem. There are other arguments that address the connection between the constitutional text and prohibitions in the Constitution-in-practice, and there is no need to rely on an obscurely worded provision with no significant history of judicial application. The hard question, when a controversy arises over a proposed constitutional prohibition with no obvious textual home, is how to determine if the proposal ought to be accepted. And on that question, the ninth amendment provides no help whatsoever. Lawyers are practical people, and a tool without a practical use is going to stay in the drawer.

The reader may worry that my conclusion violates the common law rule of interpretation that one should not render any part of a written legal instrument meaningless if that can be avoided. I think not. Viewed in their original historical context, treating the ninth and tenth amendments as a package deal, that together "make clear that the adoption of the Bill of Rights did not alter the plan that the Federal Government was to be a government of express and limited powers, and that all rights and powers not delegated to it were retained by the people and the individual States," does not render either amendment meaningless. It simply turns out that the specific part of that concern that the ninth amendment addresses has not been historically important. The constitutional text has a surprising number of provisions of which that can be said. The third amendment, for example, is full of meaning, but there has been little occasion for making use of its clear prohibition on making homeowners provide living space for military personnel in peace time.[20]

---

[19] *Griswold v. Connecticut*, 381 U.S. 479, 491 (1965) (Goldberg, J., concurring).
[20] *Griswold*, 381 U.S. at 529–30 (Stewart, J., dissenting).

The Tenth Amendment. Article II of the Articles of Confederation stated that "Each State retains its Sovereignty, freedom and independence, and every Power, Jurisdiction and right, which is not by this confederation expressly delegated to the United States in Congress assembled." The absence of any parallel provision in the proposed Constitution attracted severe criticism during the ratification process, and when in the First Congress Madison introduced what eventually became the Bill of Rights, he included a provision that he described as intended to answer those concerns. Madison's draft was very close to the text of the tenth amendment as ultimately ratified, and failed to include Article II's "expressly." Madison conceded that his proposal might be thought "superfluous" since it was "unnecessary" to announce a principle already evident from "the whole of the instrument," but he explained that "there can be no harm in making such a declaration."[21]

In *McCulloch* v. *Maryland*, Chief Justice Marshall reasoned that the text of the original Constitution and the Bill of Rights deliberately avoided any "phrase in the instrument which, like the articles of confederation, excludes incidental or implied powers; and which requires that everything granted shall be expressly and minutely described." Madison's failure to follow Article II's language, Marshall argued, was intended to avoid carrying over Article II's limiting substance.

> Even the 10th amendment, which was framed for the purpose of quieting the excessive jealousies which had been excited, omits the word 'expressly,' … thus leaving the question, whether the particular power which may become the subject of contest, has been delegated to the one government, or prohibited to the other, to depend on a fair construction of the whole instrument. The men who drew and adopted this amendment had experienced the embarrassments resulting from the insertion of this word in the articles of confederation, and probably omitted it, to avoid those embarrassments.

Some modern scholars think Marshall was wrong about the amendment's original meaning, but as a matter of constitutional law Marshall's reading has prevailed. Supreme Court opinions have observed that the tenth amendment "added nothing to the instrument as originally ratified" and described it as "a truism." That description of the amendment's language reflects the settled conclusion that it cannot be read as a prohibition with legal force that limits the powers the federal government is otherwise authorized to exercise. The tenth amendment's importance lies in its confirmation, in the text of the written Constitution, that the enumeration and police power principles are critical to the solution of constitutional problems.[22]

The Eleventh Amendment: Congress and State Sovereign Immunity. In 1793, *Chisholm* v. *Georgia* ruled that a private plaintiff from South Carolina could sue

---

[21] 1 Annals of Congress 459 (1789).

[22] *McCulloch* v. *Maryland*, 17 U.S. (4 Wheat.) 316, 406–07 (1819); *United States* v. *Sprague*, 282 U.S. 716, 733 (1931); *United States* v. *Darby*, 312 U.S. 100, 124 (1941) (the "amendment states but a truism that all is retained which has not been surrendered").

Georgia, in the Supreme Court as trial court, for a breach of contract claim notwithstanding any claim that the state enjoyed immunity from suit. The justices wrote seriatim opinions offering different rationales for the decision, but except for a lone dissenter they agreed that the case was properly before the Court in light of Article III's extension of the "judicial Power . . . to Controversies . . . between a State and Citizens of another State," and its grant of "original Jurisdiction" to the Court in "all Cases . . . in which as State shall be Party." Two justices went further, in an apparent attempt to ban the idea of sovereignty altogether from constitutional thought. Justice James Wilson wrote:

> To the Constitution of the United States the term SOVEREIGN, is totally unknown. There is but one place where it could have been used with propriety. But, even in that place it would not, perhaps, have comported with the delicacy of those, who ordained and established that Constitution. They might have announced themselves "SOVEREIGN" people of the United States: But serenely conscious of the fact, they avoided the ostentatious declaration.

Chief Justice John Jay explained similarly that sovereignty is a feudal concept which he thought entirely inapplicable in the United States: "No such ideas obtain here; at the Revolution, the sovereignty devolved on the people."[23]

Congress and the state legislatures quickly overruled *Chisholm* by adopting the eleventh amendment. The amendment's language was crafted to address the Supreme Court's specific ruling and made no reference to the states as sovereigns: "The Judicial power of the United States shall not be construed to extend to any suit in law or equity, commenced or prosecuted against one of the United States by Citizens of another State, or by Citizens or Subjects of any Foreign State." The amendment therefore could have been treated as a narrow prohibition of federal court jurisdiction over lawsuits brought against a state by a citizen of another state. In the late nineteenth century, however, the Court began to invoke the amendment "not so much for what it says, but for the presupposition of [state sovereign immunity] which it confirms." More generally, constitutional lawyers have long since accepted the terminology of state sovereignty as a means of referring to the autonomous place of the states within the American political community's federal structure. "It is an essential attribute of the States' retained sovereignty that they remain independent and autonomous within their proper sphere of authority."[24]

Under current Supreme Court doctrine, state sovereignty imposes two prohibitions on congressional legislation: the anti-commandeering principle discussed in Chapter 3, and state sovereign immunity, which ordinarily bars congressional

---

[23] *Chisholm v. Georgia*, 2 U.S. (2 Dall.) 419, 454 (1793) (seriatim opinion of Wilson, J.); *id.* at 471 (seriatim opinion of Jay, C.J.).

[24] *Blatchford v. Native Village of Noatak*, 501 U.S. 775, 779 (1991); *Printz v. United States*, 521 U.S. 898, 928 (1997). The seminal decision was *Hans v. Louisiana*, 134 U.S. 1 (1890), which held that a state is immune from suit by its own citizens.

abrogation of an nonconsenting state's immunity in either federal or state court. Neither doctrine fences off substantive areas of potential legislation from regulation by acts of Congress that are affirmatively authorized by the Constitution. They are, instead, constraints on the means by which Congress may implement federal legislation.[25] The states' sovereign immunity, furthermore, is not complete. The written Constitution establishes "certain waivers of sovereign immunity to which all States implicitly consented at the founding," which include suits by the United States and other states, and cases "in the context of bankruptcy proceedings" and in "the exercise of federal eminent domain power." The scope of state sovereign immunity is further limited by long-standing precedent, which "normally allows federal courts to award prospective relief against state officials for violations of federal law."[26]

The Fourteenth Amendment Section 5 Enforcement Power. Section 5 of the fourteenth amendment provides that "[t]he Congress shall have the power to enforce, by appropriate legislation, the provisions of this article," most importantly, the due process and equal protection clauses of section 1 of the amendment. As we saw in Chapter 2, in order to decide whether section 5 authorizes a particular act of Congress, the constitutional lawyer must determine whether the statute is actually directed toward remedying a violation of one of the prohibitions in section 1. Those prohibitions, as we have also seen, apply only to state action and not to the behavior of private individuals. It does not follow, precedent establishes, that section 5 enforcement power legislation can never address conduct that in itself does not violate due process or equal protection, but for the law to do so validly, the regulation of such conduct must be a means toward enforcing the prohibitions on state governmental action.[27]

United States v. *Morrison* (2000), for example, considered the validity of a provision of the Violence Against Women Act that gave a civil remedy to the victims of gender-motivated violence against private perpetrators. The Act's

---

[25]   An example: Congress may impose federal wage and hour rules on state governments as employers, but it may not abrogate state sovereign immunity to permit a state employee to sue an unconsenting state to recover wages that were not paid in violation of the federal rules. See *Garcia v. San Antonio Metro. Transit Auth.*, 469 U.S. 528 (1985) (Congress authorized to apply wage/hour rules to states); *Alden v. Maine*, 527 U.S. 706 (1999) (sovereign immunity bars employee private suits for unlawfully withheld overtime wages). Alden noted that state sovereign immunity would not prohibit a suit brought by the federal government on behalf of the wronged employees. *Id.* at 759–60.

[26]   *PennEast Pipeline Co.* v. *New Jersey*, 141 S. Ct. 2244, 2258–59 (2021); *Virginia Off. for Protection & Advocacy* v. *Stewart*, 563 U.S. 247, 252 (2011) (summarizing *Ex parte Young*, 209 U.S. 123 (1908)). On state sovereign immunity in state courts, see *Alden v. Maine*, 527 U.S. 706, 713 (1999) (state sovereign immunity "neither derives from, nor is limited by, the terms of the Eleventh Amendment"). Congress is authorized to abrogate state sovereign immunity when validly exercising its power to enforce the fourteenth amendment because that amendment altered the original federal–state balance. See *Fitzpatrick v. Bitzer*, 427 U.S. 445, 456 (1976).

[27]   See *City of Boerne* v. *Flores*, 521 U.S. 507, 518 (1997) ("Legislation which deters or remedies constitutional violations can fall within the sweep of Congress' enforcement power even if in the process it prohibits conduct which is not itself unconstitutional").

legislative record and express findings demonstrated the existence of widespread governmental discrimination against the victims of such crimes, and might have provided a factual basis for federal rules designed to prevent or penalize such state action. The Act's civil remedy, however, was "directed not at any State or state actor, but at individuals who have committed criminal acts motivated by gender bias" and "visit[ed] no consequence whatever on any ... public official" for what might be unconstitutional gender discrimination in the investigation or prosecution of such crimes. The Court therefore concluded that section 5 did not authorize Congress to enact the civil remedy provision.[28]

As noted in Chapter 4, the Supreme Court requires a clear indication that Congress actually intended to exercise its enforcement power before the Court can analyze a statute's authorization under section 5. The Court has explained this exception to the usual rule that Congress need not specify correctly (or at all) the enumerated power that authorizes a law as based on the need to limit the fourteenth amendment's disruptive effect on the usual relationship between the federal and state governments. "Because such legislation imposes congressional policy on a State involuntarily, and because it often intrudes on traditional state authority, we should not quickly attribute to Congress an unstated intent to act under its authority to enforce the Fourteenth Amendment." The underlying assumption is that the fourteenth amendment was originally meant to leave in place, as a general matter, pre-amendment federalism. That assumption has been periodically challenged as historically and structurally unsound, but it is well-settled in the case law.[29]

The Right to Vote: A Prohibition without a Clause? The status of the right to vote under the US Constitution is complex in rather curious ways. On the one hand, the Supreme Court "has often noted that the Constitution 'does not confer the right of suffrage upon any one,' and that 'the right to vote, *per se*, is not a constitutionally protected right.'" The text of the Constitution identifies who may vote for the members of Congress, but it does so by reference to state law – the congressional electors are those persons with "the Qualifications requisite for Electors of the most numerous Branch of the State Legislature." The Constitution's processes for select-ing the president and vice president do not guarantee popular voting at all. Several amendments prohibit the denial of the right to vote on various grounds: "on account

---

[28] *United States v. Morrison*, 529 U.S. 598, 626 (2000).

[29] *Pennhurst State Sch. & Hosp. v. Halderman*, 451 U.S. 1, 16 (1981). The argument over the extent to which the fourteenth amendment changed American federalism began shortly after the amendment was ratified in 1868. *Compare Slaughter-House Cases*, 83 U.S. (16 Wall.) 36, 78 (1873) (giving a broad scope to the enforcement power "radically changes the whole theory of the relations of the State and Federal governments to each other and of both these governments to the people. ... We are convinced that no such results were intended.") *with id.* at 125, 129 (Swayne, J., dissenting) (the Civil War "amendments are a new departure, and mark an important epoch in the constitutional history of the country. They trench directly upon the power of the States, and deeply affect those bodies. ... The construction adopted by the majority ... defeats, by a limitation not anticipated, the intent of those by whom the instrument was framed and of those by whom it was adopted.").

of race, color, or previous condition of servitude" (the fifteenth), "on account of sex" (the nineteenth), in federal elections, "by reason of failure to pay any poll tax or other tax" (the twenty-fourth), for citizens eighteen or older, "on account of age" (the twenty-sixth). But nothing in the text (except the twenty-fourth amendment) forbids the imposition of onerous requirements that have the practical effect of preventing otherwise qualified persons from voting, nor are there any provisions that expressly prevent legislative malapportionment, gerrymandering, or the use of other means by which the effect of an individual's or a group's votes is diluted. Nor indeed does the federal Constitution require that any part of state and local government be elected by popular vote except the state legislature, and even that is an inference rather than an express guarantee.[30]

On the other hand, the nineteenth-century Court recognized, in one of its earliest discussions of equal protection, that "the political franchise of voting" is to be "regarded as a fundamental political right, because preservative of all rights," and the mid-twentieth-century one person/one vote decisions, which applied a population equality norm to invalidate malapportioned electoral districts, are active parts of the Constitution-in-practice and beyond reconsideration. Shortly after the first reapportionment decisions, the Court decided *Harper* v. *Virginia State Board of Elections* (1966), which held that a state poll tax of $1.50, payment of which was necessary to vote in state elections, violated the equal protection clause. *Harper*'s use of equal protection reasoning was not entirely clear, but the decision seemed to establish the idea that strict scrutiny applies to limitations on the right to vote. However, later decisions gradually narrowed *Harper* or simply ignored it entirely, and what is at present the leading case applied a somewhat opaque standard of review unrelated to strict scrutiny.[31]

The Non-existent Emergency Clause. The written Constitution makes "express provision for exercise of extraordinary authority because of a crisis" in only one provision, the clause of Article I section 9, which forbids the suspension of the writ of habeas corpus except "when in Cases of Rebellion or Invasion the public Safety may

[30] *Rodriguez* v. *Popular Democratic Party*, 457 U.S. 1, 9 (1982). Article I section 2 and the seventeenth amendment refer to the "Electors of the most numerous Branch of the State Legislature," and Article IV section 4 states that "The United States shall guarantee to every State in this Union a Republican Form of Government." I think it is very difficult not to conclude that the guarantee clause and the Constitution's various references to the state legislatures presuppose that at least one house of each state legislature will be popularly elected, but even that is not quite express.

[31] *Yick Wo* v. *Hopkins*, 118 U.S. 356, 370 (1886). The seminal one person/one vote decisions were *Wesberry* v. *Sanders*, 376 U.S. 1 (1964) (congressional districts, decided under Article I section 2) and *Reynolds* v. *Sims*, 377 U.S. 533 (1964) (state legislative districts), which with minor tweaks supply the current rules for reviewing allegedly malapportioned districts. See also *Harper* v. *Virginia State Bd. of Elections*, 383 U.S. 663 (1966); *Crawford* v. *Marion County Election Board*, 553 U.S. 181, 190 (2008) (plurality opinion of Stevens, J.) (upholding a stringent voter ID requirement by applying a "balancing approach" requiring a court to "identify and evaluate the interests put forward by the State as justifications for the burden imposed by its rule, and then make the 'hard judgment' that our adversary system demands").

require it." Even there, it is striking to note, the text carefully frames its implicit authorization for emergency action as an exception to the express "Privilege of the Writ of Habeas Corpus." Nonetheless, the Supreme Court has repeatedly addressed questions about the extent to which (in addition to the suspension clause) the Constitution-in-practice permits governmental action during an emergency that would not ordinarily be lawful.[32]

The bedrock principle is that even the most threatening national crisis does not alter constitutional law's basic logic of authorization and prohibition or the enumeration principle. "Emergency does not create power. Emergency does not increase granted power or remove or diminish the restrictions imposed upon power granted or reserved." The Constitution does not grant or permit either Congress or the president power "to deal with a crisis or an emergency" measured by "the necessities of the case" rather than by law, nor does it permit state government to override constitutional prohibitions or valid federal statutes restricting its powers. Even during the supreme crisis of war and "at the extremes of military exigency," the view that "war silences law or modulates its voice . . . has no place in the interpretation and application of [the] Constitution." No emergency affects the obligation of American government to act in accordance with law, and above all with the law of the Constitution.[33]

The constitutional goal of creating a workable government nonetheless requires that both the Constitution's authorizations and its prohibitions take account of the possibility of a crisis that does not permit business as usual. "While emergency does not create power, emergency may furnish the occasion for the exercise of power." With respect to many prohibitions, existing doctrine dictates the appropriate analysis: For example, distinctions based on race and certain forms of interference with freedom of speech are subject to strict scrutiny, and the existence of an actual crisis might satisfy the compelling interest part of that test. When the problem involves the scope of a federal government authorization, the "constitutional question presented

---

[32] *Youngstown Sheet & Tube Co.* v. *Sawyer*, 343 U.S. 579, 650 (1952) (Jackson, J., concurring).

This section is not concerned with acts of Congress that permit the president to exercise "emergency" powers in the sense that, upon making certain findings, the president may execute that statute or others in a different manner than would ordinarily be the case. Presidents make frequent use of these statutory powers but ordinarily most of them raise no constitutional law issues since both the ordinary and the "emergency" executive powers are clearly within Congress's power to create. The emergency, which often is not what the public would view as a crisis, consists of circumstances in which Congress preferred to allow the president greater flexibility. Had Congress chosen, it could have made the more flexible set of powers the norm. Such statutes sometimes address real crisis situations but do not directly create constitutional problems, although the wisdom of affording the executive so much discretion may be doubted.

[33] *Home Bldg. & Loan Assoc.* v. *Blaisdell*, 290 U.S. 398, 425 (1934) (Hughes, C.J.); *Youngstown Sheet & Tube Co.*, 343 U.S. at 646 (Jackson, J., concurring); *Hamdi* v. *Rumsfeld*, 542 U.S. 507, 579 (2004) (Scalia, J., dissenting). Justice Scalia also quoted a version of Cicero's original words: *inter arma silent leges*, "in the midst of arms, the laws are silent."

in the light of an emergency is whether the power possessed embraces the particular exercise of it in response to particular conditions." An example will be useful.[34]

In 1947, Congress enacted rent control legislation as part of its response to an acute housing shortage resulting from the end of World War II hostilities in 1945, the consequent surge of housing needs to accommodate returning military personnel, and other economic changes due to the war's de facto end. Despite precedent holding that Congress can use its powers to prosecute war in order to address the domestic dislocation and problems caused by a war, a lower court concluded that the 1947 act was not within the war power because the war was over, in effect, and the president had issued a proclamation about the end of hostilities at the end of 1946. In *Woods v. Cloyd W. Miller Co.* (1948), the Supreme Court reversed, noting that as a legal matter the state of war continued, and holding that "the war power does not necessarily end with the cessation of hostilities." The legislative record showed that "there has not yet been eliminated the deficit in housing which in considerable measure was caused by the heavy demobilization of veterans and by the cessation or reduction in residential construction during the period of hostilities," and that the rent control law was a reasonable response to the problem. The Court agreed that measures based solely on Congress's powers over war cannot extend indefinitely beyond the end of the emergency, but insisted that there were "no such implications in today's decision." It also announced that in any future case the propriety of continuing to invoke the war powers to justify domestic governance legislation would be subject to judicial review. In a separate opinion, Justice Jackson stressed the unacceptability of holding that "war powers last as long as the effects and consequences of war for if so they are permanent," but he explained that there was "no reason to conclude . . . that the present state of war is merely technical. We have armies abroad exercising our war power and have made no peace terms with our allies not to mention our principal enemies."[35]

The Supreme Court has not articulated a comprehensive doctrinal framework for evaluating claims that a political branch or state government can use its usual powers in unusual ways to handle an emergency, and it seems likely that no such framework could exist in detail since by definition every crisis will have unique features. But the case law permits some generalizations. The Steel Seizure Case makes it clear that federal interference with personal liberty, private property, and individual rights must be authorized by Congress's exercise of its powers rather than by executive fiat. As Justice Jackson wrote, "emergency powers are consistent with free government only when their control is lodged elsewhere than in the Executive who exercises them." Furthermore, there is no emergency clause relieving the president from the continual duty of acting within the powers granted the executive by Article II or by Congress. "In a moment of genuine emergency, when the Government must act

---

[34]   *Blaisdell*, 290 U.S. at 426.
[35]   *Woods v. Cloyd W. Miller Co.*, 333 U.S. 138, 141-42, 143-44 (1948); *id.* at 147 (Jackson, J., concurring).

with no time for deliberation," it might be appropriate for the executive to take steps for which it had no formal authority such as detaining persons who posed a physical threat. But any action justified by this line of thinking would have to end, or be authorized by Congress, as soon as the moment of crisis passed. Congress too remains bound by the enumeration principle, and as *Woods* shows, its discretion to make unusual use of its ordinary powers to address a crisis is dependent on the continuing existence of facts justifying its action. The facts cannot be established simply by a legislative or executive declaration to that effect. As the Court had stated in an earlier case, "the operation of the statute would be at an end" if the federal court concluded that the crisis was over as a matter of fact, and in a controversy over the facts the constitutionally controlling judgment would be the court's, not Congress's. Finally, the unimpaired functioning of the constitutional system in an emergency means that constitutional prohibitions and the principle of asymmetry between congressional and presidential power retain their full legal force.[36]

---

[36]   *Youngstown Sheet & Tube Co.*, 343 U.S at 652 (Jackson, J., concurring); *Hamdi*, 542 U.S. at 552 (Souter, J., concurring in the judgment). The final quotation is from *Chastleton Corp. v. Sinclair*, 264 U.S. 543, 547-48 (1924) (Holmes, J.). In remanding a challenge to post–World War I rent control legislation to the lower court for factual development, *Chastleton* stated that the challengers might be able to prove that "extensive activity in building has added to the ease of finding an abode" and "if about all that remains of war conditions is the increased cost of living that is not in itself a justification of the Act." *Id.* at 548. Any decision on the continuing validity of emergency legislation past the time of obvious crisis should be highly fact-specific.

6

Identifying the Solution

Persuasiveness in Constitutional Law

Lawyers are problem solvers, and the specific job of constitutional lawyers is to solve problems that arise out of the basic political arrangements of the American political community, arrangements that include the written Constitution, the institutions of the federal government that the text authorizes and of the state governments that it presupposes, the community's commitment to limit public action by constitutional prohibitions, and the mechanism of judicial review by which constitutional law controversies are usually resolved. The previous four chapters have said a great deal about the tools and perspectives constitutional lawyers use in articulating arguments that they hope will persuade readers that their proposed solution to a problem is the right one. With those tools and perspectives in mind, what we can say about how the readers are to decide which of two or more competing solutions is in fact the most persuasive one? Are there techniques for identifying the right solution in the same way that the two-fold logic of constitutional law identifies the problem's true nature? In thinking about these questions, it is important to remember that the first readers constitutional lawyers must persuade are themselves.

A preliminary answer is that we can explain what makes an argument *persuasive* with less certainty than we can describe what makes an argument a *plausible* answer to a constitutional question. The tools of constitutional argument are a public and shared possession; they can be described in reasonably neutral terms that are broadly acceptable to constitutional lawyers of very different substantive views. Constitutional lawyers can agree, most of the time, whether a particular argument is skillfully or ineptly constructed. In order to be a plausible answer to a constitutional question, the reasoning must follow the logic of constitutional law, make cogent use of arguments from the written Constitution and from the Constitution-in-practice, take into account any perspective that applies, and the like. But an argument can be plausible; indeed, it can be highly professional and excite the admiration of its readers, and yet fail to persuade. The second Justice Harlan is a notable example of a constitutional lawyer whose craftsmanship was and is esteemed by many lawyers unpersuaded by many of his arguments. In this chapter,

I outline the considerations that constitutional lawyers are guided by, often without articulating them, in determining which of competing *plausible* answers is the *persuasive* answer.

The Role of Personal Judgment. Constitutional law is a practice of public reasoning and argument, but the sources of persuasiveness are not entirely public. Instead, in a difficult case where there are strong plausible arguments that support conflicting answers, the reasons one answer seems more persuasive than another will lie (to a very considerable degree) in the personality, intellectual predispositions, and moral and political convictions, of the person, whether lawyer or other reader, who must decide between the competing arguments. An argument that misuses the tools of constitutional law thought or suffers from serious logical flaws cannot (or should not) be persuasive, but the argument that persuades, on a question about which there can be serious disagreement, will do so in part for reasons that go beyond logic. The claims sometimes made by commentators (and by judges who should know better) that constitutional law can be freed entirely from the influence of individual judgment, moral commitment, and political preference, by adherence to some algorithmic method – the investigation of original history, for example, or conformity to a theory of adjudication – are always wrong.

This is not a defect in the practice of constitutional law. In a difficult case that is skillfully argued on both sides, and in which there are plausible and indeed strong arguments pro and con, an individual judge's judgment about which position is more persuasive cannot be a simple matter of calculating the indisputably right answer *in principle*, as if the lawyers were arguing over a problem in Euclidean geometry, which can have only one defensible solution. In that situation, the conscientious reader, whether the judge or the judge's reader, must seek the solution that satisfies logic and reason, but his or her ultimate conclusion on which solution best does so will be shaped by personal judgment about which position makes the most sense of the arguments and of the Constitution. And the same is just as true of the lawyer debating in his or her own mind which of several alternative arguments to advance in a brief or letter of advice or commentary on some public issue. The goal of the practice of constitutional law is to discern the most persuasive answers to constitutional questions, but in Justice Cardozo's words, "we can never see" the questions or the answers "with any eyes except our own."[1]

The inextricable connection between which lines of constitutional law reasoning seem most persuasive and the personal judgment of the individual person who is evaluating them is no recent discovery. The very subject matter of constitutional law is political – it is, after all, the law governing the political authority of the various instrumentalities of American government, and it deals constantly with issues that are political or that are related to politics. Political matters are inherently contestable and, in a reasonably free society, regularly contested. Sophisticated constitutional

---

[1] Benjamin Cardozo, *The Nature of the Judicial Process* 13 (New Haven, CT: Yale University Press, 1921).

lawyers therefore have always recognized as inevitable the influence of an individual's political, social, and moral perspectives on his or her conclusions in difficult
constitutional law questions. Chief Justice Marshall made the point long ago,
writing about the controversy over Congress's power to create a national bank that
he would return to over a decade later in writing *McCulloch* v. *Maryland*: "The
judgment is so much influenced by the wishes, the affections, and the general
theories of those by whom any political proposition is decided, that a contrariety
of opinion on this great constitutional question ought to excite no surprise."
Constitutional law is not geometry, and the lawyers who must ask and answer
constitutional questions are human beings rather than computer programs. Their
judgments will reflect these truths, just as the individual lawyer's "wishes, affections,
and general theories" will reflect the social limits of plausibility in his or her age.[2]

In offering his observation that differing judgments on the solution to a difficult
constitutional law problem are inevitable, and that disagreement is inevitably linked
to the differing personal commitments of those trying to decide, Marshall did not
mean to imply that constitutional law is "just" politics, that all constitutional law
arguments are equally plausible, or that there are no right answers to constitutional
questions. The context of my quotation from him is his discussion of the debate
between Hamilton and Jefferson over the national bank bill's constitutionality in the
dueling opinions they provided President Washington in 1791. Marshall included
very substantial parts of both opinions, not at the time generally available, in his
biography of Washington so that the reader could make his own judgments about
who was more persuasive, but for himself, Marshall had no doubt that Jefferson's
reasoning and his conclusion were dead wrong, not because he thought Jefferson's
political views mischievous (although he did think that) but because he thought
Jefferson's constitutional law arguments were unpersuasive.

We seem to have gone in a circle, from the unavoidable influence of personal
"wishes, affections, and general theories" on the constitutional lawyer's judgment to
the same personal considerations weighing on the judgments of those who read the
lawyer's reasoning, but the circularity is not logically vicious, and does not imply that
the arguments are mere window dressing for conclusions that are defensible only on
other grounds. The role of personal judgment is instead an unavoidable aspect of the
kind of reasoning that constitutional law inherited from the common law. Common
lawyers have generally resisted as futile and indeed misleading any attempt to make
legal arguments deductive, proceeding from sharp-edged premises to supposedly
ineluctable conclusions. And they have done so even when dealing with an authoritative written document such as a statute or, in this country, the written Constitution.
Instead, the paradigmatic form of common law argument is what we have called the
argument from precedent, which starts with a judicial decision – itself an amalgam of

---

[2]   4 John Marshall, *Life of George Washington* 243 (Chelsea House 1983) (orig. ed. Philadelphia: C.P.
Wayne, 1804–07).

facts, expressed legal principles, and arguments from prior precedents – and then asks whether the problem the lawyer must solve fits within the scope that the decision seems to demand as precedent. In a genuinely difficult case, however, the right solution cannot simply be deduced from the precedents – that is what makes the case difficult.

There are, of course, a great many questions in constitutional law that have clear answers, but we are not usually puzzled or concerned about what makes the proposed answer to such a question persuasive. Even obvious answers that do not seem to require any reflection, however, sometimes rest on arguments that are assumed to be correct, often beneath the consciousness of the constitutional lawyer unless what is "obviously" correct is questioned. Consider the following. In discussing the presidency, Article II section 1 states in part: "neither shall any person be eligible to that Office who shall not have attained to the Age of thirty five." If a brilliant thirty-year-old, someone acclaimed for wisdom beyond her years, were elected president, is there really no constitutional law argument that she can lawfully take office? Consider the following.

Constitutional provisions, *McCulloch* v. *Maryland* teaches, usually announce fundamental principles of government rather than narrow rules. The thirty-five age requirement *looks* at first glance like a specific rule, but it hardly seems doubtful that its original purpose was to ensure a certain degree of sophistication and judgment, which our thirty-year-old possesses in full measure, and perhaps to prevent the election of a youthful heir to a popular president and thereby ward off the danger of incipient monarchy. The thirty-five year figure is thus very different from the Article I section 3 requirement that each state have *two* senators. That each state must have equal representation is indeed a principle (so important that it is exempt from the Article V power of amending the Constitution), but the decision that there should be specifically two senators per state was close to arbitrary. In contrast, the choice of thirty-five was really a guess at roughly the age the framers thought would usually ensure an adequate degree of maturity. Inaugurating our exceptional but underage president-elect therefore seems to accord with the purpose of the Article II age requirement, *and* the fundamental principle that the holders of constitutional office in the political branches are chosen through democratic politics – after all, the people have chosen *her*.

The argument just sketched out is – in *my* judgment – entirely unconvincing. But that is not because it has an undeniable logical flaw, as if it were a defective proof in geometry. I reject this particular argument because it seems to me too clever, too obviously a manipulation of the modes of constitutional law reasoning to circumvent what seems – we might even say "feels" – like a provision in the written Constitution that ought to be read as a simple rule rather than an invitation to fact-specific debates over specific cases. Counterarguments such as the powerful observation that the basic goal of maintaining a workable government might be imperiled by converting the thirty-five year requirement into a principle of adequate maturity seem to me to support my judgment, but they do so by appealing to my judgment rather than by showing a patent flaw in the argument I am rejecting. The counter-arguments, to sum it up, *persuade* me and the arguments for the thirty-year-old president do not.

It is important not to misunderstand the role that personal judgment plays, in this example and in the practice of constitutional law generally. It is true that "we can never see" constitutional law problems "with any eyes except our own," but that does not mean that we are supposed to propose resolutions to those problems in order to promote our individual political and moral "wishes, affections, and general theories." When constitutional lawyers ask themselves which of competing answers is most persuasive, if they are acting conscientiously within the bounds of traditional practice, they are not making a choice about which answer they *prefer* for extra-legal reasons. The ultimate purpose of constitutional lawyers' practice is to solve constitutional law problems by determining and applying the answers that fidelity to the Constitution-in-practice demands.

Since the roles that most lawyers play in the system usually provide a context in which the lawyer must address a constitutional problem, the answers conscientious lawyers give are not always those they would have reached in the abstract. The litigator, for example, has an obligation to construct those arguments that most persuasively advance the client's interests, and even judges, whose duty is to come to the right judgment in the case before the court, must take into account constraining aspects of constitutional law thinking – for example, vertical precedent or rational basis analysis – that may preclude basing their judgment on the constitutional answer they would have thought most persuasive in the absence of those constraints. But in every context, the final goal of the practice of constitutional law is to enable and require government to fulfill the constitutional commitments of the American political community, not to advance the extra-legal interests of the lawyer.

And what about judges who deliberately act to advance personal ideological beliefs or partisan political allegiances while cloaking these objectives in the language of constitutional law practice? Many critics of the Supreme Court's decisions clearly assume that some of the justices – almost always the ones whose decisions the individual critic dislikes – can be described in this way. That assumption I believe to be quite wrong, but the criticism is wrong-headed in a different sense as well, for two reasons. First, the critics are asking for what no approach to legal decision making can provide, "a set of rules so palpable and constraining that they will be proof against chicanery, evasion and disingenuousness. But no set of rules is proof against that. ... The use of rules to coordinate human enterprises of every sort assumes a generous and honest attitude." As Charles Fried, whom I am quoting, went on to say, the traditional practice of constitutional law "assumes intelligence and good faith – that is a strength, not a weakness, and more shame to him who abuses it." In the event of such abuse, it is not our traditional practice that is flawed, but the faithless justice (or any other constitutional lawyer expected to "say what the law is") who is a cheat.[3]

Second, criticism of the Supreme Court that rests on showing a correlation between the "wishes, affections, and general theories" of the justices and the decisions they reach misses the point Chief Justice Marshall made long ago about judgment. We can assume confidently that there will be such a correlation, at least on the high Court with its steady diet of highly contested and contestable questions to answer, and proving the assumption to be true proves nothing of significance about the practice of American constitutional law. Criticism of the Court that serves the interests of the American political community, its constitutional system, and the Court itself, focuses on the cogency of the arguments the justices offer for their decisions, not on the (inferred) reasons why they offer the arguments or reach their conclusions. Does this opinion identify in a clear, logical fashion the questions that the problem before the Court presents? Does the justice writing the opinion construct the answers reached using the traditional tools of constitutional law argument in a plausible fashion, respecting the limits on any given kind of argument? Does the opinion deal skillfully and respectfully with serious arguments to the contrary, a question that can be answered affirmatively even if the critic is personally persuaded by the arguments for a different answer? The practice of constitutional law is itself the proper standard of critical evaluation for the work of the justices and indeed of all constitutional lawyers.[4]

Persuasion and Adversarial Thinking. We are left, then, with the question of what can be said about persuasiveness in addition to the observation that in difficult cases smart constitutional lawyers acting in good faith will sometimes disagree. Perhaps the most basic point is that persuasiveness depends on remembering that *constitutional law is always a form of adversarial thinking even when it is taking place entirely inside the constitutional lawyer's mind.* The requirement that both sides be heard by a neutral decision maker is not only the core of procedural due process. It is the essential prerequisite for evaluating the persuasiveness of a constitutional law argument, regardless of whether you are an advocate writing a brief, a counselor giving advice, or a judge deciding a case. On any question of any difficulty whatever, there will be (by definition!) more than one line of reasoning that has something to commend it. The most persuasive answer will be supported not only by the affirmative arguments that support it, but also by the fact that it takes into full account the concerns advanced by arguments that support other conclusions. "Good legal

---

[3] Fried, *Order and Law: Arguing the Reagan Revolution – A Firsthand Account* 66–67 (New York: Simon & Schuster, 1991); *Marbury* v. *Madison*, 5 U.S. (1 Cranch) 137, 177 (1803).

[4] *Cf.* Frank H. Easterbrook, Foreword to Antonin Scalia & Bryan A. Garner, *Reading Law: The Interpretation of Legal Texts* xxiii–xxiv (St. Paul, MN: Thomson/West, 2012) (discussing the role of "professional norms – including norms about interpretive method" in producing significant levels of agreement among judges even on the Supreme Court and in exposing the "misuse of these rules by a crafty or willful judge ... as an abuse of power"). Judge Easterbrook had statutory construction immediately in mind, but I believe his observations apply in constitutional law as well.

thought and writing . . . involve the articulation of arguments that can be made both ways . . . and their arrangement in a structure that leads to a conclusion that fairly reflects the force of opposing arguments."[5]

The precise manner in which the constitutional lawyer engages in adversarial thought varies, depending on the lawyer's role. An advocate is not neutral about whose interests he or she is ethically bound to serve, but it would be irresponsible to choose among available lines of reasoning supporting the client's cause any but the ones most likely to persuade the court. And in making that choice, the responsible advocate must dispassionately weigh the potential arguments for and against a constitutional law conclusion that would advance the client's position in the litigation. Only by doing so can the advocate make an informed decision about the constitutional claim that is most likely to persuade the judges, who are by virtue of their office supposed to be indifferent as to the client's interests. A lawyer giving advice on a contestable constitutional law issue may have a similar ethical duty. The question whether there are responsible legal arguments that advance the advisee's goals requires the advisor to make judgments about how judges, regulators, or critics would evaluate the positions the advocate is considering in deciding what advice to give.

In contrast, a judge's ethical obligation is not to advance the goals of any of the parties, but to decide which answer to the constitutional law question before the court is the most persuasive to him or her as a judge. As *Marbury* v. *Madison* taught long ago, judicial review is a duty that rests in part on the judge's personal, sworn obligation to make decisions "agreeably to the Constitution" as the judge – not Congress or the president or anyone else – understands the Constitution. A lower court judge must obey the rule of vertical precedent, of course, and a Supreme Court justice is limited by the demands of stare decisis, but those are factors that go into the judge's decision about which answer is most persuasive: The question of persuasiveness, all relevant factors considered, belongs to the individual judge. Even so, however, there is a parallel in the judge's thinking to the advocate's reflection "which argument do I think the court is mostly likely to accept?" Unless the judge is criminally corrupt, he or she will resist any bias toward one of the parties, but if intellectually honest, he or she will also recall that the influence of personal "wishes, affections, and general theories" is inevitable but not itself a basis for decision. The responsible judge will therefore evaluate the persuasiveness of the conflicting

---

[5] James Boyd White, *Living Speech: Resisting the Empire of Force* 73 (Princeton: Princeton University Press, 2006). On the parallel roles adversarial thinking plays in individual reflection and fair public debate, see Stuart Hampshire, *Justice Is Conflict* 8–10 (Princeton: Princeton University Press, 2000): Just "procedures and institutions . . . all involve the fair weighing and balancing of contrary arguments. They are all subject to the single prescription *audi alteram partem* ('hear the other side') [which defines] the principle of adversary argument. . . . In the ever-recurring cases of conflicts of principles, adversary argument and then a kind of inner judicial discretion and adjudication are called for. In private deliberation, the adversary principle of hearing both sides is imposed by the individual on himself as the principle of rationality."

arguments to the imagined audience of the opinion's readers: "which argument do I think my readers, many of whom have very different personal commitments than my own, are most likely to accept?"[6]

Nonlawyers sometimes think that the adversarial quality of legal thought, the professionally skillful lawyer's ability and insistence on considering the arguments on either side of an issue, is a sign of ethical callousness or a professional willingness to serve as a hired gun for any position. The opposite is the truth in all areas of law but above all in the practice of constitutional law. *Intellectual honesty is an essential prerequisite to responsible constitutional law argument and decision,* and intellectual honesty demands that the lawyer recognize and give full weight to the arguments that count against her ultimate decision about what constitutional answers to advocate, advise, or adopt.

An illustration of the Supreme Court justifying a decision through overt adversarial reasoning is *United States* v. *Nixon* (1974), the Watergate tapes case. President Nixon argued that the federal courts could not compel the president to turn over records of confidential presidential records that a district court needed in the course of a criminal prosecution. According to Nixon, the courts were obliged to recognize an absolute executive privilege against compelled disclosure because of "the President's need for complete candor and objectivity from advisers" in order to carry out the duties of the office. The Court found more persuasive the counterargument that according the president a qualified privilege for confidential discussions that could be overcome by a specific judicial need for information would meet the president's legitimate constitutional concerns. Furthermore, qualifying the ordinary executive privilege would not preclude recognizing a more robust privilege if the president asserted a "need to protect military, diplomatic, or sensitive national security secrets" rather than a general interest in confidentiality.[7]

As this brief summary indicates, the Court's reasoning took Nixon's argument seriously, and conceded as much to the argument as was consistent with its decision that the confidentiality needs of the Article II branch of government did not automatically override the adjudicatory needs of the Article III branch. Even in requiring the president to disclose the tapes, furthermore, the Court reasoned that the judiciary could respect "the very important interest in confidentiality of Presidential communications" by requiring the "production of such material for in camera inspection with all the protection that [the] district court will be obliged to provide." The *Nixon* opinion thus invites its readers to decide for themselves if they agree with the Court's evaluation of the strengths and weaknesses of the arguments on both sides, and precisely in doing so the opinion renders its conclusion more persuasive.[8]

---

[6] See *Marbury* v. *Madison,* 5 U.S. (1 Cranch) 137, 180 (1803) ("Why does a judge swear to discharge his duties agreeably to the constitution of the United States, if that constitution forms no rule for his government? if it is closed upon him, and cannot be inspected by him?").

[7] *United States* v. *Nixon,* 418 U.S. 683, 706 (1974).

[8] *Id.*

The Role of the Written Constitution. The Constitution-in-practice extends far beyond the semantic content of the written Constitution, and as we have seen, even a strong argument focused on the constitutional text does not always prevail, particularly against a counterargument firmly rooted in Supreme Court precedent. Nevertheless, an element necessary to making a line of constitutional law reasoning truly persuasive is that the argument must take into account the axiomatic authority of the written Constitution. There must be some sense in which the argument can rightly claim a connection to the constitutional instrument, even if the connection is remote. The absence of a plausible link to the document is a presumptive reason to reject the argument. The Court's decision in *Erie Railroad Co. v. Tompkins* (1938) that there is no general federal common law applicable in ordinary civil actions demonstrates this point. The decision required the Court to repudiate an almost century-old precedent that the federal courts had followed in a large number of cases, no small matter in a legal system that rests on stare decisis. Among the justifications the Court gave for retrospectively condemning as wrong many of its own decisions was that the written Constitution gives Congress "no power to declare substantive rules of common law applicable in a state. ... And no clause in the Constitution purports to confer such a power upon the federal courts." The precedents rested on an argument that was inconsistent with the written Constitution.[9]

Two important parts of the Constitution-in-practice will illustrate the ways in which the presence of a discernible connection to the written Constitution can enhance the persuasiveness of lines of reasoning that depend in large measure on arguments from precedent. As we saw in Chapter 5, despite its long pedigree in the case law, the dormant commerce clause doctrine has been attacked as the product of an illegitimate transformation of a clause that authorizes congressional action into a prohibition on (some) state legislation. But limiting the clause to an affirmative, power-authorizing role would create a serious tension between the Constitution-in-practice and the written Constitution's historical purpose of eliminating state economic protectionism.

> Without the dormant Commerce Clause, we would be left with a constitutional scheme that those who framed and ratified the Constitution would surely find surprising. That is so because removing state trade barriers was a principal reason for the adoption of the Constitution. ... In light of this background, it would be strange if the Constitution contained no provision curbing state protectionism, and at this point in the Court's history, no provision other than the Commerce Clause could easily do the job.

Given the *McCulloch* principle that the written Constitution is a charter of "great outlines" and "important objects," the dormant commerce clause's role in

---

[9]   *Erie Railroad Co. v. Tompkins*, 304 U.S. 64, 78 (1938) (Brandeis, J.). The original precedent *Erie Railroad* rejected was *Swift v. Tyson*, 41 U.S. (16 Pet.) 1 (1842).

addressing a core original meaning concern strongly supports adherence to the long line of precedents employing the doctrine.[10]

Critics of substantive due process sometimes assert that the very label is an oxymoron, on the assumption that process means procedure and that procedure and substance are invariably contrasting notions in law. If the doctrine's relationship to the wording of the due process clauses were actually this antagonistic, it would be somewhat surprising that the doctrine seems firmly embedded in constitutional law despite repeated attack. However, the charge that substantive due process is entirely untethered from the text of the clauses is itself unconvincing. Even on the assumption that "process" in the constitutional text is a synonym for "procedure" (an assumption that the text does not self-evidently require), "procedure" and "substance" are not terms with rigidly fixed and utterly distinct meanings.[11] More importantly, the phrase "due process of law" has long been understood to stem from Magna Carta's reference to "the law of the land," and the Supreme Court concluded well over a century ago that given the American constitutional context of limited legislative as well as executive power, that language "must be held to guaranty ... the very substance of individual rights to life, liberty, and property." (See the discussion in Chapter 5.) Whatever the merits of other criticisms of it as a general concept, substantive due process is connected to the text of the due process clauses by original meaning and structural arguments that are long-standing and defensible.[12]

Fidelity and Freedom in Dealing with Precedent. As we have seen, the Supreme Court like other American courts sometimes exercises the authority to overrule its own decisions, and modifications to the scope and application of precedents and doctrines are common. But the strong presumption in constitutional law, inherited from the common law, is that the Court will give stare decisis effect to its own decisions, while the rule of vertical precedent requires all lower courts to follow the Court's decisions even as it obliges them to apply the decisions to situations that the Court itself did not consider. The Constitution-in-practice largely consists of rules and doctrines that have been built up over time through decisions that build on prior precedent even as they extend or adjust the earlier rulings to accommodate new considerations or difficulties. Argument from precedent necessarily involves both fidelity to the precedent and its meaningful adaptation to a new situation. A useful

---

[10] *Tennessee Wine & Spirits Retailers Assoc.* v. *Thomas*, 139 S. Ct. 2449, 2460 (2019). The phrases from *McCulloch* are found at 17 U.S. (4 Wheat.) 316, 407 (1819).

[11] See, e.g., *Jinks* v. *Richland County*, 538 U.S. 456, 465 (2003) ("the meaning of 'substance' and 'procedure' in a particular context is 'largely determined by the purposes for which the dichotomy is drawn'"); *Mistretta* v. *United States*, 488 U.S. 361, 392 (1989) (referring to "the logical morass of distinguishing between substantive and procedural rules"); *Shady Grove Orthopedic Assocs., P.A.* v. *Allstate Ins. Co.*, 559 U.S. 393, 419 (2010) (Stevens, J., concurring in part and concurring in the judgment) ("The line between procedural and substantive law is hazy, and matters of procedure and matters of substance are not mutually exclusive categories with easily ascertainable contents.") (citations omitted).

[12] *Hurtado* v. *California*, 110 U.S. 516, 531–32 (1884).

analogy to the constitutional lawyer's duty to combine fidelity and adaption in handling constitutional precedent lies in the task of a novelist who is part of a group of writers writing a "chain novel" to which each contributes a chapter in turn. "Each novelist aims to make a single novel of the material he has been given, what he adds to it, and (so far as he can control this) what his successors will want or be able to add." In doing so, the individual writer has a duty to further develop in a convincing fashion the narrative of the novel, and thus a degree of creative freedom, but also the obligation to make sense of what he or she has received. The writer cannot, for example, rightly ignore "a subplot treated as having great dramatic importance or a dominant and repeated metaphor." To do so would be inconsistent with the writer's place in a collaborative endeavor.[13]

A court dealing with precedent or with some other authority works with a similar combination of freedom and obligation, with the opposing caveats that the Supreme Court *can* overrule itself (and thus reject an important aspect of the constitutional law the current justices have been given) and that lower courts cannot adopt conclusions that the Court's decisions forbid. The persuasiveness of a constitutional argument will often depend on the extent to which it seems to display fidelity in general to the relevant cases and other authorities while adopting whatever change or extension the Court thinks appropriate. The line of decisions that led from the *Plessy* v. *Ferguson* (1896) acceptance of separate-but-equal racial segregation to *Brown* v. *Board of Education* (1954) illustrates the role of continuity in persuasiveness, and also the capacity of precedent-based argument to accommodate radical change over time. Largely because of the principled *and* strategic work of the NAACP Legal Defense Fund's lawyers, the Supreme Court was first persuaded to insist that the separate-but-equal doctrine, taken on its own terms, required genuine material equality in graduate education, then to recognize that equality is not simply a matter of dollars and cents in the educational, political and social worlds, and finally, in *Brown* and subsequent cases, to reject racial segregation itself as inherently unequal. At each step, the Court's reasoning was rooted in the precedents as they stood at the time of decision, although by the end of the process all that remained of *Plessy*, the precedent from which the decisions began, was the first Justice Harlan's dissent.[14]

"Think things, not words." The persuasiveness of a constitutional law argument is closely related to the extent to which it takes realistic account of the extra-legal facts that the problem at hand involves. The risk that legal rules and doctrines will not be well-adapted to the human world they govern is pervasive. Disconnection from the facts is a particular danger in constitutional law, which is decisively shaped by a Court that by design is chiefly responsible for explicating general rules of law

[13]   Ronald Dworkin, *Law's Empire* 229–31 (Cambridge, MA: Belknap Press, 1986).
[14]   *Plessy v. Ferguson*, 163 U.S. 537 (1896); *Brown v. Board of Education*, 347 U.S. 483 (1954). For a more detailed discussion of the legal road that led from *Plessy* to *Brown*, see the excursus at the end of this chapter.

rather than applying them to specific fact patterns. Constitutional lawyers therefore must give special attention to the fit between a line of reasoning and the factual situations it will address. Justice Holmes once admonished that lawyers should not be "contented with hollow forms of words. . . . We must think things not words, or at least we must constantly translate our words into the facts for which they stand, if we are to keep to the real and the true." An argument that satisfies that demand gains in persuasiveness. Consider *South Dakota v. Wayfair, Inc.* (2018). An earlier decision, *Quill Corp. v. North Dakota* (1992), had concluded that the dormant commerce clause did not permit a state to require an out-of-state seller to collect and remit sales taxes unless the seller had a physical presence in the state; simply shipping mail-order goods into the state was insufficient to impose the obligation to collect and remit the taxes. Estimates of the lawful tax revenue loss due to the physical presence rule ranged from $8 billion to $33 billion nationally per year.[15]

The *Wayfair* Court noted that in *Quill*, the justices had been troubled that "without the physical presence rule" state taxes might burden interstate commerce "by subjecting retailers to tax-collection obligations" in many different states, but the Court reasoned that this concern no longer matched reality. The "administrative costs of compliance, especially in the modern economy with its Internet technology, are largely unrelated to whether a company happens to have a physical presence in a State. . . . Modern e-commerce does not align analytically with a test that relies on the sort of physical presence defined in" *Quill*. "Between targeted advertising and instant access to most consumers via any internet-enabled device, a business may be present in a State in a meaningful way without that presence being physical in the traditional sense of the term." The Court therefore concluded that its understanding of current facts undermined its precedent, repudiated the physical presence rule, and overruled *Quill*.[16]

Another good example of the Supreme Court following Justice Holmes's admonition with respect to a different kind of fact is *Cohen v. California* (1971). The Court reversed a conviction under a state criminal statute that prohibited conduct disturbing the peace or quiet of any person by deliberate and "offensive conduct"; the conduct in question was wearing a jacket into a courthouse with a visible expletive referring to the military draft. The state argued that it was not interfering with the petitioner's ability to express his political opposition to the draft but simply trying to eliminate a particularly offensive word unnecessary to serious debate and indeed unhelpful in such debate. Justice Harlan for the Court responded by pointing to the established free speech principle that the constitutional prohibition "is designed and intended to remove governmental restraints from the arena of public discussion." That fundamental constitutional purpose is clearly implicated by government punishment for expressing a view on a major issue of public debate even if the

[15]   Oliver Wendell Holmes, Law in Science and Science in Law, 12 *Harv. L. Rev.* 443, 460 (1899); *South Dakota v. Wayfair, Inc.*, 138 S. Ct. 2080, 2088 (2018); *Quill Corp. v. North Dakota*, 504 U.S. 298 (1992).
[16]   138 S. Ct. at 2093, 2095, 2099.

expression was "what otherwise might seem a trifling and annoying instance of individual distasteful abuse of a privilege." Furthermore, Harlan reasoned, the state's argument took too narrow and unrealistic a view of what matters in public discussion. "We cannot sanction the view that the Constitution, while solicitous of the cognitive content of individual speech has little or no regard for that emotive function which practically speaking, may often be the more important element of the overall message sought to be communicated." If the first amendment's protection of freedom of speech is to correlate realistically with how people actually speak and listen, it must extend to the full range of human communication.[17]

Authority beyond the Precedents. The reader with a taste for reading the details in footnotes will have noticed that occasionally this book names the author of an opinion of the Court, a situation in which standard legal citation form does not require a name. The practice is not an idiosyncrasy of your author but reasonably common in Supreme Court and other opinions, in briefs, and elsewhere. The explanation of the practice – not just of unnecessarily including a judge's name in a citation, but of naming individual judges in other situations as well as if the individual were an authority simply as that particular individual and not as the mouthpiece of a court – is that some individuals *are* authorities in their own right. The constitutional lawyer constructing the most responsible and persuasive argument for a conclusion may strengthen the argument by showing that it builds on the thinking of judges, and occasionally of other individuals, who are important in constitutional law for their influence, insight, or wisdom.

Let's look at part of footnote 36 at the very end of Chapter 5:

> *Youngstown Sheet & Tube Co.*, 343 U.S at 652 (Jackson, J., concurring). ... The other quotation is from *Chastleton Corp.* v. *Sinclair*, 264 U.S. 543, 547–48 (1924). (Holmes, J.).

Citation form required the footnote to mention Justice Jackson's name since his opinion in *Youngstown* was a concurrence, but there was good reason to mention his name in the text, as I did, so that Jackson himself became part of my argument. Why? Jackson's *Youngstown* concurrence is itself high authority, not just in the sense that it has almost supplanted the official opinion of the Court as embodying the meaning of the Steel Seizure Case as precedent, but also because Jackson and his Steel Seizure concurrence, in particular, are known as the source of "as much combination of analysis and common sense as there is in this area." And including Justice Holmes's name in the citation to his opinion for the Court in a case that many constitutional lawyers would scarcely recognize not only brings the weight of that controversial genius to bear, but also changes the case itself from an aging and little-known decision to a precedent that must be reckoned with.[18]

---

[17] *Cohen* v. *California*, 403 U.S. 15, 24, 25, 25–26 (1971).
[18] *Dames & Moore* v. *Regan*, 453 U.S. 654, 661 (1981) (Rehnquist, J.).

This is not (or not just) name-dropping. The practice of constitutional law, as I hope the reader is persuaded by now, is a disciplined form of intellectual inquiry and argument. But (once again) constitutional law is not Euclidean geometry and in dealing with a difficult problem, constitutional lawyers of equal skill may disagree on the most persuasive solution, and also recognize that the arguments for and against differing solutions are powerful. In such a case, the process of determining which solution is the most persuasive will involve the exercise of some degree of personal judgment – "this makes the most sense *to me.*" The same is equally true, of course, of past constitutional problems and the lawyers who wrestled with them. To know that the reasoning that went into a decision persuaded, indeed was written by, a Jackson or a Holmes is to have an additional reason for trusting the reasoning, not just because it has precedential authority but because the author makes the argument more likely to be right.

The existence in law of an element of personal authority, along with the force of stare decisis and the intrinsic persuasiveness of a line of argument, goes far back in the common law prehistory of constitutional law, at least as far as the tenure of William de Bereford on the Court of Common Pleas (1292–1326), who over his long career on that royal court played a major role in shaping the common law of the high Middle Ages and beyond. By the time Chief Justices Ellsworth and Marshall persuaded their colleagues of the value of speaking through a single opinion of the Court – and in Marshall's case further persuaded them to allow him the lion's share of the speaking – the habit of recognizing the views of certain judges as especially weighty was long since firmly lodged in common law tradition. By appropriating that bit of the tradition for constitutional law, Marshall in fact became the first American constitutional judge likely to be named in a line of argument because his name itself is a kind of authority.

No judge is without critics, fortunately, and so by definition there can be no authoritative list of which American judges have special status in constitutional law. (Contrast precedents, where in most areas of constitutional law, it would be possible to draw up a relatively uncontroversial list of the leading decisions as of the present.) The list of judges that follows is half playful, but anyone who reads much constitutional law will quickly find the names on it familiar.[19] Chief Justice Marshall (1801–1835) certainly would head any reasonable list, and his learned friend and colleague Joseph Story (1812–1845) should be there as well; Story's three-volume treatise entitled *Commentaries on the Constitution* (1833) is the almost official restatement of the constitutional law of the Marshall era Court. Even the most intellectually gifted of the justices in the succeeding period are lesser figures, or deeply implicated

---

[19]   The dates are of years as service as federal judges, on the Supreme Court except in the case of Learned Hand. Three of the justices made notable contributions to constitutional law before they were appointed to the Court. Holmes and Cardozo each served for many years on the highest courts of Massachusetts and New York, respectively, and Jackson was a great solicitor general and then attorney general of the United States.

in the Supreme Court's moral and legal failures. The exception is John Marshall Harlan (1877–1911), whose dissenting positions on civil rights, congressional power, and substantive due process have generally been vindicated by later decisions. The reader knows Justice Holmes (1902–1932), and his frequent ally Louis D. Brandeis (1916–1939) also merits special recognition. Their contemporary on the Court, Charles Evans Hughes (associate justice 1910–1916; chief justice 1930–1941), was a major figure in the center chair, while Benjamin Cardozo (1932–1938) is better remembered as a great state-court common law judge than for his brief if lustrous tenure on the Supreme Court. Learned Hand (district and then appeals court judge 1909–1961) is one of the few American judges never to serve on the Supreme Court to merit his own parenthetical in a citation. Of FDR's many appointments, the two who stand out as constitutional lawyers (of very different views), are Hugo L. Black (1937–1971) and Robert H. Jackson (1941–1954). John Marshall Harlan II (1955–1971), grandson of the first Justice Harlan, is a figure of special note because of the respect he continues to receive from lawyers who sharply disagree with many of his substantive conclusions. Of course, I have omitted many other outstanding constitutional lawyers who served as justices and judges, as well as all non-judges, and my decision to stop the list before it extended to those who have been on the bench in my time as a lawyer does not imply that there have been no great constitutional lawyers in recent decades.[20]

Let us turn from individual judges to individual opinions. The pre-Marshall Supreme Court's small number of constitutional decisions were generally announced by each participating justice writing a "seriatim" opinion, and there is no fixed convention about which to cite or quote, except that as we saw in Chapter 3, Justice Samuel Chase's opinion in *Calder v. Bull* (1798) is the long-established foundational precedent on the meaning of the ex post facto clauses of Article I sections 9 and 10. Chief Justice Marshall accompanied his successful maintenance of the practice of a single opinion "of the Court" by an attempt to minimize the number of separate opinions and abided by his own preference; Marshall himself only wrote a single dissent in a constitutional case in almost thirty years on the bench. Since Marshall's day, the frequency with which justices have filed concurrences and dissents has become astronomically higher, although some justices have claimed to be reluctant to write separately and may even have meant it. Separate opinions, often with complicated relationships to the opinion of the Court ("concurring in part, and dissenting in part" and the like), are common on the modern Court.[21]

---

[20] Although the point seems obvious, perhaps I should add that inclusion on a list of great constitutional judges implies no judgment on the individual's moral stature or political wisdom: There is no necessary correlation between a judge's personal character and his or her influence on constitutional law. Great judges do not escape the beliefs and limitations of their era, social class, and the like. We are discussing the weight a judge carries as an authority in law, not looking for personal heroes.

[21] *Calder v. Bull*, 3 U.S. (3 Dall.) 386, 390–91 (1798) (seriatim opinion of Chase, J.).

What is the significance of a separate opinion in constitutional law? In some cases, as we have seen, the justices are unable to muster a majority to join an opinion of the Court, in which event the rule in *Marks* dictates that the opinion concurring in the Court's judgment that has the narrowest reasoning is to be treated as stating the rationale of the decision. That opinion is often but by no means always the lead or plurality opinion. On occasion, furthermore, there is an official opinion of the Court that does not in fact state the reasoning accepted by a majority of the justices, and this can be determined by a close reading of the concurring opinion(s). *National League of Cities* v. *Usery* (1976) held, by a bare majority of the justices, that the federal structure prohibited Congress from imposing federal minimum-wage and maximum-hour standards on state and local agencies as employers. The opinion of the Court explained the rule as a categorical one, applying to congressional interference with the "integral governmental functions" of the states, but a concurring justice filed a short opinion implausibly asserting that "the Court's opinion ... seems to me" to adopt "a balancing approach." The Court subsequently followed the concurrence and treated *National League of Cities* as ordaining a balancing test, and then in *Garcia* v. *SAMTA* (1985) decided that this test was unworkable and overruled the decision.[22]

Where there is a true opinion of the Court, one that presents a rationale for the decision on which a majority of the justices agree, separate opinions play several roles. For the justice who is writing, a dissent or a concurrence in the judgment is sometimes said to be an appeal to the future, a presentation of the reasoning that the writer thinks the Court should have adopted and hopes that it will eventually endorse. One of the dissents in *Garcia* expressed confidence that the federalism principle the Court was rejecting would "in time again command the support of a majority of this Court." At the most basic level, a separate opinion that rejects the Court's reasoning may lessen the decision's weight as precedent by vigorously presenting counterarguments, and thus inviting future litigants to adopt its approach in asking the Court to rework or reject the decision. Aside from attempting to weaken the force of stare decisis, the justice may also seek to direct the Court's future decisions away from the direction taken in the majority opinion, or limit the precedent's scope by showing its flaws, or prevent the majority's reasoning from further ensconcing a precedent the writer thinks erroneous into "the tissue of the law."[23]

---

[22] *National League of Cities* v. *Usery*, 426 U.S. 833, 851–52 (1976) (Rehnquist, J.); *id.* at 856 (Blackmun, J., concurring). Justice Blackmun also wrote the opinion of the Court in *Garcia* v. *San Antonio Metro. Transit Auth.*, 469 U.S. 528 (1985), which overruled *National League of Cities*. Then-Associate Justice Rehnquist noted in his *Garcia* dissent that references to "the 'balancing test' approved in *National League of Cities*" were in fact "*not* identical with the language in that case." *Id.* at 579–80 (Rehnquist, J., dissenting).

[23] *Garcia* v. *San Antonio Metro. Transit Auth.*, 469 U.S. at 580 (Rehnquist, J., dissenting); *Radovich* v. *National Football League*, 352 U.S. 445, 555 (1957) (Frankfurter, J., dissenting). See, e.g., *Nat'l Fed'n of Indep. Bus.* v. *Sebelius*, 567 U.S. 519, 707 (2012) (Scalia, Kennedy, Thomas & Alito, JJ.,

Concurring opinions by justices who genuinely agree with the Court's stated rationale can serve several different purposes. In the leading commerce clause case *United States v. Lopez*, for example, two members of the five-justice majority filed concurring opinions for almost diametrically opposite reasons: one concurrence explained the limited scope of the decision and argued that *Lopez* did not put in question existing doctrine, while the other portrayed *Lopez* as the first step in a fundamental reconsideration of the doctrine. A concurrence also affords the writer an opportunity to address a related issue that the Court did not consider, dispute assertions made in other separate opinions, stress the importance of the facts and the procedural posture of the case to the Court's decision, or explain an apparent inconsistency between the concurring justice's agreement with the Court and prior opinions.[24]

The justices, then, have a variety of reasons for writing separately even when there is a controlling opinion of the Court, and when they do, other constitutional lawyers can and do use those opinions, often for the purpose the writer had in mind, to limit, expand, explain, or attack the Court's opinion in the case. Separate opinions sometimes come to eclipse the official opinion of the Court. A good example is Justice Brandeis's discussion of freedom of speech in *Whitney v. California* (1927). Brandeis sharply disagreed with the majority on the merits but concurred on

dissenting) ("The values that should have determined our course today are caution, minimalism, and the understanding that the Federal Government is one of limited powers. But the Court's ruling undermines those values at every turn."); *Whitney v. California*, 274 U.S. 357, 374 (1927) (Brandeis, J., concurring on procedural grounds) (noting that "this court has not yet fixed the standard by which to determine" the permissible scope of governmental interference with free speech and discussing the reasoning that should guide the Court in future cases in reaching "sound conclusions on these matters"); *Reed v. Town of Gilbert*, 576 U.S. 155, 183 (2015) (Kagan, J., concurring in the judgment) (arguing that the Court should apply "our content-regulation doctrine with a dose of common sense" rather than in the majority's overly rigid manner); *Church of the Lukumi Babalu Aye v. City of Hialeah*, 508 U.S. 520, 564 (1993) (Souter, J., concurring in part and concurring in the judgment) (arguing that the Court should reexamine a troublesome precedent in "the next case that would turn upon its application"). The dissenters in *Sebelius* further underlined their attempt to undermine that decision by the unusual device of having all four sign the dissent.

[24] *Compare United States v. Lopez*, 514 U.S. 549, 574 (1995) (Kennedy, J., concurring) ("the Court as an institution and the legal system as a whole have an immense stake in the stability of our Commerce Clause jurisprudence as it has evolved to this point. *Stare decisis* operates with great force in counseling us not to call in question the essential principles now in place"); with *id.* at 585, 602 (Thomas, J., concurring) ("In an appropriate case, I believe that we must further reconsider our 'substantial effects' test . . . I think we must modify our Commerce Clause jurisprudence"). See, e.g., *Heart of Atlanta Motel v. United States*, 379 U.S. 241, 293 (1964) (Goldberg, J., concurring) (concluding that the 1964 Civil Rights Act was constitutionally authorized by section 5 of the fourteenth amendment although the Court did not reach that question); *Roman Catholic Diocese of Brooklyn v. Cuomo*, 141 S. Ct. 63, 70–71 (2020) (Gorsuch, J., concurring) (disagreeing with two dissenting opinions over the significance of a concurrence in an earlier case); *Kansas v. Glover*, 140 S. Ct. 1183, 1194 (2020) (Kagan, J., concurring) (contrasting "this strange case, contested on a barebones stipulation" with future "cases with more complete records"); *Roe v. Wade*, 410 U.S. 113, 167–68 (1973) (Stewart, J., concurring) (explaining his reasons for dissenting in *Griswold v. Connecticut* which he now accepted as precedent).

procedural grounds. Within a very short period, it was clear that the Court had adopted Brandeis's reasoning: Already in *Stromberg* v. *California* (1931), the opinion of the Court cited Brandeis's concurrence equally with the *Whitney* majority opinion as authority, and by the time it decided *United States* v. *Caroline Products Co.* (1938), the Court was invoking the Brandeis opinion to the exclusion of the majority's as *the* authoritative opinion in *Whitney*. The Court eventually clarified the law by expressly overruling *Whitney* without in the least putting Brandeis's reasoning in question. In other instances, a concurrence proves more influential than the majority opinion although the latter retains its precedential force. A well-known example is the second Justice Harlan's concurrence in *Katz* v. *United States*, which introduced the principle that the fourth amendment protects "reasonable expectations of privacy." Despite criticism, Harlan's reasoning is a settled part of fourth amendment law although the opinion of the Court is also sometimes cited.[25]

The same process can occur with dissents as well, although when it does the precedential force of the majority's reasoning and disposition obviously must evaporate entirely, regardless of whether the Court formally overrules the decision. The first Justice Harlan's lone dissent rejecting the constitutionality of de jure racial segregation in *Plessy* v. *Ferguson* (1896) remains important in equal protection debate, while the majority opinion has been consigned to ignominy. Justice Holmes's dissent in *Abrams* v. *United States* (1919) is universally recognized as the wellspring of Supreme Court thought on first amendment freedom of speech; although the Court has never formally repudiated the actual decision, it is Holmes's opinion and not that of the 1919 majority that is a constitutional authority. In *United States* v. *Darby* (1941), the Court relied on what it described as "the powerful and now classic dissent of Mr. Justice Holmes" in *Hammer* v. *Dagenhart* (1918), in rejecting *Hammer*'s commerce clause analysis and overruling the decision outright.[26]

Even when a separate opinion has not achieved a kind of quasi-precedential authority as a result of its subsequent treatment by the Supreme Court, it may well be valuable for the constitutional lawyer, both in thinking through a problem and in constructing a plausible solution. The justice writing an opinion for the Court is often under some pressure to write a constrained or even least-common-denominator

[25] See *Whitney*, 274 U.S. at 375–79 (Brandeis, J., concurring). The early citations to Justice Brandeis's concurrence were *Stromberg* v. *California*, 283 U.S. 359, 368 (1931); and *United States* v. *Caroline Products Co.*, 304 U.S. 144, 152 n. 4 (1938), and the decision overruling *Whitney* was *Brandenburg* v. *Ohio*, 395 U.S. 444, 449 (1969). On *Katz*, see, e.g., *Byrd* v. *United States*, 138 S. Ct. 1518, 1526 (2018) (reasonable expectations test, "derived from the second Justice Harlan's concurrence in *Katz* ... supplements ... the traditional property-based understanding of the Fourth Amendment"). See *Katz* v. *United States*, 389 U.S. 347, 362 (1967) (Harlan, J., concurring).

[26] *Plessy* v. *Ferguson*, 163 U.S. 537, 559 (Harlan, J., dissenting) ("in view of the constitution, in the eye of the law, there is in this country no superior, dominant, ruling class of citizens. There is no caste here. Our constitution is color-blind, and neither knows nor tolerates classes among citizens."); *Abrams* v. *United States*, 250 U.S. 616, 627–31 (Holmes, J., dissenting); *United States* v. *Darby*, 312 U.S. 100, 115–17 (1941) (overruling *Hammer* v. *Dagenhart*, 247 U.S. 251 (1918)).

discussion of the issues, one that will not provoke unwanted concurrences or risk losing someone else's vote or even the majority. In contrast, a justice writing a concurrence or dissent can, if he or she chooses, write more discursively and explain more of the individual perspective on constitutional law that informs the opinion and the justice's constitutional thinking more generally. A good example is Justice O'Connor's concurrence in *McCreary County* v. *ACLU* (2005), which held that a governmental display of the Ten Commandments violated the establishment clause of the first amendment. O'Connor joined the opinion of the Court, which itself relied heavily on her separate opinions in earlier establishment clause cases. She wrote separately to explain her understanding that the original purpose of both the establishment and free exercise clauses was to keep "religion a matter for the individual conscience" and that the first amendment as a whole embodies "an idea that was once considered radical: Free people are entitled to free and diverse thoughts, which government ought neither to constrain nor to direct." O'Connor's reflections in *McCreary County* carry with them no institutional authority even of an oblique kind, but they enrich the body of thought with which the constitutional lawyer can work, and in that sense may have a persuasive authority of their own.[27]

Living Speech. In a powerful book on the role of speech in legal thought, James Boyd White contrasts two ways that lawyers, and human beings generally, use the power of speech. One is characterized by "the reiteration of clichés, formulas, slogans – dead language really," empty speech that "does not open itself up to argument, as an opinion should, but closes [argument] off." The other form, "living speech," "affirms the value of the individual mind and experience," both of the lawyer and of the reader, and in doing so invites the reader to look at the problem at hand through the lawyer's proposed solution but without pretending to impose on the reader the lawyer's answers by rhetorical force, impersonal logic, or unreasoned emotion. Precisely because a legal argument so constructed respects the adversarial nature of legal reasoning, and thus enables the reader to question the lawyer's assumptions and his or her line of thought, the argument gains in persuasiveness.[28]

A good example – in my judgment – of what Professor White means by living speech can be seen in Justice Souter's dissent in *Printz* v. *United States* (1997), which applied the anti-commandeering principle to invalidate a provision in an act of Congress requiring local law enforcement officials to carry out a federal duty. In part because he had joined *New York* v. *United States* (1992), which invalidated a different federal law imposing an obligation on state legislatures, Souter wrote separately from the other *Printz* dissenters. He began with a concession. Unlike the majority, he explained, Souter did "not find anything dispositive in the paucity of early examples of federal employment of state officers for executive purposes," but "neither would I find myself in dissent with no more to go on than those few early

[27]   *McCreary County* v. *ACLU*, 545 U.S. 844, 881–82 (2005) (O'Connor, J., concurring).
[28]   James Boyd White, *Living Speech: Resisting the Empire of Force* 16, 85, 84 (Princeton: Princeton University Press, 2006).

instances" of federal commandeering on which the main dissent put great weight: "[T]hey do not speak to me with much force." *Printz*, Souter continued, was a case "I have found closer than I had anticipated, [and] it is The Federalist that finally determines my position," and he named the four numbers of *The Federalist* that persuaded him to dissent.

In four sentences, Souter thus accomplished several objectives. First, he disavowed the overly confident tone in which both the opinion of the Court and the principal dissent were written *and* the reliance that each, to opposite effect of course, put on conflicting arguments from political practice. Souter did not attempt to refute the warring arguments of the other justices, but by alerting readers to his own reservations he suggested that they evaluate with caution those arguments. Second, Souter introduced the argument that chiefly swayed his mind, an argument from original meaning based on *The Federalist*, which he then went on to discuss in some detail. Finally, by inviting readers into his own mind, Souter appealed to each reader's own judgment: He revealed that he moved from an initial sense that the answer was fairly clear (he does not expressly say *which* answer seemed clearly correct to him) to a conclusion justified not by the other opinions' emphatic certainties by a careful reading of the relevant *Federalist* numbers, a reading that he outlines so that the reader can ponder and accept or reject. His dissent is characterized throughout by openness about his own judgments and by the implicit but clear recognition that it is the constitutional lawyer's burden to persuade the reader.[29]

Living speech of the sort that Justice Souter displayed in *Printz* is often easier to practice in a separate opinion than in an opinion of the Court, where the writer must speak for the institution, or a brief, where to some extent the writer must get himself or herself out of the way of the judicial reader's attention. But the elements of respect for the reader and honesty about difficulties that Souter showed in *Printz* are part of what can make an otherwise merely plausible constitutional law argument the most persuasive one. The fact that Souter's opinion was a *dissent* is a reminder that persuasiveness involves an appeal to judgment and that judgments of persuasiveness can diverge, and on difficult problems will often differ.

The Influence of the Historical Moment. As a general observation, a constitutional law argument's persuasiveness and even its bare plausibility require that the reasoning remain within the bounds of what most people find thinkable in the historical moment that the argument addresses. As a matter of sociological fact, individual human beings find it difficult to maintain beliefs that are at odds with the assumptions and certainties that dominate the social world around them. Modernity, with its sometimes bewildering range of apparently incompatible world views, eases the difficulty by allowing the individual more easily to band

---

[29] *Printz* v. *United States*, 521 U.S. 898, 970–71 (1997) (Souter, J., dissenting). See also *New York* v. *United States*, 505 U.S. 144 (1992).

together with others of like perspective. But a constitutional lawyer trying to decide if a particular argument is persuasive cannot adopt a position that is too far afield from what most competent constitutional lawyers would think plausible, at least if the lawyer seriously intends to influence the judgment of judges and other decision makers.

The historical moment in which a proposed argument is considered affects its persuasiveness in two distinct ways. Some constitutional law arguments that can be stated in the abstract will simply be unthinkable in the view of most or all competent constitutional lawyers at a given moment. A century before the decision, the arguments that persuaded the Supreme Court to hold state bans on same-sex marriage unconstitutional in *Obergefell* v. *Hodges* (2015) would have appeared completely incredible, perhaps even incomprehensible, to virtually all constitutional lawyers. What is thinkable changes – witness *Obergefell* – and one of the recurring themes of American constitutional history is the interaction between the efforts of advocates of change in the law to bring a proposition within the realm of the plausible, and broader changes of belief within the American political community as a whole. *Obergefell* is again an obvious example.[30]

The second way in which the historical moment affects the persuasiveness of an argument relates to its specifically political context. We sometimes speak of judicial review and of the Supreme Court as "counter-majoritarian," but a candid review of the Court's history shows that its decisions, by and large and with some exceptions, remain clearly within the boundaries of what national political opinion will tolerate. It is not simply a coincidence that the Court's decisions rejecting the constitutionality of de jure racial segregation came after many national political leaders had concluded that segregation was a Cold War international embarrassment and a national political majority had turned against segregation. A negative example of the same phenomenon is the Court's decision to backtrack from its 1940s protection of free speech in *Dennis* v. *United States* (1951), decided at the height of McCarthyism.[31]

None of this is to suggest that it is wrong or pointless for a constitutional lawyer or judge to advance an argument that goes against commonly shared views or deeply embedded political realities. The Americans, lawyers and non-lawyers alike, who refused to accept the constitutionality of racial segregation in the long years between *Plessy* v. *Ferguson* and the 1950s were right, as a matter of both constitutional law and political morality, and their resistance was a key factor in moving public opinion as well as the views of the justices. Constitutional law is one of the modes of debate by which the American political community considers arguments for and against

---

[30]   See *Obergefell* v. *Hodges*, 576 U.S. 644 (2015).

[31]   See Mary L. Dudziak's groundbreaking book, *Cold War Civil Rights: Race and the Image of American Democracy* (rev. ed. Princeton: Princeton University Press, 2011). See also *Dennis* v. *United States*, 341 U.S. 494 (1951); Martin H. Redish, *The Logic of Persecution: Free Expression and the McCarthy Era* (Stanford, CA: Stanford University Press, 2005).

significant change. And as we saw in Chapter 3, the existence of the constitutional text sometimes provides a foothold in constitutional law for arguments in support of change, even if political and legal institutions are not, or not yet, responsive. Consider this example. In *Bradwell v. Illinois* (1873), the Supreme Court rejected Myra Bradwell's argument that the Illinois supreme court had deprived her of a privilege of United States citizenship guaranteed her by the fourteenth amendment when it refused to admit her to the bar because she was a woman. The opinion of the Court based the decision on the exceedingly narrow interpretation of the privileges or immunities clause the Court had just adopted in the *Slaughter-House Cases* (1873). Three of the four dissenters in *Slaughter-House* concurred in the judgment in *Bradwell* in an opinion asserting that even under their expansive view of the clause, the exclusion of women from the practice of law was constitutional because it accorded with "nature itself" and "the general constitution of things."[32]

The fourth *Slaughter-House* dissenter was Chief Justice Salmon P. Chase. Chase was terminally ill and died three weeks after the decision in *Bradwell* was announced. He wrote no opinion, but the Court's reporter of decisions recorded an unusual statement from him: "The CHIEF JUSTICE dissented from the judgment of the court, *and from all the opinions.*" Chase, it seems, disagreed not only with the majority's evisceration of a provision of the fourteenth amendment but also with the concurring justices' smug assumption that the amendment allows discrimination on the basis of sex, at least if judges think the discrimination appropriate. It would be a century before the Court adopted Chase's view on gender discrimination, but I do not think it was pointless for him to take the position he did in *Bradwell.* Not all changes in constitutional law are good ideas, of course, but in this instance, when we look back it is Chase, not his eight colleagues, whose perception of constitutional principle was correct.[33]

Persuasion and Justice. Cases such as *Bradwell v. Illinois* and the school segregation decision *Brown v. Board of Education* (1954) pose another important question about persuasiveness in constitutional law. What is the relationship between an argument's persuasiveness as a matter of constitutional law and the justice of the outcome the argument would produce? Does a constitutional law claim become more powerful because it can lay claim to the moral high ground? The briefs filed by the plaintiffs in *Brown* were largely devoted to demonstrating that *Plessy v. Ferguson* was wrong and should be overruled on the basis of arguments from precedent and original meaning, but they also clearly articulated a moral claim. "We submit that

---

[32] *Bradwell v. Illinois*, 83 U.S. 130, 141–42 (1873) (Bradley, J., concurring in the judgment). See also *Slaughter-House Cases*, 83 U.S. (16 Wall.) 36 (1873).

[33] *Bradwell*, 83 U.S. at 142 (dissenting statement of Chase, C.J.) (emphasis added). Chase's decision to make his dissent known is itself significant: He sometimes refrained from expressing public disagreement with a decision because he thought that "except in very important causes dissent [is] inexpedient." Diary entry (January 16, 1865) in 1 *Salmon P. Chase Papers* 517 (John Niven ed. Kent, OH: Kent State University Press, 1993). On interpreting Chase's views, see Richard L. Aynes, *Bradwell v. Illinois*: Chief Justice Chase's Dissent and the Sphere of Women's Work, 59 La. L. Rev. 521 (1999).

this Court cannot sustain these school segregation laws under any separate but equal concept unless it is willing to accept as truths the racist notions of the perpetuators of segregation and to repeat the tragic error of the *Plessy* Court supporting those who would nullify the Fourteenth Amendment and the basic tenet of our way of life which it incorporates." Obviously the briefs' authors hoped to appeal to the consciences of the individual justices whose judgments would inevitably be influenced by their "wishes, affections and general theories," but can we say more? Were the constitutional law arguments in the briefs more persuasive *as constitutional law arguments* because of their claim to lead to the more just outcome?[34]

Before considering an overall answer to this question, three cautions are in order. The first is obvious: Human beings disagree, sometimes sharply, about issues of morality and justice. Few will doubt that the plaintiffs and their lawyers in *Brown* v. *Board of Education* had justice on their side, but *Brown* was decades ago. Constitutional lawyers dealing with issues that are controversial morally as well as legally in the present lack the benefit of long hindsight to know what constitutional law arguments will come in time to stand for simple justice to most people in the American political community. The morality of abortion is a matter of tremendous moral importance to many Americans, to mention an obvious example, but Americans (including American constitutional lawyers and judges) are deeply divided both about the moral questions themselves and about the role of moral answers in the public life of the community. Any consideration of the role of morality in thinking about what makes a constitutional argument persuasive must keep our moral divisions in mind.

We must also keep in full view, second, the basic tenet of the written Constitution that the American political community is firmly committed to encompassing people of widely differing religious, ethical, political, and social perspectives. In the late-eighteenth-century world, at least in those parts shaped by European cultures, religion was the most obvious source of division, and founding-era Americans were entirely familiar with had been the standard response of European and most colonial-era American governments to religious divisiveness, the attempt to avoid disunity by suppressing religious disagreement. Constitutional lawyers happily do not often need to address current-day problems that implicate the last clause of Article VI, but in the context of the late 1780s, it was one of the original Constitution's most radical provisions: "[N]o religious Test shall ever be required as a Qualification to any Office or public Trust under the United States." Added to the Constitution almost immediately thereafter, the first amendment's prohibition on any "establishment of religion" and its guarantees of religious free exercise, freedom of speech and press, and the rights of assembly and petition underlined the founding-era commitment to creating a national government that would be

---

[34]   Brief for Appellants in Nos. 1, 2, and 4, and for Respondents in No. 10 on Reargument, *Brown* v. *Board of Education*, Nos. 1, 2, 3, 5 (October Term 1953), at *65. See *Brown* v. *Board of Education*, 347 U.S. 483 (1954).

open to persons of sharply differing moral and political views. And the Constitution-in-practice, through the fourteenth amendment, has brought the state governments fully within that commitment. "If there is any fixed star in our constitutional constellation, it is that no official, high or petty, can prescribe what shall be orthodox in politics, nationalism, religion, or other matters of opinion." A constitutional law argument about an issue that is currently controversial, which rested on appeal to a broad American moral orthodoxy, might be less persuasive, not more, by virtue of the appeal.[35]

The final caution is well illustrated by an anecdote that Judge Learned Hand liked to repeat about an interchange with Justice Holmes.

> I remember once I was with [Holmes]; it was a Saturday when the Court was to confer. It was before we had a motor car, and we jogged along in an old coupé. When we got down to the Capitol, I wanted to provoke a response, so as he walked off, I said to him: "Well, sir, goodbye. Do justice!" He turned quite sharply and he said: "Come here. Come here." I answered: "Oh, I know, I know." He replied: "That is not my job. My job is to play the game according to the rules."

Holmes's response was not that justice is irrelevant to law, or is a subjective matter of opinion, and he did not deny that justice is one purpose of adjudication. His point concerned the proper role of the judge in the system, which is not to pursue justice directly, but "to play the game according to the rules," to carry out his or her "job." The same is true of all constitutional lawyers. The preamble to the written Constitution names "Justice" as the next goal after the purpose of establishing "a more perfect Union," and constitutional law pursues that goal by solving problems through the tools of the Constitution-in-practice. In doing so, the practice of constitutional law addresses issues of justice not by directly imposing one of the many moral, political, and religious commitments that divide Americans but through the forms of legal reasoning that are shared by American constitutional lawyers.[36]

Part of the two-fold logic that informs all constitutional law is the proposition that there are no extra-constitutional authorizations of federal power, and no extra-constitutional prohibitions on legitimate exercises of federal or state power. That there are pressing moral reasons why a branch of the federal government should take some action does not in itself give a constitutional justification for that action, and if the government should act without any claim to constitutional authorization, the action would be lawless. Similarly, a governmental action with an affirmative legal basis, whether constitutional authorization or a state's police power, is

---

[35] *West Virginia State Bd. of Educ.* v. *Barnette,* 319 U.S. 624, 642 (1943) (Jackson, J.).

[36] Learned Hand, *The Spirit of Liberty* 306–07 (Irving Dilliard ed. 1960). In interpreting Justice Holmes's meaning, I have followed Professor Michael Herz's persuasive discussion in his article on the use (and misuse) of the anecdote. See Michael Herz, "Do Justice!": Variations of a Thrice-Told Tale, 82 *Va. L. Rev.* 111 (1996).

constitutionally lawful if no prohibition of the Constitution-in-practice forbids it even if you or I think the action unjust.

All of this acknowledged, it does not follow that a conscientious lawyer must ignore the claims of extra-legal justice, or seek to exclude ethical considerations from constitutional law thinking. The existence of serious moral disagreement in the American political community should not be allowed to obscure the existence of agreement among most Americans on many important issues in political as well as individual ethics. Furthermore, as discussed previously, constitutional law argument is one of means by which moral change occurs in this political community. A constitutional lawyer wrestling with a problem that involves what he or she thinks a pressing moral need or a blatant injustice has, I believe, a duty of individual conscience, and as a member of the political community, to search for a path in constitutional law that addresses the need or injustice. The basis in constitutional law must be there, or achieving the morally desirable outcome is beyond the constitutional lawyer's remit *as lawyer* and demands a political resolution. That is what it means "to play the game according to the rules." The persuasiveness of a constitutional law argument advanced in good faith therefore *cannot* rest on an invitation to step outside the domain of constitutional law.

What a good faith argument *can* do is attempt to show how the lines of legal reasoning it advances point to an outcome that satisfies the professional and even technical judgment of the constitutional lawyer about the law *and also* allow a moral conclusion that the lawyer believes the American political community should endorse, and indeed embody. The logical structure of the argument starts with law and then moves to justice: "The problem at hand poses this constitutional law question, and the answer I propose addresses all the legal concerns the question brings up. *Furthermore*, what I propose as the technically correct constitutional law answer also addresses the injustice or potential injustice that I think the problem also presents. Adopting the proposed answer will make the American political community more just than would the opposing view and that is a good reason for resolving any remaining doubts in favor of my answer."

It is important to be clear that we are discussing the way a persuasive constitutional law argument is put together, not the motivations of the lawyer who constructs it. The lawyers who wrote the NAACP Legal Defense Fund briefs in the series of cases leading from *Plessy* v. *Ferguson* to *Brown* v. *Board of Education* no doubt knew that racial segregation was a moral evil – and therefore believed that *Plessy* must be fundamentally wrong – long before they built the specific arguments that pushed the Supreme Court step by step from accepting *Plessy* as settled law (whether the decision seemed to individual justices good or evil on some extra-legal scale) to the point that the Court was ready to reject *Plessy* altogether as a precedent. In each case, some and perhaps by the end all of the justices started with the sense or intuition that the plaintiffs were right, morally as well as legally. For both lawyers and justices, beliefs about justice (rooted in each person's "wishes, affections, and general theories") may have preceded reasoning about the legal issues. But the briefs and the opinions of the Court were necessarily written the other way round.

The history of constitutional law shows many examples of arguments that seemed convincing, at the time or later, because they gave answers that were technically well-constructed but also to some extent because they were morally convincing. In *Marbury v. Madison*, Chief Justice Marshall justified judicial review itself in part on moral grounds: If a judge were obliged to render a decision against his considered view of the correct constitutional law answer, his congressionally prescribed oath to decide cases "agreeably to the Constitution" would be "worse than solemn mockery. To prescribe, or to take this oath, becomes equally a crime." The first Justice Harlan's dissent in *Plessy* derives much of its power from his scathing treatment of the majority's moral indifference or hypocrisy. "The thing to accomplish was, under the guise of giving equal accommodation for whites and blacks, to compel the latter to keep to themselves ... No one would be so wanting in candor as to assert the contrary." No one, except of course (Harlan left unspoken) his colleagues. Justice Holmes's dissent in *Hammer v. Dagenhart* excoriated the moral consequences of the majority's invalidation of the federal Child Labor Act – thus permitting "the evil of premature and excessive child labor" that leads to "ruined lives" – even as Holmes insisted that the Court's decisions must be based on law. "I should have thought that if we were to introduce our own moral conceptions where in my opinion they do not belong, this was preeminently a case for upholding the exercise of all its powers by the United States." Justice Jackson capped his careful legal justification of the Court's judgment in the Steel Seizure Case with the admonition that although the institutions of "free government . . . may be destined to pass away . . . it is the duty of the Court to be last, not first, to give them up." And in *Brown v. Board of Education*, Chief Justice Earl Warren wrote a deliberately low-key opinion that avoided moral denunciations of the patent injustice of segregation, but Warren nonetheless included a clear moral appeal. "To separate [Black children] from others of similar age and qualifications solely because of their race generates a feeling of inferiority as to their status in the community that may affect their hearts and minds in a way unlikely ever to be undone."[37]

In each of these opinions, I believe that the persuasiveness of the constitutional law reasoning was strengthened by the judgment of most readers, at least in hindsight (Harlan and Holmes were dissenting!), that the opinion presented a compelling argument for the justice of its conclusion as well. The reader of this book should not conclude, however, that such arguments are the exclusive prerogative of decisions in past eras on matters now universally regarded as momentous. The

---

[37] *Marbury v. Madison*, 5 U.S. (1 Cranch) 137, 180 (1803); *Plessy v. Ferguson*, 163 U.S. 537, 557 (1896) (Harlan, J., dissenting); *Hammer v. Dagenhart*, 247 U.S. 251, 280 (1918) (Holmes, J., dissenting), *overruled by United States v. Darby*, 312 U.S. 100, 115–17 (1941) (relying on "the powerful and now classic dissent of Mr. Justice Holmes" in *Hammer*); *Youngstown Sheet & Tube Co. v. Sawyer*, 343 U.S. 579, 655 (1952) (Jackson, J., concurring); *Brown v. Board of Education*, 347 U.S. 483, 494 (1954).

dormant commerce clause problem before the Court in the 2018 decision discussed earlier in this chapter, *South Dakota* v. *Wayfair, Inc.*, was not trivial, but clearly it was not an issue of the same gravity as the constitutionality of de jure racial segregation. The opinion of the Court nonetheless supported its decision to reject the physical presence rule with the observation that the rule was "not just a technical legal problem" but also that it was "unfair and unjust" because it "allow[ed] remote sellers to escape an obligation to remit a lawful state tax" that others could not. "It is unfair and unjust to those competitors, both local and out of State, who must remit the tax; to the consumers who pay the tax; and to the States that seek fair enforcement of the sales tax, a tax many States for many years have considered an indispensable source for raising revenue." The dormant commerce clause legal principle and the concerns of justice converged, and the Court's reasoning was more persuasive as a result.[38]

The reader also should not conclude that only Supreme Court justices – or lawyers involved in a great moral movement – can hope to make their arguments more persuasive because they lead to more just outcomes. As stated in the Preface, one of the premises of this book is that the task of the constitutional lawyer is not radically different whether on or off the Supreme Court. If the Court's members believe that the moral justice of a constitutional law conclusion makes the legal reasoning leading to it more persuasive, then the rest of us may act on the same belief. Precisely because there is and can be no American moral *orthodoxy*, for each of us (constitutional lawyer or not) there will be a moral gap between what the Constitution-in-practice requires and forbids, and what you or I believe the American political community should do and refrain from doing. But this does not make constitutional law and justice alien to one another, rather it reflects the fact that constitutional law is, just as much as democratic politics, a means by which the community seeks to "establish Justice."

Are There Right Answers in Constitutional Law? This chapter is framed in terms of what makes constitutional law arguments *persuasive*, not what makes them *right*. My reason for doing so rests on Chief Justice Marshall's wise observation quoted near the beginning of the chapter. On difficult questions, constitutional lawyers of the highest intelligence and professional expertise will often disagree over which answer is the right one. "A contrariety of opinion on [a] great constitutional question ought to excite no surprise." Marshall was not suggesting that the answer to such a question is whatever anyone chooses, but neither was he implying that the right answers reside in some "brooding omnipresence in the sky" distinct from the work of the constitutional lawyers who seek to answer the questions.[39]

---

[38] *South Dakota* v. *Wayfair, Inc.*, 138 S. Ct. 2080, 2095–96 (2018).

[39] 4 Marshall, *Life of George Washington* 243 (Chelsea House 1983) (orig. ed. Philadelphia: C.P. Wayne, 1804–07). I have borrowed the famous "brooding omnipresence" image Justice Holmes used in rejecting the idea that there is a general common law abstracted from the common law of particular

Yes, there *are* right answers, even to difficult constitutional questions, but they do not exist outside the practice of constitutional law. The authority of the written Constitution is axiomatic, but as we have seen, the constitutional text does not contain on its face the solutions to many problems it creates and that we must somehow solve. The reader will recall the question of who presides over the impeachment trial of the vice president. I believe that the answer I proposed (the president pro tem of the Senate presides) is the right answer, but not because that answer is an inexorable deduction from the words of Article I section 3 (no argument is) or can be found in original meaning materials outside the text (there is no historical evidence that anyone thought about the problem). The answer is built out of the materials and with the tools provided by the Constitution-in-practice, and seems to me the most persuasive of the plausible arguments.[40]

The right answers to *all* difficult questions in constitutional law are the same. Each must be the product of a conscientious attempt to use the methods of the traditional practice to find the answer that seems the most faithful to the fundamental law of the American political community, a law that includes both the written Constitution and the methods and substance of the practice itself. The right answers, in other words, emerge from the work of those engaged in the practice of constitutional law. The fact that competent practitioners sometimes disagree over which answers are correct results from the kind of intellectual inquiry constitutional law involves. The tasks of finding the right answer and of persuading oneself and others that it is the right answer are, in the end, the same task.[41]

6.1 EXCURSUS: THE ROAD FROM PLESSY TO BROWN

Plessy v. Ferguson (1896) upheld a Louisiana law requiring railway companies to provide "equal but separate accommodations for the white, and colored races" in passenger trains. Over the lone dissent of Justice John Marshall Harlan, the majority asserted that the only question was whether the law was a reasonable regulation in light of the legislature's broad discretion to take into account "the established usages, customs, and traditions of the people . . . with a view to the promotion of their comfort." "Gauged by this standard," the majority thought (or claimed to think), the law was constitutionally unobjectionable. Segregation treated both races equally since each was

---

jurisdictions. See *Southern Pacific Co. v. Jensen*, 244 U.S 205, 222 (1917) (Holmes, J. dissenting). On the debate over federal common law in which Holmes was participating, see the appendix.

[40] Nothing rides on the verbal difference between saying that there is a *right* answer to a given constitutional question, or that there is a *better* or *best* answer among those under consideration. The search is for the answer that ideally will persuade all those who consider it, but when the question is genuinely difficult, there is no way in principle to eliminate the possibility of better arguments, not yet considered, that would lead to a different answer.

[41] "The disagreement that remains after a case has been fully argued and considered is not unique to the law, nor is it a defect. It is the inevitable concomitant of the effort to confine the variety of human experience within general rules." Lloyd L. Weinreb, *Legal Reason: The Use of Analogy in Legal Argument* 127 (2nd ed. New York: Cambridge University Press, 2016).

equally separated from the other, and the challenger had no basis in law for assuming that "the enforced separation of the two races stamps the colored race with a badge of inferiority. If this be so, it is not by reason of anything found in the act, but solely because the colored race chooses to put that construction upon it." Harlan's response was a bitterly sarcastic statement of political and social truth. Racial segregation, he wrote, rests "on the ground that colored citizens are so inferior and degraded that they cannot be allowed to sit in public coaches occupied by white citizens. That, as all will admit, is the real meaning of such legislation as was enacted in Louisiana." Harlan dismissed the insincere promise of equal material treatment with the same force and accuracy. "The thin disguise of 'equal' accommodations for passengers in railroad coaches will not mislead anyone, nor atone for the wrong this day done."[42]

After the Supreme Court made it clear in *Giles v. Harris* (1903) that it would not intervene to prevent the disenfranchisement of Black voters in blatant disregard of the fifteenth amendment, the regime of pervasive racial segregation in the South and some border states appeared safe from serious political or legal challenge. Occasionally, segregationists went too far for the Court to stomach: In 1917, for example, *Buchanan v. Warley* struck down a municipal ordinance enforcing residential segregation. But *Buchanan* was a due process decision and rested on the property right of an owner to sell his home; the Court was careful to acknowledge *Plessy*'s authority and distinguish it. The process of unraveling *Plessy* began when a brilliant constitutional lawyer, Charles Hamilton Houston, became the first full-time attorney employed by the National Association for the Advancement of Colored People (the NAACP) in 1934.[43]

Houston decided that "unequal education was the Achilles heel" of racial segregation. "By demonstrating the failure of states to even try to live up to the 1896 rule of 'separate but equal,' Houston hoped to finally overturn ... *Plessy v. Ferguson*." Unsurprisingly, there was a wealth of evidence to show the emptiness of the claim of equality: "Southern states collectively spent less than half of what was allotted for white students on education for blacks; there were even greater disparities in individual school districts." However, rather than begin with grade school segregation, which he knew would be an extremely charged issue, Houston designed a strategy of attacking segregation in law schools first, thus pressing the Court to rule repeatedly against segregation in a less explosive setting. After Houston moved to the role of senior advisor in 1939, Thurgood Marshall, later of course Justice Marshall, took over Houston's role as chief NAACP lawyer as well as his strategic plan. From 1940, Marshall was legal director of the NAACP Legal Defense and Educational Fund (the LDF).[44]

[42]   *Plessy v. Ferguson*, 163 U.S. 537, 550–51 (1896); *id.* at 560, 562 (Harlan, J., dissenting).
[43]   *Giles v. Harris*, 189 U.S. 475, 488 (1903); *Buchanan v. Warley*, 245 U.S. 60, 79–80 (1917).
[44]   NAACP History: Charles Hamilton Houston, http://www.naacp.org/pages/naacp-history-charles-hamilton-houston. See generally Rawn James, Jr., *Root and Branch: Charles Hamilton Houston, Thurgood Marshall, and the Struggle to End Segregation* (New York: Bloomsbury Press US, 2010).

Houston's strategy worked. In 1936, the NAACP won *Pearson v. Murray*, in which the highest court in Maryland held that the state's exclusion of African Americans from the University of Maryland Law School was unconstitutional under *Plessy*. "The state has undertaken the function of education in the law, but has omitted students of one race from the only adequate provision made for it, and omitted them solely because of their color." The court concluded that the state's offer to provide the plaintiff with financial support to study law out of state did not satisfy the *Plessy* requirement that if a state imposed racial segregation, the facilities it provided or permitted had to be equal. In *Missouri ex rel. Gaines v. Canada* (1938), the Supreme Court accepted that logic and rejected the state's offer to pay the plaintiff's tuition at an out of state law school. The Court also rejected the argument that a state statute authorizing a future law school at Lincoln University, a state-supported all-Black institution, cured the state's present failure to treat the plaintiff equally. And in *Sipuel v. Board of Regents* (1948), the Court rejected an attempt to distinguish *Gaines* and held that Oklahoma could not refuse to admit the petitioner to the state's only public law school solely on the basis of her race. One of the LDF's successful voting rights cases was also directly significant for its war on educational segregation. In *Smith v. Allwright* (1944), the Court accepted the principle that the constitutionality of racial exclusions is to be measured by their practical effect: It held that the fifteenth amendment prohibited the "private" Texas Democratic Party's exclusion of Black voters from Democratic primaries because the state had in effect adopted the party's racially discriminatory policy as its own.[45]

In 1950, a unanimous Court rejected two state educational arrangements designed to meet the *Gaines* decision that *Plessy*'s "separate but equal" had to involve material equality as well as racial separation. *Sweatt v. Painter* went beyond *Gaines* to conclude that the actual creation of a new law school for African Americans could not satisfy the state's equal protection obligation because the new school would unavoidably have far less to offer. Even more significantly, the Court confronted and directly rejected the *Plessy* majority's claim that segregation is even-handed since whites are as segregated as African Americans. "This contention overlooks realities." In *McLaurin v. Oklahoma State Regents for Higher Ed.*, a federal district court originally ordered the plaintiff's admission to the doctoral program in education at the University of Oklahoma. The university "complied," but did so in accordance with a new state law requiring that the instruction of African American students within the university was to be on a segregated basis.

And so sixty-eight-year-old George McLaurin was made to sit at a desk by himself in an anteroom outside the regular classrooms where his course work was given. In the library, he was assigned a segregated desk in the mezzanine behind half a carload of

---

[45] *Pearson v. Murray*, 182 A. 590, 594 (Md. 1936); *Missouri ex rel. Gaines v. Canada*, 305 U.S. 337, 350–52 (1938); *Sipuel v. Board of Regents*, 332 U.S. 631 (1948); *Smith v. Allwright*, 321 U.S. 649, 662–65 (1944).

newspapers. In the cafeteria, he was required to eat in a dingy alcove by himself and at a different hour from the whites.

The Court made quick work of the state's argument that this satisfied its constitutional obligation. "Appellant, having been admitted to a state-supported graduate school, must receive the same treatment at the hands of the state as students of other races."[46]

The LDF's briefs in *Sweatt* and *McLaurin* did not explicitly call for the Court to overrule *Plessy* v. *Ferguson*, and the Court's decisions were still in theory reconcilable with *Plessy* as a bare holding. An amicus brief in *Sweatt*, arranged by Marshall, went further. Pointing out that *Plessy*'s reasoning, "palpably preposterous" when written, no longer had any defensible place in the Court's constitutional thinking given its more recent decisions, the amici stated that *Plessy* should therefore be overruled. "Segregation *is* discrimination." In the next round of challenges, the LDF moved to grade-school segregation and to a direct attack on *Plessy*, and in 1954 *Brown* v. *Board of Education* rejected the idea of separate but equal as wholly inapplicable to public education at any level. "Separate educational facilities are inherently unequal." Later decisions quickly demonstrated that *Brown* had repudiated *Plessy* entirely.[47]

The NAACP/LDF campaign to secure the rejection of *Plessy* v. *Ferguson* and thus end de jure racial segregation was premised from the beginning on the lawyers' conviction not only that segregation was politically and morally evil but also that in principle *Plessy* v. *Ferguson* was wrongly decided as a matter of constitutional law. But *Plessy* was a well-entrenched precedent, and it would have been pointless in the early 1930s to argue that the Supreme Court should overrule the decision and thus in one fell swoop delegitimize legal and social arrangements in a third of the country. Houston and then Marshall therefore brought a series of cases in each of which the challengers' argument was persuasive in part because it merely asked the Court to take seriously what the precedents up to that point had said. The result was that after *Sweatt* and *McLaurin* nothing was left of *Plessy*'s original rationale and the decision no longer had any force as a precedent. The practice of constitutional law, no less than the moral courage of many Americans, was an essential part of the road that led from *Plessy* to *Brown*.

---

[46]   *Sweatt v. Painter*, 339 U.S. 629, 634 (1950); *McLaurin v. Oklahoma State Regents for Higher Ed.*, 339 U.S. 637, 642 (1950). The block quotation is from the classic account of the struggle to overturn *Plessy*, Richard Kluger, *Simple Justice: The History of Brown v. Board of Education and Black America's Struggle for Equality* 336 (New York: Alfred A. Knopf, 1975).

[47]   Brief for Amici Curiae in Support of Petitioner, *Sweat v. Painter*, No. 44 (October Term 1949), at *21–22; *Brown v. Board of Education*, 347 U.S. 483, 495 (1954).

Conclusion

Constitutional Law as Problem Solving

Why should we play the game according to the rules? The central purpose of this book has been to describe the practice of constitutional law, not to justify or critique it. The focus has been entirely on what constitutional lawyers and judges *actually do* in attempting to solve constitutional law problems. I have simply assumed that what I am describing is what constitutional lawyers and judges *ought to do*. Most of the time, indeed, there is no need to go further. Lawyers are practical people with problems to solve and questions to answer, and as a practical matter lawyers with a constitutional problem that needs to be solved through law "ought" to engage in the practice I have described because if the lawyers don't, whatever they say will not be recognizable as a legal argument. Depart too obviously or too radically from the recognized practice and you render yourself ineffective: your brief won't fly with the judges, your advice will be ignored or subject you to ridicule, the higher court will reverse your decision.

Even the justices of the Supreme Court, whose "higher court" can only act through the cumbersome Article V amendment process, are constrained by the need to persuade colleagues and provide meaningful guidance for lower courts, and by their preference for praise rather than scorn in the profession, the law reviews, and the media. And all constitutional lawyers, including the justices, must submit the arguments they endorse to the inner tribunal of their own judgment, shaped as it is by the common law culture of American law. We play the game according to the accepted rules because it is the only game in town, for practical purposes, and the rules are what define the game.

There is no need, therefore, when writing a brief or thinking about what advice to give or determining whether judgment should be for the plaintiff, to ask why the rules and principles that structure the practice you are engaged in should be your framework of thought and decision. But since this book is describing the practice of constitutional law, not actually solving a constitutional problem or answering a constitutional question, it seems appropriate to add to the description a brief account of why I think the traditional practice of constitutional law with its

eighteenth-century roots ought to be the means by which lawyers address twenty-first
-century problems *in principle*. In this conclusion, therefore, I give you my prescriptive opinion about what should be, not just my descriptive views about what is.

As we saw near the beginning of this book, the authority of the written
Constitution is not a matter that can be meaningfully stated as a question of
constitutional law. The text's authority is axiomatic. And as we saw at the end of
Chapter 2, so is the basic postulate of the Constitution-in-practice's completeness
that all constitutional law problems can be resolved by constitutional law means.
Constitutional lawyers start from the authority of the document and the legal
answerability of constitutional law questions: They do not, cannot, and need not
prove either as constitutional lawyers.

But what about the modes of reasoning and argument that I call the practice of
constitutional law? Why do I think that constitutional lawyers, including judges and
justices, ought to understand themselves as bound in their work by the traditional
practice? My answer begins where this book began. As a matter of history, and within
a remarkably short period of time, American lawyers and politicians accepted the
applicability of common law styles of reasoning to constitutional law questions. The
texts of the original document and of the Bill of Rights invited as much with their
many references to ideas and institutions derived from the common law. The fact
that the practice of constitutional law emerged in the founding era in a form
recognizably ancestral to our practice today goes some way toward suggesting that
our practice is faithful both to the assumptions embedded in the text and to the
original meaning of Article VI's designation of the Constitution as "the supreme
Law of the Land," law to be applied to specific situations using the familiar tools of
lawyers.

The claim of our traditional practice to authority seems to me also to draw
strength from the fact that the logic and forms of argument of constitutional law
that emerged in the founding era have dominated American constitutional debate
ever since: They have long since become woven into the operations of American
government and not just in the federal courts. Any contention that the practice
should be seriously altered would have to demonstrate why the American political
community should abandon a familiar, widely understood, and by now elaborately
articulated mode of resolving fundamental political disagreements for some new
method that is untried and unfamiliar to all but its proponents.

Traditions, of course, can be perverse, and the fact that an evil practice is long-
standing is no reason to preserve it. The practice of constitutional law has sometimes
led in the past to monstrous decisions, and perhaps far more often has failed to rectify
obvious injustices. Some would-be reformers of constitutional law regard the practice as too backward-looking, too enmired in professional and class norms to deserve
respect. But constitutional law has also been, often enough, one of the means by
which the American political community has sought to eliminate social evils and
achieve a greater degree of justice. To be sure, the historical record of the practice of

constitutional law is mixed from almost any imaginable moral or political viewpoint, but that is an inevitable consequence of the role of constitutional law in the community, which is not to impose on the community higher standards of justice from outside than those that the community will recognize and accept as its own.

Constitutional lawyers and judges – even those sitting on the Supreme Court – are servants of the constitutional system rather than in control of it. Those who would free constitutional law from the backward-looking constraints of traditional forms of argument so that it can be the leading edge in a movement of social transformation ask of it something no imaginable version of constitutional law can deliver, and forget as well that there are likely to be other Americans with very different social agendas and no reason to accept or respect radical change in the practice. In a community committed to including persons of radically different political, moral, religious, and ethical views, it is not a vice but a virtue that constitutional law is resistant to being adopted as a mere tool by a particular and contested perspective.

Conversely, those who fear that the accepted practice of constitutional law is already too unconstraining because its forms of argument are not deductive proofs or immune to disingenuous or manipulative misuse have fallen prey to the fallacious assumption that constitutional law conclusions must be either the product of almost-algorithmic logic or disguised and purely political choices. This is a false dichotomy "that rests on a mistake ... and on too grim a view of human nature and of human intelligence." The common law-like forms of reasoning that traditional constitutional law practice employs "will not seem much of a method if what you are looking for is a set of rules so palpable and constraining that they will be proof against chicanery, evasion and disingenuousness. But no set of rules is proof against that. The use of rules to coordinate human enterprises of every sort assumes a generous and honest attitude." The possibility (and no doubt at times the reality) of constitutional lawyers, and most distressingly judges, who make intellectually dishonest arguments or act in bad faith is irrelevant to the question of whether the practice of constitutional law is so defective that it should be abandoned.[1]

I do not mean to suggest that the main justification for the traditional practice of constitutional law is negative, dependent on the fact that in practice it has no serious competitors. I think the traditional practice deserves continued adherence because it reflects in a deep and satisfactory way the relationship between the American political community and the written Constitution. As we have seen, the constitutional text by itself *cannot* address in a direct and uncontroversial way all the myriad of problems that its provisions and arrangements present. The practice of constitutional law has therefore generated the Constitution-in-practice which makes a practical reality out of the notional authority of the written Constitution by giving the community shared understandings about what arguments count and why, and forms of reason that in one

---

[1] Charles Fried, *Order and Law: Arguing the Reagan Revolution – A Firsthand Account* 67 (1991) (New York: Simon & Schuster).

direction reach back to the early Republic and before that to history of common law in England, and in another direction take into account the ongoing history of the complex set of public institutions that make up American government. The Constitution-in-practice has a structure that can be explained in terms of how constitutional lawyers at their best frame and develop their arguments. The practice is the bridge we have built between our official charter and our political life.

The ultimate justification for the practice of constitutional law that this book describes thus is that the practice is a proven, workable means of carrying out a task necessary to the American political community. All communities must develop accepted mechanisms for resolving disputes among their members, and no political community can persist unless it has the means for solving the problems that arise when a dispute puts in issue fundamental questions about the community's structure and decisions and commitments. The practice of constitutional law is the means the United States has evolved to solve such problems, imperfectly all too often, but successfully as a rule, and over time. The central goal of the Constitution, as we have seen, is to create and maintain a workable government – and the reader will once again recall that in this Republic government is workable only when it is both effective *and* obedient to the community's basic commitments. The practice of constitutional law addresses that goal by providing intellectual tools that are powerful enough to solve even the most difficult constitutional problems and to do so by preserving both the effectiveness of American government and the humane ideals American government is meant to serve.

The Constitution of the United States of America

We the People of the United States, in Order to form a more perfect Union, establish Justice, insure domestic Tranquility, provide for the common defence, promote the general Welfare, and secure the Blessings of Liberty to ourselves and our Posterity, do ordain and establish this Constitution for the United States of America.

ARTICLE I

Section 1

All legislative Powers herein granted shall be vested in a Congress of the United States, which shall consist of a Senate and House of Representatives.

Section 2

The House of Representatives shall be composed of Members chosen every second Year by the People of the several States, and the Electors in each State shall have the Qualifications requisite for Electors of the most numerous Branch of the State Legislature.

No Person shall be a Representative who shall not have attained to the Age of twenty five Years, and been seven Years a Citizen of the United States, and who shall not, when elected, be an Inhabitant of that State in which he shall be chosen.

Representatives and direct Taxes shall be apportioned among the several States which may be included within this Union, according to their respective Numbers, which shall be determined by adding to the whole Number of free Persons, including those bound to Service for a Term of Years, and excluding Indians not taxed, three fifths of all other Persons. The actual Enumeration shall be made within three Years after the first Meeting of the Congress of the United

States, and within every subsequent Term of ten Years, in such Manner as they shall by Law direct. The Number of Representatives shall not exceed one for every thirty Thousand, but each State shall have at Least one Representative; and until such enumeration shall be made, the State of New Hampshire shall be entitled to chuse three, Massachusetts eight, Rhode-Island and Providence Plantations one, Connecticut five, New-York six, New Jersey four, Pennsylvania eight, Delaware one, Maryland six, Virginia ten, North Carolina five, South Carolina five, and Georgia three.

When vacancies happen in the Representation from any State, the Executive Authority thereof shall issue Writs of Election to fill such Vacancies.

The House of Representatives shall chuse their Speaker and other Officers; and shall have the sole Power of Impeachment.

Section 3

The Senate of the United States shall be composed of two Senators from each State, chosen by the Legislature thereof, for six Years; and each Senator shall have one Vote.

Immediately after they shall be assembled in Consequence of the first Election, they shall be divided as equally as may be into three Classes. The Seats of the Senators of the first Class shall be vacated at the Expiration of the second Year, of the second Class at the Expiration of the fourth Year, and of the third Class at the Expiration of the sixth Year, so that one third may be chosen every second Year; and if Vacancies happen by Resignation, or otherwise, during the Recess of the Legislature of any State, the Executive thereof may make temporary Appointments until the next Meeting of the Legislature, which shall then fill such Vacancies.

No Person shall be a Senator who shall not have attained to the Age of thirty Years, and been nine Years a Citizen of the United States, and who shall not, when elected, be an Inhabitant of that State for which he shall be chosen.

The Vice President of the United States shall be President of the Senate, but shall have no Vote, unless they be equally divided.

The Senate shall chuse their other Officers, and also a President pro tempore, in the Absence of the Vice President, or when he shall exercise the Office of President of the United States.

The Senate shall have the sole Power to try all Impeachments. When sitting for that Purpose, they shall be on Oath or Affirmation. When the President of the United States is tried, the Chief Justice shall preside: And no Person shall be convicted without the Concurrence of two thirds of the Members present.

Judgment in Cases of Impeachment shall not extend further than to removal from Office, and disqualification to hold and enjoy any Office of honor, Trust or Profit under the United States: but the Party convicted shall nevertheless be liable and subject to Indictment, Trial, Judgment and Punishment, according to Law.

Section 4

The Times, Places and Manner of holding Elections for Senators and Representatives, shall be prescribed in each State by the Legislature thereof; but the Congress may at any time by Law make or alter such Regulations, except as to the Places of chusing Senators.

The Congress shall assemble at least once in every Year, and such Meeting shall be on the first Monday in December, unless they shall by Law appoint a different Day.

Section 5

Each House shall be the Judge of the Elections, Returns and Qualifications of its own Members, and a Majority of each shall constitute a Quorum to do Business; but a smaller Number may adjourn from day to day, and may be authorized to compel the Attendance of absent Members, in such Manner, and under such Penalties as each House may provide.

Each House may determine the Rules of its Proceedings, punish its Members for disorderly Behaviour, and, with the Concurrence of two thirds, expel a Member.

Each House shall keep a Journal of its Proceedings, and from time to time publish the same, excepting such Parts as may in their Judgment require Secrecy; and the Yeas and Nays of the Members of either House on any question shall, at the Desire of one fifth of those Present, be entered on the Journal.

Neither House, during the Session of Congress, shall, without the Consent of the other, adjourn for more than three days, nor to any other Place than that in which the two Houses shall be sitting.

Section 6

The Senators and Representatives shall receive a Compensation for their Services, to be ascertained by Law, and paid out of the Treasury of the United States. They shall in all Cases, except Treason, Felony and Breach of the Peace, be privileged from Arrest during their Attendance at the Session of their respective Houses, and in going to and returning from the same; and for any Speech or Debate in either House, they shall not be questioned in any other Place.

No Senator or Representative shall, during the Time for which he was elected, be appointed to any civil Office under the Authority of the United States, which shall have been created, or the Emoluments whereof shall have been encreased during such time; and no Person holding any Office under the United States, shall be a Member of either House during his Continuance in Office.

Section 7

All Bills for raising Revenue shall originate in the House of Representatives; but the Senate may propose or concur with Amendments as on other Bills.

Every Bill which shall have passed the House of Representatives and the Senate, shall, before it become a Law, be presented to the President of the United States; If he approve he shall sign it, but if not he shall return it, with his Objections to that House in which it shall have originated, who shall enter the Objections at large on their Journal, and proceed to reconsider it. If after such Reconsideration two thirds of that House shall agree to pass the Bill, it shall be sent, together with the Objections, to the other House, by which it shall likewise be reconsidered, and if approved by two thirds of that House, it shall become a Law. But in all such Cases the Votes of both Houses shall be determined by yeas and Nays, and the Names of the Persons voting for and against the Bill shall be entered on the Journal of each House respectively. If any Bill shall not be returned by the President within ten Days (Sundays excepted) after it shall have been presented to him, the Same shall be a Law, in like Manner as if he had signed it, unless the Congress by their Adjournment prevent its Return, in which Case it shall not be a Law.

Every Order, Resolution, or Vote to which the Concurrence of the Senate and House of Representatives may be necessary (except on a question of Adjournment) shall be presented to the President of the United States; and before the Same shall take Effect, shall be approved by him, or being disapproved by him, shall be repassed by two thirds of the Senate and House of Representatives, according to the Rules and Limitations prescribed in the Case of a Bill.

Section 8

The Congress shall have Power

> To lay and collect Taxes, Duties, Imposts and Excises, to pay the Debts and provide for the common Defence and general Welfare of the United States; but all Duties, Imposts and Excises shall be uniform throughout the United States;
> To borrow Money on the credit of the United States;
> To regulate Commerce with foreign Nations, and among the several States, and with the Indian Tribes;
> To establish an uniform Rule of Naturalization, and uniform Laws on the subject of Bankruptcies throughout the United States;
> To coin Money, regulate the Value thereof, and of foreign Coin, and fix the Standard of Weights and Measures;
> To provide for the Punishment of counterfeiting the Securities and current Coin of the United States;
> To establish Post Offices and post Roads;

To promote the Progress of Science and useful Arts, by securing for limited Times to Authors and Inventors the exclusive Right to their respective Writings and Discoveries;

To constitute Tribunals inferior to the supreme Court;

To define and punish Piracies and Felonies committed on the high Seas, and Offences against the Law of Nations;

To declare War, grant Letters of Marque and Reprisal, and make Rules concerning Captures on Land and Water;

To raise and support Armies, but no Appropriation of Money to that Use shall be for a longer Term than two Years;

To provide and maintain a Navy;

To make Rules for the Government and Regulation of the land and naval Forces;

To provide for calling forth the Militia to execute the Laws of the Union, suppress Insurrections and repel Invasions;

To provide for organizing, arming, and disciplining, the Militia, and for governing such Part of them as may be employed in the Service of the United States, reserving to the States respectively, the Appointment of the Officers, and the Authority of training the Militia according to the discipline prescribed by Congress;

To exercise exclusive Legislation in all Cases whatsoever, over such District (not exceeding ten Miles square) as may, by Cession of particular States, and the Acceptance of Congress, become the Seat of the Government of the United States, and to exercise like Authority over all Places purchased by the Consent of the Legislature of the State in which the Same shall be, for the Erection of Forts, Magazines, Arsenals, dock-Yards, and other needful Buildings; – And

To make all Laws which shall be necessary and proper for carrying into Execution the foregoing Powers, and all other Powers vested by this Constitution in the Government of the United States, or in any Department or Officer thereof.

Section 9

The Migration or Importation of such Persons as any of the States now existing shall think proper to admit, shall not be prohibited by the Congress prior to the Year one thousand eight hundred and eight, but a Tax or duty may be imposed on such Importation, not exceeding ten dollars for each Person.

The Privilege of the Writ of Habeas Corpus shall not be suspended, unless when in Cases of Rebellion or Invasion the public Safety may require it.

No Bill of Attainder or ex post facto Law shall be passed.

No Capitation, or other direct, Tax shall be laid, unless in Proportion to the Census or enumeration herein before directed to be taken.

No Tax or Duty shall be laid on Articles exported from any State.

No Preference shall be given by any Regulation of Commerce or Revenue to the Ports of one State over those of another: nor shall Vessels bound to, or from, one State, be obliged to enter, clear, or pay Duties in another.

No Money shall be drawn from the Treasury, but in Consequence of Appropriations made by Law; and a regular Statement and Account of the Receipts and Expenditures of all public Money shall be published from time to time.

No Title of Nobility shall be granted by the United States: And no Person holding any Office of Profit or Trust under them, shall, without the Consent of the Congress, accept of any present, Emolument, Office, or Title, of any kind whatever, from any King, Prince, or foreign State.

Section 10

No State shall enter into any Treaty, Alliance, or Confederation; grant Letters of Marque and Reprisal; coin Money; emit Bills of Credit; make any Thing but gold and silver Coin a Tender in Payment of Debts; pass any Bill of Attainder, ex post facto Law, or Law impairing the Obligation of Contracts, or grant any Title of Nobility.

No State shall, without the Consent of the Congress, lay any Imposts or Duties on Imports or Exports, except what may be absolutely necessary for executing it's inspection Laws: and the net Produce of all Duties and Imposts, laid by any State on Imports or Exports, shall be for the Use of the Treasury of the United States; and all such Laws shall be subject to the Revision and Controul of the Congress.

No State shall, without the Consent of Congress, lay any Duty of Tonnage, keep Troops, or Ships of War in time of Peace, enter into any Agreement or Compact with another State, or with a foreign Power, or engage in War, unless actually invaded, or in such imminent Danger as will not admit of delay.

ARTICLE II

Section 1

The executive Power shall be vested in a President of the United States of America. He shall hold his Office during the Term of four Years, and, together with the Vice President, chosen for the same Term, be elected, as follows

Each State shall appoint, in such Manner as the Legislature thereof may direct, a Number of Electors, equal to the whole Number of Senators and Representatives to which the State may be entitled in the Congress: but no Senator or Representative, or Person holding an Office of Trust or Profit under the United States, shall be appointed an Elector.

The Electors shall meet in their respective States, and vote by Ballot for two Persons, of whom one at least shall not be an Inhabitant of the same State with themselves. And they shall make a List of all the Persons voted for, and of the Number of Votes for each; which List they shall sign and certify, and transmit sealed to the Seat of the Government of the United States, directed to the President of the Senate. The President of the Senate shall, in the Presence of the Senate and House of Representatives, open all the Certificates, and the Votes shall then be counted. The Person having the greatest Number of Votes shall be the President, if such Number be a Majority of the whole Number of Electors appointed; and if there be more than one who have such Majority, and have an equal Number of Votes, then the House of Representatives shall immediately chuse by Ballot one of them for President; and if no Person have a Majority, then from the five highest on the List the said House shall in like Manner chuse the President. But in chusing the President, the Votes shall be taken by States, the Representation from each State having one Vote; A quorum for this Purpose shall consist of a Member or Members from two thirds of the States, and a Majority of all the States shall be necessary to a Choice. In every Case, after the Choice of the President, the Person having the greatest Number of Votes of the Electors shall be the Vice President. But if there should remain two or more who have equal Votes, the Senate shall chuse from them by Ballot the Vice President.

The Congress may determine the Time of chusing the Electors, and the Day on which they shall give their Votes; which Day shall be the same throughout the United States.

No Person except a natural born Citizen, or a Citizen of the United States, at the time of the Adoption of this Constitution, shall be eligible to the Office of President; neither shall any Person be eligible to that Office who shall not have attained to the Age of thirty five Years, and been fourteen Years a Resident within the United States.

In Case of the Removal of the President from Office, or of his Death, Resignation, or Inability to discharge the Powers and Duties of the said Office, the Same shall devolve on the Vice President, and the Congress may by Law provide for the Case of Removal, Death, Resignation or Inability, both of the President and Vice President, declaring what Officer shall then act as President, and such Officer shall act accordingly, until the Disability be removed, or a President shall be elected.

The President shall, at stated Times, receive for his Services, a Compensation, which shall neither be encreased nor diminished during the Period for which he shall have been elected, and he shall not receive within that Period any other Emolument from the United States, or any of them.

Before he enter on the Execution of his Office, he shall take the following Oath or Affirmation: – "I do solemnly swear (or affirm) that I will faithfully execute the Office of President of the United States, and will to the best of my Ability, preserve, protect and defend the Constitution of the United States."

Section 2

The President shall be Commander in Chief of the Army and Navy of the United States, and of the Militia of the several States, when called into the actual Service of the United States; he may require the Opinion, in writing, of the principal Officer in each of the executive Departments, upon any Subject relating to the Duties of their respective Offices, and he shall have Power to grant Reprieves and Pardons for Offences against the United States, except in Cases of Impeachment.

He shall have Power, by and with the Advice and Consent of the Senate, to make Treaties, provided two thirds of the Senators present concur; and he shall nominate, and by and with the Advice and Consent of the Senate, shall appoint Ambassadors, other public Ministers and Consuls, Judges of the supreme Court, and all other Officers of the United States, whose Appointments are not herein otherwise provided for, and which shall be established by Law: but the Congress may by Law vest the Appointment of such inferior Officers, as they think proper, in the President alone, in the Courts of Law, or in the Heads of Departments.

The President shall have Power to fill up all Vacancies that may happen during the Recess of the Senate, by granting Commissions which shall expire at the End of their next Session.

Section 3

He shall from time to time give to the Congress Information of the State of the Union, and recommend to their Consideration such Measures as he shall judge necessary and expedient; he may, on extraordinary Occasions, convene both Houses, or either of them, and in Case of Disagreement between them, with Respect to the Time of Adjournment, he may adjourn them to such Time as he shall think proper; he shall receive Ambassadors and other public Ministers; he shall take Care that the Laws be faithfully executed, and shall Commission all the Officers of the United States.

Section 4

The President, Vice President and all civil Officers of the United States, shall be removed from Office on Impeachment for, and Conviction of, Treason, Bribery, or other high Crimes and Misdemeanors.

ARTICLE III

Section 1

The judicial Power of the United States, shall be vested in one supreme Court, and in such inferior Courts as the Congress may from time to time ordain and establish. The

Judges, both of the supreme and inferior Courts, shall hold their Offices during good Behaviour, and shall, at stated Times, receive for their Services, a Compensation, which shall not be diminished during their Continuance in Office.

Section 2

The judicial Power shall extend to all Cases, in Law and Equity, arising under this Constitution, the Laws of the United States, and Treaties made, or which shall be made, under their Authority; – to all Cases affecting Ambassadors, other public Ministers and Consuls; – to all Cases of admiralty and maritime Jurisdiction; – to Controversies to which the United States shall be a Party; – to Controversies between two or more States; – between a State and Citizens of another State, – between Citizens of different States, – between Citizens of the same State claiming Lands under Grants of different States, and between a State, or the Citizens thereof, and foreign States, Citizens or Subjects.

In all Cases affecting Ambassadors, other public Ministers and Consuls, and those in which a State shall be Party, the supreme Court shall have original Jurisdiction. In all the other Cases before mentioned, the supreme Court shall have appellate Jurisdiction, both as to Law and Fact, with such Exceptions, and under such Regulations as the Congress shall make.

The Trial of all Crimes, except in Cases of Impeachment, shall be by Jury; and such Trial shall be held in the State where the said Crimes shall have been committed; but when not committed within any State, the Trial shall be at such Place or Places as the Congress may by Law have directed.

Section 3

Treason against the United States, shall consist only in levying War against them, or in adhering to their Enemies, giving them Aid and Comfort. No Person shall be convicted of Treason unless on the Testimony of two Witnesses to the same overt Act, or on Confession in open Court.

The Congress shall have Power to declare the Punishment of Treason, but no Attainder of Treason shall work Corruption of Blood, or Forfeiture except during the Life of the Person attainted.

ARTICLE IV

Section 1

Full Faith and Credit shall be given in each State to the public Acts, Records, and judicial Proceedings of every other State. And the Congress may by general Laws prescribe the Manner in which such Acts, Records and Proceedings shall be proved, and the Effect thereof.

Section 2

The Citizens of each State shall be entitled to all Privileges and Immunities of Citizens in the several States.

A Person charged in any State with Treason, Felony, or other Crime, who shall flee from Justice, and be found in another State, shall on Demand of the executive Authority of the State from which he fled, be delivered up, to be removed to the State having Jurisdiction of the Crime.

No Person held to Service or Labour in one State, under the Laws thereof, escaping into another, shall, in Consequence of any Law or Regulation therein, be discharged from such Service or Labour, but shall be delivered up on Claim of the Party to whom such Service or Labour may be due.

Section 3

New States may be admitted by the Congress into this Union; but no new State shall be formed or erected within the Jurisdiction of any other State; nor any State be formed by the Junction of two or more States, or Parts of States, without the Consent of the Legislatures of the States concerned as well as of the Congress.

The Congress shall have Power to dispose of and make all needful Rules and Regulations respecting the Territory or other Property belonging to the United States; and nothing in this Constitution shall be so construed as to Prejudice any Claims of the United States, or of any particular State.

Section 4

The United States shall guarantee to every State in this Union a Republican Form of Government, and shall protect each of them against Invasion; and on Application of the Legislature, or of the Executive (when the Legislature cannot be convened) against domestic Violence.

ARTICLE V

The Congress, whenever two thirds of both Houses shall deem it necessary, shall propose Amendments to this Constitution, or, on the Application of the Legislatures of two thirds of the several States, shall call a Convention for proposing Amendments, which, in either Case, shall be valid to all Intents and Purposes, as

Part of this Constitution, when ratified by the Legislatures of three fourths of the several States, or by Conventions in three fourths thereof, as the one or the other Mode of Ratification may be proposed by the Congress; Provided that no Amendment which may be made prior to the Year One thousand eight hundred and eight shall in any Manner affect the first and fourth Clauses in the Ninth Section of the first Article; and that no State, without its Consent, shall be deprived of its equal Suffrage in the Senate.

ARTICLE VI

All Debts contracted and Engagements entered into, before the Adoption of this Constitution, shall be as valid against the United States under this Constitution, as under the Confederation.

This Constitution, and the Laws of the United States which shall be made in Pursuance thereof; and all Treaties made, or which shall be made, under the Authority of the United States, shall be the supreme Law of the Land; and the Judges in every State shall be bound thereby, any Thing in the Constitution or Laws of any State to the Contrary notwithstanding.

The Senators and Representatives before mentioned, and the Members of the several State Legislatures, and all executive and judicial Officers, both of the United States and of the several States, shall be bound by Oath or Affirmation, to support this Constitution; but no religious Test shall ever be required as a Qualification to any Office or public Trust under the United States.

ARTICLE VII

The Ratification of the Conventions of nine States, shall be sufficient for the Establishment of this Constitution between the States so ratifying the Same.

AMENDMENT I

Congress shall make no law respecting an establishment of religion, or prohibiting the free exercise thereof; or abridging the freedom of speech, or of the press; or the right of the people peaceably to assemble, and to petition the Government for a redress of grievances.

AMENDMENT II

A well regulated Militia, being necessary to the security of a free State, the right of the people to keep and bear Arms, shall not be infringed.

AMENDMENT III

No Soldier shall, in time of peace be quartered in any house, without the consent of the Owner, nor in time of war, but in a manner to be prescribed by law.

AMENDMENT IV

The right of the people to be secure in their persons, houses, papers, and effects, against unreasonable searches and seizures, shall not be violated, and no Warrants shall issue, but upon probable cause, supported by Oath or affirmation, and particularly describing the place to be searched, and the persons or things to be seized.

AMENDMENT V

No person shall be held to answer for a capital, or otherwise infamous crime, unless on a presentment or indictment of a Grand Jury, except in cases arising in the land or naval forces, or in the Militia, when in actual service in time of War or public danger; nor shall any person be subject for the same offence to be twice put in jeopardy of life or limb; nor shall be compelled in any criminal case to be a witness against himself, nor be deprived of life, liberty, or property, without due process of law; nor shall private property be taken for public use, without just compensation.

AMENDMENT VI

In all criminal prosecutions, the accused shall enjoy the right to a speedy and public trial, by an impartial jury of the State and district wherein the crime shall have been committed, which district shall have been previously ascertained by law, and to be informed of the nature and cause of the accusation; to be confronted with the witnesses against him; to have compulsory process for obtaining witnesses in his favor, and to have the Assistance of Counsel for his defence.

AMENDMENT VII

In Suits at common law, where the value in controversy shall exceed twenty dollars, the right of trial by jury shall be preserved, and no fact tried by a jury, shall be otherwise re-examined in any Court of the United States, than according to the rules of the common law.

AMENDMENT VIII

Excessive bail shall not be required, nor excessive fines imposed, nor cruel and unusual punishments inflicted.

AMENDMENT IX

The enumeration in the Constitution, of certain rights, shall not be construed to deny or disparage others retained by the people.

AMENDMENT X

The powers not delegated to the United States by the Constitution, nor prohibited by it to the States, are reserved to the States respectively, or to the people.

AMENDMENT XI (1795)

The Judicial power of the United States shall not be construed to extend to any suit in law or equity, commenced or prosecuted against one of the United States by Citizens of another State, or by Citizens or Subjects of any Foreign State.

AMENDMENT XII (1804)

The Electors shall meet in their respective states and vote by ballot for President and Vice-President, one of whom, at least, shall not be an inhabitant of the same state with themselves; they shall name in their ballots the person voted for as President, and in distinct ballots the person voted for as Vice-President, and they shall make distinct lists of all persons voted for as President, and of all persons voted for as Vice-President, and of the number of votes for each, which lists they shall sign and certify, and transmit sealed to the seat of the government of the United States, directed to the President of the Senate; – the President of the Senate shall, in the presence of the Senate and House of Representatives, open all the certificates and the votes shall then be counted; – The person having the greatest number of votes for President, shall be the President, if such number be a majority of the whole number of Electors appointed; and if no person have such majority, then from the persons having the highest numbers not exceeding three on the list of those voted for as President, the House of Representatives shall choose immediately, by ballot, the President. But in choosing the President, the votes shall be taken by states, the representation from each state having one vote; a quorum for this purpose shall consist of a member or members from two-thirds of the states, and a majority of all the states shall be necessary to a choice. And if the House of Representatives shall not choose a President whenever the right of choice shall devolve upon them, before the fourth day of March next following, then the Vice-President shall act as President, as in case of the death or other constitutional disability of the President. The person having the greatest number of votes as Vice-President, shall be the Vice-President, if such number be a majority of the whole number of Electors appointed, and if no person have a majority, then from the two highest numbers on the list, the Senate shall choose the Vice-President; a quorum for the purpose shall consist of two-thirds of the whole number of Senators, and a majority of the whole number shall be necessary to a choice. But no person constitutionally ineligible to the office of President shall be eligible to that of Vice-President of the United States.

AMENDMENT XIII (1865)

Section 1

Neither slavery nor involuntary servitude, except as a punishment for crime whereof the party shall have been duly convicted, shall exist within the United States, or any place subject to their jurisdiction.

Section 2

Congress shall have power to enforce this article by appropriate legislation.

AMENDMENT XIV (1868)

Section 1

All persons born or naturalized in the United States, and subject to the jurisdiction thereof, are citizens of the United States and of the State wherein they reside. No State shall make or enforce any law which shall abridge the privileges or immunities of citizens of the United States; nor shall any State deprive any person of life, liberty, or property, without due process of law; nor deny to any person within its jurisdiction the equal protection of the laws.

Section 2

Representatives shall be apportioned among the several States according to their respective numbers, counting the whole number of persons in each State, excluding Indians not taxed. But when the right to vote at any election for the choice of electors for President and Vice-President of the United States, Representatives in Congress, the Executive and Judicial officers of a State, or the members of the Legislature thereof, is denied to any of the male inhabitants of such State, being twenty-one years of age,* and citizens of the United States, or in any way abridged, except for participation in rebellion, or other crime, the basis of representation therein shall be reduced in the proportion which the number of such male citizens shall bear to the whole number of male citizens twenty-one years of age in such State.

Section 3

No person shall be a Senator or Representative in Congress, or elector of President and Vice-President, or hold any office, civil or military, under the United States, or under any State, who, having previously taken an oath, as a member of Congress, or as an officer of the United States, or as a member of any State legislature, or as an executive or judicial officer of any State, to support the Constitution of the United States, shall have engaged in insurrection or rebellion against the same, or given aid or comfort to the enemies thereof. But Congress may by a vote of two-thirds of each House, remove such disability.

Section 4

The validity of the public debt of the United States, authorized by law, including debts incurred for payment of pensions and bounties for services in suppressing insurrection or rebellion, shall not be questioned. But neither the United States nor any State shall assume or pay any debt or obligation incurred in aid of insurrection or rebellion against the United States, or any claim for the loss or emancipation of any slave; but all such debts, obligations and claims shall be held illegal and void.

Section 5

The Congress shall have the power to enforce, by appropriate legislation, the provisions of this article.

AMENDMENT XV (1870)

Section 1

The right of citizens of the United States to vote shall not be denied or abridged by the United States or by any State on account of race, color, or previous condition of servitude–

Section 2

The Congress shall have the power to enforce this article by appropriate legislation.

AMENDMENT XVI (1913)

The Congress shall have power to lay and collect taxes on incomes, from whatever source derived, without apportionment among the several States, and without regard to any census or enumeration.

AMENDMENT XVII (1913)

The Senate of the United States shall be composed of two Senators from each State, elected by the people thereof, for six years; and each Senator shall have one vote. The electors in each State shall have the qualifications requisite for electors of the most numerous branch of the State legislatures.

When vacancies happen in the representation of any State in the Senate, the executive authority of such State shall issue writs of election to fill such vacancies: Provided, That the legislature of any State may empower the executive thereof to make temporary appointments until the people fill the vacancies by election as the legislature may direct.

This amendment shall not be so construed as to affect the election or term of any Senator chosen before it becomes valid as part of the Constitution.

AMENDMENT XVIII (1919)

Section 1

After one year from the ratification of this article the manufacture, sale, or transportation of intoxicating liquors within, the importation thereof into, or the exportation thereof from the United States and all territory subject to the jurisdiction thereof for beverage purposes is hereby prohibited.

Section 2

The Congress and the several States shall have concurrent power to enforce this article by appropriate legislation.

Section 3

This article shall be inoperative unless it shall have been ratified as an amendment to the Constitution by the legislatures of the several States, as provided in the Constitution, within seven years from the date of the submission hereof to the States by the Congress.

AMENDMENT XIX (1920)

The right of citizens of the United States to vote shall not be denied or abridged by the United States or by any State on account of sex.

Congress shall have power to enforce this article by appropriate legislation.

AMENDMENT XX (1933)

Section 1

The terms of the President and the Vice President shall end at noon on the 20th day of January, and the terms of Senators and Representatives at noon on the 3d day of January, of the years in which such terms would have ended if this article had not been ratified; and the terms of their successors shall then begin.

Section 2

The Congress shall assemble at least once in every year, and such meeting shall begin at noon on the 3d day of January, unless they shall by law appoint a different day.

Section 3

If, at the time fixed for the beginning of the term of the President, the President elect shall have died, the Vice President elect shall become President. If a President shall not have been chosen before the time fixed for the beginning of his term, or if the President elect shall have failed to qualify, then the Vice President elect shall act as President until a President shall have qualified; and the Congress may by law provide for the case wherein neither a President elect nor a Vice President shall have qualified, declaring who shall then act as President, or the manner in which one who is to act shall be selected, and such person shall act accordingly until a President or Vice President shall have qualified.

Section 4

The Congress may by law provide for the case of the death of any of the persons from whom the House of Representatives may choose a President whenever the right of choice shall have devolved upon them, and for the case of the death of any of the persons from whom the Senate may choose a Vice President whenever the right of choice shall have devolved upon them.

Section 5

Sections 1 and 2 shall take effect on the 15th day of October following the ratification of this article.

Section 6

This article shall be inoperative unless it shall have been ratified as an amendment to the Constitution by the legislatures of three-fourths of the several States within seven years from the date of its submission.

AMENDMENT XXI (1933)

Section 1

The eighteenth article of amendment to the Constitution of the United States is hereby repealed.

Section 2

The transportation or importation into any State, Territory, or Possession of the United States for delivery or use therein of intoxicating liquors, in violation of the laws thereof, is hereby prohibited.

Section 3

This article shall be inoperative unless it shall have been ratified as an amendment to the Constitution by conventions in the several States, as provided in the Constitution, within seven years from the date of the submission hereof to the States by the Congress.

AMENDMENT XXII (1951)

Section 1

No person shall be elected to the office of the President more than twice, and no person who has held the office of President, or acted as President, for more than two years of a term to which some other person was elected President shall be elected to the office of President more than once. But this Article shall not apply to any person holding the office of President when this Article was proposed by Congress, and shall not prevent any person who may be holding the office of President, or acting as

President, during the term within which this Article becomes operative from holding the office of President or acting as President during the remainder of such term.

Section 2

This article shall be inoperative unless it shall have been ratified as an amendment to the Constitution by the legislatures of three-fourths of the several States within seven years from the date of its submission to the States by the Congress.

AMENDMENT XXIII (1961)

Section 1

The District constituting the seat of Government of the United States shall appoint in such manner as Congress may direct:

A number of electors of President and Vice President equal to the whole number of Senators and Representatives in Congress to which the District would be entitled if it were a State, but in no event more than the least populous State; they shall be in addition to those appointed by the States, but they shall be considered, for the purposes of the election of President and Vice President, to be electors appointed by a State; and they shall meet in the District and perform such duties as provided by the twelfth article of amendment.

Section 2

The Congress shall have power to enforce this article by appropriate legislation.

AMENDMENT XXIV (1964)

Section 1

The right of citizens of the United States to vote in any primary or other election for President or Vice President, for electors for President or Vice President, or for Senator or Representative in Congress, shall not be denied or abridged by the United States or any State by reason of failure to pay poll tax or other tax.

Section 2

The Congress shall have power to enforce this article by appropriate legislation.

AMENDMENT XXV (1967)

Section 1

In case of the removal of the President from office or of his death or resignation, the Vice President shall become President.

Section 2

Whenever there is a vacancy in the office of the Vice President, the President shall nominate a Vice President who shall take office upon confirmation by a majority vote of both Houses of Congress.

Section 3

Whenever the President transmits to the President pro tempore of the Senate and the Speaker of the House of Representatives his written declaration that he is unable to discharge the powers and duties of his office, and until he transmits to them a written declaration to the contrary, such powers and duties shall be discharged by the Vice President as Acting President.

Section 4

Whenever the Vice President and a majority of either the principal officers of the executive departments or of such other body as Congress may by law provide, transmit to the President pro tempore of the Senate and the Speaker of the House of Representatives their written declaration that the President is unable to discharge the powers and duties of his office, the Vice President shall immediately assume the powers and duties of the office as Acting President.

Thereafter, when the President transmits to the President pro tempore of the Senate and the Speaker of the House of Representatives his written declaration that no inability exists, he shall resume the powers and duties of his office unless the Vice President and a majority of either the principal officers of the executive department or of such other body as Congress may by law provide, transmit within four days to the President pro tempore of the Senate and the Speaker of the House of Representatives their written declaration that the President is unable to discharge the powers and duties of his office. Thereupon Congress shall decide the issue, assembling within forty-eight hours for that purpose if not in session. If the Congress, within twenty-one days after receipt of the latter written declaration, or, if Congress is not in session, within twenty-one days after Congress is required to assemble, determines by two-thirds vote of both Houses that the President is unable to discharge the powers and duties of his office, the Vice President shall continue to discharge the same as Acting President; otherwise, the President shall resume the powers and duties of his office.

AMENDMENT XXVI (1971)

Section 1

The right of citizens of the United States, who are eighteen years of age or older, to vote shall not be denied or abridged by the United States or by any State on account of age.

Section 2

The Congress shall have power to enforce this article by appropriate legislation.

AMENDMENT XXVII (1992)

No law, varying the compensation for the services of the Senators and Representatives, shall take effect, until an election of representatives shall have intervened.

Note. The text of the original Constitution was downloaded from the transcription of the inscribed parchment copy on display in the Rotunda of the National Archives Museum. www.archives.gov/founding-docs/constitution-transcript.

By the terms of Article VII, "The Ratification of the Conventions of nine States" was "sufficient for the Establishment of this Constitution." The Constitution was therefore "established" on June 21, 1788, when the New Hampshire convention became the ninth state convention to ratify. The first ten amendments, universally but unofficially known as "the Bill of Rights," became part of the Constitution in 1791. The ratification dates of the subsequent amendments are given with each amendment. The twenty-seventh amendment was actually one of the twelve originally proposed by the First Congress, but only met the Article V supermajority requirement for ratification over two centuries later.

Appendix: The Common Law

As an historical and substantive matter, the "common law" refers to the law that the English royal courts evolved in the medieval and early modern eras. Sir William Blackstone's treatise, published in four volumes 1765–1769, quickly became the classic summary of English common law as it existed at what turned out to be the eve of the American Revolution, and was widely influential on both sides of the Atlantic. Blackstone defined the common law as "the *lex non scripta*, or unwritten law ... that collection of maxims and customs, which is now known by the name of the common law ... probably, as a law *common* to all the realm."[1] By "unwritten," Blackstone meant that the common law was not created by acts of Parliament but was to be found in the reports of judicial proceedings and decisions and the writings of practicing lawyers.

Despite some early controversy, after independence, American courts generally continued to follow and develop the English common law of crime, property, tort, and contract, and although statutes (and administrative rules based on statutes) now supply the rules of decision in most cases, these American versions of the common law continue to serve as the backdrop to enacted law in varying ways across the states, even in Louisiana, if in a muted fashion given its civil law heritage. Although every state is theoretically free to develop its own common law without regard to the decisional law of other jurisdictions, in practice there have been strong forces pushing for uniformity in judge-made law across the states.

COMMON LAW AS METHOD: PRECEDENT

In the context of understanding what I have called the common law-like character of American constitutional law, the term "common law" identifies the distinctive methods of legal argument and reasoning descended from the practices of the old royal courts and the English bar. An English philosopher aptly described the methodological common law as an "institution whereby law emerges from the conflicts that it resolves," and a central element of common law reasoning as it

---

[1]   1 Blackstone, *Commentaries on the Laws of England* *63, *67 (1765).

eventually developed is the centrality of precedent, prior judicial decisions that ordinarily are treated as authoritative in judicial decision making if the case currently before the court is factually and legally analogous.[2] The common law understanding of adherence to precedent – a principle often referred to by the Latin phrase stare decisis ("to stand by things decided") – has not remained static over time but early American constitutional law quickly adopted a view essentially the same as that held by contemporary American lawyers. As the former solicitor general Charles Fried once put it:

> It was taken for granted [in the founding generation] that the Constitution, like other legal texts, would be interpreted by men who were learned in the law, arguing cases and writing judgments in the way lawyers and judges had done for centuries in England and its colonies. Argument from precedent and by analogy would allow the Constitution to be applied to changing circumstances. . . . That experience [of being solicitor general and "reading, editing, and sometimes writing hundreds of briefs as the head of a busy appellate law office"] taught me that, even in constitutional cases, precedent and analogy are the stuff of legal argument, and that legal argument is what moves the Court – or moves it when all involved are doing their work right. . . . This has been the texture of common lawyers' reasoning for centuries.[3]

Professor Fried went on to express his approval of this early adoption by constitutional lawyers of common law reasoning: "The authority, powers, and methods of John Marshall's judiciary were – and are – entirely appropriate" to American constitutional law." Some contemporary constitutional lawyers hold less positive views of stare decisis, which they believe detracts from the authority of the written Constitution, but as a descriptive matter, in the Supreme Court and elsewhere, the Constitution-in-practice continues to be centrally driven by what the Court once termed our common law "traditions of case-by-case reasoning and the establishment of precedent."[4]

The most significant difference between the eighteenth- and twenty-first-century views of stare decisis is that modern American lawyers usually treat a single decision by the controlling court, in constitutional law ultimately the Supreme Court, as establishing a precedent entitled to the full weight of stare decisis, at least if the issues were fully briefed and addressed by a full-dress opinion rather than decided summarily. An eighteenth-century common lawyer would likely have distinguished the weight of a single, recent case from that of an established line of decisions.[5]

---

[2] Roger Scruton, *A Political Philosophy* viii (London: Bloomsbury, 2006).

[3] Charles Fried, *Order and Law: Arguing the Reagan Revolution – A Firsthand Account* 66, 68 (New York: Simon & Schuster, 1991).

[4] *Parratt* v. *Taylor*, 451 U.S. 527, 531 (1981) (Rehnquist, J.). See also *McDonald* v. *City of Chicago*, 561 U.S. 742, 881 (2010) (Stevens, J., dissenting): In constitutional decision making, "the Court has applied both the doctrine of *stare decisis* – adhering to precedents, respecting reliance interests, prizing stability and order in the law – and the common-law method – taking cases and controversies as they present themselves, proceeding slowly and incrementally, building on what came before."

[5] On the significantly different view of precedent dominant in earlier common law thinking, see Gerald R. Postema, Classical Common Law Jurisprudence (Part II), 3 *Oxford Univ. Commonwealth L.J.* 1, 16–17 (2003).

COMMON LAW AS METHOD: THE INTERPRETATION OF TEXTS

This book is a description of contemporary constitutional law reasoning rather than an in-depth examination of how our constitutional practices came to be historically, and presents the end result of what was at first a somewhat contentious process of deciding how properly to give the written Constitution the force of law. Arguments based on semantic meaning and the common law canons of construction were never the only expository methods employed, and from the beginning it was recognized that in light of the Constitution's unique nature as the basic charter of government, the traditional canons did not always generate acceptable answers. For example, in his 1791 opinion advising President Washington that he did not think the national bank bill was authorized, Attorney General Edmund Randolph rejected as unpersuasive the argument that the bill was "improper" and thus prohibited by the requirement in Article I section 8 that an act of Congress based on implied authority must be "necessary and proper" to the execution of an enumerated power. Randolph thought that "proper" added nothing to the requirement of necessity and denied that the canon against rendering part of a text meaningless was controlling. The more plausible approach to "and proper" in his view was to treat "it as among the surplusage which as often proceeds from inattention as caution."[6]

In political settings, the argument was sometimes made early on that the Constitution should not be "construed" at all. For example, one of the Philadelphia framers, Elbridge Gerry, informed the House of Representatives in 1789 that "all construction of the meaning of the Constitution, is dangerous or unnatural, and therefore ought to be avoided." Such assertions were objections to the application of common law rules of construction in preference to reliance on what later might be called plain-meaning arguments, and their plausibility waned in the face of the repeated experience that the Constitution's words simply do not answer, or answer sensibly, many constitutional questions if only their semantic meaning can be considered.[7]

A different debate of greater historical importance concerned *which* branch of common law learning on documentary construction constitutional lawyers should use. Common law courts approached the construction of acts of Parliament somewhat differently than they treated other public documents and private legal instruments such as written contracts; in construing treaties, they took into account the interpretive principles of the law of nations (public international law). For the most part, early constitutional lawyers assumed that constitutional interpretation was analogous to statutory construction and so the same basic principles should apply, but constitutionalists who viewed the Constitution as a compact among the states

---

[6] See Randolph, *Opinion on the Constitutionality of the Bank Bill* (Feb. 12, 1791), published in Walter Dellinger & H. Jefferson Powell, The Constitutionality of the Bank Bill: The Attorney General's First Constitutional Law Opinions, 44 *Duke L.J.* 110, 127 (1994).

[7] 1 Annals of Congress 574.

generally argued that the canons of treaty interpretation were controlling, especially the rule that any delegation of power a sovereign concedes in a treaty should be strictly construed.[8] Chief Justice Marshall's opinions for the Supreme Court in *McCulloch v. Maryland* and *Gibbons v. Ogden* devoted serious attention to rebutting the compact theory and its accompanying canon of strict construction, and neither idea plays a significant role in contemporary constitutional law.[9]

THE COMMON LAW JUDICIAL TRADITION

As this book's many references to individual Supreme Court justices (and occasionally to specific constitutional lawyers in other roles) display, the history and practice of constitutional law have a personal dimension that might seem odd except for the fact that American lawyers and a fair number of other Americans are so accustomed to it. In the *Steel Seizure Case*, Justice Jackson described "the essence of our free Government" as "'leave to live by no man's leave, underneath the law' – to be governed by those impersonal forces which we call law," and then asserted that "our government is fashioned to fulfill this concern so far as humanly possible." Powerful words, in an opinion rejecting a president's exercise of a kind of personal, prerogative power, but Jackson wrote the words in an opinion that was, originally, a concurrence joined by no other justice, an entirely personal statement with no formal institutional weight at all. The Court has since adopted the analytical framework Jackson proposed, and that aspect of his opinion now has institutional, impersonal authority. But even in changing the status of Jackson's words, the Court initially explained its reason for doing so by referring to the "combination of analysis and common sense" in the concurrence, attributes of Jackson's mind before they were features of his writing.[10]

In practicing constitutional law, lawyers on and off the bench are engaged in discerning the right answers to constitutional questions by standards of reasoning that are impersonal in the sense that the standards are the common property of the American political community across time and political disagreement. But they do

---

[8] See, e.g., 1 St. George Tucker, *Blackstone's Commentaries on the Laws of England* app. Note D 141–45 (Philadelphia: Birch & Small, 1803).

[9] See *McCulloch v. Maryland*, 17 U.S. (4 Wheat.) 316, 402–05 (1819) (the Constitution is the act of the People rather than a compact among the state sovereignties); *Gibbons v. Ogden*, 22 U.S. (9 Wheat.) 1, 187–89 (1824) (rejecting a rule of "strict construction" because it would "deny to the government those powers which the words of the grant, as usually understood, import," "in support of some theory not to be found in the constitution"). "Strict construction" is dismissed as "not . . . to be taken seriously" in the already classic treatise on the canons of construction co-authored by Justice Antonin Scalia. Antonin Scalia & Bryan A. Garner, *Reading Law: The Interpretation of Legal Texts* 356 (St. Paul, MN: Thomson/West, 2012).

[10] *Youngstown Sheet & Tube Co. v. Sawyer*, 343 U.S. 579, 654–55 (1952) (Jackson, J., concurring); *Dames & Moore v. Regan*, 453 U.S. 654, 661–62 (1981) (Rehnquist, J.). That then-Associate Justice Rehnquist was one of Justice Jackson's clerks in the Term of Court *Youngstown* was decided only underscores the personal dimension of the constitutional law being made in the later decision.

so with recurrent attention to the role of individual justices and others in the shaping of the law. Commenting on a claim Chief Justice Marshall made in an 1824 case that "judicial power is never exercised for the purpose of giving effect to the will of the Judge," Justice Cardozo wrote that Marshall's own place in constitutional history shows that his comment can never be "more than partly true."

> He gave to the constitution of the United States the impress of his own mind; and the form of our constitutional law is what it is, because he moulded it while it was still plastic and malleable in the fire of his own intense convictions.

The Constitution-in-practice stems from reasoning, debate, and judgment by Marshall, and (as the reader of this book knows) many others, and while the result is not simply the work of any individual's will, not even Marshall's, the impress of individual personalities runs throughout.[11]

In this, as in other respects, the American practice of constitutional law is deeply shaped by its roots in the English common law tradition.[12] Chief Justice Marshall's critical role in the early development of our practice, for example, is paralleled by that of William de Bereford in the history of the common law. King Edward I commissioned Bereford as a judge of the Court of Common Pleas in 1292, one of the first royal judges chosen for his professional skills and accomplishments in the law.[13] Before him, appointment to a royal court almost always went to a senior government bureaucrat, often a cleric. Bereford was a judge of a different ilk: He owed his elevation to his mastery of the law, and his interests and his judgments were shaped by professional pride and expertise. Bereford was a self-confident and forceful individual, politically shrewd and utterly convinced that it was lawyers who ought to say what the law is. He was long-lived as well, and served for almost thirty-four years, half of that time as chief justice. By the time he died in 1326, no common law judge or advocate knew any vision of law but Bereford's. After him, almost all royal judges had backgrounds similar to his, and the judiciary soon became the preserve of an autonomous profession, rather than a bureaucratic or overtly political institution.[14]

Bereford was given the opportunity to shape bench and bar in a time of great legal ferment. King Edward I was later named the English Justinian because it was in his

---

[11] Benjamin N. Cardozo, *The Nature of the Judicial Process* 169–70 (New Haven, CT: Yale University Press, 1921). Marshall's remark is in his opinion for the Court in *Osborn v. Bank of the United States*, 22 U.S. (9 Wheat.) 738, 866 (1824).

[12] In the following discussion of Chief Justices Bereford and Coke, I have drawn on a lecture I gave on The Emergence of the American Constitutional Law Tradition. The lecture was published in 103 *Judicature* 24 (2019) and 52 *International Society of Barristers Q.* 41 (2020). I am grateful to both journals for their permission to use the material.

[13] On Bereford, see generally 2 *The Earliest English Law Reports* viii–xxi (Paul A. Brand ed. London: Selden Society, 1996); William C. Bolland, *Chief Justice Sir William de Bereford* (Cambridge: Cambridge University Press,1924); and Thomas Lund, *The Creation of the Common Law* 23–63, 349–55 (Clark, NJ: Talbot Publishing,2015).

[14] T. F. T. Plucknett, *The Legal Profession in English Legal History*, in Plucknett, *Studies in English Legal History* XIX 332–33 (London: Hambledon Press, 1983).

reign, and that of his son Edward II, that the common law of the realm was overhauled root and branch and began to assume its developed medieval and early modern form.[15] For the first Edward's first twenty years, legal change was centered in the high court of Parliament. The dominant judicial body was the Court of King's Bench, and the clerks in the royal Chancery held a tight grip on what cases the royal courts could and could not hear. These arrangements ensured that the views of the king and his ministers played a central role in the articulation of law. By the time Chief Justice Bereford died, all of this was in the process of transformation. The initiative for legal change now lay in the Court of Common Pleas, and neither King's Bench nor Chancery had effective control over Bereford's court.[16]

The reorientation of common law decision making toward the intra-professional norms and attitudes dominant in Common Pleas was exemplified by the link Chief Justice Bereford and his successors drew between the common law and "reason."[17] Eighteen years after Bereford died, Common Pleas heard a case, *Flaundres v. Rychman*, in which the plaintiff's lawyer invoked a Bereford decision. When one of the judges sounded doubtful, the lawyer insisted on the authority of precedent: "I think you will do as others have done in the same case, or else we do not know what the law is." Justice Roger Hillary responded that law is "the will of the Justices." To which Chief Justice John Stonor immediately replied, "Nonsense! Law is reason."[18] Over the next three centuries, this idea that law is reason was fleshed out, until Sir Edward Coke, the central figure in common law history from the perspective of early American constitutional lawyers, gave the equation its canonical formulation.[19] In November 1608, King James I convened a meeting at Westminster of judges and other high officials: James was unhappy about the Court of Common Pleas, of which Coke was then the chief justice, interfering with the work of commissions exercising the king's personal prerogative. In the course of the discussion, James commented that if law is reason, then he himself, being a reasonable and learned king, was perfectly competent to make legal

[15]   1 William Blackstone, *Commentaries on the Laws of England* *23 (1765) (English laws reached a "pitch of perfection ... [u]nder the auspices of our English Justinian, king Edward the first"). On legal changes in this era, see T. F. T. Plucknett, *A Concise History of the Common Law* 27–31 (5th ed. Boston: Little, Brown & Co., 1956); S. F. C. Milsom, *Historical Foundations of the Common Law* 99–118 (2nd ed. London: Butterworth & Co., 1981).

[16]   On Bereford's successful expansion of the role of Common Pleas, see Lund, *Creation of the Common Law* 65–126.

[17]   For example, in one case, when the defendant argued that the plaintiff's pleading error should prevent him from recovering on a debt the defendant clearly owed, Bereford sharply replied, "Reason requires that you [pay], and the law is founded on reason, and good faith demands it." *Gaunt v. Gaunt* (C.P. 1310), *Year Books of Edward II, 1309–1310*, 79, 80 (F.W. Maitland ed. London: Selden Society, 1905).

[18]   *Flaundres v. Rychman* (C.P. 1344), *Year Books of Edward III, 1344*, 377 (Luke O. Pike ed. London: Selden Society, 1905).

[19]   On Coke, see generally Christopher Hill, Sir Edward Coke – Myth-Maker, in Hill, *Intellectual Origins of the English Revolution* 225–65 (Oxford: Clarendon Press,1965); David Chan Smith, *Sir Edward Coke and the Reformation of the Laws* (Cambridge: Cambridge University Press,2014).

decisions or delegate them to his political councilors. Coke politely but emphatically disagreed.

> True it is that God has endowed your Majesty with excellent Science and great endowments of nature, but your Majesty is not learned in the Lawes of your Realme of England, and causes which concern the life, or inheritance, or goods of your Subjects . . . are not to be decided by naturall reasoning but by the artificiall reason and judgment of Law . . . which requires long study and experience.

King James was not amused. Indeed, he was enraged by what he called treason, and Coke only barely escaped imprisonment in the Tower of London. But the episode had no effect on Coke's behavior as a judge, and founding era American constitutional lawyers remembered it (in Coke's personally self-aggrandizing version) as an important milestone in the history of the rule of law: For all the king's bluster, it was Coke and the common law that had the last laugh.

The implications of Coke's position were momentous. Even when the law requires judges to give effect to an act of Parliament or of the monarch, such political acts must enter the domain of law governed by the judges' reasoned judgment before they can rightly touch the "life or inheritance or goods" of the individual. It was a bold and indeed breathtaking claim about the authority of legal reason and the scope of judicial authority, and it articulates a principle that lies at the foundation of American constitutional law.[20]

FEDERAL COMMON LAW

Founding-era debate over the existence of a federal common law of crimes revolved around its implications for the principle of enumeration, although claims that the federal courts could entertain criminal prosecutions without any basis in an act of Congress also raised concerns about the separation of powers and what we today would understand as procedural due process. There was a political dimension to the controversy as well. Federalist defenders of the controversial Sedition Act of 1798 had justified Congress's punishment of seditious libel in part on the supposed existence of a federal common law of criminal libel, while Republican critics had attacked the Act as unauthorized by any grant of power to Congress as well as a violation of the first amendment's prohibitions on abridging freedom of speech and press. When *United States* v. *Hudson & Goodwin* rejected the existence of a federal common law of crimes in 1812, the opinion of the Court was delivered by the senior Republican justice, William Johnson, who asserted that the issue was long settled in public and professional opinion. Johnson also wrote that as a matter of constitutional principle, the lower federal courts could only exercise jurisdiction

---

[20] Coke's account of the incident is in his reports. See *Prohibitions del Roy*, 12 Co. Rep. 63, 64–65. For a fuller picture, see Roland G. Usher, James I and Sir Edward Coke, 18 *Eng. Hist. Rev.* 664 (1903) (reproducing accounts by other participants).

over a criminal case if granted the authority do so by Congress, which within the limits of Article III defines their jurisdiction. Although no one wrote a public dissent, Justice Johnson noted that the decision was not unanimous, and the issue returned to the Court a few years later. The Republican attorney general declined to argue the case, explaining that he thought *Hudson & Goodwin* was controlling. "Under these circumstances," Johnson announced, once again speaking only for a majority, the Court refused to revisit its earlier decision "or draw it into doubt." Subsequent decisions treated *Hudson & Goodwin* as settling the question.[21]

The question before the Court in *Swift v. Tyson* in 1842 – were the federal courts obliged to follow state court cases in a matter of commercial law? – raised quite different issues than those debated in the earlier controversy. The case was in federal court under Congress's grant to the federal court of diversity jurisdiction over disputes between citizens of different states, and thus the jurisdictional and separation of powers concerns that had troubled Justice Johnson were not present. Furthermore, for centuries common lawyers had treated commercial law as a transnational body of private law rather than an exclusively English area of law: Indeed, as the Court noted, the New York decisions that it thought incorrect did not claim to apply a common law rule unique to New York but to "deduce the doctrine from the general principles of commercial law." In itself, *Swift* asserted little if anything more than the propriety of a federal court following its own view rather than that of a state court on an issue in a body of law common to both.[22]

Two developments changed this originally quite modest (if debatable) proposition into a large-scale constitutional problem. The federal courts gradually expanded the *Swift* rule to cover a vast range of private law issues, thus creating the judicial "police power" problem discussed in Chapter 2. This expansion, furthermore, was often justified on the ground that "the common law" in general is a general body of substantive law that transcends the decisions of any particular jurisdiction. This understanding of common law was already coming under severe attack even as the federal courts were invoking it to explain their expansive application of *Swift*, and after his appointment in 1902, Justice Oliver Wendell Holmes became the leading voice in an ongoing critique. The idea that courts "discover" the rules of a general common law was, he insisted, nonsense. "The common law is not a brooding omnipresence in the sky, but the articulate voice of some sovereign or quasi sovereign that can be identified." "It is very hard to resist the impression that there is one august corpus, to understand which clearly is the only task of any Court concerned. . . . But there is no such body of law. . . . The common law so far as it is enforced in a State, whether called common law or not, is not the common law generally but the law of that State existing by the authority of that State."

---

[21] *United States v. Hudson & Goodwin,* 11 U.S. (7 Cranch) 32, 32–34 (1812); *United States v. Coolidge,* 14 U.S. (1 Wheat.) 415, 416 (1816).

[22] *Swift v. Tyson,* 41 U.S. (16 Pet.) 1, 18 (1842) (Story, J.).

As these quotations illustrate, Holmes's primary objection to *Swift* was that he thought it rested on an erroneous understanding of law, but he also denied that Article III authorized the federal courts to act on that understanding regardless of its jurisprudential validity: "the fallacy [propounded by *Swift*] has resulted in an unconstitutional assumption of powers by the Courts of the United States which no lapse of time or respectable array of opinion should make us hesitate to correct."[23] A few years after Holmes died, the Court adopted his views and formally repudiated *Swift* in *Erie R. Co. v. Tompkins* (1938). Justice Brandeis's opinion for the Court in *Erie* quoted Holmes in describing the *Swift* rule as an unauthorized and thus unconstitutional exercise of power and explained that conclusion by invoking both the enumeration and police power principles.[24]

After *Erie*, when a federal court exercising diversity jurisdiction must decide a question of common law, it must apply the common law of whichever state is relevant to the dispute. But *Erie* should not be misunderstood as a wholesale rejection of a role for common law thinking in executing federal powers that are authorized. When a federal court must decide a case involving "a constitutional function or power" of the federal government, and so neither the enumeration nor the police power principle is at stake, in the absence of a relevant act of Congress, "it is for the federal courts to fashion the governing rule of law according to their own standards" – to create a limited kind of federal common law.[25] And *Erie* did not question in any sense constitutional law's adoption of the intellectual tools of the English common law in order to fashion the Constitution-in-practice.

---

[23] The quotations from Holmes are from, respectively, *Southern Pacific Co. v. Jensen*, 244 U.S 205, 222 (1917) (Holmes, J. dissenting); *Black & White Taxicab & Transfer Co. v. Brown & Yellow Taxicab & Transfer Co.*, 276 U.S. 518, 533 (1928) (Holmes, J., dissenting).

[24] *Erie*, 304 U.S. 64, 78 (1938): "Except in matters governed by the Federal Constitution or by acts of Congress, the law to be applied in any case is the law of the state. And whether the law of the state shall be declared by its Legislature in a statute or by its highest court in a decision is not a matter of federal concern. There is no federal general common law. Congress has no power to declare substantive rules of common law applicable in a state whether they be local in their nature or 'general,' be they commercial law or a part of the law of torts. And no clause in the Constitution purports to confer such a power upon the federal courts."

[25] *Clearfield Trust Co. v. United States*, 318 U.S. 363, 366–67 (1943).

Additional Reading

The literature on the Constitution and constitutional law is voluminous. Rather than attempting to provide a comprehensive bibliography that would likely be of little use to anyone, I suggest the following very short list of works that I believe may be particularly helpful to readers interested in exploring further the themes of this book. The list omits the many other excellent books and articles from which I have learned a great deal.

THE PRACTICE OF CONSTITUTIONAL LAW

Black, Jr., Charles L. *Structure and Relationship in Constitutional Law* (Baton Rouge, LA: Louisiana State University Press, 1969) and *The Humane Imagination* (Woodbridge, CT: Ox Bow Press, 1986)

Bobbitt, Philip. *Constitutional Fate: Theory of the Constitution* (New York: Oxford University Press, 1982) and *Constitutional Interpretation* (Oxford: Blackwell, 1991)

Fallon, Jr., Richard H. *Law and Legitimacy in the Supreme Court* (Cambridge, MA: Belknap Press, 2018)

Fried, Charles. *Saying What the Law Is: The Constitution in the Supreme Court* (Cambridge, MA: Harvard University Press, 2004) and "On Judgment," 15 *Lewis & Clark L. Rev.* 1025 (2011)

Monaghan, Henry Paul. *American Constitutional Law: Selected Essays* (Durham, NC: Carolina Academic Press, 2018)

THE WRITTEN CONSTITUTION AND THE AMERICAN CONSTITUTIONAL SYSTEM

Amar, Akhil Reed. *America's Constitution: A Biography* (New York: Random House, 2006)

Foner, Eric. *The Second Founding: How the Civil War and Reconstruction Remade the Constitution* (New York: W. W. Norton, 2019)

Graber, Mark A. *A New Introduction to American Constitutionalism* (New York: Oxford University Press, 2013)

Jackson, Robert H. *The Supreme Court in the American System of Government* (Cambridge, MA: Harvard University Press, 1955)

Rakove, Jack N. *Original Meanings: Politics and Ideas in the Making of the Constitution* (New York: Alfred A. Knopf, 1996)

THE CONTEMPORARY DEBATE OVER CONSTITUTIONAL METHOD

Scalia, Antonin. *A Matter of Interpretation: Federal Courts and the Law* (rev. ed. Princeton: Princeton University Press, 2018)

Strauss, David A. *The Living Constitution* (New York: Oxford University Press, 2010)

LEGAL THOUGHT IN GENERAL

Cardozo, Benjamin N. *The Nature of the Judicial Process* (New Haven, CT: Yale University Press, 1921)

Schauer, Frederick. *Thinking Like a Lawyer: A New Introduction to Legal Reasoning* (Cambridge, MA: Harvard University Press, 2009)

Weinreb, Lloyd. *Legal Reason: The Use of Analogy in Legal Argument* (2nd ed. New York: Cambridge University Press, 2016)

Index

Made in the USA
Las Vegas, NV
11 September 2023

77441394R00148